FREEHOLD: RESISTANCE

BAEN BOOKS by MICHAEL Z. WILLIAMSON

Freehold
Contact with Chaos
The Weapon
Rogue
Angeleyes

Better to Beg Forgiveness...
Do Unto Others...
When Diplomacy Fails...

The Hero (with John Ringo)

A Long Time Until Now

COLLECTIONS
Tour of Duty
Tide of Battle

FREEHOLD ANTHOLOGIES
EDITED BY MICHAEL Z. WILLIAMSON

Forged in Blood
Freehold: Resistance

*To purchase any of these titles in e-book form,
please go to www.baen.com.*

FREEHOLD: RESISTANCE

EDITED BY

MICHAEL Z. WILLIAMSON

FREEHOLD: RESISTANCE

A Baen Books Original

Baen Publishing Enterprises
P.O. Box 1403
Riverdale, NY 10471
www.baen.com

ISBN: 978-1-9821-2423-6

Cover art by Kurt Miller

First printing, December 2019

Distributed by Simon & Schuster
1230 Avenue of the Americas
New York, NY 10020

Library of Congress Cataloging-in-Publication Data

Names: Williamson, Michael Z., editor.
Title: Freehold : resistance / edited by Michael Z. Williamson.
Description: Riverdale, NY : Baen, 2019. | Series: Freehold
Identifiers: LCCN 2019034504 | ISBN 9781982124236 (trade paperback)
Subjects: LCSH: Science fiction, American.
Classification: LCC PS648.S3 F75 2019 | DDC 813/.0876208—dc23
LC record available at https://lccn.loc.gov/2019034504

Pages by Joy Freeman (www.pagesbyjoy.com)
Printed in the United States of America
10 9 8 7 6 5 4 3 2 1

To the Finns, the Kazakhs, the Israelis, the Apache,
and all others who fought relentlessly
against overwhelming odds.

Contents

FREEHOLD: RESISTANCE

PROLOGUE:
Invasion

There had not been an interstellar war among the colonies and nations of humanity. There hadn't been a reason for one. Eventually, though, a reason was found.

It was inevitable that colony systems with plenty of local resources, far smaller populations to demand them, and smaller bureaucracies trying to manage every facet of running them, would develop quickly.

As they did, some declared nationhood, and joined the UN. The reasons for the latter were a combination of a sense of duty to the body politic of humanity, for trade and commerce through the established agencies, and for economic support and investment. The smaller and less-funded colonies needed this more than some others.

At the other end of the spectrum, Govannon was owned by Prescot Deep Space, which was owned by a single family. They were neither colony nor nation, and did as they wished, selling raw materials to all systems, neutral and unhindered.

Grainne Colony, however, upset the routine when they declared themselves a nation, then made no effort to ask for UN membership. It would have been granted, since they were a wealthy system with a strong economy. The Parliament waited, and no request came. The Parliament enquired, and was told that the Freehold of Grainne saw no advantage to UN membership, but was happy to continue trading with members.

At this slight, various factions made snide comments, accused the Freehold of selfishness and greed for all its development costs,

1

failing to mention that had all been underwritten by TanCorp, a private entity that might be smaller than Prescot, but was just as insular.

When this failed to achieve a response, it was stated loudly in both Parliament and the media that Grainne's economy would promptly collapse without UN membership and support.

It did not. Trade continued, wealth increased, and the Freehold diplomats smoothed out political issues in trade deals that wouldn't have been necessary if the UN bureaucracy was not determined to have a say in everything and a cut for their operations.

Until the UN tried to sanction the Freehold and its ships for "noncompliance" with UN Directives.

Inconvenienced but not stopped, Freehold ships either reflagged to other nations, or simply hauled their goods into Caledonia or Novaja Rossia and traded there. NovRos especially was known for paying only lip service to UN Directives, and happily relisted anything it got as domestic production.

It took a decade, but the UN Security Council, despite protests from several members, voted to form a committee to consider direct action. This committee immediately did so, ordering the Military Bureau to prepare for a military exercise, while privately informing a handful of reliable officers it wasn't an exercise.

Nor was it successful.

The UN managed to slip an assault carrier into the Freehold system, and dropped a landing force to secure Jefferson Starport as a landhead for further incursions. Four of the ten transports never made it to ground. Two others force-landed in the wilderness. Four landed successfully and were utterly outmanned and outmaneuvered. The Freehold media railed on the hilarity of attempting to occupy a planet with fewer than two thousand troops.

As powerful governments often do, the UN reacted to the slight by doubling down.

Spider's Web

Jessica Schlenker

Part 1

1st Week February 210

Moyra Kelly stepped into the kitchenette to fetch a drink for her grandmother. A string of Irish Gaelic she didn't recognize abruptly echoed through from the living room. She hadn't heard such words since her pelvis was crushed under a horse, six or seven years ago.

She stepped back in to see what caused such a response from the normally restrained Isibéal O'Higgins.

Smoke filled the infoset's screen, suddenly backlit by a bright explosion. Pieces of a building—concrete, roofing, what Moyra could only hope wasn't a person—flung apart. A calm, measured voice spoke over the scene. *"This is the live drone feed above Heilbrun Base. UN ships have initiated an unprovoked attack on Grainne soil without warning. These ships did not declare their affiliation until after this act of war started."* Another building took a direct hit, with a cluster of bright stars flaring just before the entire building exploded from the inside. *"UN forces are demanding—"*

The infoset's signal cut off.

"The devil they're *demanding* anything. Those bloody *bastards*." Isibéal's voice dripped with venom.

Moyra agreed, mental wheels turning. Isibéal took the forgotten glass from her. Moyra apologized.

Isibéal waived it off. "You're thinking, lass." She smiled, in a not-particularly-nice manner. "Are you brewing up mischief now?"

Moyra nodded slowly. "The kettle's just been put to boil, Grandma."

"Be sure to let me know when you're ready for the teapot. I'd like a cuppa, myself."

Her concern and uncertainty must have shown on her face. "No," Isibéal said softly. "You aren't going to go along with this... this... *nonsense*. Not to save me. I'm old. I'm worn out. They destroyed my family and home once. Not again."

"Okay." It hurt to agree.

The broadcast spluttered back to life. A clean-cut male whose uniform bore the UN emblem sat in the primary seat. The room and set were different from normal, indicating the signal had been hijacked. "*This is an interim broadcast during changeover. The UN has resumed leadership of the Grainne Colony...*"

"I highly doubt that," Moyra snorted over his droning. "Can you hit record on this, so I can analyze it later? I need to... check in with some people."

"Certainly, lass." Isibéal set the record.

The *special* console never slept, and her compatriots already were filling the screens with furiously typed messages.

:: Shut up, all you lot, :: she typed. :: What the fuck do we know? And why don't we know more already? ::

:: Hespera! You heard about— :: the messages overlapped.

:: We were watching the station broadcast. Again: What the hell do we have? ::

A flurry of information replied, and she scanned it. The UN's "diplomatic" vessel arrived a few weeks ago, and one of her dabblers out on the stations had helpfully slipped a mined data chip onto the ship, as usual. Precious little information had been gleaned, but Jenkins primarily focused on blackmail material, including what might interest their *other* client. It wasn't impossible he missed something. Her clique tended to keep away from military interests, to avoid tangling with their own military.

Invading her home changed that.

:: What are we going to do? :: asked Braknck. He had yet to live up to his claimed handle over the course of their escapades, or even manage to be useful.

:: We are spiders in the web, :: she replied. :: We will do as we always do. ::

DalesOP opened a private comm. :: The hell we will, Hesp. I won't. We can't let this happen. ::

:: I know, Dal. You know Brak as well as I do. He'll flake if he thinks he's at risk of anything. ::

:: True. Trip and Dam are angry, too, though. ::

:: Dam, I trust. But do we trust them *enough*? ::

:: Dam served a term, so yes. Trip . . . I'm not sure. ::

:: Dam may have useful contacts. We're going to have to bridge where we normally avoid. ::

:: Yes. ::

Damocles appeared in the comm. :: Whatever it is, as long as it's against those UN bastards, I'm in. ::

:: Thanks for letting me ask the question, man, :: Moyra snarked. :: But good to know. Do you think Trip is solid? Brak wouldn't be. He's only in this for the money. ::

:: Trip, maybe. I'll sound him out. You know we'll have to maintain some kind of op to keep the others from being curious. At least at first. ::

:: Yeah, :: DalesOP replied. :: Wankers. ::

At least they were in agreement there, Moyra thought.

The main comm blinked, and Moyra flipped over. :: Oh shit, :: Salamander typed, :: Trip, please tell me your sister and the baby are still visiting your folks. They just bombed the dormitories at the base here. ::

:: Oh no. Oh fuck. Baby's here. Sis just headed back off maternity leave two days ago. Oh fuck. I have to tell my parents. :: Moyra felt unbidden tears fall for her friend, and thanked the heavens his baby nephew was safe—for now, at least.

:: Not unexpected, :: Damocles responded. :: They've hijacked sat feeds, and they're taking out the bases. I'm surprised they didn't immediately take a station, too. Should probably try to check with Skylight up on Skywheel Two, to see if she's okay. ::

He added in the back comm, :: A few of my boys got out. But only a few. Daks pinged me from Heilbrun. Rescue attempts are in progress. We don't have a response from Maygida. He'll try to find out how many got out at Merrill. Assbags. It's NIGHT there. ::

:: Do we know the extent of the damage? ::

:: Negative. But I would expect the UN intends to bomb the bases into oblivion. It's what I would do. ::

Main comm chatter angered Moyra. :: Shut up. All of you. The UN isn't interested in our little activities YET. Don't make the mistake of thinking that won't change. Have any of you ever LOOKED at the UN laws regarding what we do? You—we—are all in deep shit if they decide to go after us. ::

Jenkins flagged up a private comm. :: My uplink to the "diplomatic" ship hasn't been shut down. Yet. ::

:: How much access do you have? ::

:: Not enough to deploy Wrecking Ball, but I can fix that quickly. Won't even have to pull a Leroy. :: Moyra snorted at the age-old joke.

:: How far are you willing to do this? ::

:: My brother is...was...at Heilbrun. I hope he still "is." ::

:: Crap. Sorry, man. Gotcha. We need as much access as deep as we can, as fast as we can. ::

:: I'm on it. ::

Moyra flipped over to the back comm. :: Jenkins is going to play a round at the alley. ::

:: He's in? :: Damocles replied.

:: He says his brother is stationed on base. ::

:: Shit :: / :: Fuck :: came the replies.

:: There's going to be a lot more casualties before this is over, Hesp. ::

:: I know, Dam. I hope it won't be any of our guys, but... ::

:: Nuke the UN, :: DalesOP replied.

Moyra got up to stretch and check in with her grandmother. The infoset continued to drone UN propaganda on the satellite feeds.

"What do the normal broadcasts show?" Moyra asked.

"I hadn't checked," Isibéal said. She gestured with the remote, and changed over to the local news.

Air footage of the demolished military base filled the screen. Craters partially encircled by the crumbled remains of walls smoked, both fire and dust. Lights from emergency vehicles pulsated while personnel scrambled over ruins, pulling at loose bits.

"This is Action News, reporting live. Heilbrun has been targeted by apparent kinetic weapons. Witnesses report feeling the ground shake at the start of the attack, but there does not appear to be any fallout consistent with thermonuclear devices. Rescue missions are underway at this time. We have reached out to Freehold Forces

contacts for any update available, but have been unable to successfully locate a contact so far."

The screen zoomed to a particular building-*cum*-crater, as the anchor continued. *"As this was the public relations office, we do not expect a rapid official reply to our inquiries.*

"What few unofficial sources we have been able to contact at this time, as well as the known takeover of the satellite-based channels, indicate that the United Nations is attempting a second invasion. Our viewers may recall the repulsed invasion attempt at the spaceport last year.

"It appears the UN learned from the previous failure, and targeted the military forces directly. Stations located near the other Freehold Forces bases are showing similar destruction, and we have those feeds on parallel.

"We currently do not have a status on those forces stationed in locations other than the main bases.

"Here are the aerial views from other stations across Grainne."

Isibéal gestured the remote, and the infoset shut down. "I've seen enough."

Moyra thought of Jenkins, TripleShot, and Damocles, all with friends and/or family in the rubble. "Yeah. I have work to do." *Before the UN tries to turn every town and city on Grainne into more smoking rubble.*

force Majeure
Michael Z. Williamson

Part 1

The base was a hollowed-out five-kilometer planetoid. It started as a project for a remote facility for austere support training, itself a training exercise.

Then the UN invaded, and the exercise became real. It was built out in a matter of days. The passageways, spaces, even the bays were roughhewn in the silicate, the precision-machined hatches in odd contrast to the blasted and burned gray material. It contained billeting with furniture, life support, limited vat and hydroponic food production, a power plant, docking pylons and umbilici, offices for staff, cargo bays and even rec facilities.

Factory ship FMS *Force* provided most of the tools, materials and labor to convert a barren rock lacking even a chart listing into a crude but functional dock for small boats to engage in low-level resistance of the UN invaders.

Force was five hundred meters of ugly, tubular hull, stuffed with every machine tool in existence, with the ability to fabricate as many more as it needed, or anything a fighting unit might require. With days or weeks between star systems, a war could be lost awaiting resupply. *Force* and her sister ships provided assets on location, from ammo to fuel to vehicles to custom weapons, replacement boots or armor, or even a ship. If a chemical analysis and blueprints existed or could be made, she could fabricate it, as long as there was raw material in her holds.

She could build anything, but she couldn't fight. Her point defense was limited. She was possibly the best combat-support craft in human history—the base being evidence of that—but not a combatant.

Force was low on resources, and Captain Francis Yates wasn't sure what the future held. Surrender was unpalatable, but might be inevitable. Without a fleet carrier, he was stranded in-system—neither money nor engineering had yet made it possible for *Force* to have phase drive. They were stuck supporting a tiny fleet of gunboats and stealth insertion craft, who were doing something he wasn't told about, that seemed to be irritating the enemy. But he couldn't offer them much more at this point.

He ran through a mental tally of the damage so far. It was depressing and terrifying. All three ground bases, bombed with kinetic kills. Jefferson, Marou, Taniville, Westport were all occupied. The jump points were all under UN control. Half the fleet weren't accounted for. Several were IDed as lost, others as seized in-system, unable to escape. Most of those were known to have taken some level of damage in either combat or capture denial procedures. None were known to have been scuttled outright.

All this over a desire to be left alone, he thought. The videos didn't show much detail, just dust clouds over the bases. The broadcasts from the habitats documented attack, concern, occupation, and then switched to cheerful UN talking heads insisting all was well.

Control the communications and the oxygen, he reflected, *and you utterly control a space habitat.*

The groundside broadcasts lasted a bit longer, but also switched to happy propaganda. That meant the ground forces hadn't been able to stop occupation of media and presumably the minimal Freehold government.

Space Communications Tech 1 Gerry Mati broke his thoughts.

"Sir, message from Station Control for you." Mati's South Islands accent was fast but crisp.

"Got it." Yates opened his display and pulled up a headset. One kept C-deck quiet, and it just might be a sensitive communication.

"Captain Yates, go ahead Control."

The control officer said, *"Captain, I have some news."*

"Good?"

"News," the tech said evenly. *"Sleipnir is coming in system to retrieve you. They have an operation."*

Sleipnir was a fleet carrier, intended to haul non–stardrive craft where needed. They had a large reactor, a huge frame, and a sizeable crew.

He noted, "I have almost nothing to support them with." He settled his body into his couch. It would make working easier. Though he was broad enough across the shoulders the couch always felt snug, despite being programmed to fit him.

Control replied, *"That's understood. They have some resources."*

"Very well. I'll need the data and orders. Is this immediate?"

"To reduce detection profile, yes. Less signature is better."

"Then I guess action on the war is good. Shoot it over and we'll get to work."

The officer sounded wistful. *"It's been awe-inspiring to watch you and your crew work. Please relay our thanks and kudos to your crew."*

"I will. Thank you for giving us a mission and a purpose."

He didn't ask how the information got here. The boats carried some, and there were rumors of piggyback signals on the UN-controlled network and entertainment feeds. Low density, but apparently discreet and effective.

The orders and data had them reaching a point far out in the Halo in two weeks. That was a long, slow movement. It would minimize signature, though. If they boosted all out, the ship used continent-years of energy that would be easy to locate. There was nothing to hide behind in deep space.

By the end of the day, the crew detached for liaison, duty, and recreation were all back aboard. The ship unshackled and nudged free on maneuvering thrusters, then engaged drive to take them out. There were no signals, not even tightbeam. The base was as close to blackbody as possible. It was small, wrapped in a fluff of vacgel that absorbed radiation going in or coming out, and made as few transmissions as possible. It would be hard to detect or suspect, and the boat pilots would scramble the coordinates if threatened.

Force powered away gently, minimizing her own signature, bound for the war but at a very leisurely pace.

Fourteen days of her nineteen-day course elapsed. Somewhere ahead was the fleet carrier *Sleipnir*, ready to grapple them and depart system. They'd know when they got there.

Somewhere behind was a UN warship in a trajectory that

didn't match, but wasn't far off. They seemed to be conducting search sweeps. The only option was to continue slow, steady boost and hope they couldn't see *Force* against the background. Sudden variations would be more noticeable.

At this point, if anything had happened to the carrier, or they'd astrogated incorrectly, they'd have to find a way to evacuate the crew, scuttle the ship, and attempt to reach and hide in one of the habitats or on the ground.

We had our own nation, dammit. But we couldn't accept the UN requirements for membership, and we couldn't remain a colony. Now we're an entire system of refugees and rebels.

Still, orders were orders, and he represented his nation. He'd do his damndest to be part of whatever was going on, whether it delayed the inevitable, allowed time for diplomacy, or just for residents to disperse away from the invaders.

The commo contact flashed. Tech Mati swiped to accept.

"Vessel identified as FMS Force, *this is UNS* Montevideo. *You are ordered to proceed at best safe speed to Station Ceileidh and make orbit. All forces of the Grainne Colony will revert to UN control. Please respond and comply."*

The message wasn't totally unexpected. But knowing all major Freehold Forces installations were smoking craters, it was iodine in an open wound.

Yates looked across the control center at his staff, arranged in a circle, each G couch in a pie-section-shaped block of controls.

"We can't fight. Can we outrun them?"

Tactical Officer Lieutenant Rievley linked Astrogator Farana's display to his. He scrolled, swiped, and sent something back to her. A moment later it popped on Yates's display.

Farana replied, "Sir, *Montevideo* is a cruiser. She can chase us and eventually catch us."

Yates looked at the curves and decided, "Wait for their warning hail, then respond. Then dial the thrust down slowly. How long can we reasonably delay intercept?"

"No more than three days. At least one," she said, having already calculated the curves. She was tiny with a slim build. All her development had gone into her brain.

"That's our strategy. Hopefully we can get close enough for *Sleipnir* to take us."

As anticipated, the second hail was more sternly worded.

"*Ship identified as FMS* Force. *Please heed previous transmission at once. Further disobedience will be considered a hostile act and grounds for engagement.*"

"They won't even allow us our own name," he said in irritated amusement. "Comply as discussed."

Farana touched controls and the thrust curve changed, imperceptibly at first, then just barely noticeably.

Mati replied, "*Montevideo*, this is FMS *Force*. We have received your transmission. We are reducing thrust and will make most efficient way to your stated position. We are a support ship on a deep-space training and provisioning mission. We presume there is a military emergency we have not been informed of. Please advise the nature of the situation."

He watched across the arc as Farana furiously worked her screen, grid, touchpad, and even scratched some markings on a second screen with her fingertip. He knew she was plotting the best curves possible.

The transmission lag was thirty-two seconds. Thirty-two light-seconds was a good distance, but it wasn't good enough to prevent interception.

"*Ship identified as FMF* Force, *as stated before, all craft of the former Grainne Colony are reverting to UN control. This process began over a week ago.*"

Lag.

Mati replied, "*Montevideo*, this is *Force*. Under whose authority is this change?"

Lag.

"*Ship identified as FMS* Force: *This is UN authority.*"

Yates tapped a message for Mati to repeat.

"*Montevideo*, this is *Force*. As we are an unarmed support ship, we are complying with your directive. Please officially note we do so under protest and expect a hearing at an Admiralty court."

The awaited reply was, "*Yeah, whatever.*"

Mati snarked, "He seems nice."

Farana pinged for attention. Important, not critical, or she'd have spoken. He looked over.

"Astrogator?"

"Sir, I have a trajectory. It will give us two days and some to deny resources to the enemy."

He was about to reply when another message came in, coded.

"Force, *this is* Sleipnir. *Immediately proceed to Plot Point Alpha. We will rendezvous.*"

The message had cut through on priority.

Farana raised her eyebrows and said, "That's a bastard of a trajectory change on their part. As in, I can see the trail. That means *Montevideo* can, too."

"They have big reactors. Can we keep ahead of *Montevideo*?"

"For a while. Let me check drive efficiency."

A seg later she said, "I've got our best plot. They can possibly intercept short term, though."

He asked, "Can we release debris to delay them?"

Rievley shook his head a fraction and said, "Not enough to matter. If they go balls out, they can catch us, but then they have to call for recovery for themselves. I suspect they won't. Your call, sir?"

"Let me see the plot."

Farana flashed it to his comm, and he glanced over it. *Montevideo* would get within weapon range, but not reliably. Did they want to waste weaponry on a noncombatant support ship? That as far as they knew had no support? Probably not.

"I don't see a way to do better. Proceed."

Shortly, another message repeated, "*Ship identified as FMS Force, stand down or be fired upon.*"

"Ignore that. Can they hit us?"

Rievley replied, "Not reliably. Five percent chance."

"Well, this is a war. Five percent is better than fifty. Keep running."

Rievley corrected, "They might actually make ten percent."

"Still worth it."

"And they've fired."

He felt a ripple of shock. This was it, because obviously the pursuers thought it was worth wasting a missile.

"Bastards. Track?"

He could just see the man's head shake as he replied, "Not defined at this point. Other than it's in the right cone."

"Yes, please update."

"Will do."

Moments later, Farana said, "I don't like the plot curve. We're safe until recovery, but we can't drive hard enough to get away. They can keep shooting and may get a cleaner shot, especially if telemetry from this one helps their placement."

"Overboost. My order. You may go to Never Exceed power level if you need to."

"I need five percent over that to make it work, and one twenty-five percent of boost."

And that's why I'm Captain.

"Do it. But ease off as soon as you can."

"Will do. Stand by for power." She sounded the emergency klaxon and boost alert, waited barely three seconds, and eased the engines up, .5G, 1G, 1.5G, 1.8, 2.3 . . .

The entire spaceframe hummed with vibration as material was stressed beyond intended limits. His screens showed reactor temperature rising, containment holding but taking wear at a dangerously accelerated rate, driveline temperature getting into the red, and the driveline losing efficiency as he watched. Days of fuel were disappearing in seconds.

Then the boost cut.

Rievley advised, "Interception definitely below fifty percent."

"Well, that's good to know." On the one hand they wanted to avoid capture. On the other hand, marooned in deep space was only a moral win by denying the ship to the enemy, which they had much more survivable means of accomplishing.

He added, "Ignore all further transmissions. That is, I don't need to hear them unless it's a game changer. Log them for later intel."

Mati said, "All they're doing is repeating their orders and shouting."

"Well, good." If they were talking, they weren't sure of their intercept, either.

Five segs later Rievley announced, "Interception below forty percent."

"Noted."

Shortly he added, "Interception below forty-four percent."

Yates prickled. "It's up?"

"Better readings. I'm still confident."

He didn't say, *I hope so.* "Thank you. Accuracy is appreciated."

There was a long, tense pause as they awaited more data.

Eventually, Rievley noted, "Below thirty-eight percent."

"I like this trend."

Nothing happened for a long time. That was space. You tried to guess what was happening at a distance with light lag, and waited to see if you were correct.

Near the end of the div the tactical officer spoke with a much brighter tone.

"Sir, it's below thirty percent, and I'm going to state I don't think they've got a shot. Professional estimate."

"Thank you."

"In fact, I'm calling it under thirty percent on a near miss, no chance of a hit."

One-third chance of a near miss could still wreck them badly. Under these circumstances that would be as lethal as a hit, and in fact potentially worse if it was a slow death.

Long segs went by with normal watchstanding, but everyone was aware of the risk behind.

Mati reported, "*Sleipnir* wants an update."

"Give them one."

"Yes, sir. Sending them our plot curves."

"How is pursuit?"

Rievley was already replying, "Their missile just lost boost. I expect readings on an abort detonate momentarily... and there it is."

Yates let out a breath from his tight chest. "Good. That's one threat taken care of."

They still had to dock with *Sleipnir*.

They had two days and change before they reached it. He ordered repair to all damage, minimum power to nonessential services, and asked if *Sleipnir* needed anything.

Long segs later, there was a reply.

Mati said, "Sir, they say they're fine but other elements will need whatever we can spare."

"Noted." The war didn't sound promising. He wasn't going to say that aloud. But perhaps some neutral system would give them asylum? Though the number of non-UN systems was few, and those who could ignore a UN order... that was pretty much Govannon only.

Well, *Sleipnir* obviously had some kind of info and a destination in mind. For now, he and his crew were alive, had support, and there was still some sort of chain of command. The only news came from a very biased UN source, but seemed to show a pretty complete takedown and a lot of deaths of the ground forces, occupation of everything. There was no way to know what the rest of the Space Command looked like.

The insults from *Montevideo* tapered off to notional "official" sanctions that meant nothing unless they were captured, though at that point, they'd claim all kinds of theft and misappropriation of a ship they claimed title to without occupation.

"*—Command crew, you are ordered to seize control from the captain, who is committing piracy and mutiny of a UN vessel—*"

"*—Crew of the ship identified as FMS* Force, *under instruction of the UN Military Bureau, you are ordered to apprehend the command crew, hold them under arrest, and contact us for instructions on repatriation. Compliance with this directive will exempt all parties from any criminal charges—*"

He wondered what repercussions *Montevideo* might face for not apprehending them. *Force* was not a warship, she was an ungainly pile of machinery, holds and spare parts.

He followed their track, and that of *Sleipnir*. They were closing as planned, but he'd never done a deep-space docking before. No one had. Fleet carriers held orbit or station with known coordinates. Matching two orbits wasn't that hard in near space. Out here, they'd need precision measurements to get close, and then have to treat it as a single movement to intercept between them.

"I think we can resume normal watches, with an alert and sensor crew keeping an eye on the *Montevideo*'s movements. Stand by for normal rotation."

At the top of the div, First Officer Ship Commander Roy Brody came in to relieve him. Yates noted his concerns and status.

"I will be resting, but do not hesitate to call me if there is an issue. Note that you have full authority for emergency and combat orders in my absence. Use it as needed."

"Understood, and aye, sir. Rest well."

"I will." He'd try at least. Brody was very competent, but letting someone else have command authority was always like letting someone else steer you downslope on skis.

Late the next day they were close enough to match with *Sleipnir*. It was actually anticlimactic. The carrier had had three days to assume a workable position. Farana brought them up from astern. There was one long thrust correction to match orbits, and they drifted closer over two divs. One short thrust brought them almost parallel, a few hundred meters apart, *Force* a stubby tube next to the giant gantry of *Sleipnir*. A nudge closed that gap. One more slowed that and they eased into the framework.

"Force, *stand by for rendezvous and docking.*"

The entire ship clattered as it always did on hookup. It went a lot faster, though. Neither wanted to remain where enemy ships might pursue a known location, and there was a war to fight in some fashion, somewhere else.

Typically, hookup took about twenty segs. It was barely over twelve when the connection crew leader called via wire and advised, "Force, *we are engaged. Your drive is locked. I am relaying to you that phase drive is imminent. CiC should contact you momentarily, but I request you make ready.*"

"Acknowledged, *Sleipnir.*"

"*Also, we'll need your fuel to reach destination.*"

"We can transfer when you are ready." Gods, that meant things were tight. *Sleipnir* wouldn't have made it out. They'd apparently come in-system short of juice, just to catch *Force.*

Mati relayed, "All hands, stand by for phase entry. All non-phase crew make immediate restraint."

Through their network, the carrier's C-deck announced, "*Stand by for phase entry.*"

There it was. Thrust first barely felt, then increasing to full drive, likely 1.7G standard, with oscillations and vibrations as the docking hardware shifted under stress. That was followed by the shivering twists one felt as the universe changed its entire shape around one.

There had been no courtesy call or official contact from the *Sleipnir.* Just "Hurry and we'll need your fuel."

Once safely in the phase field, both ships extended fueling umbilici, connected, and *Force* also became an external tank. That was one advantage of the fleet carrier. Any resources and personnel could be easily moved between other vessels.

Shortly they were transferring fuel, what precious little they had.

It was only then the expected command call came.

"*Captain Yates, this is Captain Kacito.*" Her sharp face was familiar and a relief. They weren't alone in the dark anymore.

"Captain, first, thank you very much for assisting in our escape. On behalf of my crew and myself. And then, pleased to see you. I'd request permission to dock, but..."

"*Yes, no niceties, for which I apologize, but we are bound for an emergency point. How up to date are you?*"

"Ah, we're at war with the UN, and the Freehold has been

hit hard. We were supporting several smaller boats and helped fit out a remote base in-system."

Kacito frowned. She replied, *"That's all correct, but doesn't begin to cover the magnitude. I'll dump the entire known SitAn, and you should probably join me for a face-to-face summary."*

"Yes, Captain. At your convenience."

"As soon as we reach destination."

Watchstanding was easy in phase drive. *Sleipnir* handled everything related to the mission. All the crew had to do was maintain shipboard operations.

Three days later, they had most of their repairs accomplished, though some tweaking would take external analysis which the carrier could do for them in normal space.

Which could be soon. They were warned of phase exit, and shortly precipitated.

He decided he'd better wear Class A instead of a shipsuit, just to maintain decorum and etiquette. He rose from his couch and stretched, awaiting Third Officer Alito to relieve him.

Astrogator Farana had a quizzical look on her face as she checked her screens.

"This is interstellar."

"Farana?"

She elaborated, "Sir, we're nowhere. Not in any system."

"I see."

"But there's a facility here. A very rough one, with a single dock port. Three ships are in slow parking orbits. *Jack Churchill* is one, and two smaller craft, heavily stealthed."

"I will inquire."

A query to Fleet provided an explanation.

Command Navigator Morales came on view and said, *"Yes. Only astrogators know the location. And until the UN gets their phase drive ships online, they can't get here anyway. Though they could infiltrate or charter, buy, or steal a craft. Sorry, 'commandeer.'"*

"Well, we're in. What are we doing?"

"You'll be fabbing everything with what material you have. Should I tell the captain to expect you, sir?" he asked, reminding Yates there was a process.

"Of course, I'm on my way and available at your captain's pleasure."

Cleared for Professional Release: "Excerpts from General Jacob Huff's Journal"

Christopher and Jaime DiNote

FMF Special Warfare University Press's prepublication note: "The following are declassified excerpts from UNPF system Occupation Commander General Jacob Huff's personal journal. Artifacts were predominantly transcribed from hard-copy notebooks, and where possible, sequenced in time with recovered audio and video. GEN Huff's exact words have been preserved to the maximum extent possible. GEN Huff was wont to use an awkward mix of Grainne and Earth time references, which makes exact time and date stamps difficult to determine for many entries.

Huff #1
Journaling (21 January 210)

You journal with whatever you have on hand. It'll be a mess, with lots of handwritten notes mixed in with typed and dictated entries—I'll clean it up later. This is the one thing I don't let anyone do for me. Keeping a journal has saved my career more than once, and probably will again. Besides, memoirs lead to book tours, and potentially insurance, if the UN government decides to blame me should operational complications arise.

Huff #2
Arrival—[6 or 7 February 210]

I arrived planetside at what *should* be 0500, but locally, more like 0615, and I'm already tired. Acclimation is going to take a while. I'll adjust to the local weather, rotational period, and the higher gravity, but right now I can't show that it's bothering me.

I like my new aide-de-camp, Wing Commander Sandeep Patel-Stiles. Commissioned from Sandhurst and a career fighter pilot in both Avatars and Sentinels. He's very pleased that he has almost 1,000 hours in the Sentinel—a rare feat for air supremacy pilots these days. On his first day with me, he even said that "one vee one air-to-air is the last true home of honor," so I started calling him "the Red Baron." He might know who that was. More importantly, Sandeep knows coffee. Good coffee. I think I'll keep him.

At maybe 0630, I knocked out thirty minutes on the treadmill, because my lead Personal Security Officer—a bald, brutish SOB—won't let me run outside yet. (Note: Need to have common devices, like PT equipment, synched to the system's master network time—should encourage quicker adaptation, and ease rapport building with the locals.)

I gave myself time for hygiene and reading—well, skim and highlight. Then, I took a quick verbal prep from my new Chief, Strategic Analysis and Studies Group. I just call him "The CAG." This bloke knows his stuff and has excellent tact. He also worked stability missions right next door to the main Grainne area of operations on Mtali, so he's got some sense about the locals. He hails from field artillery, but now his primary weapon is a slate loaded with more to read than I could ever want or get through.

0800: Time for the O&I—Ops and Intel briefing. My first one on the ground here, so I have all the J-codes, special staff, civilian staff, UN, and some select Non-Governmental Organizations in person, but no press, no media embeds. That will come later.

Let's see what we have: First, an arrogant intel prick who won't ever brief me again, for starters.

"...And here on 'Grain,' we assess..."

"Grahn-YAH." I interrupted him. I couldn't stand it anymore. I even overemphasized the last syllable.

"Sir?" This idiot had no clue he'd been mispronouncing the planet's name for five straight minutes. What the *hell* is going on in my J2 shop?

"Grahn-ya, Captain. The planet you're currently standing on. Grahn-ya, not 'Grain.' Say it."

"Grainne, sir." He's not happy, and afterward, he'll be even less happy.

"That's better. It's some kind of Gaelic, right, POLAD?" It's rhetorical, I don't care if he knows. "Now say it one more time, correctly please, and continue."

Technically, "POLAD" or "Political Advisor," is an obsolete term; the UN prefers "UN Policy-External Nation Sensitivity Officer," but I can't pronounce that acronym.

I don't like to pull stunts in a public setting, but the incident was a disgrace. When I glanced over at the J2, she looked at her hands, shook her head, and with one hand stroked her eyebrow, nervous and embarrassed. We briefly made eye contact and she got the hint: "This idiot won't brief me again." She has one star, if she wants a second, she'd better figure it out.

I'm genuinely worried about things like this; if my people don't care enough about the absolute basics—like pronouncing the planet's name correctly—then I don't know how we're going to win anyone over.

On to enemy force dispositions: no remaining major ones as far as we know. We don't have extensive HUMINT networks. Vetting those takes a lot of time we don't have, even as well as this seems to be going so far. The damn Spacy took out too much infrastructure, which I'd have preferred to appropriate for our own use. We damaged some orbital constellations, a few spinners, and the system-wide relay architecture. It's a double-edged sword; you disable the opponent, but you hinder your own ability to communicate with the outside world, and engage with the populace. Worst of all, you squash the intel take.

The J3 and I will PAR the opening moves later, offline.

Shit, I zoned out. We're on the J6, but he's merely restating the obvious.

"...And we're going to have to bring in our own combat signals folks to put in infrastructure, wired terrestrial infrastructure. What the locals have is insufficient and nonstandard."

This is going long. I look over at my Chief of Staff. She nods.

"Thank you, J6, any others, brief by exception only."

Awkward silence, then a quick round of "Nothing further, sir."

My turn. "Folks, we're not alone and not afraid, we have full UN support for stability operations, governance projects, and reintegration, but we're going to do a lot of the building. Not just rebuilding, but building a cultural baseline that can fully integrate with civilization, and accept the UN mandate. Expect pushback from certain corners. This command will operate with a fair degree of autonomy, but always within doctrine, within the published Rules of Engagement, and within the Law of Armed Conflict, to the tee. To. The. Tee. Chief of Staff, go around the room, ping the outstations again, and let's get to work."

Spider's Web
Part 2

For the next several days, Moyra Kelly remained glued to her console as much as she could physically cope with. She only took breaks for necessities, including stretches to keep her hip from seizing. She kept one screen open for what had become the command channel while she worked with complex code and random chitchat on the other screen.

:: Strike in one confirmed, :: Jenkins messaged the command team.

:: Good, :: DalesOP replied. :: Initiating Breakdance. ::

Moyra switched over to private comm with TripleShot. :: Need you to get Disco Inferno ready. ::

:: With pleasure. :: Moyra could almost hear the angry staccato typing. Trip's sister hadn't been found yet. Damocles' buddy promised to keep looking, while survivors attempted to get back into some semblance of order.

Damocles continued to work furiously through his military contacts, attempting to determine who in the chain of command survived. He reported to Moyra that the damage was substantial, although perhaps less than the UN anticipated. They were going to need a *lot* of resources to have any hope of fighting back. The UN hadn't even landed much on the surface yet, although the data coming in from the now-occupied stations made it clear they were about to land in force.

Skylight, on Skywheel Two, funneled as much information as she could safely manage from every ship that showed up. She coordinated her own little network of dabblers topside, each feeding data to her and down. As soon as Moyra was able to find a place to have things sent to, she'd have them start altering everything in every way possible.

Several gutter balls rolled around while Jenkins attempted to expand from the diplomatic ship's network over to the recently arrived military transports, but one throw finally hit a couple of pins. Necessarily, progress was painstakingly slow. Between those two sources, Moyra intended to scramble the database to destroy the logistical controls in place. With DalesOP and TripleShot off playing matador for the UN's security teams, there was a fair chance they could get the deep foothold necessary to completely compromise the UN network in-system.

Then, it would simply be a matter of keeping the defensive teams distracted with surface level attacks while they worked underneath it. "Simply."

In main comm, the pre-shelling bullshit chatter continued. Braknck whined about how they hadn't gotten a good money hit in weeks, and what was taking so long.

:: Most of the cretins that cretins like us prey on aren't keen on hanging around when the UN shows up, maybe? :: TripleShot replied. :: And it's not like that ship showing up wasn't a big dance number to telegraph their intentions. ::

:: I'm broke! I can't buy Sparkle and I've been out for a day already! ::

:: Thought it was just a simple pleasure, :: Moyra snarked.

:: Fuck you, Hesp, :: Braknck replied.

:: Sorry, I have work to do. You'll have to be content with your palm. ::

The expected crude comments shut Braknck's complaints up, while he joined in trying to top them.

:: You know he'll turn us in for a bounty, :: Damocles said in the command comm.

:: Kinda counting on it, actually, :: Moyra typed, sighing. She had already dropped a note to Bowler Hat. The risk of compromising their *other* activities felt way too high, but Bowler Hat always came through when other income came slowly. He said once he preferred to pay them a retainer if it kept them from meandering into other pockets.

She doubted he would disapprove of their current focus. The UN was notoriously bad for business.

:: Laters. :: For once, she was actually headed outside of the apartment, rather than heads down in working out bugs in Salamander's project. Her brain needed the break to work through the code issue.

Isibéal met her at the door. "Be careful," she said, pressing a kiss to Moyra's forehead. She helped Moyra shrug on her backpack and arm crutches. Moyra usually shunned the power brace, because she always felt it made the pain worse. Besides, given how long it had taken to walk again, while the doctors carefully rebuilt and regrew her pelvis, she didn't want to lose the ability altogether. She saw a few people at the specialty clinic like that.

"Always," she replied. She didn't always need the crutches for walking around town. Some days, she didn't need them at all, but it was better to have them than not.

She stopped at her favorite restaurant, which was almost empty. The few patrons barely whispered to each other. More filtered in as it got closer to dinner time, but it stayed relatively quiet. She chatted pleasantly with Charles, the owner, until her comm chirruped for attention, and he faded away to let her deal with it. Salamander's application was sending notifications it shouldn't be, and she tapped into the program.

The "game" screen came up, a standard block stacking clone, harkening back to the earliest days of computers. She immediately lost the first level in the particular command structure required to flip into the "administrative" side.

She read TripleShot's frantic message, relayed by Sal. :: Troops, Hesp, troops. They're attacking Jefferson. Powered armor and armored vehicles. Lost most comm signals already. Emergency system managed to get out the alert before it got slammed shut. Let Dam know! Shutting my systems down, safeties engaged to slag if necessary. ::

:: Trip: Be safe. Stay low. Hugs. :: She loved that boy more than anything right now, and her heart twisted to think he was at risk. :: Sal: Confirm Dam has received info for relay. Did Skylight get any warning just missed? ::

:: Trip's offline; already told him about that for you. Dam received info. Has relayed. Will contact you separately. App is buggy, but best option ATM. Skylight warned of gear shifting between Three and ships, but learned of landings after shift. Couldn't comm safely. ::

Moyra ground her teeth. The app was *beyond* buggy...and still their safest networked communication. Fuck, they needed deeper access to everything. For a fleeting moment, she regretted they— *she*—had kept their focus so narrow prior to this.

They needed more. More access, more hands, more eyes, more links. Skylight's warning might have done...something. What, Moyra wasn't sure.

Sound of a crash yanked her attention up to the screens above her. She tapped out of the "game" before securing the mobile and typed a reminder. *Note: Auto time outs on access.*

Hamilton was a good div's trip northeast of Jefferson. Charles had one over-the-air station up on all screens. The newscasters looked a combination of scared and furious. "*—confirmed reports of UN troops assaulting the main downtown area now. Other stations alerted us they were being brought offline by force. We only have limited video input from citizens on the street,*" the female anchor said. "*We are relaying everything we get. Please stay inside for your own safety. We will remain on the air as long as we can. Repeat, we have confirmed reports of UN troops—*"

"Has anyone heard from family?" Moyra asked loudly. Her question broke the horrified fascination. Several shook their heads, and immediately started reaching for devices. Some voiced frustration that their network provider was down. Two managed to reach out, and Moyra got the information for the networks in use and listened to what was relayed.

A warning klaxon started playing over the infoset's speakers. "*Troops have entered our facility. I expect our broadcast will be shut down shortly. Good luck. May God and Goddess be with us all.*" The male anchor's calm voice and expression belied the import of the situation. The anchors continued talking, reiterating advice to stay quiet and inside, until the signal abruptly died. No cut screen, just black silence.

The silence echoed in the diner until someone shuffled in discomfort. Moyra just stared at the black screen. "They take control of Jefferson, and then what?" someone asked.

"If the monologues from the sat feeds are anything to go by," Charles replied, "They're a mite ticked we haven't been wholeheartedly happy to embrace their benevolent dictatorship after 'saving' us by KEWing our bases. So they're going to start in with the sticks."

Moyra waved Charles down and handed him her payment. She headed home.

Isibéal met her halfway home from the diner, while she played up her limp on the crutches. "Ah, good. I hoped you'd be on your way back."

"It got quite uncomfortable."

"Quite." Isibéal made a show of helping Moyra back home and into the flat.

The real conversation resumed as soon as Moyra verified certain pieces of equipment were still working. "Was there no warning you could share?" Isibéal asked.

"Too little, too late. We need to fix that."

She moved the mobile's connection to the encrypted hardwired lines, and then tagged into the "game."

A message from Damocles waited.

:: I have contacts who need to meet with you, in person, soonest. I can be with them. ::

:: Important ones? You'd have to be, to verify them to me. ::

:: Very. They wanted me to be "in command" but... you're better. You can make this work. ::

:: That's intimidating. ::

:: Some of the very best on offer have perished, Hesp. You've collected most of the rest. I think it's time to tug on some lines, though. And only you can do that. ::

:: If they're willing. I'll try. You know where. When? ::

:: We're en route, before Trip's message got through even. Call it a dinner date. ::

:: You're penciled in. :: Damocles and his guest weren't flying in. Dinner *tomorrow* was a land trip. Just how far out had he found this VIP? She let Isibéal know about the visitors' ETA.

She jotted down the note to Salamander about having the device screen time out of the app, regardless of security settings, along with a brief thought about the annoying code issue. She bit at her lip while she stared at the mobile's screen. They needed more hands. Regardless of this VIP, they needed more hands.

But just because *Damocles* trusted this VIP, didn't mean *she* could. Dare she risk the entire black- and grey-hat hackers by contacting them now?

Troops have entered our facility. The anchor's calm, controlled voice echoed in her mind. *Troops have entered our facility.*

Not all of the BGs would be willing to pitch in. A handful— including Braknck—would be willing to sell themselves to the highest bidder, although she expected they would regret it later. Still... she sat down to check in, and start tugging on strands.

In response to her query about possible payment, Bowler Hat requested as much information as they could possibly collect for every UN official or politician in-system. Her team would continue to collect their bounty in exchange. She provided what they had on the initial "diplomat."

She flicked through the channel updates, and dropped off a note in the main comm about a payment en route. Braknck's inane response bore little worth responding to, but he at least seemed mollified.

She gave DalesOP information on the networks which were working after the initial Jefferson invasion. He immediately dug into looking at the technical, logistical, or geological differences between those providers and those already shut down.

:: We will need to replace Trip's work until it's safe for him to come back online. Or shift to a different Op? :: DalesOP commented.

:: Don't know yet, :: Moyra replied. :: I see Dam's offline too. Sightseeing? At a time like this? ::

:: You know Dam, :: DalesOP replied.

The casual shrug she "heard" in that reply convinced her to tap the BGs. Damocles had not felt it prudent to tell even DalesOP, their mutual best and oldest friend, about the VIP needing to see her in person. Perhaps not even that a VIP had been located, and was interested in tapping their resources.

Even as she started to compose the initial query in her mind, she realized she needed to reach the whites, too. But only a handful of that crowd had the right mentality for the work in question, at least until—if—they received "official sanction." Others might be worth bringing in . . . later. Possibly much later.

Two divs later, she and Salamander resolved the most pressing bug. In between bits of that task, numerous contact queries went out to the right kind of individuals. Some ran their own networks, like she did, and others were specialists in specific gear that might be useful. All of them had useful contacts, occasionally through second and third layers.

They also did not know her as Hespera or Moyra. Those who did were riskier, given the situation. She'd respond if *they* tagged her, but for now, she needed to keep the personas and names separated.

The door read *Samantha Peterson* in an elegant script, and Moyra Kelly ruthlessly pushed the nostalgia down. Memories were for later.

She spared a few moments and burned restless energy to give the office a once over, both cleaning and verifying integrity. She settled in to review information from her mother's work with the military years ago. Damocles and his VIP-in-tow would be arriving soon, and she needed the refresher.

A polite knock roused her from reviewing the files, where she'd made notes that might be of use now. She checked the security feeds, and verified it was Damocles at the door. An older man she vaguely recognized stood by and at least one guard attended them. She buzzed them into the room.

"Miss Peterson," Damocles said. "Thank you for meeting with us under such short notice. Please allow me to introduce Colonel Naumann and Blazer Davis."

Moyra shook hands with Naumann. He did not let go, staring at her intently. "My condolences on your mother's death. I heard about her passing, although I was curious that the business continued under her name."

"Brand recognition, mainly. Most businesses care about the brand and the services provided. As I had already been a partner in the business for some time before she passed, the . . . handover was relatively seamless."

"I see."

Moyra gestured to the seats across the desk. "Please, sit."

Damocles moved to lean against the wall, but Naumann directed him to sit, with the guard at the door. "Corporal Johnson indicated he had a small network with the capability to take over most of the operations which my own team can no longer access or perform."

"Was the equipment destroyed along with the bases?"

"Most of it." He offered no details.

"Sorry, sir. I hope you had fewer casualties than feared."

He snorted and Damocles shifted uncomfortably. "Were that so, Miss Peterson. But when Johnson mentioned Miss Samantha Peterson as being a member of the network, I recognized the name. I'll trust you with what we have. Provided, of course, you can decrypt and provide the passcode."

Moyra nodded, and gestured at her screen off to the side. "I have full access to the files from the previous contract, including an encrypted passcode file. If it's the item I believe you reference, I can have that completed shortly."

Naumann smiled slightly. "You have the same efficiency." He handed her a memory stick. She took it with a raised eyebrow, and moved over to the hardened jump box. Once she verified integrity and safety of the chip, insofar as feasible, she moved over to the working machine, where she'd already transferred items of interest to enable a decryption.

She pressed her finger across the reader, and flinched ever

so slightly as it drew a droplet of blood. "Gene-key?" Naumann asked. "You don't use a neural interface?"

Moyra shrugged. "Nothing can be foolproof, but it's harder to hack a wired keyboard than other options. Nor do I want a competitor sabotaging me with a neural net virus." She tapped in the necessary commands, and watched the decryption proceed. The data file opened. "I'm in."

"Those files have the technical details for accessing the covert satellite controls and other communication points. Per previous contract, that information was not retained in-house. Now you have them. Can you leverage it to regain clandestine control of the communication networks? If so, how fast?"

Moyra considered, as she flicked through the decrypted documents, pausing at particularly interesting sections. "I cannot provide a definitive timeline at this juncture. However, the more access the better."

Naumann nodded. "Very well. What other assets are at your disposal?"

She turned to face him full on, and leaned back in the chair. "I have contacted several business associates. They range from occasional dabblers who assist in information gathering to full-time professionals such as myself. I'm waiting to hear back. My personal network already achieved minor success in a baseline infiltration of UN assets, and I have two operations engaged in low-level distractions to act as cover."

Naumann asked, "How 'baseline' is baseline?"

She phrased it for his unasked question. "With a little more time, enough to start minor electronic sabotage."

"How soon can it be major?"

"We must move carefully to avoid existing defenses and anyone actively paying attention to alerts. With more assets at my disposal, that can be more rapid."

He didn't dispute, only asked, "Is your crypto communication usable now?"

"Corporal Johnson contacted me on it when relaying your wish to meet."

"That would be a yes."

"A qualified yes," Damocles spoke up. "Our primary programmers are still resolving functionality issues. The *security* is fine, but the performance and stability are not yet there."

"We resolved the major stability issue yesterday," Moyra replied.

"Ah. I was deliberately not checking, to minimize trackable signals."

"If you swap to the encrypted lines, you can get updated." She glanced at Naumann. "If you have a phone or comm you prefer to use, I can also create an authorized installation and connection for you."

"Perfect," Naumann said. "How do you expect to disperse it later? A manual process for every individual would be...time consuming."

"Time consuming but necessary. It will need to be extremely restricted as to who can communicate with who. We don't want a single instance of compromise to take out every individual involved." She shrugged. "I, and my team, will manage the administrative aspect. The base application won't have two-way communication enabled. It's a game, and a popular one at that. It's one of our revenue streams, actually. We use it for...other purposes, generally. This is an extension of that application, enabling two-way communications for select 'players.' I can deploy those based on validated information to specific devices." She smirked. "I expect *most* individuals who are likely to partake in this already have the base application installed."

Naumann nodded. "Very well." He unlocked his military comm and slid it over to her. A few moments' tinkering, and she had him functionally on the platform. Damocles switched over to her encrypted lines and updated himself.

Further discussion solidified the *goals* Naumann had for the counter attacks, and he provided specific information with which to validate key individuals from his remaining resources. She cloned the necessary information for hooking into the covert channels, and everything else of interest.

At last, there was little left that could be discussed without further technical progress. Naumann stood. "It will be a pleasure doing business with you, Miss Kelly."

Moyra did not react. She wondered when he would admit to knowing her name. He smirked. "You're not surprised."

"Mother noted you knew our actual names, and that you tried a similar trick on her."

A genuine smile bloomed on his face. It rather disturbed her. "It *will* be a pleasure doing business with you." He glanced at

Damocles. "I will leave Corporal Johnson here with you for the time being. He'll return separately."

Standard disaster operations. Moyra nodded, and let Naumann and his guard out the door. Damocles sighed heavily as the door shut. "That was exhausting, Hesp."

"Yeah. We'll let them skedaddle away, and then I'm under orders to bring you home. Gram never forgave us for not working out. She wanted you for a grandson-in-law."

Damocles snorted. "As long as she's made dinner."

"Your favorite, even."

A Time to Fight

J.F. Holmes

Part 1

Orme, Plains District, Year 206 of the Freehold

"Warrant McClellan? We're about to de-orbit, you need to secure yourself in the passenger compartment." The shuttle crew chief sounded loath to break into the older man's reverie, but space was unforgiving.

He said nothing in response, but stood, placing his hand on the green flag of the Freehold, feeling the aluminum container underneath. It was cold in the cargo bay, but not as cold as his heart. "Jesus, John, what am going to do now? This is going to kill mum," he muttered.

The body of his brother, Senior Sergeant John McClellan, communications specialist, Third Mobile Assault Regiment, Freehold Military Forces, had no answer for him. The military standard casket remained silent, as it ever would.

"And how the hell am I going to deal with Jack? The boy will want to know. Should I tell him you're a hero, John, or just tell him the randomness of a mortar? The stupidity of it all?" Bitter tears rolled down his clean-shaven face, and he jerked as the crewwoman touched his arm.

"Sir," the crew chief said compassionately, "you have to get strapped in. As soon as we touch down, you can come back and escort your brother out."

"Aye, lass. I will," he said, slipping into his native brogue in his grief. Though Scotland was thirty Earth years behind him, he had never really left the Highlands at heart. Grainne may have become his home, but it held no joy for him now.

She turned and led him back through the hatch to the personnel compartment. He sat, cursing as the basket hilt of his *claidheamh cuil*, the backsword, caught on the harness. Then G hit with the retros, pushing him forward in the restraints. Once in atmosphere, the pilot took them in a smooth arc, dropping down to Jefferson Starport. Still the heavy push and pull made his leg ache, where tendons were badly damaged by the same mortar that killed his brother. Regen would heal the leg almost like new, but it wouldn't bring back his brother. He had family to look after now, and retirement age was a good public reason.

Half a div later, he stood with his hand on the casket again, wincing at the harsh Iolight as the ramp dropped, unused to it after his time on Mtali. Six figures in dress uniform, black boots, gold laces, black pants, and green jackets matching his own, stepped forward with precision, filing toward either side of the hold.

Logistics Warrant Leader David McClellan, Third Legion, Freehold Military Forces, stepped aside, drew the sword, edge gleaming in the harsh light of Iota Persei, and held it to his face, looking stonily ahead. The four men and two women, three to a side, stepped forward, grasped the handles just under the flag with white gloved hands, turned, and lifted. In measured step, they carried the body of his only brother out onto the apron, past the young boy who stood stiffly, trying not to cry. Next to him stood the boy's grandmother, and her face was as gray as the aluminum of the casket that bore her son.

12 March 210

"And what, exactly, do you suppose we do about them?" asked McClellan, addressing the whole town hall in general. Gathered in front of him were twenty-three men and women that represented the total adult population of Orme within thirty kilometers.

"We FIGHT!" shouted James Harrow, the man with the smallest farm in the area, and the least to lose. Even on Grainne, there were those who lived in a shack and slowly drank themselves to death. His choice, but if the war hadn't come, the neighbors might have soon interfered with his kids. As it was, they ate at others' places more than at home. A right bastard he was.

"Aye, you fight, we can do that," answered the older man. "And how do you propose to do so? That's a whole UN supply battalion, with at least a platoon of infantry to provide security."

The arm he waved was in the general direction of the forward logistics base being erected just outside of their small town. Two hundred and fifty kilometers northwest of Jefferson, Orme made a good place to service VTOLs and truck convoys, though the village itself was little more than a grain depot, the Singh's convenience/grocery store, and McClellan's farm equipment dealership. Prefab buildings were quickly growing up in the "requisitioned for government needs" wheat fields of Killian Gots's farm. The owner himself had not been seen since he went to the UN offices at Jefferson to protest. That had been two weeks ago, and rumor had it that he was "detained." Mac knew well enough what that meant: to never expect to see his friend again.

"Listen to me," said McClellan. "I've seen war, and it's not pretty. There's enough firepower in that base to sweep away the lot of us, and this is my home. I'd like not to see it destroyed."

"Are you a coward then?" asked a voice from the back of the room.

McClellan's grip tightened on the pistol he wore holstered on his belt, then relaxed. They were all tense, and getting into a duel now would solve nothing. He couldn't just let that pass, though. "I'm no coward, Miguel, and any other time I'd prove it to you. I just know what war is, and I have no desire to see you all slaughtered for no reason."

That brought an angry outburst from some of them, and Mac wished desperately that there were other veterans around him, even a reservist or two, but they had all disappeared northward three months ago when the war started. What was left were a bunch of small-town people, and he was an outsider to them. Hell, he could probably have lived here for a hundred years and still been an outsider. Being from Earth, even three decades ago, didn't help.

"Listen," he continued, "you're all farmers. Regardless of who is in charge, people need to be fed. I have some contacts in what's left of the FMF." *Maybe.* "If you want to help the war, then grow food, and I'll see what can be done about getting it to the people who need it, the ones that CAN fight effectively."

"Well, I'm not sticking around here. I'm going south, to see who will take me to fight," said Miguel. Several of the younger men stood and said they would join him, giving looks to McClellan. He just nodded; they would do what they would do.

The meeting broke up after that, the farmers somewhat mollified. Although they loved their freedom, the immediate threat of the UN base next door had brought home the war as nothing else could. Everyone, that is, except Harrow, who left cursing everyone and swearing that he would show the "goddamn UN that not everyone in this town is a pussy."

"Listen," he said to the men who wanted to go south, "stop by the dealership, I'll give you what supplies I can, and you can have one of my lifters."

As Mac returned to his warehouse, he felt the angry waves coming off his nephew, and did his best to ignore it. The boy would learn, he hoped, that sometimes rash action was worse than no action.

"*Are* you a coward, Uncle?" asked Jack, when they had gotten back to the dealership. "I know there have been attacks, and we're fighting back. I want to be part of it, not just sit here and suck up to the aardvarks. Like my dad did!" He could hear the emotion and anger in the teenager's voice.

"Jack, your dad would have agreed with me one hundred percent. There's no point to rushing off and getting yourself killed. If you're going to fight, you have to fight smart." He said it, but he could see that there was no getting through the kid's head.

The teen grew angry at the mention of his father, and shot back, "He died a hero, saving other people's lives! And I don't see YOU fighting! Just trying to make money off those scumbags."

McClellan had no answer to that. How do you explain to someone who had never seen the randomness of violence that a highly trained soldier had been killed by a black market UN mortar round? That the low-angle shot had sailed over the wall, beneath the protective anti-indirect fire screen, and gone off a meter from where Communications Sergeant John McClellan Sr. had been walking to get some chow at midnight? That thank God his brother had probably never known what hit him?

You didn't, of course; you told Jack Jr. that his dad died a hero. You also didn't tell him about the men who came at night, to pick up anything even remotely militarily useful, from trucks for transport, to industrial piping for rocket casings, to fertilizer for improvised explosives. Mac had debated bringing Jack on in this. He was a good kid and a great help around the business. The kid's hotheadedness, and the way he had started listening to that asshole Harrow, made him too much of a risk. No, better to keep him out of the loop.

Summer was coming fast, and it was going to be a tough one. True to his word, Mac had arranged secret pickups of whatever the farmers could afford to send to the guerrillas. It was getting harder, though, as the UN agencies wormed their way into the farmers' lives, measuring crop yield, registering assets, enacting strict regulations. They even put radio tags on all of the farm equipment in his dealership, down to the smallest power tool. Each sale now had to be registered through their computer system, and he had another "official" in his office every other week.

Jack came in, wearing what looked suspiciously like combat fatigues. They were a mix of green Earth and orange Grainne vegetation. That is, the pants were green and black, and the shirt was dull orange and brown.

"What's with the outfit?" he asked, and got nothing but a scowl.

Seeming to realize he might not get what he wanted by being obnoxious, the kid smiled and said, disarmingly, "Can I get your old hunting rifle out of the locker? Me and Carl want to go hunting for meat."

"Carl and I," he said absently, looking more over the books. "Remember the UN rules, no more than three rounds."

"What if we come across a ripper?"

"Make sure you hit it with your first shot," McClellan tried to joke, but the teen was already gone.

This was the tricky part. When you blackmail someone who was up to their eyeballs in criminal shit, things could go very wrong. Or right. McClellan wasn't even sure it was necessary, yet. Hopefully the man's greed would be enough, and he wouldn't have to use the videos from the escort service. It was a seriously dangerous game of poker, one he had played before. Two of the men he played against on Mtali had lost their lives.

That had been some hairy action, setting up a deal for the Special Warfare to catch a Shia arms dealer. Mac was the bait, posing as, basically, a corrupt version of himself. The deal went bad, and only his body armor saved him from the ancient Tokarev pistol. Mac's return shot blew off the man's head, the second shot catching the startled bodyguard in the crotch, then McClellan had thrown up as the SW troops came pounding into the room.

They sat in Nimbutu's office, both men smoking cigars from Earth. The UN sergeant major had offered him a joint, and Mac nodded no. "It's a cultural thing, Joseph, you understand." The real reason is that he wanted a clear head to do business. Being on a first name basis, though, with a man like this, chewed at his insides.

"Are you sure? It is just a sample, but I can get you more, in bulk."

"No, if I wanted that, I could go to just about any farmer around here," said Mac.

Nimbutu shrugged and said, "Well, on to other things. Business had been good, but I suspect that you want something more than band-aids and medicines to help out your 'farmers.' Everything, of course, comes with a price." With that, he slid a paper across the desk to McClellan.

It was a list, of course, but his eyes widened involuntarily when he read it. "These are...FMF munitions."

"Well," said the logistics NCO, "obviously your farmers don't have any UN weapons, do they? And things are not as easy to get here as they were on Mtali. This is all captured stock, set to be destroyed. Of course your friends need small-arms ammo to defend against the nasty wildlife here on Grainne."

"Aye, that's true," he muttered in response, looking the list over. Fifteen thousand cases of 4mm rifle clips. Ten thousand 7mm rounds for pistols. One *million* rounds of 11mm sniper for light machine gun. That made sense; the heavier stuff wasn't issued to be carried. The list went on, but no prices.

"I see you've been busy." Mac slid the list back across the desk, and Nimbutu used a lighter to burn it.

"I have many friends in many places. As you know from Earth and Mtali. You could say that nothing moves anywhere on Grainne without my, how do you say in English? My cut."

Now was the time to be careful. Negotiation over that amount of material would be tough. "This is a lot more than simple farmers need. Or can afford."

Nimbutu laughed, and said, "I don't want your money, David, I want my freedom."

"What the bloody hell?" said the surprised Freeholder. "Freedom?"

The African steepled his fingers, and said, "I know what you're doing, with your buying supplies from me. I know who they are going to, also. You may win, you may not. Maybe this whole planet will crash down around us. But if you do win, I want you to remember who helped you."

He opened a drawer on his desk, and McClellan tensed, feeling naked without a gun to defend himself. Though, if it came down to it, he could strangle the fat bastard before any weapon cleared the top of the desk. He relaxed when Nimbutu brought out a small cooler box, humming faintly on battery power.

"What's this, then?" asked the suspicious Freeholder.

The UN man smiled, and said, "A token of my good faith. It's a sample of a nonlethal but nasty virus that, rumor has it, the UNPF will be releasing atmosphere wide soon. To force rebels in to the clinics to be accounted for. They've used this tactic in regional rebellions on Earth. This one was modified for your atmospheric conditions. Maybe you can do something with it."

Mac put it in a pocket of his kilt, and they stood up. "I'll let you know what my friends need. I understand what you want."

"Until then, David."

Walking outside into the damp night air, to where McClellan's truck was parked, the two men ceased talking about any more deals. They stood in the loading bay while lower-ranking enlisted UN troops unloaded the boxes of foodstuffs.

"Perhaps you can introduce me to your driver?" asked the sergeant major, wiping sweat from his face. His immaculately tailored dress uniform contrasted sharply with the battle dress uniforms of the lower enlisted, who were lazily unloading the truck. Jack, hearing that they were talking about him, rolled up his window and turned the truck radio up full blast, making the frame thump with bass.

"My apologies, Sergeant Major," said McClellan. "He lost his father on Mtali, and doesn't particularly care for aard—I mean the UN military."

"Ahhh, that was a bad place, son, a very bad place. I'm sorry to hear that."

I bet you are, you son of a bitch. It had taken him a long time, but David McClellan knew who was responsible for his brother's death. The fragments they pulled out of his body were from a 120mm UN-issued mortar round, sold on the black market to religious fanatics. Sold by a scumbag like this man. If anything, he hated them more than his nephew did.

"But," continued the UN soldier, "I'm glad some of your people are coming around. Things up in the capital..." he trailed off, shaking his head.

"Well, I'm just a businessman, and I enjoy doing business with a fellow Mtali veteran," McClellan answered, nodding to the six rows of ribbons on the man's chest. Probably all bullshit, he thought. His own few ribbons were locked up in a box. The two veterans exchanged small talk for a while as the UN troopers carried used plastic cartons back onto the truck.

"Yo, Sarge, you shitbag," called a private, making McClellan cringe at the lack of military discipline, "some of these boxes is still got stuff in them."

"Jackson, I told you before, some food doesn't get used before the mandatory expiration date. Do you want the Food and Drug Administration crawling up our asses?" the sergeant major blasted back at him. The two had an argument for almost a seg, with Private Jackson eventually throwing his hands up and walking off the detail. Incredible.

"Well, got to go," said Nimbutu, offering his hand to the Freeholder. David shook it, resisting, as always, the urge to slip a knife into Nimbutu's guts. He climbed back into the truck, Jack started it, and they maneuvered to the gate, zigzagging slowly through the barriers. As always, he took note of the soldiers manning the two bunkers on either side, and the watchtower, looking for signs of any more alertness than usual. Nothing, so far. One machine gun, the ammunition locked in an ammo box. One stickyweb gun in the other bunker, and a heavy-duty tangler in the nearest guard tower. Troops with their helmets off, smoking. Even as they drove through, a male and a female lazily walked back to the MG bunker, carrying food trays.

"I don't know how you can shake that goddamned aardvark's hand. You should be fucking ashamed of yourself. Mr. Harrow says you're a traitor for doing business with them!" barked his nephew when they had cleared the gate.

"Jack, there are a lot of things you don't understand. When you get older..." Maybe the wrong thing to say. Obviously the wrong thing to say, because the boy shut up and said nothing else for the rest of the short trip.

Later that afternoon a battered farm truck rolled into the rear of McClellan and Son Farm Supply and backed up to a loading dock more permanent than the one at the UN warehouse. A man in rough, worn clothing stepped out and met Mac at the rear door. In silence, they worked together to move six crates into the truck, working up a sweat in late summer heat. When they were done, both returned to the office.

Jack was nowhere in sight, and customers few and far between, once word had gotten out that he was dealing with the UN. They had the office to themselves, but even so, the stranger ran a sweep for bugs.

"Clear," he said.

McClellan reached over and grabbed the man in a bear hug. "It's good to see you, Minstrel. We need to talk."

"Bet we do. Got a few segs?"

The two sat in Mac's office, and the resistance fighter brought him up to speed on where things sat with the UN occupation. "I don't have to tell you that they're moving out and expanding into the rural areas. Word's out that hitting their logistics is a good tactic; some people have been doing some damage."

"Not here, if it can be avoided. I've got a lead into the base, and tomorrow I put a lock on him. I'll be able to get at least ammunition for captured weapons, as well as more medical supplies. Starting with this," he said, pulling out the box Nimbutu had given him.

"What is it?" asked Minstrel.

"From what I understand, and here's some intel for you, the aardvarks are going to start using viruses. This box contains a sample of one; supposed to be a sign of good faith."

Minstrel took it and placed in a backpack. "Thanks for the info and the sample. I know a group of people who would love to get their hands on it." The FMF Blazer, for that was what he was, whatever his role now, shook his head and said, "This war is getting nasty."

David said, "War is always nasty. You were there on Mtali. You know."

"And other places, yes," agreed the younger man. "We'll take this base off the target list, for now, if you can keep a conduit open. We lost a lot of stuff in the orbital strikes."

"Give me a shopping list, and I'll see what I can do. For now, let's get you loaded up." The two men went out back, and the boxes that had come from the UN base were quickly shifted to Minstrel's truck.

"So what have we got?" Minstrel asked.

Mac ran through the inventory in his head; there was no paper record. "Primarily medical supplies. Bandages, run of the mill nanos, antibiotics." Just as valuable to an insurgency as ammunition and weapons.

"And to think, all they want in return is alcohol and prostitutes."

"Hey, it's like gold to them. Their idiot General Order Number One. No drinking, no fraternization. It's like they're a bunch of children, not soldiers."

Minstrel nodded, and asked, "Tell me about your contact. In case something happens to you."

"Well," began McClellan, "I knew of him when I was on Mtali. Slick mother, knows computer logistics systems inside and out, knows how to blackmail too. Deals in supplies, weapons, you name it, as long as the price is right."

"How come he hasn't been caught by the UN inspector general?" asked Minstrel.

"Always covers his tracks," answered Mac. "This assignment, he's like a kid in the candy store, looting a whole planet. I hate the bastards."

Minstrel nodded; he was the one who had passed along the information about the munitions that had killed Mac's brother. "It's war, David," he said. "After we win, you can do what you want with him. For now, though, we have to play it cool."

"Yes, after we win." The two men shook hands, and Minstrel climbed back in his truck, just another farmer getting replacement parts for worn-out machinery.

Force Majeure
Part 2

Away from FMS *Force*, Captain Francis Yates remembered he'd been served a decent meal, but couldn't remember what it was. The conference was in the first space inside *Sleipnir*'s docking port.

"So how do we have this handy base in interstellar space?" he asked.

Kacito explained, "A survey located it four years back, while doing phase drive tests. We, meaning the military specifically, sent a recon and study mission, determined it had potential for this, and flagged it. It was triple sealed and has been basically word of mouth only."

That was brilliant. "And without phase drive, it's unreachable."

"Unless we were to sit still and let them build a jump point, yes."

"As amazing as that is, it's not a glamorous superweapon that will win the war for us," he noted, politely probing for more information.

"No. But it's all we have. It was pretty much left alone, except for one supply mission of construction gear. We're rotating crews through to assemble it."

"We worked on something similar in-system, heavily stealthed."

"Yes. As to the war ... we fight. That's our duty and our orders. Commo is largely through contact, days out of date. We just got that update ourselves from a stealth boat *Matahourua* recovered from in-system."

"So what do we have left?"

"Two carriers—us and *Matahourua*, two cruisers—*Malahayati* and *Jack Churchill*, one factory ship—you. Two replenishment. Several gun and stealth boats. A handful of Reserve transports."

"That's all?"

Even her strong featured face softened. "As near as we can tell, everything else was destroyed, captured in-system, seized in dock, or sabotaged in lieu."

Firmly, he said, "I will fight this war. I agree with our duty, orders, and moral position. Though I have little hope for what a noncombatant support ship with a half load of material can possibly do."

Kacito acknowledged, "We're running dry ourselves. Without a material source, or a raw source and enough power, we can't do much more. We've got a list if you can scavenge. We have some gases, some silicates, a little metal, and damaged ship parts and waste."

"We'll take it."

Fabrication went on full shift rotation, producing parts for repair, spares, and support. *Sleipnir* had some wear and tear. The cruiser *Malahayati* arrived and was fitted out for the maximum stealth a ship of that class could manage, including nozzles for chilling the hull with liquid helium. She was bound for Earth space to wreak havoc. *Churchill* got much of the same, and a full complement of weapons. He—*Jack Churchill*'s crew always referred to the ship as "he"—would go back in-system and attempt to damage as much as possible, then rearm at the remote base in the Halo. Each of the gunboats and the stealths were brought to blueprint, then the engineers made whatever mods possible to push their design envelopes.

Yates had little command responsibility at this point. The ship was docked, as functional and provisioned as possible. Other than routine housekeeping, all the duty was under Fabrication Mission Commander Tirza Karanov. She kept him in the loop, but there was nothing he could offer for help, other than the use of space crew as needed.

She gave him the daily progress, noted materials used and power consumption, even though that was from carrier umbilicus, and status.

She told him, "We're taking time to find the absolute most efficient methods possible—material conversion and generation, minimal waste on all processes, because recycling takes energy."

"Yes. Fuel's the point source failure risk for everything here. They're trying to acquire more."

Looking at her notes, she said, "We can operate at this rate for another month. We can manage reduced for another month. We'll need the third month to get somewhere we can resupply and refuel."

"I'll chart that," he said. "Please give me a periodic correction to it."

"Right. Also, I'd like permission to consolidate the messes and gut NCO and officer sections for materials."

"Will that little mass matter?"

"It's not just mass. It's also energy usage and material. We'll pull conduit and reuse the cabling and controls. It reduces our maneuvering mass and consumption at your end."

"And if that's not enough, we'll all have to consolidate even more and go somewhere for asylum or surrender," he admitted. "Permission granted."

She looked determined as she said, "Especially as food beyond basic flavored glop will run short, as will minerals."

Gods, it was a depressing subject.

On the positive side, every ship here was full to capacity on everything except fuel, and tuned to the highest specs possible. They were also outnumbered at least ten to one.

The station had little to recommend it other than a circumferential path one could run around for exercise, and some larger spaces for functions. Yates rotated the crew through to let them have what R&R was possible. Under these conditions, even that was a welcome break. Duty slacked off once everything was to spec and beyond. The cruisers departed.

Spider's Web
Part 3

Moyra Kelly's grandmother Isibéal continued to record and assist in analyzing UN broadcast communications, while Moyra worked on solidifying the resistance's infiltration of the UN network and stabilizing the communication platform.

The primary news channels continued broadcasting highly sanitized news the day after the UN's hold on Jefferson was consolidated. Even the most stoic of broadcasters reported on their "approved" news stories with such sardonic tones that little could be taken seriously. Every rah-rah-UN story was accompanied by subtle derision by those voicing them. The camera crews ensured that the armed goons "off-screen" were frequently visible during those broadcasts.

The UN forces started deploying into suburbs, Moyra's included, while they "set up camp for their visit," as the broadcasters put it. Reports started coming in of residents being dumped on the street while UN troops commandeered complexes, but the UN quickly put a stop to the "resident reporting" block so popular on many of the channels. Bowler Hat cheerfully received the list of bureaucrats who made *those* decisions, and the ground networks started reporting about bounties.

Moyra quietly closed and relocated her mother's office, taking the door sign with her, along with the other items that the UN might find interesting. The office building was commandeered two days later. When they made the choice to use the in-situ wiring, without verifying the lack of data taps, Moyra felt torn between hysterical laughter and braining whichever idiot made that decision, out of sheer industry loyalty.

The choice to live in a relatively dilapidated complex helped protect her from the forced relocation, but she held her breath while the UN forces "decided" where to put their new base. Thankfully, they chose the other, more industrial side of town, to take advantage of the sturdier roads the plants had built for their use.

A week later, *sister stations* were frequently mentioned on all of the news channels, and that these *sister stations* were broadcasting "new entertainment channels." Word of mouth assisted in disseminating the decryption module design for baseline entertainment units. Moyra's black-hat hardware team ensured the modules were easy to fabricate from off-the-shelf parts, and the software to run them readily available, discretely advertised on the software marketplace as "personal weather stations." Not all infosets were compatible, but the team was working on the largest market share first.

Paper media found a quick resurgence in popularity. Difficult to track, difficult to stop, a careful balance of *useful* information and compromising information had to be maintained. Naumann and his team provided clearance as to what information could be sacrificed. Some, Moyra fed to Braknck, knowing he would eventually decide to "abandon ship" as soon as the UN started offering sufficiently large bounties for information themselves. The last thing she wanted was her identity of Hespera to be compromised. He remained unaware of Samantha Peterson or Moyra Kelly.

Moyra found herself doing as much management of "operations" as any active hacking on her part. The response from all divisions within the information-security sector overwhelmed her pessimistic hopes. She supposed that being semiofficial helped, as well as her and her mother's reputation in the communities.

With a stabilized and improved communication platform, thanks to the hardwired back door in the satellite network, her key personnel free-formed most responses to developments on the UN side. Every "freelancer" team that made contact was assigned a handler. Every "freelancer" knew their handler as "Dear Beth," and the idea that Dear Beth was in fact an AI was encouraged. When voice communications were required, voice fuzzing turned the deeply masculine DalesOP and Damocles into middle-aged women, and Moyra about died laughing the first time she heard it. The freelancers quickly outstripped her available supply of handlers, and she reached out to a select few of those "displaced" by the UN in the neighborhood.

TripleShot smuggled his important equipment out of Jefferson, and made for one of the rendezvous points that Naumann provided for Moyra to direct important personnel to if they had to evacuate. From there, he was installed in an area still controlled by the rebels and provided hardwire lines to get back to playing matador with the UN information teams.

DalesOP worked closely with a PsyOps team, having a sadistic streak a mile wide when angry. And he was angry. TripleShot looked up to him as kind of a brother, and hearing how despondent the boy was over the confirmed loss of his sister left him raging. Jenkins fed information to DalesOP, culling targets for both Bowler Hat and DalesOP's team.

Damocles resumed his military position, acting as Naumann's primary link with Moyra. The sheer volume of communication required for Moyra to maintain the ebb and flow of activity kept both Damocles and Moyra tied up significantly. Thankfully, Salamander worked well with one of the BGs Moyra had tapped, and that team was furiously providing software updates to several *hundred* applications. Every single one had to be adjusted, ever so slightly, to permit it to get "upgraded" into a two-way communication point. That team had been doing the same thing Moyra's had with software: It was already funneling SOME information to their databases. Now, it had to be functional two ways.

The UN lagged on deploying their own satellite network for communication between bases, and continued to leverage the Freehold network. With the covert channels, Moyra had access to every unencrypted file possible. AI tools, filtering the yattobytes of data into useful information, alerted her to a personal, unsecured server, which one of the bureaucrats insisted was necessary for "other purposes." She handed the task off to one of the best hackers on the planet, Dmitri Kozlov, from a long, proud lineage of "capitalistic subversives," as his grandfather was described when he fled Earth.

Kozlov reported back that the system was tied into a guest section of the UN network. The bureaucrat emailed between both the personal server and the official UN military servers. Kozlov leveraged the account to execute the most basic of social-engineering attacks. Having a list of active email accounts enabled easy targeting, and endpoints were compromised within divs.

From there, the first significant breakthrough on exploitation of the UN network started small. A personnel database, pay and leave, was...adjusted. A randomly selected record would be zeroed out, swapped with a separately selected record, or be flagged as "deceased." Personal information such as family connections were also compromised, resulting in several UN soldiers receiving automatic notifications of their approved bereavement leave, changes in marital status, or the addition/subtraction of dependents. The game of whack-a-bug, comprised of semirandom errors, was designed to be irritating and difficult to track...and very distracting. Moyra noticed communications complaining about the "glitchy" systems, with some questioning if the mismatch between Earth and Grainne time might have an effect.

Branching out from there, as fastly-slow as could be managed, the team involved in takeover of the UN control network reported a significant jackpot. The automated convoys and drones in use were on nonupgraded, known vulnerable systems, for which standard exploits existed for the past several years. They were *unpatched*. In the interest of protecting their new asset, the team deployed corrected patches, which maintained their access without permitting a secondary takeover.

Moyra tasked Jenkins with determining the UN's activated drones versus those held in inventory and reserve.

Naumann personally contacted Moyra to express his glee at this development, and provided a list of extrapolated and known "freelancers" who needed gear that might be on those convoys first. She made the command decision to leave the entire drone fleet alone for the moment. The convoys, however, were rerouted.

Moyra provided information to Kozlov, and let him pick the best matches for estimated locations versus the convoys' patterns. She alerted the military, who acknowledged.

She watched the video stream as the first convoy diverted course, and kept an eye on UN communication traffic to see if they noticed. This convoy followed in the tracks of a previous one, and so as part of the takeover, Kozlov had the convoy repeat previous grid coordinates instead of actual.

The convoy halted near the anticipated location. Kozlov had it honk once as it halted. A militia element appeared from the wood line. Kozlov released all of the hatches. The freelancers looted the convoy, leaving it empty.

Moyra confirmed they were clear. Kozlov latched the hatches back down, and put the convoy back on course. He purged the recording banks and other sensor information as it rejoined its original path.

The third convoy resumed course after being redirected.

:: Peterson, :: Dmitri Kozlov pinged, :: that convoy's back on its track. ::

Moyra frowned at the screen. :: Hold on. :: She flipped over to another system and started a search query against the email index. She pulled up a recent message, and sighed. :: They've gone to manned convoys with drone support. Message didn't get flagged by AI. ::

:: Well, hell, :: he responded. :: Time to hit the drones? ::

:: Not yet. But have a few more convoys try the same thing at the same general time into the trip. Make them think there's a hack they haven't fixed. Diversion. Get creative. ::

:: Gotcha. ::

While she had little choice but to rely on the AIs for filtering, teaching the programs what was legitimately of concern in this scenario proved tricky. She fussed with the logic code, and reran the queries against existing data. The results were fuzzier, but that allowed for a wider net of information.

Curating the information between managing team interactions became a mountainous task, and Moyra always felt a shred of relief when she went off her (irregular) shift to hand over operational control to DalesOP.

Huff #3

Lies, Damned Lies, and Aviator Math
[First Battlefield Circulation Tour, Mid-March 210]

Station Ceileidh, handling traffic from Caledonia is at only partial capacity due to a major atmosphere leak, whether sabotage
or natural causes is unknown. Repairs will take forever with
bureaucratic environmental concerns, even though it's empty space.
We're working around it, and at least it's not direct from Earth.

My vertol companies all showed up understrength. I asked
for multiple aviation brigades, but I'm getting understrength battalions, detachments, and too many hangar queens. I'm getting
war reserve materiel that's been condemned. Scrapyard worthy.
I love how the zipper-suits lie about readiness.

Here's an example of a typical conversation with them; I took
copious notes.

The commander was a Command Colonel. He was very stiff
as he reported, "Sir, we have twenty-seven Guardians, primary
aircraft inventory."

"That's how many you brought?"

"No, sir, we brought fifteen to make twelve."

"I'm sorry, what?"

"We have twenty-four primary aircraft authorized. Those other
three never leave the hangar, they're 'can' birds."

"Can...huh?"

"Cannibalized. Just parts and training benches for maintenance folks."

"You have zombie aircraft?"

"Yes, sir, basically. That takes a full colonel to approve. And
we don't deploy with everything in the unit. We have other birds
in phase depot maintenance, others have grounding maintenance
problems, so we have to borrow from other units in the meantime."

"Got it, I understand that part..."

"And we keep six back at home for training. Our full go-to-
war requirement is eighteen and two spares."

"But you brought fifteen?"

"That's because we're tasked for twelve."

"Because you're supposed to have fifteen on hand?"

"No, sir, fourteen to make twelve per the EXORD. That assumes one combat loss and a maintenance spare, but that's rainbows and unicorns math. Hence, we bring fifteen."

"Okay, how many are actually flyable?"

"Ten."

"How many sorties are you generating per day?"

"Since we started losing maintainers to the super-clap, and last week, when three outright disappeared one night and all we found were wallets, jewelry, and a patch of skin? Six, maybe seven. We're not even close to meeting tasking anymore. And let's talk about attrition, sir. We've lost two in combat so far, another is down for over-G. The pilot threat-reacted to old-timey ChiTech XVI missiles so hard he broke the bird. We have two different versions of fire-control software, two whole different variants of aircraft, so I think your staff is only counting the 'C' models, not the 'D' models."

I could feel my eyes crossing. I needed to shift topics.

"Tell me about the combat losses." When I mentioned this, the young commander hardened and tightened up. Until now, he had been very twitchy and nervous. This topic changed his demeanor. I want to talk to him offline sometime, because, unlike most of his brethren, when he talked combat he had no fear, no doubt in his mind.

"Both were lost to mod'd guided antitank missiles with seeker heads reoptimized for vertols. We've also had close calls with aerial mines, classic man-portable missiles, small arms, dazzlers, rocket-propelled grenades. I've seen air cars and other vehicles turned into armed technicals. The only really 'fancy' stuff so far has been datalink hacking, and trying to home drones in on our comms transmissions. The drones have micro-EX in them, real nasty if they get through the armor on the engines. They only need one to mess up sensor pods. None of this stuff costs more than a few thousand, maybe low tens of thousands of creds. They lose plenty of troops to do it though. Still, if you think about the trade-off, they're coming out millions of creds ahead of us."

He gave me a moment to let that sink in and continued, "Here's something else that's getting us a little worried, sir: We have to loiter in the AO much longer than we like and switch to manual reversion for tasks way too often."

"Why is that? More maintenance problems, or something else?"

"Well, the avionics guys aren't sure, but assisted nav and coordinate-seeking systems are off just enough that it's making ground coordination difficult, like the LZ isn't quite where the computer thought it was. So you make more passes to sweep the area, which means longer threat exposure."

The commander let that drop, and we switched to personnel problems. The replacements aren't rotating in fast enough, and it takes the crews too long to get checked out for combat missions because of the multi-day mandatory cultural sensitivity, proper sexual conduct, and local acclimation training requirements. Why the hell have I never had Sandeep explain aviation math to me? Why hasn't he taken it upon himself to do so? When was the air component going to fix this?

I thanked the Command Colonel for his time. "Sandeep, a word?"

A Time to Fight
Part 2

The first shots woke David McClellan from a troubled sleep. A volley of fire from a weapon he instantly identified as a Merrill M-5, set to full auto. It echoed in the distance, then a muffled CRUMP as some kind of explosive went off, one that shook his bed and sent a flash through his screened window.

As he shuffled to belt his kilt on, cursing middle age, he called for Jack, but got no response. In the distance a warbling siren started from the UN base, one he knew all too well from Mtali. More shots, another explosion, and he cursed. "Bloody idiots!"

"JACK!" he yelled again, still no answer. He slipped out of the room and knocked on his nephew's door. No answer, so he turned the handle. Locked, so with a well-placed kick, he knocked the door off. The room was empty and the window stood open. The shots across the river reached a crescendo, panicked automatic fire, finally being answered with the hiss crack of a beamer and the thuds of a heavy machine gun.

In a panic, McClellan rushed to the room he used for an office, and stared in horror at the weapons rack bolted to the wall. His own M-5 was missing, and the ammunition drawer underneath stood wide open, empty of all the 4mm clips he had.

"Holy Mary mother of God," he whispered, praying for the soul of his nephew. Then he forced his fear away and ran down the stairs. At the door to the basement, he stopped and checked to make sure he still had a certain key hanging around his neck. He did, and pounded down the stairs, then flipped on the light. The key fit into a crack, unnoticeable to casual, or even detailed inspection, opening another doorway, also impossible to see. It swung out on oiled hinges to reveal a room filled with stacks of military-grade containers, ones that Minstrel and others had cached here. Thank God Jack hadn't gotten in here. They might take him alive for just an attack with a rifle and some homemade explosives. If he had access to the stuff stored here...

He closed and locked the door, and tried to call his nephew by phone. Nothing. The gunfire stopped, though the damned siren still wailed, and emergency spotlights flickered. Only the UN would have lights like that in a combat zone.

The hardest part was waiting. If he rushed to the base, he was as likely as not to get gunned down. The whole place would be an anthill, especially as it was filled with rear echelon troops who would be in a complete panic. No, best to wait and see. His neighbors, the Singhs, came out of their shop, asking what happened. "Some damned fool attacked the base, is what. You'd best just go back inside and see what the morning brings."

They did, and he sat on his porch, looking out over the cleared fields toward the base. A vertol hovered around, sweeping the immediate area with a harsh, glaring beam, but not venturing any further. Good troops would have immediately patrolled to disrupt a secondary attack, but there was no sign of it in the night-vision glasses he placed on his face. Just white-hot figures milling around by the gate, and several motionless ones slowly fading to gray. But he pushed the fear aside, analyzed the scene with a professional soldier's eye.

Mac thought hard about things he had buried long ago. Although he retired as a logistics warrant, the first five years of his service in the FMF had been straight infantry. None of the Blazer or Black Ops crap, just regular soldiering. Squad-sized assaults on defended positions had been his specialty, until a bad fracture ended those days.

"Ah, to be young and stupid again," he said out loud. There was so much he could have taught those idiots, the primary thing being that they had no real chance as untrained civilians, even against shitty UN troops. Maybe he should have formed a militia, but that would have been too noticeable with the base right there, and all the decent guys had left. So many decisions and choices, none of them the right ones. None of them ever were.

His thoughts were interrupted by someone stumbling down the road, coming slowly from the direction of the base. Mac stepped off his porch to see who it was, and taking off the NVD, let his eyes adjust to the false dawn. The man, or more like the boy, lurched forward into the circle cast by the lone streetlight, and collapsed.

It was Carl Singh, Jack's best friend. Mac could smell cooked meat before he got within ten feet of the boy. Microwave beamer, one of the so called "nonlethal" weapons the UN was using. That buzz-CRACK he had heard was probably the unit shorting out; some jackass had set it up way too high. Mrs. Singh rushed past him, screaming, followed by her husband, and Mac let them go. There was nothing he could do for the boy, except maybe a mercy shot; he was surprised the kid had made it this far.

"Take him back to the house, and make him comfortable. Tomorrow," he said, giving them some false hope, "a UN patrol will be through here. They'll take him to the base hospital."

He knelt down by him, and asked gently, "Carl, what happened?" The boy couldn't really see; his eyes had been cooked. The smell was unbearable.

"Was Jack there? Just nod your head." Instead, the breath whispered out of him, for the last time, and his mother's screams rose even higher.

Carl's father stood, and the look of anger on his face made Mac take an involuntary step back. "I will kill them all!" he shouted, and turned to go back to his shop.

He ran up to the despondent father, and said, "Raj, wait. We need to know more, and you don't want to make your little girl lose her father, too. I'll be back here in thirty segs, go get your rifle ready."

The road to Harrow's trailer was empty this early in the morning, and McClellan knew that his truck stood out like a sore thumb. Thank God it was northward, away from the UN base. He drove with his lights on, knowing it would make no difference to a vertol's sensors, and not wanting to wreck. As he sped down the road, he fished around under the seat for the pistol in the hidden compartment. Hitting the latch, the gun dropped into his hand, and he laid it on the seat next to him. There was a battered truck in the drive, one that he recognized as the Harrows'. Slipping on his night vision, it glowed warmly, even in the summer heat, capacitors still cooling off. Bastard.

Mac slid to a stop in the gravel, barely avoiding the various debris and wrecks scattered across the front yard. The truck had barely come to a stop when he flung the door open and rushed up the porch. "HARROW!" he yelled, "OPEN THE DOOR!" and kicked as hard as he could on it. Then he stepped aside, a moment before a shotgun blast, both barrels, BANG BANG, shattered it. He shot the lock, and he entered as the door swung wide. Harrow was fumbling with the shotgun, trying to reload it, and as he snapped it shut, Mac kicked it out of his hands, pressing the pistol to the man's forehead.

"Tell me why I shouldn't," he said, filled with rage. "Carl Singh is dead because of you. Where the hell is Jack! Is he dead? ANSWER ME!"

"T-T-Tangler!" the man sobbed out. "He volunteered to act as, as a div-version, and they tangled him and we shot at them."

McClellan's heart hammered in his chest, and hope filled him. The boy might be alive after all. "Who else, you stupid fuck?" The farmer babbled the names of several of Jack's classmates, kids who weren't old enough to go fight with the guerillas. Kids easily influenced by this shit stain of a man.

"I'm coming back here tomorrow, and this place better be empty. If not, I'm going to kill you. Where are your kids?" Harrow had two twin daughters, who more often than not, were over at a neighbor's house, begging for food.

"Marcie's got 'em," he babbled, meaning the woman on the neighboring farm. "I ain't stupid enough to git 'em involved in this stuff."

"No, you're just stupid enough to get other people's kids killed," Mac answered, and, thinking of how much pain Carl Singh must have been in before he died, shot him in the forehead.

"OK, give me ten segs after you see my truck go through the gate," Mac said to Raj Singh. "Understand? Let's go over the plan again."

The man's knuckles were white on his rifle, but he nodded. Singh wasn't a veteran, but he was a hunter, which was even better in this case. "In thirty segs, I am to kill those sons of bitches at the front gate. I am to take as many as I safely can, then withdraw."

Mac could see that the man didn't like the idea of breaking off his attack. "Yes, withdraw. Your family is going to need you even more, now." They had discussed it; Singh was to take his wife and daughter to relatives even deeper into the mountains. "Come back when this all settles down, and I'll buy you a beer."

They shook hands, both fearful that a UN patrol would make its way into the town, but nothing had shown. Mac was going to go into the base on his regular supply run, and, if the distraction went well, get Jack out of the lockup. He expected there to be some killing, but surprise was on their side.

The guards at the cargo gate were nervous, on edge after the night before. They had been lulled into a false sense of security, one which an actual FMF squad could have exploited to wreck the entire base. He thought back to his days in 3rd Mob. They were good troops; maybe not Blazers, but good enough. Yeah, his old squad could have definitely taken this place. Twenty against two hundred, fair odds.

Now these bozos at the gate were playing at being soldiers. He was made to get out of the vehicle, and held at gunpoint while they searched it. "Heard you had a little bit of excitement last night!" he said while he waited. "What happened?"

The master sergeant first class snorted, and said "A couple of dumb kids learned not to fuck with the UN. We killed two, and have a prisoner to torture, uh, I mean interrogate." She laughed at that one. Then she looked at him closely.

"Say, you're a local. How do we know you weren't involved?" My God, she was dumb as a box of rocks.

"Would I show up here the next morning, with my regular supply run?" he asked, the sarcasm flying right over her head.

"Uh, I suppose not." She saw that her troops were done crawling all over the truck, and an indecisive look passed over her face.

"Listen," he said, "I'm a businessman, and I have business to do with Sergeant Major Nimbutu. I'd hate to see me late for my appointment with him, Captain," he said, deliberately mistaking her rank. With a smile, she waved him through. Mac climbed back up in his truck, and slowly made his way through the warehouse area of the base. Prefab buildings sat in orderly rows, Some even with Earth trees planted outside offices. That more than anything spoke to how long the UN planned to stay here.

He stopped in front of Nimbutu's office, hand slipping unconsciously to check that his comm was still in his pocket, and thought about the contents of the truck. Concealed in the false bottoms that he used to smuggle out supplies from the base were what any typical farm town had in abundance. Fertilizer, thirty gallons of it. Ninety-four percent ammonium nitrate, to be precise, mixed with six percent fuel oil. It was for plan "C," if everything else went to shit.

"Come in!" called the NCO in a jovial voice, and McClellan opened the door. Nimbutu sat at his desk, with his back to his "I love me wall." Numerous placards and framed letters of commendation formed a continuous wallpaper behind him. There were several weapons mounted there, even, incredibly, what Mac had recognized as a gold plated AK-74, something which must have been five hundred or more years old. He doubted, though, that the fat bastard had ever fired any of them.

What held his attention now, though, was the sword that lay across the desk. His own *claidheamh cuil,* that he had thought safely hidden away from his nephew. Nimbutu saw his eyes widen in recognition, and smiled. "Interesting weapon, this broadsword. As you can see, I'm a bit of a collector myself. This will make a fine addition. I wonder if your nephew can tell me its history?" Not waiting for an answer, he just said, "We need to talk, David. It seems our arrangement is going to change a bit." He slowly took a pistol from its shiny black holster, and placed it on the desk in front of him.

"What, exactly, do you mean?" asked the Freeholder.

"I mean, you are going to start giving me information as to who your contacts are in the remaining FMF, and in return I'll see that your nephew doesn't get sent to a re-education camp."

"I thought you were on our side; isn't that what you said? That you wanted your freedom?" He ignored the offered chair, preferring to stand, arms folded. There had been no way to get a weapon past the guards, even hidden in a container.

Nimbutu laughed, a deep belly laugh, and said, "My friend, I am on MY side! Of course, when such a card falls into my lap, I must play it! My superiors will give me another medal, and perhaps a posting back in my home country! Where I can spend my wealth—"

His bragging was interrupted by the base klaxon sounding again. Grabbing the pistol, Nimbutu stood and turned to look out his window. McClellan dove forward onto the desk, snatching at the hilt of the sword, and crashing into the big man. They both went down in a tangle of limbs, Nimbutu trying to point the pistol at David's head, Mac straining to maneuver the point of the sword to reach any part of Nimbutu's body.

They struggled silently like this for what seemed like an eternity, the pistol creeping closer to his eye, and the UN soldier grinning as he used his superior weight to press home his attack. McClellan headbutted him in the nose, and, as the other man winced in pain, used the basket hilt to hit him across the face.

Nimbutu went down in a welter of blood, and started to cry out, a cry that turned into a gasp as Mac pinned him to the floor, the point going through his belly and grating on the concrete. Again and again, consumed by a killing rage, the Freeholder plunged his sword downward into the now-still body.

What finally brought him to his senses was the passing of the base Quick Reaction Force vertol screaming overhead, and the whine of an infantry carrier's capacitors moving full out. He cleaned the blood off the sword, and found the scabbard sitting in a corner. The pistol was a non-standard-issue H&K A6, with two extra magazines. That meant a hundred and twenty rounds to get him into the holding facility and get them both out of the base.

He glanced up at the weapons on the wall, and grinned. The AK-74 hung from brackets, with a bandolier hanging from one peg. He knew many such "trophy" weapons were reproductions, and this could very well be one. Locking the door to the office, he lifted the weapon off the pegs, then pulled a magazine from the pouch. Flicking one round out, he looked the stamp on the back. "JCA 203." Jefferson City Arms, Freehold year 203. Yep, reproduction. "Fake ass poser," he muttered to the corpse. Even the "gold plating" was vapor coating.

Then he thought better of using the rifle. It would be loud, and pretty damn obvious. The H&K had a built-in suppressor, and the holding area was only two blocks over. Stepping back out to the truck, ignored by people rushing by to the front gate, he opened one of the containers, throwing the food out and pulling out the false bottom. Inside were UNPF uniform pants and blouse. He stepped back inside and quickly skinned out of the kilt, buckling the sword around his waist. Not unusual, since he wore lieutenant colonel rank and they were notorious for eccentricity. Unlocking the back door to the office, which he knew led to the loading bay of the warehouse, he glanced around, and saw no one. Picking up a tablet from Nimbutu's desk, he opened the door, stepped out into the bright Iolight, closed the door behind him, and walked toward the holding area.

No one paid any attention to him as he walked confidently into the military police office. Attitude, he had found, could get you anywhere. Now he just had to hide his Grainne accent, and pull this off.

The woman behind the desk was a civilian contractor, with a patch on her shoulder that said WACKENHUT SECURITY. He'd seen them before; many of the base functions were contracted out, but this was ridiculous.

"I'm here for the prisoner. Transfer back to UNHQ," he said, as abruptly as he could.

The woman glanced down at her tablet, and then back up at him. "I'm sorry, Colonel, but he was scheduled to be interrogated here at the base at 1700 today. There is no transfer order, I'm going to have to call my..." She stopped when she saw the barrel of his pistol pointed at her head.

"How many others are in the building?" he asked. "Don't be a hero, lady. Just answer me."

Instead, she reached for the stunner hanging on her belt, almost smiling as if daring him, reaching at the same time for a panic button hanging around her neck. He fired, once in the chest, a loud POP that knocked her back out of her chair and onto the floor. *Shit shit shit*. He hadn't wanted to do that. She started to scream, and he shot her again, through the mouth.

Her cut-off scream brought the sound of running boots down a hallway, and a burly guard in the same shit-brown uniform burst through the door to his right. The man seemed to stop in his tracks, and then swung a stun baton hard at McClellan's arm. With a numbing CRACK, the baton hit, and the gun fell to the floor.

Dodging sideways, he dragged left-handed at the sword, trying to clear it from the scabbard, even as the guard hit him again with the stunner, trying for his head. Mac managed to free the sword, and swung it in a vicious backhand that caught the man across the throat, even as the emergency alarm sounded inside the holding area. His attacker slowly fell to the ground, grasping at his throat, even as his other hand had squeezed his own panic button.

Reaching down, Mac pulled a blood-soaked security key card from the man's belt, hoping there were no retinal scanners. The open doorway showed a long hallway, lined with cells. "JACK!" he yelled, running forward.

"UNCLE DAVE! IN HERE!" his nephew shouted back. He was in the last cell on the left, and the two hugged through the bars, tears running down the older man's face. Even as he tried to work the lock, his nephew kept apologizing for getting captured.

"Stand back!" Mac said urgently, and tried a card against the scanner. He heard shouts outside, and stopped to pull out his comm. Punching in a number, the thirty kilos of explosives in his truck detonated, sending a fireball into the sky. Not a huge distraction, but hopefully it gave them some time.

The door refused to budge. He tried another card, then a third. He flipped it over. They were unidirectional. BUZZclick. His nephew stumbled out, and McClellan caught him. He could see the teen had been viciously beaten; strands of tangler still wrapped themselves around his face.

"Jack, pay attention. We're going to head out this back door and make a run for it. Do you remember when this was Gots's farm? The draw in the southeast corner?"

The boy nodded, and McClellan continued, "We're going to head for that, it's only about two hundred meters. I have an aircar sitting in the woodlot beyond."

Outside, the alarm changed tone, to one Mac recognized as *infiltrators in the base.* He had heard it enough on Mtali. "Time to go, lad."

Jack McClellan looked at his uncle in amazement. He had called Mac a coward, and the man had fought his way into a UN base to rescue him. "Uncle," he started to say, but he was cut short.

"Jack, listen to me. You go to Hanging Rock, find a man named Joe Carpender, if he's still alive. Tell him that you're Jack McClellan's son, and he'll take care of you. Hell, maybe you'll even learn to fight properly. Now go! Walk like you're supposed to be here, and then run like the devil for that draw." And he shoved him to the back door, handing him the bloody security card.

"But..."

"No buts. I told you there was a time not to fight, and a time to fight. This is my time to fight. Yours will come. Now GO!"

His words were punctuated by shouts from the front of the office, and David McClellan's last glance at his nephew as he turned to stride away from him, toward battle, a giant of a man, pistol in one hand and *claidheamh cuil* in the other.

He could almost hear the pipes playing.

■   ■   ■

Huff #4

Worry About the Hinterlands... [Early March 210]

If this fool says "governance" one more time, I'll shoot him myself. Since I can't actually do that, I nod. Then I nod again sagely, like generals are supposed to, and briefly make eye contact with the UN Agency for Rural Development toady lecturing me.

"It's problematic. Yes, General, problematic. Given the lack of medical records and registration, we can't tell for sure what the true civilian inoculation rate is, especially with the number of claimed religious exemptions our workers encounter."

I've counted fifteen "problematics" in thirteen minutes. I quit counting how many times he said "governance," but I'm sure it will exceed fifty before the briefing is through.

He does have a point, though, even if he did smother it in buzzwords. These people bear a striking resemblance to what I've read about North Americans during the "Prohibition" era. There's cooperation, and there's "*cooperation*." The first is genuine. The second is meant to keep lawful authorities satisfied yet ignorant while figuring out how to make them go away fastest. We're getting lots of the latter, very little of the former. It seems many of the native farmers and merchants don't care for UN business practices.

Then, apart from three significant cities, most of the huge single continent is sparsely populated. Lots of towns under 50,000, but that's big enough for significant rebel activity and support. There are thousands of smaller settlements, too blasted many for us to maintain a presence in more than a few. That needs to change.

From a military standpoint, the pacification phase of this is quite doable; not easy, not with the resource shortfalls, red tape, and second-class troops, but nothing insurmountable. However, we aren't getting effective civilian control and local cooperation. They call us "aardvarks" among other, less pleasant epithets.

[*1.5 divs later*] Tonight, we broke out formal dress and hosted a reception at the house, honoring the UN Chief of Mission and her role in the system-wide compliance effort. I had a feeling the CoM wanted to talk about rapport with local farmers, given the wretched briefing I took this afternoon. I don't even think she knows what day of the week it is, honestly.

The CoM directs every UN civilian, every credit spent, every nonmilitary contract and sanctioned NGO throughout the system. Because this is a peacekeeping operation, I take direction from her when it comes to anything touching reconstruction, cultural, or economic policy, and I pay for her security. This bill eats into my forces. Luckily, my actual orders, responsibilities, and authorities, come from BuMil and SecMil, but I know better than to make an enemy of the ambassador.

Officially, the UN frowns upon military antiques like formal receptions as inegalitarian, yet no one turns down the invitations. We accomplish a lot at these things, and people tend to misunderstand this: Business gets done when people are well lubricated. In this instance, I wanted the CoM to spool down from panic mode, and get her claws out of my Regional Commanders' freedom of action. If she had her way, every platoon would have an embedded "advisor" and an armored convoy for protection every time one of them had to take a piss.

I spotted Ambassador Trudeau before she noticed me, so I gestured for Sandeep to get two glasses of wine and to rejoin us after I opened the discussion. General Order One gets "modified" when it comes to political work, and this was *work*.

"Ambassador! It's great to see you! My aide will be back momentarily with some red. Your preference, right?" My smile was practiced, and real enough—she is attractive and carries herself without the pinched look of most UN senior civilians.

"General Huff. Yes, thank you." (*Perfect timing, Sandeep!*) She was stone faced, but gracious.

I started the parley: "You're thinking about Orme, aren't you?"

Her face softened, but her smile was predatory. "Orme had a lot of potential, don't you think?" She then went on about the attack on the supply base. Somehow, she knew an insurgent prisoner escaped. She knew the body of the second day's attacker—the farm-equipment salesman who blew the place up with a VBIED and chopped people up with a goddamn Scottish broadsword—was identified as an Earth native and FMF retiree. She even knew this man had been dealing in contraband with senior base personnel.

"General, you have a corruption problem in your ranks, and thanks to that, you're endangering civil progress here! You're jeopardizing the entire project!"

She wasn't entirely wrong; the base sergeant major was behind a lot of compromising activity, some of it outright disgusting, and this made the base vulnerable to begin with. The condition of his body, the sheer rage unleashed on him, told me he'd made some personal enemies, and for all our sakes, we need to know what he was really doing. With any luck, we'll also find out who's leaking information to the CoM.

Sandeep attempted to politely redirect the conversation, but Ambassador Trudeau wasn't having it. I was in for a long night, and there wasn't enough wine to make it tolerable.

The Danegeld

Marisa Wolf

Part 1

"Grainne ship Graci, *upon docking Captain Ananda Romdee and First Officer Cal Goderitch are required to report to the officer of Acquisitions, Logistics, and Technology. Acknowledge."*

"Hello to you too, Greendoor Station," Ana replied, taken aback by the unfamiliar brusque tone after being out of her home system for months. "Captain Romdee, receiving your message. What is this in reference to? I have a schedule to keep."

"You have a required meeting, Graci. *Jump points are closed per order of the United Nations Interim Governance Authority. You will dock and remain docked until your meeting is complete."*

Goddamned UN. Babies in uniforms had been up her ass for months enforcing every piece of the rules and regulations they could pull up on their slates, and they'd taken the long way home to avoid as many interactions as possible. Now the UN was issuing orders from stations in Grainne space. Retirement had lasted barely a month, but if Ananda had realized how many officious, useless little UN ninnies were going to pop up in every station, she might have tried harder to make it stick.

If not for the fact her wife was still dead, and her husband had become infinitely more annoying with the loss of Graciela. A fact all spacers knew by heart—no matter how good the captain, the void needed only the smallest of mistakes to kill you. So too it had been with the ocean—Gracie had grown up fishing the sea, but one terrible storm had taken her off to the depths. Better to keep both herself and Cal occupied and afloat rather than rattling around their old home with a vital piece missing. Only Graciela and shared work kept them together over the years; she should have known retirement couldn't hold them without their Gracie.

"Closing jump points?" Sammy leaned back from nav, blowing out her breath. "That's fun."

"It's like they can't help being stupid about how big space is." Ana shrugged, forced herself to sit up straight, and sent her acceptance of the meeting. "Tell your father to get ready for a meeting. I'm gonna make sure Hank and Tico have everything stowed safely for our visit."

Sammy nodded, flicking through the docking course once more. No need for showboating when the UN had a lock on them, and always better to be careful when the agency was trying to throw their weight around. Ana watched her wife's daughter for a moment, then pushed the warmth away and swung out toward the main body of her craggy hulk of a ship.

Sammy sent the slow-burn signal through the ship, letting the three other members of their crew know it was as safe to move about as it ever was. Ana turned the first corner and found the corridor full of Tico.

"We're stowed." As usual, their cargo master anticipated her, confirming that all remotely questionable goods were squirreled into the cubbies, bolt holes, false bulkheads, and hollow bottoms they'd spent months creating and covering. Never a precaution they'd used in Freehold space, but the sheer number of inspections they'd weathered lately had them all jumpy.

"Good. Because when we dock, Cal and I are summoned for a meeting with UN Acquisitions."

"I thought Sam was taking the old girl in slow." He thumped the closest wall with the affection of a lifelong spacer. Not for the first time, Ana congratulated herself for stealing him from her uncle's—well, nephew's now, she supposed—ship. After more decades than she'd count, they had a strong understanding of each other's priorities.

One, fuck everything but safety. Treat the ship well, and the ship would keep them alive. Two, profit. Three, take care of family—blood and ship. Four, extra fuck off to the UN and anyone who got in the way of one through three.

"They don't need to know how fast we can be. And no

one's in a rush to be lectured, again. What'd you leave on the manifest—the persimmons, crate of gems, frozen fish?"

"And the embroidery. Why go to NovRos and not pick up glamorous tapestries?" He gave a mocking half bow, as though presenting their goods to the Acquisition nerd waiting on Ana and Cal.

"Good. Not going to offer them anything they don't ask for, but be ready to poison that fish if they try and commandeer anything."

"Your wish is my task list, Cap." Tico whistled his favorite off-key aria as they passed each other, and they both knew the tune would be stuck in her head until they docked.

"Spacers Romdee and Goderitch, welcome. Please, sit." This UN man looked competent—shipshape, cleanly pressed uniform, his eyes steady on hers. Unfortunate—she preferred her UNers bumbling or plain ignorant, even pompous left her plenty of room to navigate. "I'm Lieutenant Colonel Josiah Severson. Appreciate your taking the time."

Ana smiled, all friendliness with nothing to hide, even showing a hint of frustration—as any honest trader would, schedule getting yanked about by an admin—as she sat. Cal gave his charming grin, leaned forward to press his elbows on the back of the second chair, and lounged comfortably. Neither remarked on how much choice they'd had about the meeting.

"Can we get you anything to drink, maybe some refreshments?" Severson leaned forward attentively as he took his seat.

"Cocoa would do, thank you. Or coffee. We'll have some time to make up after this meeting," she said, careful to show mild interest.

"I hope to make it worth your while, spacers." He pressed a button, and a moment later an aide slipped in with a tray, steaming mugs of coffee neatly balanced. The response had been so fast he must have prepared ahead.

The officer had done his homework, and Ana forced herself not to tense with worry. It did her no good to spiral into all the possibilities of what he might want with them. He'd tell them soon enough.

"You need some persimmons?" Cal offered, projecting casual amusement as he took his mug.

The man shook his head in half amusement, half disgust. "Not that kind of deal, Goderitch."

"We're all ears," Ana prodded, not gently, and gave a nod of thanks to the aide for the coffee before the woman slipped out.

"Your rig's new to you, is that right?"

Cal put in, "We've been in this work longer than you've been walking space stations, so—"

"You misunderstand me." The officer held up a hand to interrupt Cal, his attention still focused on Ana. "This isn't part of your inspection, and I'm not questioning your professionalism. On the contrary, I have a proposition."

"The rig's new," Ana allowed, holding the mug close to her mouth without sipping. Smelled good, and fresh. While the jump point had been bureaucratically locked down from this end, the UN still had supply coming in. "We tried retiring. It didn't take."

"Spacers belong in space," he agreed, smile too broad. "You owe quite a bit, to be just starting out."

"We made a good deal, and most stops made us a bit more black in the ledger."

"'Most' is a generous claim. You owe more than you did before, when you factor in your expenses. The debt plus your age plus all the growing tension..." He tsked a bit, and Ana drank her coffee to hide the downturn in the corners of her mouth. "That's a lot to balance. What if I told you there's a way I could cut your debt?"

"I've plenty of years in me still, and so does the ship. We don't have anything in the holds the UN needs worth that kind of pay."

"Not yet." He sipped his coffee, looking pleased with himself.

"You have something you need us to move?" She let doubt color her tone, and put the mug down. "You have newer, faster ships than ours. And plenty of them, far as I can tell."

"We have any number of ships." He waved his free hand dismissively. "You have a ship that's gone system to system, and unless I miss my guess, capable of orbit to land." The smugness in his tone indicated he wasn't guessing.

"We have a lighter." Leaning her chin in her hand, Ana made it a casual declaration. The shuttle had exactly the rickety air she wanted it to, making it seem an unlikely contender to go to ground on a regular basis. "I haven't had as much time to fix it up as I'd like."

"I imagine it does just fine, Captain." Severson paused to drink again, enjoying the conversation far more than his guests. "We have a great deal of material we need to get to ground, and you know Grainne airspace well enough."

"It's more expensive to fuel those on-planet landings and takeoffs, not even considering the safety of it, Colonel."

"You know what spacers say," Cal offered, grin widening.

"Yes, safety above all." The UN official interjected the sanitized version before Cal could continue, eager to get on with it. "We pay well, Captain. And you may have noticed, even former Freehold ships are not immune to the rules and regulations of UN space. This could ease many of your troubles at once."

Ana knew exactly what he meant, and thought Cal had figured it out as well. The UN had decided to put down on Grainne, and more likely than not that meant their ships were taking potshots from residents. Did this Uno think Freeholders would bother to run a transponder before firing?

Of course, if they did get shot down, well, the UN only lost a load of cargo, not a ship and crew on top of it. Smart of them to pay well, with that kind of upside—they'd still come out ahead.

"Colonel Severson, you're asking us to run goods for you, and take on a lot of risk to do so. Why, exactly, would we do that?"

"Risk, Captain Romdee?" Severson chuckled, a good-natured sound, and put his mug on his desk. "I've heard quite a bit about the *Graci*, and of course your previous berth. The *Rom's Horn*, wasn't it? Both seemed adept at getting where they needed to go without undue attention. I have utter faith you and your small crew can figure it out."

Ana blinked. She hadn't expected him to show his stick so blatantly, calling them out as smugglers. He must have caught the change in her expression, as he hurried to follow up with the carrot.

"We're buying up bad loans across Grainne—some economic stimulus for your struggling colony." The word colony grated, but Severson continued airily, "The rates on yours aren't the most forgiving, given the... quality of the establishment you partnered with. We acquired your loan. If you give us one year of service, we call it paid off. The schedule will be a full one, but we'll cover your fuel costs and other expenses, and in two years—Earth years, at that—your ship is yours outright, and we'll renegotiate your pay as an independent contractor."

Instant rejection flooded through her on a wave of bile. She wanted to tell him no, knock over the coffee, and storm out in a righteous fury before he could clean up. But the deal...

A handful of months, and they'd pay off the ship. Graciela's island, their leverage, would be theirs again. She'd counseled any number of younger family members through tough times or shitty jobs with her father's old advice: "You can do anything for six months." What difference did a few more make?

Even playing delivery boy for the UN.

"I'll talk this over with my crew." Ana inclined her head. The risk wasn't worth the shiny reward, but Cal had a stake in their ship, and the crew had a vote. They needed to weigh the offer—and the consequences of rejecting it—before committing to anything.

"I'm eager to hear your decision. Docking fees are on the UN while you consider. I've already taken the opportunity to let the dockmaster know."

Meaning they couldn't just unhitch and drop into space. Too mild for threat, too heavy-handed to be anything else. Typical UN.

Cal waited until they got back to the ship to say anything, which Ana silently blessed him for. There were some stations where she couldn't shake the feeling of being watched, for good reason. Never before in Grainne space, but the UN's sticky fingers meant a first time for everything.

"Of course we take it."

She leaned back against the airlock, closed her eyes for a second, giving him all the permission he needed to double down on his point.

"How is it a question? This is the kind of deal that changes our lives. We've been running on the edge. Now every trade is gravy from here out. Take a few more risks. Don't need to worry about inheritance."

"You're worried about inheritance." Her voice was too flat to be a question. Cal had never been the conservative one, and was lucky enough a gambler to come out ahead more often than not. But it was always about the gamble, for him. "The kids still have an entire island to carve up between them, worst case if we somehow lose our leveraged one, and we have plenty of time to pay off the ship. We're not desperate."

"This isn't desperate, Ana. It's sense. Couple months dropping supplies around Grainne, get in some visits with the family, guaranteed walk-away-with-the-ship. What's to discuss?"

"The UN's making moves on our home, and you want to run their errands?"

"UN's always making moves somewhere, pretending they got weight. What they do have is resources, so I say we take 'em. Pick up and drop off, do some boring work for a few months, and then fly off with our own ship."

"And not make any money in the meantime," she reminded him.

"And not pile up any expenses, either. There are worse things—you know there'll be months we only break even up here, staying in-system while the jump point's closed."

"Why are they buying up all the Freehold loans?" Did they think it would give them some real say in local matters? She was sure the loans looked risky from some cushy UN office, but Freeholders weren't stupid—very few, in her experience, made bad bets with their money, having a pathological hatred of debt.

"Ana. I say this with love—who cares?" He crossed back to reach for her hand. "They're a bunch of spoiled morons who think they can blow and bluster the house down. Let's run their goods and take their money. This will all be over before a year's out, and we'll be free and clear."

"Will we? They're *on* Grainne, Cal. We do this, we work for them, and we always work for them. We're theirs."

"The UN?" The noise deep in his throat was pure scorn. "They can't hold on to shit. They're annoying, not dangerous. Worst of it comes out, we take their money, take the kids, and scamper. You know they can't catch us."

"Let's talk to the crew." She let go of his hand, pushed upright from the door, and started walking without looking back at him.

"Yeah, sure, but Ana—it's our call. We run goods for a few months, maybe some fall off along the way that we sell to keep the income moving, and we have no chance of losing Graciela's island for the kids. I know they're not *your* kids—"

"Don't you dare," she snapped, picking up her pace until her hip's warning twinge radiated down to her knee. Fragged old joints, taking the wrong time to make themselves known. Better to think about that than her urge to throttle her husband.

"I love every one of those monsters, and always have. They're yours, and Graciela's, and that makes them mine." She didn't miss that flash of his smile. He'd roped her on that one, and knew it. "And I love you."

"But you don't like me," he finished dutifully, repeating her refrain for her. Then, that hint of a smile stretching full on, he added, "Because you know I'm going to win."

"Fucking danegeld." Hank slammed a hand down on the crate Tico had just loaded, making everyone scowl. "Remind me why we're doing this?" He ran his other hand over his bald scalp, the bulk of him radiating disgust.

"Because the UN aren't Vikings, and our one ship isn't going to make them so strong they'll keep coming back." Cal rocked on the balls of his feet, ready to drop the lock and get the show on the road. "We get our ship, and whatever of their goods we want to keep. Win-win, Hankers."

"Fuck off." Hank took his hand off the crate, but his tone was too dark for the usual banter. He'd been the most reluctant to sign on to this idiot scheme, reading the entirety of an ancient Kipling poem to them repeatedly, and Ana couldn't dismiss the creeping discomfort he was correct. They needed the money, sure, but if the UN won out, insane as she told herself that was, where could her crew and family go? NovRos? Run forever? Serve as permanent gofers for a smug and over-regulated occupying force?

She buried the thought yet again, down with Graciela's face, and reminded herself of the payoff. The ship would be theirs, free and clear. No matter how bad the aftertaste, she could swallow it.

"Hank." She pitched her voice to carry, and he turned toward her. Lifting one shoulder and both eyebrows, she silently asked if he'd finished what they discussed. He snorted and stalked off to the front of the shuttle, which meant yes, but he was still mad about it.

Fair enough. The manifest passed for exactly as it had been when they'd accepted delivery of it, despite the difference in several numbers. Every crate perfectly sealed, UN stamped, though the *Graci*'s various cubby holes were getting overfull. She'd have to find an excuse to go home and offload, or a buyer that didn't leave her wanting to vomit.

"Let's do it." At her signal, Cal and Tico moved smoothly,

the former cycling the lock and lining up the gangplank and the latter getting the servos loaded.

"You're late." The UN lackey on the ground yanked the card from her hand and barely glanced at it before glaring at her. "We've been out here for two hours." The snap in his voice didn't cover the hunch to his shoulders, or how twitchy his men were.

"You set the meeting, and changed it twice," she replied, voice level as she stared over his left shoulder. "Some reason your base doesn't work?"

"Someone keeps shooting at us," he snarled, hand half lifting toward his holster. "Maybe you heard? Your feral asshole country-men can't seem to keep their hands off their firearms. You all forget sex exists, got to blow things up to feel good?"

"Ready for the shipment?" Ana kept her eyes fixed in the middle distance, face neutral. She had never longed so strongly to ram the butt of her gun down on someone's forehead, which after a lifetime with Cal really said something.

"Have your crew unload it, we'll keep watch."

She wanted to needle him, ask if he knew how big the preda-tors got on this side of the mountains. But she barely trusted them with their weapons, no need to add an excuse for one of them to take a shot at her crew because a shadow flickered.

She gestured back to the ship, and heard the whine of the servo lifters as Tico responded. Ana regretted the time she and Hank had spent doctoring the documents and seals when the sergeant tossed the card back to a lackey who barely looked at it. Pride of work was all well and good, but this group made it insultingly easy. A distracted amateur could have skimmed off these idiots. The growing pile of UN goods siphoned away and stowed throughout her ship from the first month of runs was still a win, but not nearly as satisfying.

She felt some measure of justification when the sergeant examined each pallet loaded into their truck and checked it off the manifest. Would have been better if he'd cracked open even a single crate to ensure, but deliveries remained sealed until they reached base. Maybe they didn't trust their own troops, or didn't believe anyone could reseal and stamp their packages so perfectly. She couldn't imagine they had anyone with Hank's eye for detail or the intricacies of their own electronic seals.

Ana exchanged a look with Tico as he maneuvered the next

load down the gangplank. He'd noticed the mood, and had none of his usual attempts at banter. No sense provoking twitchy soldiers with none of the discipline instilled in a Freehold child. For a moment she allowed herself to picture Graciela's oldest son Seb, how quietly proud and exhausted and confident he'd been after his first year of military training. Had these striplings ever experienced that level of rigor?

She cut that line of thinking short—did it matter? The UN soldiers were here, regardless. Armed. Outnumbering the Freehold force. Muttering about her and her crew, and about her fellow citizens. Covering all of her expenses, patting her on the head.

Fuck.

"Making good time?" Cal asked as he strolled down to her, grinning at the clustered UN soldiers as though none of them had a care in the world on this blindingly sunny day.

"Everyone is very efficient." She kept her voice neutral, her body relaxed. No point in adding to the tension Cal ignored.

"That's the UN in a nutshell, isn't it? Handling their business. Sergeant Norris, a pleasure to meet you." Cal waved and took a few steps in the younger man's direction, dropping his hands loose at his sides. "Senior Corporal Tennison said if I saw you, to tell you he'd gotten better at poker, but is still shit at spades."

The UN man swiveled away from Tico and faced Cal fully, sudden interest replacing some of his twitchiness. "He's still shit at poker. Where'd you see Tennison?"

"Northern slopes. He bargained for extra parkas. Lost a few rounds of poker." Cal laughed, so genuinely the sergeant cracked half a smile. "You're right—if that's him playing better, he must have been shit to start."

"The worst," Sergeant Norris agreed.

"You're smart to be on your guard out here—sorry the meet had to change. Orders all around, eh."

Norris grunted, a comfortable sound. Ana still wanted to bash him, but she marveled at Cal's ability to put even the tetchiest ass at ease. At least at ease enough to not shoot her people because a branch cracked.

The Prayer Wheel

Jason Cordova

"Shuttle *Iwaneka* is clear of the release point, minimal thrust initiated," Orbit Control Specialist Arika Santiago announced in a flat, monotone voice as she stared unblinkingly at the display before her. A quick glance to her left revealed that Lieutenant First Class Wes Borland was matching her pronouncements to the slate he held in his hand. Not entirely unsurprising, but still insulting to the young engineer. She bit down on what she wanted to tell the aardvark and instead refocused on the task at hand. "Shuttle *Kona* has lifted from surface and will tether in ten seg—ah, seventeen minutes. Next shuttle scheduled to enter atmo in twenty minutes. Bro, comm. Skywheel Three. Open tether. Repeat, open tether. Message ends."

"Concur," the UN officer said after a long inspection of his notes. He beamed a happy smile in her direction. "On schedule and within the release variables. I'll give you colonials credit: you sure make things run on time."

Unlike you pigs, Arika didn't say. She grunted instead, and swapped a glance with Assistant Orbit Control Specialist Andy Mather, who was doing his best to be invisible, obviously to avoid any attention at all from Borland. It had definitely taken too long. Everything seemed to be behind schedule now. Nothing the occupying soldiers did after taking control of Skywheel Three had improved her working environment. Of course, the UN representatives promised otherwise when they had boarded but since the fancy-suited rep left, the soldiers had taken a very *laissez faire* approach to some things, and a totalitarian one to others. Arika wanted to correct the issues, but inefficiency oftentimes led to problems for the UN, which she was all for.

Arika had been working on Skywheel Three since she became a certified aeronautical engineer six years before. It was an arduous process, since almost nobody wanted to work on a skywheel. The jump points were where the real money was at, her instructors had told her continuously as she worked twice as hard to make it through her individual classes. There had been no changing her mind, however.

Ever since she was a little girl, working on a skywheel was her dream. Watching the massive structure turn overhead as she looked out her bedroom window every night filled her with a sense of wonder that nothing else could hope to match. Nearly invisible in the daytime, it was only at night when they became apparent to all others on the surface of Grainne as their control lights showed as wisps. Most people thought little about them except that they were a cheap and efficient way to move ships to and from space. Arika was not most people.

"Well done, Arika," Lieutenant Borland said as he moved slightly away from her seat. She heard him curse as he lost control of his slate again. She withheld a smile. The UN had been on the skywheel for long enough now that all Freehold personnel knew who was microgravity (emgee) adept, and otherwise. The lieutenant was a flounder.

"*Skywheel Three, this is UNSS* Guy Mollet, *preparing to transfer storage goods to Temporary Holding Facility, Jefferson,*" a voice crackled over the comm. Arika growled softly. The United Nations Ships and United Nations Support Ships received priority over all others, and their continued abuse of this power caused many headaches in Control. She swore there was a little bit of joy in their voices every time they took a priority slot.

"*Mollet,* this is Skywheel Control." Arika kept the irritation from her voice. Maintaining a professional demeanor was what had kept her in charge of the skywheel after the others let their hatred show. They'd all been transferred groundside. "You have the tether schedule, I assume? Relay the coordinates so a release vector can be figured."

"Let's remember our jobs here, okay?" Borland murmured in her ear, his hot breath on her exposed neck. She withheld a shudder as he rubbed her arm. Fish out of water or not, microgravity allowed for people to sneak up on one another without making noise.

Oh my Goddess you stinking hairy window-licking ape get the hell away from me before I puke! she screamed internally.

"Rog, Lieutenant," a robotic voice replied. It took her a moment to realize that it was hers. "Our jobs are to support the ships in space and ensure that everyone gets where they're going in a safe and timely manner."

"Right," he smiled and gripped her upper arm tightly. She winced but managed to avoid flinching, though it was a close thing. "Let's remember our duty. The rewards are... very beneficial if we all do our jobs right."

I'm going to slit your throat in your sleep one night, you disgusting Earth pig.

"Yes, sir," Arika nodded as she reached across the console and began to calculate the necessary release point so the supply shuttle could achieve an optimal flight path toward the provisional UN base. Jefferson had different flight rules now that the UN was in charge, and they oftentimes conflicted with their other stated rules. Arika couldn't make heads or tails out of most of their regs, but predetermined flight paths were something she could wrap her mind around. And, when convenient, manipulate.

She paused a moment, pinged Docking Control One at the end of the twenty-kilometer Tether One and informed them, "Schedule adjustment, military priority, sending now."

Payload Manager Rostom replied, *"Well, short notice is better than none. Thank you, Control. Received."*

He obviously wasn't saying what he thought.

Mental math told her that the supply shuttle would need to achieve a minimum acceleration of 0.13 km/s^2 upon entering the atmosphere with a linear speed of 25 km/s. It would remain on the tether for 1.77 segs before release and reach the preferred flight line for Jefferson, with the momentum aided by the skywheel saving the shuttle over fifteen thousand credits on fuel over a direct landing. Her delicate fingers flew over the screen as she double-checked her math. It was only for record. Her math was almost always perfect.

The *Mollet's* supply shuttle attached itself to the proffered tether and it changed vector toward the surface of Grainne, the acceleration almost imperceptible to the naked eye as the engines cut back to conserve fuel.

"All that in your head? You're going to go far, as long as you have the right support *behind* you," the officer said with a stupid grin. Arika swallowed back the angry retort and simply nodded. That was all she could do. She dared not speak another word. There was no telling what would come out of her mouth if she did.

"Specialist?" a head popped into the small, confined control room. Arika snapped around to see who called her and very nearly sighed with relief.

"Senior." Arika nodded as her counterpart floated into the room. Senior Technician Tammie Darden flicked an annoyed look at Borland before turning her full attention back to Arika.

"How're things?"

"Quiet," Arika admitted after a moment of thought. Granted, the UN was shipping hundreds of thousands of tons of supplies and equipment down to the surface every day, but it paled in comparison to what a skywheel could handle. Before the invasion Skywheel Three used to handle five times this amount. The UN soldiers on board thought the crew was accomplishing something when in reality they were hindering. "I have two shuttles on right now, and a satisfactory window until the next scheduled arrival. Adjustable mass distribution is negligible, less than one percent. Easy shift."

"Get those shuttles off the tether and you can hit the rack," Tammie said as she slid into her seat on the sister console opposite Arika's. "You are relieved."

"Rog," Arika acknowledged as the senior technician buckled her safety harness and settled in at her station. Focused on the display, she felt rather than saw Borland drift away from her and back to the safety position where the UN staff usually observed from. The tightness in her shoulders eased as she realized that she would not be executed for murdering the lieutenant. *If they could read minds, I'd be shot in an instant*, she thought as the last shuttles from her shift released from their tethers. Satisfied, she transferred Control over to Tammie. "System. Control Specialist Santiago has been relieved. Duty station now occupied by Senior Control Specialist Darden. Time, date, and transmit. Have a good night, Tams. Night, Andy."

Darden replied, "Night, Arika."

Mather said, "See you next rotation." He was on alter half shift and would be off the next day.

Arika swam past the lieutenant in emgee, who did not even look in her direction as she reached the passage. She gave him one final withering look before she pushed off and began to drift toward the outer ring of the skywheel. As she coasted slowly down the tube, she felt feathers of gravity affect her as the centrifugal force of the station started to push her to the deck. Once she was able to walk instead of float, she quickly moved to the berthing quarters for the assigned skywheel crew.

She passed a few female UN soldiers loitering in the passage, and with the exception of a snide comment they left her alone. The women of the occupying forces she understood. There was a certain attitude between the UN and Freehold personnel on the station, most of which began at dislike and worked downwards from there. The UN mostly left the station personnel alone, however, since the skeleton crew was the only reason that the skywheel was able to function at all. If the UN wanted to save credits and keep landing supplies in an efficient manner on Grainne, then the crew of the skywheel were essential.

Which was why Lieutenant Borland's behavior both infuriated and confused her. When there was nobody around except for her he was a brash, abusive, and utterly contemptible human being who would not leave her alone. If someone else was in the room, such as Senior Tech Darden, then his behavior was completely different. Like a submissive and kicked puppy, and it was in this state that Arika almost felt pity for him. This, in turn, made her even angrier.

She entered her small cabin and sealed the hatch behind her. The UN had the override key, naturally, but it still gave her some semblance of privacy. It was her escape from the demands of her job and the overbearing presence of the UN, even if only for a little while. Arika needed it now more than ever before.

Breathing a sigh, she turned and looked at the single decorative piece in her tiny room—a wall-mounted Buddhist prayer wheel, a relic brought to the Freehold when her ancestors fled Earth generations before. Mass mattered, and the less aboard, the more could be transferred.

Stripping off her work coveralls, she tossed them into the corner to join a growing pile of dirty laundry. Normally a fastidious neat freak by nature, the clothes pile was her small way of rebelling against the UN. Though they *were* beginning to smell stale, she noticed as she went over to pick them up off the deck. She stuffed them into her laundry bag and made a mental note to get them all scrubbed before her next scheduled duty shift.

Her personal comm started blinking, telling her that she had a missed call. Surprised, she grabbed the device and flipped it on.

She pulled up the missed call and saw there was a message. Immediately the smiling face of Ranil Kotelawala came on the screen.

"Hey Arika, give me a call sometime. I got a new job. We should meet up soon and sosh it. I'll bring the drinks. Your place sound good? Call me."

The message ended and left Arika in the silence once more. A wry smile creased her face. A few months before Ranil had just been another prospective lover, a young worker who transported goods as a day laborer on the planet's surface. The duo quickly became friends instead and would remain so after he managed to get hired on at the skywheel just before the invasion. Since getting to the station, he was far too busy working maintenance to actually visit often.

During the initial stages of the occupation, every single employee of Skywheel Three had been subjugated to a questioning and DNA background check. She didn't understand why until Ranil informed her they were looking for veterans. Since neither Arika or Ranil were, they were cleared to work on the station. More than a few employees were moved groundside in a support manner after the UN found out they'd served in the FMF.

It was funny, really. Arika knew that one could not throw a stone in Jefferson without hitting a vet, given its close proximity to Heilbrun Base. It was hard to find any qualified engineers who weren't. She was one of the rare exceptions. She called Ranil back and he answered almost instantly.

"Hey," he smiled. Not for the first time she studied his lean face and marveled at the odd attractiveness of the younger man. He wasn't bulky and overly muscular as most maintenance workers were. No, the allure lay in his leopard-like build, slim yet powerful. Arika was also a sucker for eyes, and Ranil's seemed to pull her closer when she gazed into them. *"Got plans tonight?"*

"I have plans," she acknowledged with an impish smile. "I was hoping that they would involve you."

"Ask and ye shall receive, lady. What time?"

"Give me five segs to get cleaned up," she said as she quickly glanced about her room. Her own little private rebellion would need to go, she realized as her eyes lingered on the pile of clothes in the corner.

"I have some 'shine they cooked in Life Support," he offered. Arika sighed and quietly chuckled.

"Pretty sure that's not what the water condensers are for."

"*I won't tell if you don't.*"

"Deal," Arika agreed. "See you soon."

Quickly changing into the sexiest outfit possible, she sat at the edge of the bed and waited. Impatient, she stood back up and quickly walked over to her closet. Pulling the hatch open, she checked her reflection in the vanity mirror inside. Satisfied for the moment, she closed the hatch and hurried back to the bed.

"Shit!" she cursed as one of her breasts slipped out of the top. As she reseated it, there was a knock at her hatch. She stared at the source of the sound, aghast. "Are you serious right now?"

Then she nearly tripped as she hurried toward it. She yanked it open and there stood Ranil, somehow managing to look dashing in an old pair of gray coveralls. In one hand he held a large, dark green bottle. In the other were two coffee mugs.

"Mind if I come in?"

"Get in before someone sees you," she hissed, blushing brightly and yanking him inside. She poked her head out into the passageway but fortunately she could see no one else. Slamming the hatch shut, she hurriedly secured it.

"Everything okay?"

"Yes, fine, good," she replied and moved across the room to her bed. She sat down on the edge as Ranil got comfortable on the deck. With a sigh, she accepted an offered cup and waited as he poured what she presumed to be alcohol into it.

"I heard this was good stuff," he told her and filled his cup. He raised it up and sniffed. "Mech shine. Call it Old Greaser Number Seven."

Arika took a small sip and realized that maintenance workers should stay away from brewing. However, it was the first drink of alcohol she'd had in months, and after burning away her taste buds it wasn't really that bad. She drank it quickly, since it seemed to be that sort of booze.

"How's tricks?" She asked. Ranil smiled and shrugged.

"How's your end of things?"

"Slow," she admitted as she held out her cup for more. Ranil half crouched and poured. "The UN is inefficient as hell. They insist on doing things in the most inefficient and difficult manner, and then congratulate themselves when it almost goes right. Idiots."

"Inefficiency is good," Ranil said after pouring her a second drink. He continued after he sat back down. "That mass distribution on the deliveries has to be very precise. If we got the mass wrong, how much would that affect your trajectory?"

"Depends on how much," she replied as she stretched languidly across the bed. Ranil did not seem to notice, however. His eyes were far away, thinking about something else. Arika scowled. She was *not* going to throw herself at him, but she was not above pushing her breasts up to the point of screaming for more attention while she lay on her side. Experience told her that a man could not help but to look at cleavage. He was genetically predisposed to it. "Grams matter, you know."

"Does everyone in Control see it, or only you?"

"Ranil, I'm lying half-naked on my bed," she declared, exasperated. "I'm wearing a thin, see-through tank top and shorts. No shoes or socks. I painted my fucking nails. Do you *really* want to talk about work? Because if you do, let me throw on a sweater and scream in frustration before we do. Okay?"

Ranil smiled. "I'm sorry, I was trying to not jump your bones before we talked. I didn't want to presume anything."

"Presume all you want. Talk less. There are other things you should be using your mouth for, mister."

Later, as they lay entwined together on the deck, Arika murmured softly under her breath as Ranil ran a finger along her spine. She could feel his strong arms around her and the heat of his body on her chest. His hand moved to the nape of her neck, then the back of her head, where his finger ran along her shortly clipped hair. A sigh of contentment escaped her lips.

"You ever think about growing your hair out and using a static pin to hold it in place when you're in micro-G?" Ranil asked as he continued to trace her features with his fingers, moving from the back of her head to her jawline. Arika murmured softly under her breath.

"Not womanly enough for you?"

"That's not what I meant," Ranil chuckled, his deep voice rumbling in his chest. "I just like something to hold on to..."

Arika giggled. "As tempting as that sounds, I'm not sure I like you having *that* much control."

"You didn't seem to mind when I had you in that one position," he reminded her.

"That was because if I'd flexed my hips I could have crushed your balls," she countered and gently pecked him on the lips. "Then you'd be of no use to me."

Ranil smiled and looked into her eyes for a long time, silent. Arika, unused to such scrutiny from her part-time lover, squirmed uncomfortably. She reached down and tickled his hip. This broke the odd spell which had come over Ranil.

"Hey," she prodded. "What're you thinking about?"

"Well," he began, then paused. His eyes were filled with uncertainty, she saw. "You know I trust you, and I really like what we do in your spare time. I mean, I like you a lot, and I trust you completely..."

"Ranil, you are *not* about to propose marriage to me!" Arika snapped as she bolted upright. Quickly disentangling herself from the sheets and her lover, she rose to her feet. She felt her hands begin to shake.

"Relax, Arika." Ranil chuckled and propped himself up on one elbow, opting to remain lying on the deck. "I'm not going to propose marriage. Hadn't even crossed my mind."

"Oh, so now I'm just a piece of meat to you?" Arika asked as her eyes narrowed dangerously. "Your late night fling? Am I not even worth marrying?"

"No! I mean, yes...wait...are you messing with me?"

"Of course I am," she laughed and grabbed her underwear from the edge of the bed. She tugged them on and then grabbed her shorts before sitting down next to Ranil on the deck. He looked around his immediate vicinity, found her shirt half-buried under his pants, and offered it to her. She gratefully accepted and put it on. "Sometimes you're too easy."

"I'll remember that," he muttered as he rolled onto his back. Arika slipped down next to him. She kissed him again before settling back on top of the sheet.

She apologized. "I'm sorry, I couldn't help it. You looked so confused there for a moment and I had to keep it going. Tell me...what were you going to say?"

"I don't know," Ranil said. He gave her a very strange look, one which she had never seen on his face before. "It's weird..."

"No weirder than you wishing I had hair to pull when riding me from—" she reminded him and his sudden laugh cut off the rest of what she was about to say.

"Okay, fine," he exhaled slowly. His eyes flicked to her right before they met hers steadily. "Do you love your home?"

"Well, in a way," she allowed as she thought back to her childhood. "I mean, summers were always nice, and we could go swimming in the creek if it got too hot. Dad usually gave us a rifle in case a ripper showed up, but we only saw one once. You could say I love my home, yeah."

"No, not your childhood home," Ranil shook his head slowly. "Not what I meant."

"Then what did you mean?"

"Freehold," he stated simply. "Grainne. Do you love your home?"

"What?" Her confused question seemed to agitate him. His face grew cloudy and suddenly the happy-go-lucky technician was gone.

"The Freehold of Grainne!" he clarified. "Do. You. Love. Your. Home?"

"Yes, I love Freehold. It's my home. Now tell me what's going on?"

"How hard would it be for a supply load to accidentally get tossed into the wilderness instead of the 'mistakes' you've made with smaller payloads in the sea?" he asked instead, his entire body language changing on her as she scooted away. It was as if Ranil had flipped a switch in his mind. He had gone from seductive to intense to... she wasn't entirely certain. It was a focused man before her now. Not playful, not endearing, yet not exactly terrifying. It was unsettling.

"It'd be really hard, because it would mean both the computer and I screwed up somehow," she replied uneasily. The sudden change had thrown her completely.

"Just go with this for a moment," Ranil continued, oblivious to Arika's inner turmoil. "What if someone entered in the incorrect mass, and the computer *and* Control missed it? Could that happen?"

"Well... yeah, maybe."

"Trapped up here, with no way to fight against our oppressors... did you ever think that you could have a more active role in the war?" he asked. Arika was shaking her head before he had even finished asking the question.

"No, there's no war anymore," she said as she crossed her arms. "It's an insurrection."

"Fine, call it whatever you like," Ranil allowed. A flicker of annoyance crossed his face, fast enough that Arika wasn't certain if she had seen or imagined it. "You going to just sit up here for the entire war, or are you going to do your part?"

"My part?" she asked, dumbfounded. "I'm doing my part."

"Can you do more?" he asked. It took Arika a moment for the two seemingly separate conversations to merge within her head. When they did, though, her eyes widened in shock.

"That..." her voice trailed off as she began to process the possibilities.

"It's almost certain that only you would detect the change in mass during our window," Ranil told her. He was intense, urgent. "You already confirmed that. The UN would have to be watching you very closely to catch you."

This made Arika scowl. "Lieutenant Borland watches me like a hawk."

"Because he suspects you?" Ranil asked, looking at her oddly. Arika swallowed nervously and shook her head.

"No," she replied. "It's because he keeps dropping not-too-subtle hints that spreading my legs for him would earn me favor in the eyes of the almighty UN."

"So he has no idea. Good. Now, do more," Ranil stood suddenly. Arika, caught off guard by the surprise move, nearly face-planted. He grabbed his clothing and got dressed. "Imagine how bad it would be for *all* if those supplies were looted in some places that are a bit more difficult to get to?"

He left, leaving a stunned Arika behind.

Arika locked the hatch behind him and then began to pace the room, stopping every so often to spin her prayer wheel. Her fingertips felt the ancient leather facing of the wheel each time it rotated. The faint fragrance of incense and spices from ages past wafted into her nostrils. It might have been only a memory, or the smells could be real. She was never certain. Either way, she felt her anger dissipate with each rotation. As usual, her ancestor's wheel reminded her to remain grounded, even while in space.

Especially in space, she thought as her eyes scanned the cabin. They took in the disheveled bed, the organized closet, and the lack of photos of any family members. Those she had destroyed as the UN was boarding the station. The theory at the time was that while the invaders might be able to track her family down eventually to use against her, there was no reason for her to make it easy for them.

Ranil's words had weight. He had pointed out the one great flaw to her scheme: There really was no risk in the little things she was doing on the station. The UN was losing almost nothing with her occasionally sending a few tons of equipment into the sea. With as much as was being shipped through the skywheel, one- or two-tonne shipments were pathetic. She needed to up the ante.

If that man can do what he says he can, it wouldn't hurt to send the occasional transport to the wrong location for the FMF to pick up instead, she realized. *The only problem would be getting it past Borland. How do I do that?*

She fell into the messy bed and stared up at the ceiling, deep in thought.

The perfect opportunity came three days later.

"Shuttle *Andrei Davich*, cleared from tether," Arika called out as the computer informed her that the small UN transport had released into space. Segs later a small blip appeared on her screen as a new payload was attached. She checked it against the manifest and saw that it reported as weighing a little over fourteen thousand tonnes. However, the sensors informed her that it was actually slightly less than fifteen thousand. The difference, she noticed, was almost eight hundred tonnes.

It was almost too easy. It would appear as though someone simply entered in the numbers wrong, and at a quick glance it all looked fine.

"Payload One-Zero-Seven attached to tether," she announced aloud as a quick swipe across the board cleared the incorrect information on the sensors. "Load good, descending to surface now."

"Ah, the armament payload from the UNS *Juneau*," Borland nodded as he floated over to her station. He glanced at his payload checklist and chuckled. "That's a lot of ammo. Nonlethal, of course. But then, nobody ever said that nonlethal had to be painless."

Mather turned, opened his mouth, and she shook her head a fraction. He closed up and faced back to his station.

"Just over fourteen thousand tons," she murmured as the calculations came on the screen. The computer suggested a release speed of $2.17/km^2$ per second at 202.7 mil angle. Arika knew this was wrong and instinctively tried to correct it before stopping herself. The entire point of the mistake was to lose the cargo. She ran the math in her head and realized that the release point, due to the mass discrepancy, would actually be 5.5 mils early and way too slow. The UN was about to lose almost two hundred million creds worth of material . . . on the slopes of Braided Bluff, she realized as her mind mapped the trajectory. She held in her smile. The resistance would probably get to it long before the UN could, even accounting for the nearby base. "Release of Payload One-Zero-Seven . . . now."

The payload released precisely on schedule. It accelerated as the automated craft began its preprogrammed flight. A warning flashed on Arika's display. She glanced down and saw, without much surprise, that the craft did not have the velocity or angle to maintain an optimum flight path. Or any flight path, the computer confirmed a second later as the lander's engines ran dry and it began to wobble. The onboard sensors attempted to compensate for the lack of momentum given from the skywheel but simply did not have enough fuel.

"Lieutenant?" Arika called out to Borland, who turned around in confusion. They both watched as the payload glided gracefully across the sky. The computer beeped another warning as the preprogrammed path of the cargo yawed to the left at exactly the correct time. Segs seemed to stretch into eternity as two pairs of eyes tracked the flight of the automated cargo shuttle. A new projected path appeared in the screen, showing that the cargo was about to fall over fifty kilometers short of its target landing zone.

"*What the hell?!*" Borland shouted as he watched the payload land gently on the slopes of the range. "Oh fuck. The fucking rebels are gonna get that before we can send out search and rescue! *Fuck!* How did this happen? I don't understand . . ."

"Doublechecking the depot numbers now," Arika said as she brought up all information on the cargo. She made a show of scanning the numbers—which now said precisely what they were supposed to, courtesy of Ranil's computer magic—and shook her head. "Lieutenant? That payload was precisely what it was registered to be, mass and everything. Could have been a technical issue on the tether, releasing it too early. I'm not certain. It doesn't appear—"

Borland began to curse under his breath. "Fuck. Seen this on Mtali."

"Excuse me?" she asked, half turning in her restraint harness to look at the UN soldier. That was news to her. She had no idea that Borland had spent any time on the war-torn world of Mtali.

"Well..." he breathed out slowly. It was obvious to Arika that the lieutenant was reluctant to share the tale, so she decided to goad him a little. She even used the typical UN moniker which everyone on the skywheel insisted on using.

"Wes, you can share with me," Arika said in the gentlest voice she could manage. "I trust you with stuff..."

"Equipment went missing all the time on Mtali," he admitted after a second of contemplation. "I knew some guys who were implicated in the scheme. Turns out it was on the logistics end of things. They were reporting more equipment lost than actually was occurring, then turning around and selling the extra to the rebel factions on the planet for a pretty penny. Charges were brought up after the war but I'm pretty certain that nobody important served any real jail time."

"That's...horrible," she lied. In truth it was the most beautiful thing that Borland had ever said to her. It was as though every wicked fantasy and prayer she had ever played out in her mind had come true. She kept her concerned face on the lieutenant while she cheered internally. "You think that's what happened here? A mass variation due to someone pilfering equipment?"

"Maybe? I don't know," Borland admitted. "There's going to be an inquiry. Let's check the logs and see if there are any discrepancies."

They spent the next fifteen segs confirming what the backup list told them. The cargo shipment was supposed to mass 14,890 tonnes. In reality, the station system had logged the mass at 14,089. This caused some initial alarm for Arika, who had forgotten that the transmitted manifest would differ from what the log read. However, this merely incensed Borland further.

"Are you kidding me? The fucking *Juneau* is pilfering goods?"

"What do you mean?"

"The updated manifest was sent from the *Juneau* right before we picked up the payload," Borland reminded her. He pointed to the screen. "See? Whoever doctored the mass of the payload on the other end didn't know that we had a copy of what was expected. Once they figure out who did, they'll be punished for stealing eight hundred tonnes of arms as well as the loss of the entire payload."

"Can't you retrieve it?" she asked, genuinely curious now. It wouldn't do for her to go through all the risk of ignoring the mass discrepancies if they could easily mount an operation to fetch it. "The cargo, I mean?"

Borland was shaking his head before she finished. "No, we can't. Fucking heads are gonna roll."

"That's . . . that makes no sense," she admitted. "Accidents happen."

"If everything works right, there are no accidents."

"Uh . . ." she shut her mouth. The sheer ignorance of the statement was lost on Borland. The power which the UN wielded over all created a dissonance toward the colonies they ruled. A minor, honest statement like that carried further in weight than all the false promises in the universe.

"I mean, accidents happen," Borland said in a near-panicking voice. "But not into unpacified areas."

"Five segs until the *Novogorsk* joins the tether and leaves atmo," she replied after checking with the manifest. "Simultaneous tether with the transport shuttle *Aries* in orbit. Mass variance between the two is fifteen tons. Adjusting the distribution . . . now."

"The *Aries*?"

"Free trader," she responded as she punched in the final commands to shift the balance of the skywheel slightly to compensate for the lighter *Aries*. It was a mere five hundred kilograms worth of ballast, but it was enough to ensure that the free-floating nature of the skywheel and the stable orbit remained intact. "Outbound for Novaja Rossia."

"Ah, right," Borland nodded as he pushed his way over to the exit hatch. "You colonists still allow this sort of barter. That's another thing we need to clamp down on eventually. Damn it. I need to go file the report on the lost cargo before the *Juneau* somehow jackrabbits out of here."

Any sympathy she might have had for potentially getting Borland in trouble disappeared at that moment. She had allowed herself to forget that he and his kind had invaded her home. Ranil's words echoed in her ears. *Do more.*

"Rog, Lieutenant," she replied absently as Borland disappeared out of the compartment. Her mind drifted back to the next arms shipment. Could she drop the next one into the sea as well? Or should she send it to the FMF out in the wilderness?

Not yet, she decided after watching the two shuttles link up with their respective tethers. The mass distribution was perfect, as she expected, and the skywheel continued to turn. She would have to find a way to let Ranil know without the UNPF getting wind of it. *But how?*

In the meantime, she had to focus on the task at hand. Lying convincingly to whoever came asking questions about the payload being lost would be much easier than linking up two shuttles with massive mass disparities. *Especially if they're anything like Borland*, she thought.

Arika's father had a penchant for ancient sayings. One of his favorites, often told while he was imbibing a vintage port, was "when the shit truly hits the fan, you'll know it." She had never understood precisely what that meant until the day she stumbled upon a dead Tammie, two dead guards, and Ranil standing over all three while holding a bloody knife.

It had been a hectic week. Three more large supply drops had fallen into the hands of the rebels. One during her third shift, and two during Tammie's. Borland had freaked out but there was little he could do. It was obvious to everyone that there was a problem on the *Juneau*. At least, that was the rumor, courtesy of Ranil and Arika's careful planning.

Which all came crashing to the ground the moment she saw Tammie's body.

"Wha—" she began before Ranil moved with the fluidity of a ripper. He clamped his free hand over her mouth and somehow pulled her out of the passageway and into the small alcove next to Tammie's berth. She squeaked through his iron grip as his eyes bore into her.

"Ssh," he hissed and looked around quickly. There was nobody in the immediate vicinity. "Don't scream. I'm not going to hurt you. I found some aardvarks handling Tammie. Looked like they were staging an 'accident,' so I tried to stop them. Killed these two, but a third ran off. Guards are probably coming. It's time to blow this fucker out of the sky."

She tried to tell Ranil that she wouldn't scream but all that came out sounded like a bunch of incoherent mumbling. Ranil quickly apologized and removed his hand from her face.

"Not going to scream," she gasped as quietly as she could

manage given the circumstances. She looked out onto the passage deck at Tammie's body. "Poor Tammie…"

"She'd been doing what you were doing," Ranil told her as he dragged her back into the cubby. He looked wildly around. "UN caught on. She wasn't as good at hiding the evidence as you were. I heard that they were going to talk to her, but someone else decided to make it an accident. This is good."

"Good?" Arika asked, dumbfounded. "My coworker is *dead!*"

"I'm sorry, but she knew—shit," he stopped.

"She knew shit?"

"Hey, you!" a voice ordered loudly from behind her. Arika half turned and spotted a squad of UN goons standing in the passageway. She opened her mouth to speak but Ranil easily pushed her back down the alcove. Stumbling, Arika managed to keep from falling flat on her face. She pulled herself back upright through sheer determination and gave Ranil a withering look.

"Quit staring and move!" Ranil screamed at her as he hefted the blood-covered knife in his free hand. Arika ran as quickly as she could manage in the lower gravity. The UN guards bounded after her, though more ungainly. Their inexperience in space showed. Her lead grew with each step.

"Halt or we will fire!" One of the UN guards shouted. Arika almost stopped until she heard Ranil shout back at them.

"You can't discharge a lethal firearm on a pressurized station, morons!" Actually, they could, but she assumed he was betting they didn't know that.

A loud *snap!* echoed down the passageway. Arika looked over Ranil's shoulder and saw the guards pull out stun batons.

"Yeah, those could hurt," Ranil stated. He motioned at Arika without taking his eyes off the UN. "I don't want to you be involved. Move!"

Ranil turned to follow her, so Arika decided that it was time to put even more space between herself and their pursuers. With each step gravity grew slightly less, and her emgee experience helped their lead grow. The UN guards pursuing them were doing decently well, but they were neophytes.

Ranil passed her but instead of being alarmed, she recognized his plan immediately. She knew that while she was skilled in emgee, Ranil lived in it. Whatever training he had before arriving on the station showed as he monkeyed up the handholds and pushed off, using the almost nonexistent gravity to move faster. She bounded off the deck and grabbed Ranil's outstretched arm. He expertly maneuvered her to another stanchion as the guards closed the distance. She bounced off the wayside slightly and flipped up to the overhead next to her companion.

"On three," he said as he began to count down. On "three" both shoved as hard as they could on the handholds, propelling them deeper into emgee. After nearly twenty-five meters of nothing else to grab, they reached the first set of stanchions just before Control. Ranil snagged her hand as he managed to catch the second grip of the set. He motioned for her to wait a moment as he readjusted his grip.

"What are you planning?" she asked as the UN reached the red line. His smiled grimly and reached into his coveralls. He pulled out a small remote device and passed it to her.

"Hold this for me," he said as he locked eyes on the approaching guards. "Don't mess with anything yet. I have to kill some aardvarks."

Arika watched as Ranil flexed his muscles and pushed off from the wayside as hard as he could. She gasped. Every single spacer knew from training that one typically took it easy in space when flying around in emgee. It was dangerous and required caution at the utmost. She had seen more than a few injuries during training, all of which had been relatively minor. But, if one wasn't too careful, a spacer would end up with a collection of broken bones.

Ranil didn't seem to care as he flew at the UNPF armed with only his tiny knife. As surprised as Arika was by his sudden attack, the guards were even more shocked to see the diminutive man rocketing down the passageway at them. Other than stun batons, they were not equipped for close-quarter combat. All eight tried to slow their approach but Ranil had picked his contact point perfectly.

The UNPF, unable to slow or halt their momentum, were fed into the grinder that was Ranil.

Ranil, a quiet and mostly unassuming man, mowed through the UNPF as if they were floating targets and not living, breathing human beings. He stabbed two through the throat, then broke the neck of another. One of the guards trailing in the rear managed to disarm Ranil with a lucky shot from his stun baton and was rewarded by Ranil crippling him with thumbs into his eyes. The last uninjured guard cracked Ranil brutally across the chest with his own baton, stunning him. Off-balance and helpless, there was little the mechanic could do to protect himself from his attacker.

Suddenly Arika was there, driving the knife into the exposed neck of Ranil's assailant. She screamed incoherently and wrenched the sharp blade to the side. Blood erupted from the jagged wound and the guard, stunned by the sudden rear attack, bled out faster than she anticipated. Her entire upper body coated in blood, Arika yanked the knife from the wound and pushed the dead guard aside. Maneuvering carefully, she pulled herself up to where Ranil floated.

There was little she could do for the man. The UN guard had crushed Ranil's sternum and broken both arms. The blunt force trauma to Ranil's formerly handsome features was enough to cause her to sob. She gently pulled him close.

"Who are you?" she whispered as she cradled Ranil's twitching body in her arms.

"Just...a man...who loves...his...home," he struggled with every breath. His eyes flicked to the remote she held in her hand. "Password...to...detonate...is...your...birthday."

"My birthday?" she asked, shocked. "How did you know my birthday?"

"I...loved you."

Ranil shuddered one final time and quit breathing. His lips turned cyanotic. His hands grew limp in hers. Arika, unable to do anything for her lover, was helpless as he suffocated in her arms.

"I love you too," she cried into his still chest.

The device in her hand was a stark reminder that the mission still remained. Taking down the skywheel would be childishly easy. However, Arika wanted to do more than that. She wanted men and women in the UN who were like the detestable Lieutenant Borland to pay for attacking her home.

The length of the skywheel was just over 40 kilometers. If her memory served correctly, the current positioning of the tethers were about 640 and 140 mils respectively. Calculating the speed of the tethers, she realized that if she blew it at that moment then the skywheel would hit the planet's oceanic surface area almost flat. It would create a huge wave, but that would be it. Her mind raced. The very edge of the tether would impact and the rest of the skywheel...would take out Jefferson City.

"That won't do at all," she muttered under her breath as she did more mental calculations. If she could manage to let the planetside tether hit the water at an 83 mil angle, the mass of the skywheel would allow the tether to buckle. This would potentially shorten the amount of reach the tether would have. It would also knock Control out of a stable orbit as it and the other tether would remain in space.

No, not eighty-three mils plus, she corrected herself. *Seventy-two mils plus. Mass won't be an issue. Velocity and mass . . . yeah, 72.22245 at a speed of 2.25km/s². They'll get a tsunami about two segs after impact, and the air pressure wave would be about a seg or so out . . . the very edge of the tether should strike the shoreline, which would create an impact crater. How deep? Deep enough I guess. Should reach my target area. Will it be too much and affect Jefferson City? Maybe. I don't know. Damn it, think.*

Either way, if she wanted to do the most damage to the UN, then she had to wait another eighteen segs until the angles were just right. That would be easy enough. As long as she avoided the roving patrols wandering the station, it should be simple enough.

"Hey you!" an accented voice yelled out from down the passage. She turned her head and spotted three UN guards in riot gear. They handled their nonlethal firearms with obvious unfamiliarity. "Don't move!"

Of course, nothing is ever easy on a skywheel, she thought as she gently pulled Ranil's still form to the proper position. She gingerly placed both feet on the dead man's chest. "I'm sorry Ranil, but you'd understand better than most."

Arika shoved Ranil away from her and toward the guards, who were carefully making their way through microgravity. The force of her push gave her some momentum away from the guards. While not the most effective way to escape, it did hamper her pursuers and got her moving at a faster velocity than the men behind could immediately match. It would give her precious segs, and that was all that she needed.

Her brain continued to count down the time when she would blow the tethers of the skywheel. The detonations would have to be triggered in seven segs—assuming that none of the UN soldiers got wind of what she was attempting and braked the rotation against the flywheel. She frowned and thought about that possibility for a moment as she drew closer to Control.

Most aardvarks don't take a dump without permission, she reasoned as she grabbed a stanchion near Control's entry. Her momentum nearly flipped her over but as she performed a twisting maneuver she was able to get her feet back beneath her. Arika's legs flexed and they cushioned her, absorbing the impact. Finally stopped, she risked a quick look back toward the men chasing her. A smile creased her face. They had gotten caught up in the zero-G section, as she expected, and Ranil's body had brought any progress to a halt as the UN tried to figure out how to chase her down.

"Too late," Arika whispered and ducked inside Control. She secured the hatch—something the UN would never allow, and turned to Mather.

"Emergency conditions, right now!" she said.

"Yes, ma'am," he agreed. "What do you need? You were away."

Very firmly, she said, "I was. Evacuate."

"What, now?"

"Yes. Pod. Now."

He nodded with a "Yes, ma'am," and scrambled out.

She reached her station. Quickly scanning the readouts she saw that her estimation of the tethers had been spot-on. The tethers were at 702 and 75 mils. She'd almost cut it too close.

She opened the station comm channel and announced, "This is Control. Emergency, emergency, emergency. Collision imminent. Real world. All personnel evacuate. All personnel evacuate. All personnel evacuate."

There were only seconds, but the regular crew drilled on emergency procedures, would account for each other, and climb in the rescue pods without hesitation. Maybe they'd take some UN goons, maybe not. That was up to them.

Arika was not afraid to die. Dying blind, alone in space, however, was something that was unnerving. Being in Control helped alleviate her fears. She could see everything, courtesy of the consoles. A quick look at the tether display told her it was time.

"There is one love," she began to whisper, remembering her mother's favorite prayer. "One power. One presence. There is a single eternal source of all of life. An amazing wellspring of strength, courage, and comfort. A place of pure potential. A life of infinite possibilities.

"That life is my life. That power flows through my own veins.

That presence is deep within me. An eternal source of strength that is my true self. A pure potential that I am now aware of.

"In this moment I reclaim my power."

Arika detonated the bombs.

Skywheel Three was in the shadow of Grainne when the bombs blew. They were shaped charges which exploded internally, damaging the structural integrity. They did precisely as Ranil had promised Arika: made the skywheel inoperable. Thanks to Arika's precise calculations *when* the detonations occurred, the rotation of the skywheel was destabilized enough to truly make an impact on the world below.

However, the detonations were small and internal and therefore invisible from below. Nobody could foresee the consequences—except for Arika Santiago.

At 0421 UN time the first tether of the skywheel struck water forty-two kilometers off the coast. Jefferson City, located four kilometers inland, was hit by the overpressure wave of the falling tether at 2.12 divs. Every man, woman, and child in the area was woken by the hurricane winds which ripped through, some clocking over eighty kilometers an hour on the UN sensors. The permanent structures in the city were not harmed. Much of the damage was limited to poorly installed polycarb windows and uprooted trees. There would be one civilian death reported later: an elderly man out walking struck and killed by a falling tree.

As the populace of the city began to crawl out of bed to try and figure out what was going on, the twenty-meter tsunami caused by the initial impact was diffused by the underwater breakers located just offshore. It slowed and boiled in the marsh and farmland between the city and the coast, though some wealthy mansions on the cliffs to the north took hard splashes. It did cause some minor issues upriver, jostling barges and piers. None of the water made it into Jefferson City proper.

The UN facility outside the city, though, was close to the coast.

UN troops were tossed from their bunks as the overpressure wave struck their camp. Temporary housing units, built of thin polymer, buckled as the storm winds tore into them. Gear and soldiers were thrown out of their beds and into the open as the wind slammed through. Many were injured by haphazardly flung debris. Some were killed as they struggled to stand up amidst flying shards.

As bad as this was, though, it was over as suddenly as it arrived. The general alarm belatedly erupted into the predawn sky, warning everyone of an impending... something. The unwounded survivors counted their blessings and tried to help their fellow soldiers out. Since officers were housed on the far side of the base away from the sea in more permanent housing, they suffered little when compared to the enlisted personnel. A few windows were dismounted, and one housing unit had its roofing torn off, but otherwise they survived unscathed.

Officers poured out of their lodging to issue conflicting commands. What initially started out as a mess quickly devolved into chaos. More than one high-ranking officer stated that things could not get any worse.

They thought wrong.

The tsunami hit. Muted as it was, it was still a five-meter surge from the river.

Debris sloshed through the already wrecked base. Carried by the force of the water, it did not cause many deaths itself. This merely delayed the relief effort and churned the base into muck.

The third act of Arika's perfectly executed surprise attack struck at 2.26 divs as the remains of the tether, folded over due to its flexible nature, reached the planet's surface at long last.

Thousands more died as the monomolecular filament tether, which was over four hundred meters wide where thickest, slammed directly across the runway. While low in mass and density, it still had enough to matter. Everything caught beneath it was instantly crushed. Fragments of the tether exploded outward upon impact, slaughtering hundreds of flight personnel who were trying to organize an evacuation of the survivors. It shredded everything not already destroyed. The results were catastrophic.

Through it all Arika watched from Control, where everything had begun. The compartment maintained a small reserve of emergency power, the charges having severed the main power line and backups. One solitary monitor remained active, tracking the progress of the tether's damage. She glanced back at the detonator in her hand. It was mere segs before the last set of bombs exploded. Still in orbit around the planet, her time was short. She was happy, though. She was able to watch her childhood dream kill hundreds, maybe thousands of invaders.

Do you love your home? She heard Ranil ask her.

"I love my home," she whispered back.

You did good, Ranil said. Arika started to cry. He chided her gently. *There's no need to cry, my love. This is a great victory.*

"I'm not crying because I'm sad, you idiot," she giggled softly as she closed her eyes. For a moment she could swear that his scent was there with her in the room. Fleeting, but tangible. A soft smile touched her lips. "I'm happy, though I wish we had more time together."

We have all the time in the universe, love. Besides, Control doubles as a rescue pod.

■ ■ ■

Huff #5

The Skywheel [Mid-March 210]

Pandemonium. That's the only word for what's happening on this base. You can't call this "consequence management," because most of the base has been atomized, the coast has new geologic features, and thousands are dead. I'll order the J4 to get reconstruction underway, on this same spot, because I'll be *damned* if we concede this ground!

[Reviewer's Note: Source document missing two pages, likely torn out deliberately; extant entry picks up four days later.]

Destroying Skywheel 3, from any material standpoint, makes little tactical or operational sense. We have two remaining skywheels to compensate for 3's loss with little slippage in timetables or capacity. The attack itself had to have taken immense effort and resources. Strategically, the real pain for us is the near-total loss of Main Operating Base Unity and thousands of personnel: military, civserv, contractor, and NGO. Now, those useless NGO sacks of shit are bailing out of the whole system.

The survivors are severely traumatized; I haven't escaped unscathed either. Regaining our footing, our momentum? That won't happen overnight. Nothing—not even the worst carnage I saw on Mtali compares to watching a 400m-wide space tether slamming into an active runway at shift change. Clever bastards. The nightmares are awful. In one, I'm on the runway and the end of that tether, with that sickening sound of the filament approaching supersonic speeds, slams right into me. Sandeep suggested I see Behavioral Health twice before I told him to stuff it. A lesson I learned early in my career: never talk to those people, don't take pills, don't let anyone get a single damn data point they could sell to the administration. I'll send others to them, but I can handle this.

It took a few days to reconstruct the events. I was staying in the DV quarters on Unity for a troop visit and to catch a shuttle up to Skywheel 3 that morning. Once the initial shock wave formed after the first end of the tether hit the water, Baldy snatched me out of my room. I learned later that he was awake outside when his emergency comms went off and saw "slivers of light" in the early morning sky. Since we were set to travel to the Skywheel in a few hours, he'd been listening in on traffic and security messages, doing his job. A shuttle broadcasted an emergency message on the open "guard" frequency while on approach, just as explosives detonated. That pilot will get a commendation very soon. The second he mentioned "debris from the station falling out of orbit," Baldy moved out. He's only required to protect me, but he helped Sandeep and some of the key staff make it as well. We reached the shelter at exactly 0440, just in time to see the tether unfold and fall. That's when he tackled me into the bunker. The tsunami warning sounded soon enough and we stayed put until it passed. It was the most structurally sound building on the base, but even those thick walls could barely muffle the impact...or the screams. The worst sound, though, was the silence.

The recovered Skywheel crew don't know anything, of course. I wouldn't expect them to. This is as likely one of our busybodies' screwup as theirs.

We had to wait a few days for the water to recede enough for me to get back to my office on Commerce Street in the "Green Zone." The double hit from the attack caused notable damage even 40km away, and I wasn't sure what to expect in Jefferson. Luckily, the damage on Commerce was mostly superficial and hard to notice above the battle damage from our initial strike. More windows blown out, more fire-suppression water and foam everywhere, bookcases knocked over. Nothing terribly important or irreplaceable, but one item caught my eye. On the wall behind my desk, I hung a family shadow box I received on my commissioning day. Among other heirlooms, it contained a flask handed down father to son for centuries. The box had fallen and the glass shattered, the flask lying on the ground. I noticed the light wear and tarnish, but the embossed lion emblem with the words "Pro Rege, Pro Patria, Pro Lege"—*For King, For Country, For Law*, remained bright and clean. I think I'll keep it a bit closer for the time being.

Spider's Web
Part 4

Moyra Kelly, her critical and essential equipment, her grand-mother, and the local handlers all relocated to one of the newer safe houses. It was based in what was essentially a refugee camp, further up into the mountains to the south of Jefferson, and across the rivers. Being so close to the primary UN base, while having its benefits for potential espionage, seemed risky for other reasons. Friendly fire at this juncture could ruin much of Moyra's logistics, and while she had *some* disaster and successorship planning in place... that was a less than optimal scenario.

Moyra quickly realized that "refugee camp" belied the construction and organization of the smaller town. The portion that she moved into was, by Freehold standards, somewhat slapdash built, but functional enough. Her grandmother settled into assisting the town's leadership with resettling others fleeing Jefferson and her own Hamilton. Half mountain resort, half mining town, and a whole lot of boiling hatred for the UN, made for an interesting place to expand operations.

Moyra barely managed to ensure all of her equipment made the relocation without issue and that the provided encrypted hard lines were to her satisfaction before the next disaster struck. DalesOP provided a rundown of the actions that he and Damocles managed while she was out of contact for three days during the transition.

Skylight frantically advised the command team that Skywheel Three was going down, and that they had no contact with bridge staff. Some escape pod beacons were heard, and rescue ships were already en route.

Moyra relayed Skylight's information to one of the sister stations for dispersal, along with Skylight's belief it was caused by UN forces attempting to take over full operational control. From there, the story made it to the news despite the UN's filtering. Between the devastation of the anchoring lines and the damage to the UN's base "Unity," the resulting disorganization actually *assisted* their cause. A rallying cry, the obviousness to other citizens that there *were* people fighting back, and less piecemeal than perhaps the UN was pretending... the team establishing new contacts with freelancers became rather busy. In turn, this left Moyra, Damocles, and DalesOP reviewing two-way applications nearly nonstop, on top of their other duties.

The UN forces dithered about taking complete control of a skywheel to use for their landing operations, but the information that Moyra pulled indicated they were more than a bit surprised at the aggressive defense. Two days later, Moyra saw the order come down to preserve the resources they had on hand, which meant that dedicating more personnel for a skywheel which "these crazy people" might take down immediately was a tactic the UN could ill afford at the moment.

Skylight was, temporarily, safe.

Damocles relayed that, while blaming the UN was useful, Naumann had reason to believe it was caused by Freehold personnel denying the asset to the UN. Skylight took small comfort from the idea her friends went down fighting.

In the background, Moyra felt the constant need to slowly spin down Hespera's network without setting off Braknck too much. Bowler Hat paid handsomely for every UN bureaucrat's name, and Moyra understood the life expectancy once a bureaucrat's name appeared with a bid was often measured in days, if not segs. Whenever a handler got word that a contract was being fulfilled, the team worked to ensure that UN surveillance of the area and several others failed at the same time.

The income helped keep Braknck in line, but she suspected he was getting antsy. Every time the UN upped their bribery for information, he made noises that worried her. Main comm's chatter remained primarily restricted to comments about what was heard on a sister station. He remained unaware that several of the team had relocated physically and anything else outside of Jenkins's role in acquiring the information about the initial bureaucrat.

Between the group's income streams, some of which were drying up just from normal ebb and flow, and her own personal income, she and her grandmother were doing well enough. The reactivated military contract provided other income, as well, permitting her to focus on the actual tasks at hand. She suspected the town council for the "resort" also had *other* responsibilities. As long as they didn't conflict with hers, she didn't care enough to expend precious energy figuring it out.

Huff #6

Public Nudity [3rd Week March]

HOW THE HELL DID THIS HAPPEN?

One minute, I'm in the car, reviewing some notes. Next thing I know, my driver is tangled, and I've got some Grainne bitch yanking me out of the seat, carrying me off like I'm a fucking monkey, shoving a gun in my face, stealing my briefcase, and yelling at me like some secondary-school bully, to strip.

Yes, I looked like an idiot. That's not what worries me—I'm worried about how the lapse happened. I've fired most of the personal staff, the XO, the local MP Commander. His commander. His commander's commander. They all lodged labor complaints. I don't care. Sandeep and Baldy survived the purge. Baldy was lucky, he was on a three-day pass, his counterpart—not so much.

Counter-Intel found two more of the security detail dead and stripped, with their secure communications crypto material missing. The bodies were displayed purposefully; the rebels wanted us to find them. The staff had to scramble to get me new security. This shook everyone up, but was completely overdue. I can't believe my own complacency.

Every local national is banned from the compound until I say otherwise. I need to talk to the Provost Marshall, and see when she thinks it will be appropriate to ease off.

Star Crossed

Kacey Ezell and Robert E. Hampson

December 207. Three Years and Two Months Before the Invasion.

Dr. Reagan Meacham looked at the results one more time. His heart shattered into billions of tiny pieces, like stars flung through the black outside his porthole. He put his head down for a moment and closed his eyes.

"Reagan."

Her voice came through the small intercom speaker above his workstation. Reagan pressed his lips together for just a second, then swallowed hard and answered in a voice clear of any devastation.

"Yes, love?"

"It's midcycle. Food's ready in the galley. Come eat."

"I'll be right there," he said.

"Really?" she asked, tinny laughter echoing through the speaker. *"You mean I won't have to call you eight more times as usual? Are you feeling well?"*

Despite everything, Reagan grinned. That was his Tessa: finding dry humor in the most unlikely of moments.

"I was at a stopping point anyway, saucy girl," he said. "I'm going to put this mess away and I'll be in the galley in five minutes."

"Hurry," she said, her tone still clearly joking. *"Otherwise I might eat all this food myself."*

"So it's early yet, but I think these numbers are encouraging," Tessa said as Reagan finished the last bit of what had been a very good sandwich. For ship food, at least. At least the ship's breadmaker could produce a passable loaf.

"Sounds like it," Reagan replied, wiping his mouth one more time. He crumpled his napkin in his hand and stood to take his plate to the cleaner/storage unit built into the bulkhead of the galley. When he and Tessa had first boarded the ship, he'd thought the galley unbearably crowded. But since they'd arrived on station and the transit crew had left, it was almost luxuriously spacious.

The ship was officially designated UNRV *Korielle*, but for over five Earth-standard years, he and Tessa had called it "home." Tessa (Dr. Tessa Asano, if they were being professional about it) had received a grant to study jump point formation. His task, on the other hand, was to study the results of long-term exposure to jump point side effects and phase drive usage on human neurophysiology. They'd dreamed about taking this research trip together for years, even before they fell in love, when they were just two post-doc students at the Max Planck Institute on Earth.

They'd been on-station for almost an E-year, since 207 for him, 2555 CE for Tessa. For the last six Earth months, they'd been the only occupants. If they had an emergency, or drifted too far from their approved station, a "system pilot" crew would come over from Jump Point One Control. However, that would take time which could be critical in an emergency, so during those first three months, the transit crew also trained them in basic shipboard maintenance, piloting and navigation. Naturally, Tessa excelled in piloting and navigation, leaving Reagan to muck out the hydroponics and tissue culture tanks and to care for their small colony of mice. Unfortunately, their only real research subjects for the effects of jump point effects on the brain were himself and Tessa.

"How did the latest test results turn out?" Tessa asked as he finished the galley cleanup.

"Not too bad." It wasn't a complete untruth, Reagan thought. "An 'N' of two doesn't do us much good for publication. I'd be happier if we could get at least *one* of the sensor packages back!"

"It's only been two months since we sent the last one through. You know that the ships we asked to carry them were scheduled for Mtali and Meiji at the very least before headed back to Grainne." Reagan was already headed back to his lab, but Tessa's voice followed him via the comm clipped to the collar of his shipboard

coverall. *"You're just being impatient! We have more than two years left to gather your data. After all, I have to wait for the ships, too."*

"I know, but we asked the last one—the one headed directly to Sol? We asked her to pass the package off at the jump point to someone coming back through right away." He knew he was being petulant, but there was also an underlying anger. She didn't know it, but if his test results were true, they didn't *have* two years.

CHIME. The incoming jump alert sounded throughout the ship.

"Patience, my love," she said lightly. *"Let's see if your wishes have been granted."*

Reagan reversed direction, and headed to the communications station instead of his laboratory. *"Ident coming in."* Tessa was already decompressing the ship's identification and jump log squirt by the time he arrived. *"Freighter* Bob, *Grainne Registry, Registry number forty-two. Cargo: Nunya."* She paused a moment while he continued to read the infodump. A crackle come over the comm, sounding remarkably like a snort. *"Why do you Grainiacs do that? The last three Grainne-registry freighters through here gave their registry number as forty-two, and what's 'Nunya'?"*

Reagan laughed. You had to grow up in the Freehold to understand the Freeholder response to rules and regulations. "Look, Earth makes the ships report registry and cargo. The Freehold does not. So it's a rebellion thing. Earth needs a number? Give them a number, but one that is meaningless, or perhaps the most meaningful of all! They want to know your business? Tell them 'Nunya' as in 'Nun'ya business.'"

"Oh-kay," she drew out the syllables. *"So what about the name? Bob?"*

"Well, they do need their own unique name to identify themselves to others. In this case, the metadata on their jump-squirt says that they're the 'Anson MacDonald.'"

"Right, that means exactly zero to me." Now Tessa was sounding petulant.

"Look, sweetie, you're the one with access to the computer core—you *could* look it up..." He paused a moment, to see if she would react, but realized it was also somewhat petty, and continued before she could answer: "Twentieth-century, classic speculative fiction. 'Anson MacDonald' was the pen-name of Robert Anson Heinlein. Called 'Bob' by his friends. Okay?"

He was met with silence.

"Sweetie? Tessa? Are you mad at me?"

"Huh? No, oh, no, not that. I was distracted. 'Bob' just sent a squirt in our direction in addition to their omni arrival broadcast."

"Wait, what? They sent something to us?"

"Oh, yes, my love. They have your sensor package. The tissue packs will have to go to Orbital and back to us on the supply run, but they squirted all of the data."

"Oh, my dearest sweetest Tessa, I could kiss you!" In his enthusiasm, Reagan had forgotten.

"Yes, dear, I know you could," her voice came back sadly. *"I know."*

After a preliminary glance, the data from the sensor pack looked encouraging. Not quite encouraging enough for Reagan to forget about the results of his latest shipboard test, but encouraging enough that he was able to summon some enthusiasm for Tessa's benefit.

"So the sensor pack data correlates with what we're seeing on board?" she asked.

"Mostly, yes," he said, scrolling through the readout, his eyes never leaving the screen. "There are some deviations, of course, but well within the accepted range. And when we control for differences in age and health conditions..." he trailed off, swallowed hard, forced himself to continue in a lighthearted tone. "It's early yet. But it appears that our hypothesis isn't entirely off base. We may be on the right track, here, Tessa."

"So that's good news," she said.

"Very good news."

"Good. So what else is the problem, then? Because something's on your mind. Is it the other information Bob *sent? About the tensions between Earth and Grainne?"*

"A little," he lied, grateful for the excuse. It wasn't that the news *didn't* concern him, it was just that it wasn't nearly the first thing weighing on his mind. "I just don't see it turning out well. The UN doesn't like upstart planets who won't fall in line. Take a look at Mtali, for example."

"That's a totally different situation. The UN and Grainne both value science," Tessa said, her tone reassuring. *"I don't think we have anything to worry about."*

✧　　✧　　✧

In the darkness, her skin slid over his in all the delicious silkiness of sex. He breathed her name and tasted her lips as they laughed against his. She tasted like sunshine and chocolate. He groaned and pressed up into her as she caught his lip between her teeth...

Reagan woke, gasping in the dark. His sweaty hair stuck to his forehead, and his heart felt close to hammering out of his chest. Desire still thundered through him like a mag-train, and he groaned as he realized that it had been a dream. Tessa wasn't here with him, in his tiny shipboard bunk. He blinked bleary eyes and forced them to focus on the chrono readout.

Time to get up. She was probably already at work. He should join her.

With another groan, he forced himself up and over to the tiny cleaning unit as the last vestiges of his erotic dream faded in his mind.

Reagan had a bit of time to wait for the latest model to complete its simulation run, so he pulled up the draft research report that he and Tessa were preparing for the Max Planck Institute on Earth.

Biophysics of Phase Drive vs. Jump Point
Neurological Stress—Q7 Technical Report,
MPI Fellowship Contract M8000-27-C-93514.
Prepared by Meacham, R, MD, MPH, PhD
and Asano, T, PhD, MBA, PE

Neurological analysis of Jump Shock has been limited by the availability of biological samples from high-order nervous systems. During the Q1–Q4 pre-deployment preparation at the Institute, the study team designed and prepared a sampling package consisting of physics sensors and self-contained tissue cultures. Deployment and training during Q5 slowed progress, but sixteen sampling packs were launched into Grainne Jump Point One during Q6.

Q7 progress: We have distributed eight sensor packs to ships departing the Grainne system en-route to Earth, Mtali and Meiji, as well as secondary stops along the way. So far, only one package has been returned, having traveled only once each direction through the Earth-Grainne

Jump Point. So far, results confirm findings from onboard samples retained on RV *Korielle*, as well as the local drone-deployed sensors.

Biological findings: Jump Shock appears to be an inflammatory response to tissue heating during reintegration into normal space. Magnetic resonance suggests accelerated hydrogen spin and precession similar to that produced by electromagnetic radiation in the microwave through X bands, however, the physics sensors have not detected radiation in that domain. Scanning electron microscopy does show tracks from an elevated flux of delta-particle paths consistent with high-charge-and-energy (HZE) atomic nuclei with all electrons stripped off. Unusually for HZEs, the measured molecular weights of the nuclei exceeded that of most galactic cosmic radiation (GCR) components. The unusual HZE flux could result in abnormal beta and delta ionization tracks and point-source degradation of chromatin resulting in inflammation and auto-immune disorders. See attached confidential medical report AsanoTMPI00631.

Physical findings: Sensors deployed inside the jump point at the time of re-emergence have confirmed that HZE flux is elevated above that of the background cosmic radiation. Interaction of these particles with biological tissue will result in damage, albeit most likely temporary.

Astrophysical findings: Jump points do not conform to Morris-Thorne-Weaver or Einstein-Rosen wormhole physical predictions. Current theory suggests a convolution of M-space membranes, but does not account for the unusual HZE flux. We remain concerned that the unusually massive HZEs may interact with exotic-matter lensing in Phase Drive which may require additional shielding around the phasing shunts.

Anticipated Q8 progress: In the next performance period, we anticipate completion of milestones 3.2.5 and 3.2.6a regarding analysis of the physics sampling packages. Progress on milestone 3.2.6b will depend on the return of addition sampling packs and correlating findings with the number of phase drive transitions and jumps.

Problems and Concerns:

Reagan had left this part of the report blank. Anything he wrote, Tessa would also see and he was uncertain just how much to reveal of his own worries. A soft *ping* sounded in the larger chamber outside his lab. The need for both space and high-tech instrumentation meant that the lab was located in the engineering section of the *Korielle*. He'd been running the simulation on the main engineering console—after all, it wasn't doing much while they just sat here taking measurements. Oh well, he'd get to that in a moment. He needed to finish this report and get it submitted before the funding agency got upset. After a few minutes additional thought, he decided to be honest, yet circumspect:

Problems and Concerns:
    I remain concerned about Dr. Asano's health. She is
not improving. Please see attached medical report.

It's not like the Institute could do anything other than recall them to Earth, and Tessa *was* getting her work done. He'd just have to wait and see how they reacted when they read the report. That is, *if* they read it. It was just a routine progress report, after all!

A featherlight touch brushed against the back of his neck, and Tessa's laugh pulled him from his reverie.

"You're so deep in thought," she said. "Are the secrets of the human brain unraveling themselves?"

"Not quite," he said, smiling anyway. "What are you doing?"

"Taking a break," she said. "We got a comm from our supply courier. They're within twenty-four standard hours out. They said they had our hard-copy samples, too."

Reagan leaned back in his chair, feeling the joints and muscles in his spine pop as he stretched his arms overhead.

"That's good news," he said. "I wasn't expecting them quite so soon."

"I don't think they were expecting it either. But there's been a lot more traffic between Earth and Grainne recently, because of the political stuff. So maybe that has something to do with it...though I'd think the opposite would be more true, rather."

"Not if you understand human nature," Reagan said, smiling at his own cynicism. "Conflict always creates commerce, which increases communication and interaction. Or maybe it's the other way around. In any case, they go hand in hand...in hand, I guess."

"That's a lot of hands."

"Always is."

"I wonder if they'll have more news about the situation, then?"

"I almost guarantee it."

The work went on, and Reagan and Tessa settled into a groove. Two Earth years passed, with more of the sensor package results coming in at unpredictable intervals. They even had a transit crew take them through the jump point twice in that time, running comprehensive tests on themselves in comparison with the sensor-package numbers.

Reagan ran his own analyses of their condition as well, usually when Tessa was deep in her own work. He continued to get the same heartbreaking result, every time. He knew he needed to share those results with Tessa...but he just couldn't bring himself to do it.

Not yet, he told himself. *Not yet. I can confirm the data one more time...*

"Reagan! Can you go check the receiver relays?" Tessa's voice through the intercom speaker sounded worried. Reagan looked up from the analysis report he was preparing and blinked.

"Sure, love. Is something wrong?"

"The point just went totally dark. It has to be something with our receivers. Can you see if they're loose or something? I can't imagine any other explanation. It doesn't make sense to just shut the point down, unless..." she trailed off, and horror began to seep into Reagan's mind.

"They're invading," he whispered. "The UNPF is invading my home."

"They wouldn't do that," Tessa said. *"The UNPF is just that, a peacekeeping force! Why would they invade Grainne?"*

"Haven't you been paying attention to any of the news reports I've been reading to you?" Reagan asked, his tone heating up more than he would have liked. "The media's been all over blackballing the Freehold. The thing with the refugees, the protests in Jefferson...all the reports on how Freeholders' 'basic civil rights' are being denied!" he broke off angrily, fingers still in the air from his air quotes.

"Reagan...I know you're worried. But it's not my fault," Tessa said softly. Reagan let out a curse and scrubbed his hands over his face.

"I know," he said. "I'm sorry. It's just...I never imagined it would come to a war. You don't understand the Freehold, my darling. This isn't going to go well for anyone, but especially not Earth."

Her body lay in a cradle, unmoving, eyes closed, lower face covered by the respirator. He'd shaved her head twelve weeks ago in order to fit a new induction cap, and small tufts of hair had grown out between the points where the neural pickups contacted her scalp. He'd have to trim that back soon.

He started at the neck, gently scrubbed her down to the toes, then back up to her face, careful not to disturb the respirator or neural contacts. The supportive gel from the life-support tank still clung to her skin in places, and he took care to remove all traces, despite the fact that she'd be going back into the tank once he was done.

As he worked, he thought of the news from Earth, from Grainne. Tessa said it didn't involve them, but it would. If they got called back to Earth...Well, that just didn't bear thinking about at the moment. If he got too upset, he could injure her. This was supposed to be about relaxation, about care...about love.

As he got to each limb, he gently flexed it, running through the full range of motion to help maintain muscle tone and joint flexibility. He followed the soap with a mild disinfectant, paying particular attention to pressure points, and places where skin would be in contact with other materials. Once he finished washing, he reached for the plastic flask that he'd brought from the laboratory. He'd paid his way through college on Grainne as a masseur, and he knew he was good at it. His clients particularly liked that he compounded his own massage oils.

He gently massaged the warm, but unresponsive flesh, hoping and praying that this time, he'd get a reaction. Unfortunately, the test results had told him that it wasn't to be.

"You know, you don't have to do that. The gel has nanocytes for skin preservation and tissue repair." Tessa's voice coming from the intercom speaker startled him. He'd been working in silence, lost in his own thoughts.

"I know, dear, but I *want* to do this. If I can no longer hold you under the stars, talking about galactic empires and making love until daybreak, then I will do this as the next best thing."

It had started as a tingling feeling in her hands and feet a few years ago, shortly after their arrival on station. Within a week she had muscle weakness, and soon after that, could no longer stand in gravity. Reagan spun down the habitat section, risking his own neuromuscular health to preserve her mobility. A week later she woke up gasping for breath, and he had to put her on the respirator.

The medical diagnostic readout said Guillain-Barre Syndrome—an autoimmune disorder that attacked the motor and sensory nerves. Nano treatments proved ineffective. Sure, they could repair existing nerve damage, but repairing damage was pointless when the disease just continued to progress. Five hundred years of Earth medicine hadn't even made a dent in figuring out what caused it in the first place, and had even taken giant steps *backward* as innovation took a back seat to "necessary care" for the ever-growing (and aging) population.

Was it the proximity to the jump point? An undiscovered consequence of the jump drive or phase drive? Perhaps one of the reasons why vessels sent out to develop new jump points sometimes didn't return? Reagan and Tessa were out here in search of scientific knowledge, but he'd personally forgo this particular bit of scientific truth just to have his love back.

He still hadn't told her about encrypted order 7773.3–4, the order that downgraded her from "human" to "biological specimen." He couldn't.

February 210

CHIME!

"Another ship through the jump point. One, two, three . . . Reagan, dear, I think you'd better take a look at this."

"What?" They'd gotten another of their sensor packs back yesterday, and Reagan was totally immersed in his analysis of the neural tissue simulations. He'd been comparing the results with their own data from the two jumps they'd made a few months back. It was now obvious to him that they shouldn't have taken those jumps—never taken the risk with Tessa's condition. She had just been so set on getting firsthand readings that he'd agreed. She could get so much more from her direct neural interface with the ship's sensors than any autonomous package they could deploy.

"That's six ships in the last three hours. This doesn't look good." She paused a moment, then continued. *"Oh, and now there's a ping from Orbital. We've got a message from Earth."*

"On my way." Despite the small size of their research vessel, it still took time to get from his laboratory just off the Engineering compartment to the Communications station at the bridge. If he'd been wearing his own neural induction rig, he could have tapped directly into the console from Engineering, but it didn't feel right. Tessa was integrated with the systems; activating his own interface would have felt like invasion of privacy.

By the time Reagan arrived at the communications console, he could see two annunciators blinking in addition to the incoming message light. One indicated that the message required an immediate reply, the other that they had a request from one of the ships that had just come through the jump point. It was close enough that communications lag was down to a few minutes, so they were requesting real-time communication.

"Okay, message from Earth, first," he said, keying in his personal decryption code.

To: Asano, T, Meacham, R, UNRV *Korielle*
From: Beck, M., Max Planck Institute
        RECALL NOTICE

Drs. Asano and Meacham, I regret to inform you that your fellowship grant has been terminated due to revocation of your certificate of need for the RV *Korielle*.

You are to return immediately to Earth, a UNPF transit crew has been sent on the UNSS *San Diego* to return the *Korielle* to the Earth system. Upon arriving in the Earth system, you are to debark immediately at Station Pulau Bintang and await transport to Earth. Due to the volume of outbound UN personnel and inbound refugees, you are allowed only one kilogram of personal gear, not to exceed one-thousand cubic centimeters in volume. You will leave ALL UN, MPI, and personal equipment aboard the *Korielle*, no exceptions. All research samples are to be destroyed, and all instrumentation disconnected prior to jump, per UN Research Council Specification 4473.3–4 (Autologous biological specimens).

This recall is effective immediately. Please understand that this is for your own protection. However, failure to comply with this recall or instructions of the UNPF will subject you to disciplinary action under UNRC Resolution 140077.23 section 225, paragraph 14a4 (State of Emergency).

This recall is recorded as Notice To Fellows MPI-30150742.1.1 in accordance with UN Charter, Munich, Bavarian UN Prefecture, Earth.

Reagan's eyes clung to the phrase "Autologous biological specimens." He couldn't look away, and the words on the screen remained as a haunting afterimage when he closed his eyes.

"No," he whispered. "We can't do that."

"Reagan . . . love . . ."

"I lied," Reagan said, tears overflowing his lower lashes and streaming down his face. He could feel a scream building inside him, a scream so powerful it would burst capillaries and windows alike and vent this whole stupid tragedy to the vacuum of space if he let it out . . . "You're not getting any better. All the tests say so. I've known for months, since the day we got the first sensor pack from that Earth ship. I just couldn't face it, Tessa, so I lied to you."

She said nothing, her silence accentuated by the subliminal hum of the ship's speakers.

"I'm so sorry," he whispered.

"Let's see what the freighter has to say," she said, her tone gentle. Was this forgiveness? Reagan hoped not. He absolutely did not deserve her forgiveness, and the thought of it made him writhe inside.

He nodded, and flipped open the comm channel from the freighter.

"Research Vessel Korielle, *this is UNSS* San Diego. *Be advised that we are on an intercept course in accordance with Recall Notice MPI30150742.1.1 under the authority of the United Nations Peacekeeping Forces. Your assigned return crew will arrive on your vessel in approximately three Earth-standard days. You are advised to use this time to make final recordings of your research results and prepare for return to Earth per the terms of the recall notice. Your acknowledgement of this message is required."*

"Acknowledged," Reagan said into the comm, his voice rough. "Thank you."

He had no idea why he was thanking them. Manners, he guessed. He certainly didn't *feel* particularly grateful.

"*Well*," Tessa said, her voice filling the silence left behind. "*There we go. Three days.*"

"How?" Reagan gasped, "How are you...so calm?"

"*Reagan. Do it.*" A hint of her anger and indomitable will came through her voice, and Reagan felt his shoulders straighten despite himself.

"All right," he said, and keyed in the command to open the comm channel from Orbital once again. He felt a shift in the air current behind him as she manipulated the life support functions of the ship to "kiss" him, and his eyes threatened to spill over one more time.

To: Asano, T, Meacham, R, UNRV *Korielle*
From: Beck, M., Max Planck Institute
re: RECALL NOTICE MPI30150742.1.1

Drs. Asano and Meacham, request you immediately forward your reply to the recall notice issued immediately prior to this communication. Your reply should contain a summary of your research and findings to date, including a detailed description of tests or trials ongoing such that <garble> may be continued at a later date.

Your immediate attention is required and appreciated.

"*What was that?*" Tessa asked.

"They want our data—"

"*No, the weird glitch in the message. The recall notice was crystal clear, we shouldn't be getting any kind of astrophysical interference with this transmission...so why a glitch?*"

"I don't know," Reagan said, "I just figured—"

The communications console beeped, and the text of the reply order disappeared from the display, which went completely dark. A female voice not Tessa's issued from the ship's speaker:

"*If you're hearing this, then you likely already know. The UN invaded the Freehold of Grainne and destroyed our major military facilities. The UN says the war is over. We say the UN hasn't got a clue what war is. We intend to show them.*"

"Wherever you are, whatever you've got, if you're with us, we want you. Do what you can with whatever you have and remember that while any single freedom-loving Freeholder lives, there is still hope.

"Stay safe, or make it count. We'll be here."

"What . . ." Tessa asked again, sounding entirely unsettled. *"Was that?"*

"Encoded message," Reagan said, as the comm display blinked back into existence. A text of the reply order scrolled back into place, with actual words where the garbled bit had been. "They must have sent it to anyone with a Freehold origin secure comm key. They buried it like a virus in the code of the reply order . . ."

Despite his own misery, Reagan felt a quick burst of pride in his uncowed countrymen and countrywomen. He wasn't political, and he'd loved working on Earth with some of the best scientific minds in the galaxy, but the magnificent defiance of that message struck a chord in him. While any freedom-loving Freeholder lived, there was . . .

"Tessa!" he said, his eyes going wide as an idea ignited in his mind. "I know what we're going to do."

"What?" she asked. *"What do you mean?"*

"Start evasive maneuvering now, love. We can't be boarded by that freighter!"

"Why not?"

"Because, my darling. I'm not leaving you, and you're not leaving this ship. Ergo, we're not going back to Earth. Ever."

"Research Vessel Korielle, *check your course coordinates . . . no changes were authorized!"*

"Negative, *San Diego*, you ordered us to prepare for intercept. We've programmed in an intercept course of . . . oh . . ."

Two Earth-standard days later, Reagan snorted a laugh as he listened to Tessa perfectly don the persona of the ditzy, book-smart professor with zero attention to detail. She sent him another air-kiss and continued transmitting the conversation through the ship's intercom for his amusement.

"San Diego, I . . . uh . . . there seems to have been an error in calculation."

"You don't say, Korielle."

"Yes, well . . . I'm an astrophysicist, not a navigator. But no

need to worry. Our course takes us directly to the entry for Jump Point One. We are scheduled for reentry into the Earth system per the terms of the recall notice. You can meet us back in-system. I do apologize."

"*Roger,* Korielle," the freighter's comm officer responded. Even across the comm line, his long suffering tone was clear enough to make Reagan stifle another laugh. *"Please stand by while I advise Control of our change in status. Continue on your programmed course for now."*

"Are you sure? I could try and correct—"

"NO! Just…continue on your current course, Korielle. *Don't touch anything. UNS* San Diego *out."*

"You ought to be ashamed of yourself," Reagan said, once the line went dead. Tessa's laughter echoed through the speakers. "Generations after generations of feminists are rolling in their graves at you, a respected astrophysicist and research scientist playing the dumb broad to get your way."

"We use what weapons come to hand," Tessa reminded him. *"And those dead feminists can roll all they like. I'm still a respected astrophysicist and research scientist, no matter how dumb I play on the comm line."*

"Right," Reagan said. He kept his tone light, even if her mention of "weapons coming to hand" was a rather sobering reminder of their situation. "So how long do we have?"

"We'll be at the jump point in another six hours."

"Perfect. Just enough time to broadcast our results to everyone who might be listening. At this point, I'm not all that interested in keeping our science proprietary."

"I agree," Tessa said. *"Let's put it out there, hopefully someone will pick up where we leave off."*

So that was what they did. Reagan took the time to put the finishing touches on the most comprehensive report possible. Thanks to the interruption, their findings weren't as complete as he would have liked, but in the end, he was proud of the product that he and Tessa had produced, and hoped that someday, someone *would* pick up where they left off and continue to make interstellar travel even more safe and useful for the human animal.

After the report was finished, he had just enough time to take the final section and enter it as a technical note to be automatically published on the scientific 'net once the main report was decrypted back at Max Planck. He entitled the note: "A Demonstration of Jump Point HZE Particle Interaction with Exotic Matter Lensing in Phase Drive, Asano, T. and McGuiness, R., Freehold Science Alliance, Grainne." He deployed the last of their sensor suites to monitor the jump point in their wake, and keyed them all to append their observations and rebroadcast the note once the "experiment" was completed. He programmed the whole package to broadcast out just before they entered Jump Point One, then Reagan headed to the galley and fished out the bottle of honest-to-goodness champagne that they'd brought. It was in a special pack, of course, and the cork didn't give its characteristic *pop* when he opened it, but it was bubbly and celebratory nonetheless. He poured it into a plastic cup and raised it to the ceiling.

"To you, Tessa, my love. To you and eternity."

"Right back atcha, babe. Enjoy the taste for me."

He did, first sipping, and then downing the champagne. Then he took himself off to his cleaning unit and shaved his head bare before heading to the sickbay. Once there, he shucked off his clothes.

"This isn't creepy, is it?" he asked her, even though they'd already discussed it. "I just want to feel your skin next to mine one more time."

"It's not, love. Cuddle away. I'll be waiting for you here in the ship," she said. As ever, her humor buoyed him up as he pulled himself into the too-small cradle that held her unresponsive form. He spooned up against her, wrapping his arms around her and just reveling in her warmth for a moment. Then he kissed the back of her neck, right where she always kissed him with the airflow, and reached up to pull on his own induction cap.

He felt a slight tingle as the leads contacted his scalp, and then...

He *was* the ship. He could feel every wire, every surface, every bit of data flowing throughout the entirety of the machine. The subsonic vibration of the phase drive replaced his heartbeat, and the whoosh of the life-support scrubbers became his breath. And his mind...

Hi, she said, and it was like it was his own thought. Never, not even at their most tender, not even when he hadn't been able to tell where his body left off and hers began, had he ever felt so fundamentally, so *intimately* close to her. She was all around him, inside him. He was all around her . . . they were intertwined, fused . . .

Inseparable. Forever.

That was the point, right?

Right, she said, and he knew that he'd never be alone again.

I should have done this a long time ago, he thought. She replied with humor that manifested as the memory of her lovely laugh.

It's almost time, she said. *We're approaching Jump Point One now. Destination is set for Earth, and the phase drive is keyed to activate on the jump signal. Are you ready?*

For you? Always.

With a single thought, they activated the jump drive.

Together.

■   ■   ■

Huff #7
And now JP1!

J4 is all but apoplectic right now. We expected a supply shipment this morning, mainly for the reconstruction efforts at Unity. Instead, we received word that a suicide mission, carried out by our own scientists, collapsed Sol Jump Point Six, (locally, Jump Point One). This was a genuine strategic surprise—the bad kind. We had absolutely no indications and warnings of an imminent attack through available sources.

I wonder if we're making a so-called "Devil's Deal" with these Jump Points. Dr. Meacham's research indicated some unsettling long-term effects of Jump Point usage. I'm not a doctor, but I know that autoimmune disorders and chronic inflammation aren't conducive to building a fit force. The UN may have a workable defense budget right now, but what happens when everyone out here starts filing disability claims in a few years?

On the other hand, if we can't resupply our forces quickly, they won't have to worry about disability. The way things are going right now, the medical consequences of long term Jump Point use may very well be the last thing we should worry about. We don't have the necessary in-system fabrication capabilities yet to build up our material advantage, and the *Force* is the rebel's lifeline. We need to find *Force—captured is preferable to destroyed*, and then we can upend the playing field until JP6 is running again. The sooner we accomplish our mission here, the sooner we can start understanding, and dealing with, dangerous exposure.

Spider's Web
Part 5

The destruction of Skywheel Three and JP1 encouraged the UN to deploy the satellites held in reserve, over the accountants' protests. Moyra Kelly watched the email traffic in real-time as the UN brass correctly argued that the only reason the Freehold satellites had been left alone was that the resistance either didn't have the force projection (yet!) to take them down, or were otherwise using them. Ergo, the UN needed to move to their secured satellites. That way, if they detected the resistance using the sats, the UN could knock them down without blowing their own communication structure. The accountants wailed about budgets, but operational sanity prevailed.

Moyra cursed as that cutover occurred, and she lost access to that flow of information. The other network links remained unaffected by the change, but it meant that any new sites the UN brought online were likely to be less visible to the resistance forces. She enabled active reading of the hardwire monitoring located in her old office building, as well as the infiltrated hardwire taps being built into the UN bases' networks.

The accountants and bureaucrats insisted that local contractors were a better use of funds for base construction over importing UN personnel. Moyra, via the handlers, instructed all contractors who responded to the work bids to arrive on location absolutely spotless but with lots of bags until notified otherwise. UN troops found it difficult to ensure every contractor was clean, especially after the first few weeks. Apart from a minor infraction here and there, the troops found nothing to indicate security concerns.

A boring month of checking every contractor over and finding nothing encouraged the guards to get lazy about checking. After several days, random contractors were provided extra hardware to start slipping into the buildings. Moyra ensured that none smuggled twice in a row, or even within a week.

Jenkins found and forwarded on a communication chastising everyone to be on their best behavior for the UN general's upcoming dog and pony show. The guest list, comprised of multiple UN bureaucrats, went to Bowler Hat. Moyra understood there were some very unhappy people looking forward to that information.

Given the influx of nonmilitary brass about to occur, Moyra decided it was time to give them a taste of reality.

:: I think it's time the drones start getting glitchy, :: Moyra told Kozlov.

:: Just glitchy? ::

:: We want them to stop trusting their equipment, all of it. They're complaining about the "cursed" network. But I want to hold the drone vacation plan in reserve for now. ::

:: One of the models they've got uses a similar control frequency and encryption scheme to the one our people are using most. We can target those for "glitching," without giving away the rest, I think. ::

:: Sounds good. If there are any remaining windows in the commandeered structures, that is probably the place to start. ::

Force Majeure
Part 3

Captain Yates, commanding FMS *Force* was actually off watch during normal ops when Kacito pinged from *Sleipnir.*

He took the call, offered greetings, and asked, "Good news or bad news?"

"Well, it's news. We apparently have a trade balance on file with Prescot."

"How?"

"One of the clandestine elements apparently managed to board and seize a UN ship. Cruiser."

He took a moment to process that. They'd hijacked a warship?

"Fuck. That's impressive."

"Very," she said with a nod. *"Prescot bought it and there's an open account for nonmilitary materials. It's all marked for industrial use and bought by a cover. Besides, they don't let the UN look at their documents."*

"Aha. Materials we can convert."

"Exactly. We're taking you in-system to get it."

"I'm waiting for 'some limitations apply.'"

"Yeah, it's neutral, there's UN ships in system. They can't have you in space long, and you have to transfer and leave before the UN decides to argue what constitutes military materiel given our capabilities. Once you have it aboard, they can shrug. We can probably only do this once. So we'd like you to get the most mass possible."

"And then? Pick us up on the far side?"

"You'll need to fabricate fuel for us. If anything goes wrong, none of us go home."

That again. "Got it. Then back here?"

"Back here with as much fuel as you can juice us with to continue operations, mass we can convert, and spares for the small craft. After that, we're taking you home."

Home. That was . . . "Are we fighting head to head?"

"No, we're dropping you far out in the Halo again. You're to support the ground and habitat resistance with whatever we can smuggle in. At least one stealth boat is ready. They'll bring raw material in, take finished goods out."

"Fuel is the tough part then, too. And food," he noted. Everyone knew it, but they dare not forget it.

"Yes. They've got some resources to help with that."

Once again they grappled to the carrier. At least they were going somewhere. To Farana he commented, "Sitting dead in space as a factory is certainly within our duties, but it's wearing on the crew."

"That it is, sir. Just so you're aware, *Sleipnir* has locked my system. Even if we had star drive, I couldn't tell you where we were going, and I can't get any reading from them at all. I have no idea where we are, how we got here, or how we're leaving."

"That's reassuring, actually."

"Yes, sir. It's 'not my problem.' At the same time, I'm damned sure curious. But I suspect even if we win we'll never know."

He thought and replied, "I wouldn't say never. At some point it's bound to be discovered or compromised, either through intel or advanced tracking. Secrets never last. But I do hope you're around long enough to satisfy your curiosity."

"Thank you, sir. And you also."

They were warned of phase entry, made entry, and were cut off from any sensors at all, since *Force* was never intended to enter this plane of space. All they could do was hang on for the ride.

They precipitated into normal space. After some scans and calculations, Farana announced, "This is Govannon's outer belt. Space density is within safe levels, but high compared to background. Tactical reports we're already acquiring mass via our shields. They can configure to sweep to maximize that, as we aren't facing an imminent threat."

"Rievley, please do."

The tactical officer replied, "Will do. Though even that is less than we're consuming. There's not much to acquire out there."

"No, but it all helps."

Shortly, Rievley said, "Sir, small vessel. Identifies as Prescot Deep Space Resources liaison boat *Dylan*. Operations Officer Frank Leyden would like to speak to you personally."

"At once. This is Captain Yates."

"Welcome, sir," Leyden replied with a notable British lilt to his accent. *"We were advised you needed power and mixed resources. Is that correct?"*

"Yes, sir. We don't know what we'll need to fabricate."

"It is understood that this cargo is being transferred for the purpose of fabricating support and operating materials for former Freehold vessels, not for fabricating munitions or war materiel. I understand you claim status as stateless persons and vessels, awaiting a diplomatic resolution to said status."

"That is also correct." Mostly. Yates had just lied about not fabricating war materiel, as they were damned sure going to do that. But, the Prescots were now clear. As soon as it was reasonable for them to know from elsewhere that rule had been broken, all further supplies would cease. The legal fiction was a favor, once only.

"Perfect. We can commence material furnishment at once. With your permission, I will coordinate with your retrieval crew."

"Please do, and thank you very much, Operations Officer."

"You are welcome. Prescot appreciates the opportunity to service you as a customer, and we hope you will return again soon. If there are any discrepancies or issues against manifest, please feel free to contact me at once."

Damn, they were ballsy. The man had fed him the legalese to agree to so Prescot could furnish raw materials to a military fabrication vessel in wartime, and were willing to face the UN's lawyers and bureaucrats over it.

On the other hand, the UN couldn't run this outfit if they took over, and couldn't last a week without the gigatons of materials they supplied.

Leyden apparently dumped an entire menu of goodies to Logistics and Supply Section. It was mere segs before Karanov called.

"Captain, we're going to need retrieval boats and nets. Anything we have that can recover and hold masses of material. We'll feed it into holds and davits as fast as we can, but I suspect we'll have to strap them on the outside and carry them ourselves while we depart under, shall we say, duress."

"We'll do so at once. I gather the materials are in containers and will have to transfer to our holds?"

"No, sir. Their transshipment engineers already sized the containers and units to fit our stowage doors exactly."

Damn. It was pretty clear whose side Prescot was on in this fight. They couldn't overtly offer weapons or precursors, but they were all in on raw materials.

"That's very kind of them," he said in massive understatement. "Use whatever you need."

Materials Handling and Retrieval Section suited up and went to work. It was always fascinating to watch them, and Yates linked his visuals in.

External Section were tethered on or in cabled tugs, nudging loads into the huge bays. They were nudging very carefully, because these loads were massive chunks of raw metal and semirefined organics. *Force* could intake raw gas from outer atmosphere, or harvest planetoids through the belly hatches and mining jigs, but having concentrated material was a huge plus.

Two Prescot tugs brought in huge arrays of material. Each was tethered to a large barge frame with canisters attached.

Force received iron, aluminum, magnesium, titanium, copper, zinc, tin, some gold for circuitry. There was semiprocessed petroleum base material in a solid black block, wrapped in an envelope to prevent outgassing. Another chunk was pure carbon. There were custom-made tanks of hydrogen, helium, oxygen, nitrogen. The handlers nudged them in quickly but carefully. Internal Section were all suited and tethered along the loadways, latching or clamping or attaching hoses and conduit, as called for.

Meanwhile, a fueler arrived and docked, with the correct matrix of reactor elements.

Karanov called. *"Sir, I told them we'll fill the entire forward hold with fuel bricks. Once we're full of material internally, do we want to use the jacks to attach external pods? There's plenty more on account, and they're happy to let us take it."*

"We absolutely do, but let me check numbers on our safe margin, and on our maneuver margin." He pinged two others. On duty now was 2nd Astrogator Patrick Mathews. He also called the engineer.

"The discussion is external mass, capacity, boost safe margins, reactor safe margins. We can expect pursuit at some point."

Engineer Eric Anderson said, *"Sir, we can do that calculation for you after we hash out a few things between us. In the meantime, take it all. We can always leave it behind, tagged for credit, or jettison it if we must. We're here now, we may not be again. I am comfortable if you go thirty percent over rated capacity for a few segs."*

"Thank you. Please discuss amongst yourselves and let me know. Commander Karanov, you heard?"

"I did, sir. We'll take it all. I'm pushing for as much fuel and nutrition elements as they can give us."

"Yes, continue."

The small Prescot command boat lurked in the area, obviously monitoring activity. Likely, it was to document that only raw materials were being furnished, as per contract. It contacted them twice per shift. He'd seen one of those boats before on a supply mission. The lower deck was cabins for crew with kitchen and toilet. The upper deck was a dome for visual observation, and equipped with every sensor known to man. Behind it all was an engine. They were pure business.

They were two and a half days into loadout when the Prescot control boat pinged them between scheduled calls.

"Captain Yates, Second Officer Jacqui Llew. Be advised UN vessel en route. Cruiser Mumbai. *We cited client privacy, but they apparently aren't accepting it."*

"Understood, thank you. We should probably depart and not consume more of your time. Your hospitality has been beyond gracious."

"Noted. Please advise of your course. We'll sling what we can your way. Take what you can, we'll recover the rest and deduct the fees, credit the balance."

"I will transfer this channel to my lead and second navigator at once." Second Astrogator Mathews was on duty. He sent a call to Farana.

Mathews got to work on departure profile. Farana arrived, looking groggy.

"Sir?" she asked.

He summarized the plan to catch thrown cargo, then asked, "How reliably can we intercept?"

"I will need a few segs, please, for a reliable approximation."

"Do so."

Farana chugged caffeinated cocoa and sucked at a tube of apple sauce, while drawing in her plot space.

Finally she said, "If they throw it correctly, we'll be picking up a load about twice a div for the next three days. After that, reliability drops off, even with the reusable drive units they're using."

"I didn't know they had those."

"They just made them. They have engines to spare."

"Damn, we should have asked."

"It would be hard to justify. That implies using them on other small craft. Gunboats. Missiles."

"Yes. Still, we'll take the leeway."

"This assumes we don't have to go to hard boost to avoid intercept. You have the best case numbers."

"Understood. Operations, how safe is it to have load crew operating under boost?"

Operations Officer Lt. Commander Kaciri swiped at his board and said, "They'll have to be in tethered pods. Boost will have to remain under three G or you risk losing them. Maneuverability will be harder due to pendulum effects. Inside crew will have to be tethered or doing it all by waldo. You know how movement under boost is."

"How effective can we be?"

"No one's tried it. I can't guess, sir. If you demanded a guess I'd say thirty percent would be good."

"Let's do it. Commander Karanov, what do we most need?"

"*Carbon and volatiles. We have plenty of metal. We need source for plastics, gas and food again. After that, more fuel. After that, rare earths.*"

"We'll get on it."

Loadmaster Senior Sergeant Cheung Ortega remained focused on his task. He didn't want to get squashed by a mass that could shift relative at any moment. He didn't want to think about the risk of tether failure and hoping to last long enough for Prescot to recover him, even with a spare oxy bottle.

This was the second mass of a very long shift. The first had been a mass of rare-earth elements, essential for electronics and other fabrications. That was belted to the hull with a mesh of cables.

The cargo inbound was a custom-fitted tank of ultracompressed mixed hydrocarbons—methane, ammonia, some water and oxygen. It was probably either scooped from the local gas giants, or postprocess residue, recovered and valuable. Though given Prescot's industrial base, it was entirely possible it was a comet they captured to reduce space clutter and processed into sellable material.

"This is why we earn the big creds," he muttered. On the plus side, the stuff was fitted and ready to stow once it closed. On the negative side, it was all one mass at once, big enough to smash chunks of the ship, and no one had ever done a load under boost before.

He clicked and asked, "How's it looking from your side, Jansen?"

Load Handler Specialist Kitaira Jansen replied, *"Steady. I'm awed they came up with these maneuver units that fast. Can we buy some of their fabrication tech?"*

"I think we'd have to hire their brains. The tech isn't that complex. What do you have for closing rate?" And god, did she have a sexy voice. Good looking, amazing sounding. She could make a fortune acting.

"Nine five zero seconds to retrieval contact. Rate is just a shade over a second."

"That's what I'm showing. Grapple Section, How's alignment?"

Load Handler Sergeant Budi Patterson said, *"This far out it looks fine. It might change, though."*

"Right. But smaller corrections now are better than big ones later." A mass this size moving at 1 m/s would still wreck the ship. Or, it might miss entirely.

He announced, "I'm going to start adjusting the jacks." Then he touched his controls and slowly closed the front legs to create a cage. Helm was going to have a fuck of a time adjusting for this much mass this far off-center, but that wasn't his problem. Just to report it accurately.

He wanted to close the grapples a bit at a time, like catching a baseball. Ideally, he'd latch closed as the tank stopped at the front gantry.

Of course, these legs were made to settle and attach to a planetoid, not to cage a solid mass. But it was workable in theory.

Rate of approach slacked off slowly, and the curve seemed correct. Alignment looked perfect.

"Load, this is C-Deck, Astrogator Mathews. How's the time-frame on your retrieval?"

"C-Deck, time to contact is eight four three seconds."

Mathews replied, *"Noted. We will need to adjust boost or abort due to pursuit."*

That was the other risk. If the ship had to boost, his tether, and Jansen's, were probably going to snap. They might also get burned by the reactor emissions or the stinger field astern the ship.

Or they might all get vaporized by a UN ship that knew better than to waste time ordering surrender.

If they aborted, they'd all be inside and secured in under a seg. But they really needed the material. He checked all the plots, tried to remember what he knew of astrogation and handling.

"C-Deck, this is Load. if you can maintain attitude exactly, reduce thrust to close distance, resume to match current closure rate, we can do it. Otherwise we'll abort when you say so. We'll need a seg total from abort to boost."

"Load, C-Deck. I can do it. It's going to be hell on your stom- achs and tethers." And he sounded so cheerful about it.

"C-Deck, Load understands. Break. Did everyone get that?"

The channel was open, not dedicated. Patterson and Jansen agreed, *"Understood."*

"Load, this is C-Deck, stand by for strong maneuvers."

Immediately, thrust dropped and so did the sensation of gravity.

He hadn't visualized how the maneuver would take place, but now he did. Oh, fuck.

Then thrust came back, building quickly to double what it had been, squeezing him down in his pod. His feet throbbed, legs ached with his calves cramping. Everything in his guts settled hard. He panted for breath and felt the helmet grinding into his shoulders.

The change in tension on the tether caused oscillations, and he heard it thrum, but it was a low tone, which he figured meant it wasn't close to breaking. Then the whole cage swayed and swerved.

He knew his vitals were jumping, but he watched his screens for the recovery load and his connections.

Thrust dropped off to what it had been. It was now only 603 seconds to recovery. More importantly, everything was still in perfect alignment. Except him, though the cage steadied out until it was again directly astern of the thrust line.

He did have to adjust a grapple. It had shifted under power. That was concerning. He logged it for maintenance.

"C-Deck, this is Load. Still on track. Five nine one seconds. Do you wish to maneuver again?" *Please don't.*

Mathews replied, *"Load, C-Deck. We're good. What is your secure time once you have contact?"*

"If I do it right, a few seconds."

"Understood. When complete, get inside fast then advise."

"We will recover and board and advise soonest. Will do."

The load was visible by eye now, occluding stars as it approached.

Jansen advised, *"I show point seven three meters per second now."*

"Confirm," he agreed. "Patterson, how's alignment from your end?"

"Still perfect."

Damn, they were good.

Taking a measurement, he closed the grapples a bit more. The mass should slide right inside on a slow approach. Once in, the ship would have limited leeway to increase thrust to match, while the cargo engine dropped the rate of approach. Then he'd close the rear and tighten the jacks until the mass was locked down.

Here it came. He confirmed a closing rate of .536 m/s.

He really didn't dare tighten up anymore yet. He'd have to be fast when it hit, though.

It now was a huge blot on the sky, coming up astern. He wondered about any sort of eddy effect from the stinger, and yes, it wobbled slightly, but its flight controls corrected.

Then it was within the frame measurement of the ship, closing at .249 m/s.

Its thrust dropped off, and a flash on his screens asked him if he'd like to take manual control.

Would he? It was as perfect as it could be. He had little experience driving an engine by remote. He was, though, responsible for it.

He let it alone.

Now at .109 m/s and just about to enter the cage. He checked all his figures and placement, took visuals from the cameras, and tightened just a touch.

Half in, .004 m/s. He wanted it to hurry up, but dare not nudge it. It would take a lot of thrust to change vector, and then he'd have to change it back. This was textbook.

Almost. He saw it just as Patterson shouted.

"Pending contact inboard up!"

Hitting his controls fast, he opened the jacks there a couple of meters. He punched for adjustment control rather than override and quickly guessed time. Mass, time, thrust, duration, adjustment, enter and activate.

The maneuvering engines glowed and he watched the vector change.

With a relieved sigh he brought the jacks back in, then a bit more.

The rear of the load was in enough he felt comfortable starting to close the cage. More. More.

There.

"All stop!" he ordered.

"All stop!" "All stop!"

Gods, that was perfect.

"Get inside, I'm tightening the latches."

"*Yes, Senior.*" "*Aye, sir.*"

That was it. He checked again. Yes, secure.

"C-Deck, Load. Mass is secured and latched for thrust. I need a few seconds to get inside."

"*Load, C-Deck, understood.*"

He wound the spool until he rode back inside the dark shadow of the hatch and into the lit mounting bay, then hustled ass to get out, scramble across the deck, and into a flat position on the stern bulkhead. He latched his line. secure.

Mathews nodded to Yates. "That's it. We need to boost now, sir. And I mean ten segs ago."

"Order the crew to prepare, boost when he's in."

"Aye, sir. And he's in."

The alert sounded, Brown counted down, Ortega informed them, "*Load is inside and dogged. Crew accounted for.*"

Mathews opened the engines.

Force powered on into the dark.

Behind them, a UN ship not burdened with kilotonnes of material closed the gap.

Mathews ran calcs on his screen and reported, "Sir, *Mumbai's* closure rate puts them here in two days."

"That's cutting it very close."

"Yes, sir. They'll be in firing range about the same time we match course with *Sleepy.*"

At least the UN continued the formality of stand-down orders. On the other hand, they'd use that in any tribunal to insist Yates and his officers were well aware of the proclaimed status, and probably charge them with piracy.

Commo Tech Brown said, "Sir, *Sleepy* has made contact."

Mathews said, "Connect me, please."

"Connected."

Shortly the astrogator said, "I have a course correction. I can increase boost with your permission."

Yates nodded. "Go."

"Thank you. Commo, standard warning."

Brown announced, "All hands, this is C-Deck. Battle stations. Battle stations. Stand by for thrust and combat maneuvers. Secure and report."

After all, there was no point in waiting to make corrections later, when they'd use less fuel and thrust now.

Yates told Mathews he could go to 105 percent, and it felt like it.

Boost tapered back to standard.

Mathews reported, "Well, sir, we'll rendezvous in 1.73 divs now. We corrected, she corrected. We'll definitely be ahead of *Mumbai*. It's still going to be close, though. They might overboost themselves . . . and they are."

That was a tactical question.

"How long is their safe margin at that boost?"

Rievley said, "I'd say a couple of divs. Searching. Yes, their own forces' estimate is seven hours."

"Then wait until they reach redline and boost again as needed. Force them to risk damage to pursue."

Mathews said, "Attrition-damage chicken, sir. A worthy game."

A bit over two divs later, *Mumbai* backed off the thrust. Third Officer Alito on watch followed Yates's directive, and *Force* boosted again.

When he came back on shift and checked status and log, Rievley informed him, "Sir, we've gained just over five more segs of lead."

"Very good. Though they'll be shooting as we depart."

"Yes, sir. But not before."

"Well done."

They closed in on their new rendezvous fast.

Rievley reported, "Sir, we have sensor contact with *Sleepy*, and the UN is going schizo."

Brown brought up audio.

"*—Freehold . . . former Freehold vessels identified as FMS* Force *and carrier . . . carrier identified as a former Freehold vessel, you are ordered to cease all maneuverings and thrustings and stand down.*"

"I would love to tell him about ceasing thrustings," Yates muttered. He got some laughs with that. He added, "Apparently they didn't know *Sleipnir* was here. They may even have thought they accounted for her."

Mathews asked, "Should I continue thrusting the horse, sir?"

He laughed. "Indeed you should. Advise them we have external loads."

"Yes, sir. Rendezvous imminent. Ten thousand kilometers and closing."

"Lieutenant Brown, wave off Prescot and thank them."

"Yes, sir."

Yates looked at the tactical display and ran figures in his head. "It seems like the UN closed the gap a bit."

Rievley said, "Slightly. They can shoot. I don't give them a chance in hell of hitting. We'll need to grapple fast, though."

Yates watched as trajectory lines and intercept envelopes moved in the display. It was going to be close. Very close.

It was frustrating as hell to be perpetually fleeing pursuit. And yes, scary. He was cold with clammy sweat.

Sleipnir pinged in.

"We're ready for you, Force. *Request permission to assume control at one hundred kilometers."*

Yates nodded, "Permission granted."

Mathews replied, *"Force* acknowledges *Sleipnir* will assume remote helm at one zero zero kilometers."

Rievley announced, "Sir, given flight time, if they don't fire now, they will not have time to reach us, much less acquire target."

"What about beam weapons?"

"They will not get close enough for a shot that can penetrate our shield or hull."

"Well done."

"Sir, *Sleepy* has remoted."

"Thank you."

He trusted his crew and the math. Nevertheless, he felt itchy during the entire matching, mating, securing sequence.

It went fast. The contact was rougher than before, with some jostling and impact he hoped wasn't damaging the docking cradle.

Segs later, Mathews noted, "We are just reaching the enemy's maximum range for beamed weapons."

From *Sleipnir* came the instruction, *"All hands and attached hands stand by for phase insertion."*

Yates checked the advisories of his crew, and his own harness.

Then they entered phase and the UN ship ceased to be a problem.

Releasing a long-held breath, Yates said, "I will authorize two drinks per crewmember, as soon as they are off shift."

"Understood, sir."

"I'm going aft for a shower." He changed channels and ordered, "First Officer Brody, please relieve me."

"On the way, sir."

Dear Diary

Rob Reed

Dear Diary,

Today is my birthday. On parts of Earth I'd be "Sweet Six-teen" and have a lavish party. Here where the years are longer, my 10th birthday would have put me well on the path to adult-hood. I celebrated my last birthday with my family. Then the UN invaded and my life changed forever.

From Notes in My Diary—April 1, 209 (One Year Earlier)

"Wake up, Birthday Girl, breakfast will be ready soon!" Mom said as she ordered my bedroom lights on. I crawled out of bed, took a quick shower, and got dressed.

I passed my little brother, Tomas, in the hall. He snapped my bra strap so I smacked his head in return. "Watch it," I said. "I'm still bigger than you."

Mom made my favorite breakfast. As we ate we outlined plans for the day. Dad was headed to Jefferson Utility Services, where he was chief engineer, while Mom would spend the day doing military reserve training at Heilbrun Base. That left Tomas and I on our own. On my birthday.

"Kassie, can you take Tomas with you today?" Mom asked.

"Do I have to? I was going to patrol the park with the gang."

"Yes. Keep him out of trouble. I'm sure you'll have some alone time with Davee later," she teased. I blushed.

Davee was the leader of our small gang. Although we liked each other, there was nothing romantic between us . . . yet. I hoped hav-ing Tomas along today wouldn't ruin anything Davee had planned.

Mom brought out a pair of brightly wrapped gifts. "We'll do your presents now since I won't be home for dinner," she said. The distance between our condo in Jefferson and the base made commuting a challenge.

"This is from me," she said as I unwrapped the first. It looked like an old-fashioned hardcover book with "My Diary" on the front. I tried to open the cover, but it was locked.

"You need to imprint it to you," Mom said. She explained how. The title morphed to "Kassie's Diary." I opened it to find a tablet comm with a stylus tucked into a narrow compartment.

"I'm introducing these from Earth. The girls there love them," Mom said. She was a professional influencer. With two kids, she specialized in youth trends and often started the fads my friends got caught up in.

I still wasn't sure what to do with this. I mean, I had a comm already...

Mom saw my confusion. "Whatever you put in this diary is totally private. It can't connect to anything. You can record audio, video, type on the virtual keyboard, or draw with the stylus. It's secure against anything, even nosy little brothers."

"Hey!" Tomas said, as Mom and I laughed. She'd had a younger brother too.

I still wasn't sure, but I acted enthusiastic, smiled, and thanked her.

"This is from both of us," Dad said. Under the wrap was a metal security container. Inside was a Callahan 8.5mm. This was my favorite of the pistols I'd tried at the range.

"Oh, wow! Thanks." I examined the gun for a bit before putting it back in the case and handing it to Dad.

"What do you want me to do with this?" he asked.

"I thought you'd put it in the safe."

"It's your pistol. We'll install the security box in your room. You can transport it in a range bag until you start wearing it holstered."

"About that..." Mom said.

"Yes," Dad said. "You need to practice more. We want you to be confident and understand the responsibility. I don't think it will take long until you're ready to carry."

I was surprised. I mean, I was pleased that they trusted me with the pistol, but the thought of carrying a weapon was slightly unsettling as well. It was so very...adult.

"When do I get my own gun? I'm old enough," Tomas asked.

I think he was half joking, but Mom answered him seriously.

"When you are responsible enough for one," she said. "It's not about age, it's about maturity."

"How will you know when I'm mature enough?"

"It's how you behave. When you start doing your chores without being told, pay more attention to your studies, stay out of trouble..."

"Stop harassing your sister," I interjected.

"...and stop harassing your sister," Mom agreed. "We'll know."

Tomas went quiet and looked thoughtful. After a few more divs of chatter, we headed out. Even with Tomas in tow, I had the feeling it was going to be a good day.

We got to Liberty Park early. Tomas bought chocolate ice cream cones for my birthday. When we finished we went to the restrooms to clean the melted drips.

Back outside, the gang was there. Davee, a year older than me, Jon and Mackey.

"Happy birthday!" they all said, and I blushed a bit. They had more gifts. Garnet earrings, a credit chit for some loads, and a bar of Russian-recipe chocolate.

"So, how about we patrol the park now?" Davee said, breaking up the awkward pause.

He had Jon and Mackey take Tomas in one direction while we headed a different way. This let the two of us have some time alone.

"So, fun birthday so far?" Davee asked.

I suddenly realized we were at the entrance to the labyrinth. I knew what went on in there, of course, even if I hadn't done that yet. Although the way I was feeling...

My thoughts must have been on my face because Davee took my hand. "You want to go in with me?" he asked, a comical parody of a leer on his face. I felt the blush go up my neck to my cheeks.

Davee laughed and then I did too. It felt good.

"Not now," I said. "I do really like you though."

"And I like you too. Maybe soon?"

"Maybe. Probably not as soon as you'd like, but maybe soon," I said.

He kissed me and I kissed him back. That felt good as well. I broke the connection before I changed my mind. "We should head back, we've covered enough ground."

"Yes, yes we have," he said. I knew he wasn't just talking about the park. "We've definitely covered a lot of ground today."

This was my best birthday ever and I was excited to see what happened next. The future seemed bright and full of promise.

I had no idea how wrong I was.

The early days of the war the next February were chaotic and confusing. Mom was on duty when the first attack came. We didn't hear from her that day. Dad was at work, checked in, and said he would have to stay at the plant. "Will you be okay?" he asked.

"Yes," I said, but I wasn't sure.

Tomas and I holed up in the condo with my pistol loaded and ready. The building shook from distant explosions and the smell of smoke filled the air.

The channels showed images of burning buildings, bodies in uniform, and UN troops in power armor rampaging around the starport. The feeds went dead early the second morning. A perky blond announcer came on a bit later. When she basically said, "We are from the UN and we're here to help," I turned it off.

Nothing from Mom. I was scared. I called Dad, who said not to worry.

When Dad returned two days later he wouldn't tell us what happened to him. "You don't want to know," was all he said. We'd seen enough to be relieved he was back and were frantic with worry for Mom. By now I'd learned the explosions we'd felt were from orbital strikes on our bases.

It was too late to flee the city so we were trapped behind enemy lines. The UN started road blocks and checkpoints around Jefferson and in the northern industrial area. They required everyone to register and backed it with random door-to-door searches. At least I thought they were random, until they showed up at our door.

"Open up! This is the UN Civilian Assistance Program. You are required to admit us," the voice on our door caller demanded.

"OK, just like we discussed," Dad said. He opened the door to a balding, middle-aged man dressed in a slightly rumpled business suit escorted by a pair of armed UN soldiers in full body armor.

"I'm Supervisor Stewart with the UN Civilian Assistance Program," he said. "I need to register you so we can help meet any needs you have."

"We're fine, thank you," Dad said.

"This is not a request," Stewart said. He referred to the hand-held data device he carried. "This is the Fields residence, correct? You are Mr. Sanford Fields, this would be Ms. Kassie Fields, and I assume this is Tomas. Where is Mrs. Tamara Fields?"

"My wife is in the military. We haven't heard from her since the invasion," Dad answered.

"That matches our records. We are still processing prisoners and compiling casualty reports and we'll inform you when we have information on her status."

What a cold-blooded son of a bitch.

I was surprised they knew so much about us. Dad had considered lying about Mom's military service but decided they probably knew already. It turns out his hunch was correct.

The bureaucrat went through the process of registering us. We provided our names, birthdates, and DNA samples. In return we were issued UN identification and ration cards.

I claimed to be 12 years old. Dad wanted them to think I was an adult and that would make me over 18 on Earth. I borrowed some of Mom's clothes and was wearing my hair and makeup in more adult styles. We didn't try the same trick with Tomas. He didn't look nearly old enough.

"We need to secure any weapons you have for safety," Stewart said next.

Dad unlocked the safe under the watchful eyes of the soldiers. "We just have this hunting rifle and my handgun," he said. "My wife took her service weapon with her."

Stewart looked at me. "Where's your handgun?" he asked, obviously clued into the fact that most adults carried, or at least owned, a gun.

"I don't like guns," I said.

Stewart removed the guns from the safe and handed them to one of the soldiers. He gave Dad a receipt. "The handgun is contraband. You may be compensated for the rifle if it is found to be particularly suitable for sporting purposes. Is this everything?" he asked.

"Yes," replied Dad.

"We'll see," Stewart said, as one soldier activated a scanner and went from room to room. He stopped in the hallway outside my bedroom, "Got a hit." He broke through the wall with his stunner rifle butt and then pulled a pistol out of the hole he'd made.

"OK, that's mine," I said. Stewart took the gun and looked at me. "I thought you didn't like guns?" I shrugged. He didn't give me a receipt.

The soldier went into my room and his scanner got another hit.

"Hold on," I said. "That's a hidden safe. No need to break the wall. Just press...there," I said, pointing to a specific spot. The soldier did so and a secret panel opened to reveal a metal security container securely mounted in the wall.

Stewart said, "Open it," so I complied, and stepped aside. He reached inside and pulled out some antique jewelry Mom had given me and my diary. "Please open this as well," he said.

I unlocked it and gave it to him. He briefly inspected the tablet and stylus before closing it and handing it back to me. "My daughter has one just like it," he said. It was the most human thing he'd said and it surprised me.

"I believe our business is concluded," Stewart told my Dad. "Here's my information if you need any assistance. I'll contact you later about setting up education for the child. We had planned on using local schools but since so many people homeschool that wasn't viable."

"We homeschool," Dad said.

"And do you have proof of teacher certification, and the required curriculum in all subjects? I thought not. We'll be in touch.

"Oh, and Mr. Fields, one more thing. Those ration cards are only good as long as you continue your duties at the power facility. We need you to keep the lights and heat on for the public's benefit. You should return to work tomorrow."

They left and I let out a deep breath. Thinking about Stewart's last comment I had a better understanding as to why we were selected for this "random" sweep.

"How did they know so much about us?" I asked.

"They likely have my employment records," Dad said. "The rest is probably from social media and maybe some informers. We tried to destroy as much as we could but once information is out there it's impossible to call it all back. I was expecting to be identified as a critical worker."

"They really are concerned with the utilities, aren't they?"

"It's not for our benefit," Dad said. "Sure, we need power and heat, but that's a side issue. What they really want is a stable power grid so they don't have to draw as much upon their own resources. If the power is on, they exert more control, because they can also turn it off at will."

The whole experience was unsettling and didn't make me feel any better. It was my turn to make dinner so I busied myself in the kitchen as Dad discussed what we should expect in the near future. None of us mentioned my pistol, safely hidden behind the security container in my bedroom wall. The one they found was Mom's spare.

I walked Tomas to the UN-run school every weekday. They offered transportation but I wanted to spend more time with him. He had become very moody and withdrawn since Mom had gone missing and I worried about him.

The school was in the Gray Zone of the main UN perimeter. This area also included the occupation government offices and concessions run by local residents. We weren't allowed into the more secure area for UN offices and UN civilian housing without a valid reason and an escort.

I introduced myself to Tomas's teacher the first day. I told him that our mother was missing, that Tomas was having a difficult time, and that I hoped spending time with children his own age would help.

The teacher, Mr. Connelly, was just a few years older than I was supposed to be. He had a warm personality and a friendly smile. I would have found him attractive, if he wasn't an aardvark. As it was, I had to keep myself from flinching at his Earth accent.

"Call me John," he said. "We'll take good care of Tomas and I'm glad to see he has a sister who looks out for him so much."

I made small talk with Connelly whenever possible over the next few days. I showed interest in Tomas's classwork and also expressed my frustration with how much time it took me to go through the main gate every time I dropped Tomas off or picked him up.

Connelly suggested I stay the whole school day so I'd only have to go through security once. "You can help in the classroom or audit some of other classes. That will also let you spend more time with Tomas."

I'd hoped he'd make this exact offer. I didn't want to seem too eager so I "thought about it overnight" before agreeing.

I spent the next week at the school. The students were a mix of UN dependents as "role models" and Freehold kids. I was appalled by the low expectations placed on the students. The curriculum was designed to pass everyone so no one put in more than the absolute minimum effort. Many did less.

I had Connelly help me get my diary cleared through security so I could use it to take notes. Since it couldn't connect to any networks it was eventually added to the blanket list of approved items. It helped that several of the decision makers were familiar with the diaries as they were currently very popular with kids on Earth.

What no one knew was that we'd completely hacked the "unhackable" diary. A "friend" added a chip that would allow network connections, but only when specifically triggered. It was invisible to scans. They added a concealed memory sector, too. When they finished I had an improvised covert intelligence-gathering device disguised as a simple kid's toy.

I was now ready to spy on them.

"Do you have anything good for me?" Davee asked. We were alone in the kitchen. I had begged off staying with Tomas at school today claiming errands to run.

Davee was now more than just my boyfriend. He was also my "reporting official." Someone he knew online asked him to get data, and he'd agreed. That's all I knew. When he agreed, he was given a data dump on how to run a clandestine resistance cell focused on intelligence collection.

The DIY spy manual contained instructions on basic tradecraft and descriptions of what kinds of information to gather and the types of people to target. It also included tips on social engineering, personality hacking, blackmail, honey traps, and other useful techniques to manipulate sources. If anything happened to Davee, I'd take over, so we copied the material to my diary and I spent late nights learning about the intelligence trade.

Davee recruited our gang and a handful of other kids for his cell. The UN didn't understand the difference between a typical undisciplined and ill-behaved Earth child and the more independent Freehold youth. That was going to bite them.

My insertion into Tomas's school led to our first operation. The school's location inside the UN perimeter was ideal. I used my diary to run sniffer programs that recorded the details of network traffic, radio frequencies in use, and any other activity in the EMF spectrum. I didn't know what was useful, as most transmissions were encrypted, and I had no way to break the encryption. Still, I was tasked to collect the information, so it had to be helpful to someone.

We also reported on any troop or police activity we saw, the habits and routines of UN personnel, and even what rumors were circulating among the UN contingent. I was such a fixture at school by now that the staff would forget I was there and their gossip became a valuable intelligence source.

We maintained tight, compartmentalized security. Only Davee knew his handler in Freehold intelligence and no one outside the cell, not even Dad or Tomas, knew of our spy work. I split my time between school with Tomas and taking care of family business around Jefferson. This let me conduct electronic monitoring and observe UN activity at multiple locations. I don't know how much our efforts helped, but it was something. We were fighting back.

About once a week I'd turn in what I'd collected, usually via dead drop or brush pass. Davee was paranoid about surveillance so we very rarely met in person. This was the first time I'd seen him in what felt like forever.

"Not much this week," I told Davee as I handed him a chip. "Here's the latest EMF info. Someone shot down another Guardian. Number twelve we've accounted for."

"Well now that business is done, what's next on the agenda?" he said.

I stood and led him to my bedroom. "Soon" had arrived a while back under the stress of the occupation. We had a pleasant div before I had to pick Tomas up at school.

They say you can get used to anything eventually and our lives settled into a new routine. We lived our lives and conducted what resistance we could manage. Skywheel Three was destroyed, and everyone drove past to see the ruined remnants of the base. UN troops in power armor threatened to open fire on us while they searched the debris for survivors, and we ducked and ran. We hadn't had anything to do with it, but it proved the Freehold was still fighting, and it proved the UN could be hurt.

A week later, Supervisor Stewart announced himself at the door. We'd had no contact with him since our registration so this was unexpected. Dad answered the door and Stewart entered, with a single UN soldier as bodyguard. I noticed the soldier now carried both lethal and nonlethal weapons.

"There is no good way to say this so I'll be direct," Stewart said. "It is my solemn duty to inform you that the UN has received confirmation that Grainne Warrant Leader Tamara Fields was killed in action during the initial engagement. There were no remains recovered and no other information is available."

Dad stood there, stunned. Tomas let out a wail and ran from the room. I heard someone sobbing and realized it was me when I felt the tears roll down my face. Stewart started to say something when Dad interrupted him. "Get out. Now." Stewart nodded, motioned to his escort, and the two men left us to our grief.

The news of Mom's death changed things. Although we knew it was likely, we hadn't really accepted that she was gone until faced with the reality. Tomas and I grew even closer as he clung to me for emotional support. Dad, on the other hand, became more withdrawn. While he didn't exactly neglect us, he seemed to be going through the motions and acted like a man bearing a terrible burden.

The next crisis came three weeks after the memorial service we'd held for Mom. Dad dealt with grief with by burying himself in his job. He worked longer shifts and took fewer days off. I compensated by taking on more responsibilities for us all.

Because of Dad's long workdays I wasn't concerned when he missed dinner one night. It wasn't until the next morning that I realized he'd never returned at all.

I tried Dad's comm. When he didn't answer I called the power station. No one had seen Dad since he left the day before.

I knew the UN had questioned Dad over some power outages that made the UN look bad. One had even interrupted a propaganda broadcast on the status of the pacification. Dad blamed the problems on the facilities damaged in the invasion, the lack of spare parts, and a critical shortage of trained personal. He thought he'd convinced the UN it wasn't sabotage, but now I wasn't sure.

The UN knew they'd face a revolt at the utility if they arrested Dad. But, if they grabbed him in secret, no one would know who to blame. They could then install their own hand-picked engineer.

Dad had also received death threats from people who called him a collaborator. "They don't understand," he'd said at the time. "If we don't keep the power on, people will die." I'd heard reports of suspected collaborators vanishing. Could that be what happened to Dad?

I called City Safety and made a missing person report. I gave the investigator the details along with our investigation insurance information. He asked a few questions and promised to keep me informed. They were "collaborating" too, to keep doing what they could.

I then called Davee's emergency burner comm from my emergency burner comm. I told him Dad was missing and filled him in. He offered his sympathy and said he'd be in touch. I knew he'd reach out to his intelligence contact but I didn't know how long that would take.

I thought of a third possibility: What if Dad found out he was targeted and went into hiding? In that case I knew he wouldn't contact us. I understood about keeping secrets for everyone's safety. Whatever the reason, Dad was gone, and I had no idea if he'd ever return.

By then it was almost time to pick Tomas up from school. I dreaded telling him about Dad.

At the school I was surprised to be met by Supervisor Stewart along with Connelly.

"Ms. Fields," Stewart said, "We know your father is missing. His name is flagged on the network and I've read the report you filed."

"I need to pick up Tomas. I don't even know how I'm going to explain this to him."

"Kassie," Connelly said, "we've already told Tomas."

"What! You had no right to do that!"

"We had our counselor there to help him process his feelings.

He . . . didn't take it well. We had to sedate him. He's in the infirmary."

"Bring him to me! I need to take him home and take care of him."

"That's another issue, Ms. Fields," Stewart said. "As a limited adult you aren't old enough to have sole custody of a minor. Tomas is now a Ward of the State and will be staying with foster parents."

"You can't do that!" I screamed and flung myself at Stewart. Stewart's bodyguard pulled me away. All my self-defense training fled my brain as I flailed uselessly in his arms.

"I'll excuse that because of the circumstances," Stewart said. "But, just this once. You can see Tomas tomorrow."

I realized I was not making the situation better. After a few segs of deep breathing I calmed myself enough to nod agreement. "OK," I said. "Tomorrow. I'll hold you to that."

"I'll have this officer escort you home," Stewart said.

"No," I said. I looked at Connelly. "John, can you take me home? I want to get some of Tomas's things for you to bring him tonight. It might help him."

I thought Stewart would protest, but he didn't.

Connelly said, "Sure, I'll be glad to help."

Connelly met me at the main gate. I slipped into the passenger seat of the ground vehicle and gave him a tearful smile. "I'm sorry I yelled back there. It's not your fault. It's that just with my dad, and now Tomas, I'm overwhelmed."

"It's okay, I understand," he said. "I care about Tomas too."

"I know you do. Thank you for agreeing to take him his things. It means a lot."

We made the short trip in silence. Connelly waited in the living room as I made up a bag for Tomas. In addition to clothes and toiletries I included a few favorite toys. He was probably too old for them now, but something familiar might make him feel better.

I handed Connelly the bag and gave him a parting embrace. I held him a couple beats too long for a friendly hug, released him, and sent him out the door. The flirting wasn't really necessary but might prove useful later. I hoped.

I then called Davee's new burner and left him a message about what happened.

✧   ✧   ✧

The next morning I headed to the UN compound to spend the day with Tomas at school.

I was refused entry at the gate and given a number to call. I called from a café across the street. I was not surprised by who answered.

"This is Supervisor Stewart. Is that you, Ms. Fields?"

"Yes, you know it is. I want to see Tomas."

"We need to minimize the disruptions to his schedule. You'll be allowed to see him this afternoon, after school, for two hours."

"What! He's my brother, he needs me!"

"What he needs now is time to adjust to his new living conditions without being distracted by his sister. Let's start with this first visit and see how it goes. Your behavior will make a difference."

I had never wanted to kill anyone as much as I wanted to kill Supervisor Stewart right at that moment. I lowered the comm and took a deep breath, than another, and another. After a bit I brought the comm back up. Stewart was still on the line. I knew he would be.

"Ms. Fields?"

"Supervisor Stewart," I said with icy calmness. "What time this afternoon and where?"

We agreed on a quarter div after class, in the classroom. I had to translate from Earth clock, which wasn't even adjusted to our day cycle.

I headed home. I had plans to consider.

Once home I investigated my legal options. It turned out I really didn't have any. Since we were under UN occupation, UN law prevailed, and it was stacked against us. There were some papers I could file and arguments I could make but I could tell from my research that it would likely be pointless. I set aside the idea of getting any help from the legal system.

My visit with Tomas was one of the most painful experiences of my life. We talked, held each other, and cried. The hardest thing I ever had to do was let him go when our time was up. I told Tomas that I loved him and that I'd see him soon. I then got up and left. I could hear his voice calling my name as I walked down the hallway.

✧　　✧　　✧

When I got home there was a message on my comm from an unknown contact. It just said, "Go to last birthday's meeting spot." I knew who it was from and where to go.

I headed straight to the park and found Davee near the restrooms. Was it really only a year ago?

Davee led me through the remains of the labyrinth. The greenery was neglected and dying and, under the UN, it was no longer a make-out spot. It could still serve as a place for a private conversation though.

"I met with my contact," he said. "Your dad may have been abducted. Supervisor Stewart has been pressuring Freeholders to collaborate by threatening their families. Several who have refused have gone missing. No one knows if they are even still alive."

I couldn't help it, I let out a sob.

Davee took my hand. "There's more. Stewart is also sending Freehold children to Earth. We don't know if they are hostages or if there is some other reason."

My heart beat even faster. I wondered if it would explode.

"We have to get Tomas out," I said. "Now."

"I know," Davee agreed. "We'll figure something out. My contact says if we can rescue Tomas she can put you both in hiding outside the city. It won't be safe for you here anymore either."

We walked and talked until afternoon turned to evening. I'd had the beginnings of an idea earlier and the two of us hashed it out until we had what we thought was a workable plan. We only had our limited training and a few resources to draw on. They'd never see us coming. We hoped.

The next day Davee and I made our separate preparations to free Tomas. We planned to try that night. I didn't want to wait for him to get shipped to Earth.

In the morning I filed a Petition of Custody with the Clerk of the Court at the occupation government building. It took all morning. Waiting. Being referred. Explaining again. More waiting. Before I left the Zone I stopped by the school and asked to see Tomas. They wouldn't let me and I made a small scene before leaving.

I returned home, made some food, and ate without tasting it. As I went over my copy of the legal paperwork I noticed the date. Today was my birthday and this was my birthday meal. I cried as I cleaned up.

I changed out of Mom's clothes into one of my own outfits. I made up my lips and eyes in bright colors instead of in the subdued tones currently fashionable. I pulled my hair into a ponytail and added fingernail extensions for the first time in ages. When I looked in the mirror I saw the girl I'd been before the war.

I had a little time so I pulled out my diary and made entries updating everything that had happened up to now. I wanted there to be a record.

Davee arrived and told me all was ready on his end. By now school had ended for the day so I called Connelly. I made sure my ID would show up on the call.

"Kassie?" he said.

"Oh, John," I said, letting some emotion seep into my voice. "I tried to see Tomas and they wouldn't let me. I miss him so much."

"I know, I heard. Tomas misses you too. You'll have another visitation soon."

"The house is so empty. Without Dad and Tomas, I'm going out of my mind. I'm so alone. I need to be with someone."

"Would you like me to come over and keep you company for a while?"

"Oh, yes, could you? I really need a friend right now."

"I'll be right there."

I ended the call and looked at Davee. We were committed.

When Connelly arrived I greeted him with a hug. "I'm so glad you're here."

We sat on the living room couch. "Oh, John, hold me, please." He put his arms around me. I buried my face in his chest. We sat like that for a while. Then I nuzzled his cheek and licked his ear. I looked up, expectantly, offering my lips for a kiss.

He pulled away. "Kassie, what are you doing? This isn't right."

This wasn't working how I'd planned. He was off script. I wasn't sure what to do.

"I think I should go," he said, and stood to leave.

"Wait! It's about Tomas. I need your help to save Tomas," I blurted out.

He stopped. "Save Tomas from what?"

"Supervisor Stewart is going to send Tomas to Earth. I can't let him do that!"

I showed Connelly what I'd discovered in the documents from the custody challenge I'd filed. "Tomas isn't a Ward of the State. This shows Stewart has full legal guardianship. He can legally send Tomas off-planet. He's done this to other children already. I can't tell you how I know. You have to believe me."

Connelly scanned the files. "That son of a bitch!" he exclaimed. "He has done this before! The other kids Stewart said were Wards of the State never stayed long. Stewart had an explanation each time. They transferred to another school, or he found family for them in another region, or they ran away, or something. This makes so much sense now. He's been abusing the system this whole time!"

He went back to the paperwork and looked at it more slowly. I could see his anger build as he read the documents.

"Kassie, I didn't know about this. I swear. What Stewart is doing is wrong. This... this isn't why we're here. We just wanted to help. Taking children away from their families is against everything we stand for."

Connelly looked at me. I mean, he really looked at me. He took in my hair, my makeup, my clothes. I could see the wheels turning in his head.

"What were you up to tonight? How old are you really, anyway?"

Caught in the act. Nothing to do but confess and hope I don't blow it.

"I'm not eighteen Earth years old," I said, doing the conversion from Grainne years to Earth years to make it easier for him. "I was born April first, year two hundred on our calendar. Today is my birthday. I'm ten so that would make me just over sixteen Earth years old."

"Sixteen?" he said. "So you were trying to..."

"Blackmail you, yes. There's a camera, and I have... a friend, in case you gave me any trouble. Davee, come out." I flushed red and hot. I was embarrassed, and relieved I didn't have to follow through.

Davee emerged from where he'd been waiting. He had my pistol in his waistband. "Hi, Teach."

"You know just the allegation would wreck me, right? And with video I might have gone to jail," Connelly said.

Davee smiled. "Then it's a good thing we didn't need it. How do you think it would play if we used our calendar and said she was ten?"

Connelly looked pale. "Yes, that's a good thing. Now, how can I help you keep Tomas? All you had to do was ask." He looked at the documents again. "This is evil."

I went over Connelly's part in the plan to get Tomas off the UN base. We came up with a cover story that we'd abducted him at gunpoint to explain his involvement. I was vague on the details of what we'd do after we left the base and Connelly was wise enough not to ask questions.

We had Connelly call Tomas's foster parents to invite Tomas over for dinner that night. He said Tomas's sister had made his favorite meal and begged him to give it to her brother. The problem was there was only enough food for two. Connelly was very persuasive so they agreed and set a time.

Davee headed out to meet his contact and get in position for their part in the plan. He took my pistol as I wouldn't be able to get it through base security.

We passed through the main gate without a problem. At the gate for the secure housing area Connelly signed me in as his guest. The guards reminded me I either needed to leave by curfew or stay until morning.

"That's not a problem. I may want to spend the entire night," I said, as I ran my fingers through Connelly's hair. He stammered, the guards chuckled, and we were in.

So maybe my first plan wouldn't have really caused that much outrage. The UN had these laws, but they only applied to certain people.

We parked and Connelly led me to his apartment in a modular housing complex. I had to wait there while he retrieved Tomas. If Connelly was going to betray me, that would have been the time to do it. I suffered through many agonizing segs as I imagined UN soldiers bursting into the apartment to arrest me.

The door finally opened and Tomas saw me. He cried my name and threw himself on me for a full-body hug. He buried his face in my blouse and sobbed. My own tears made rivers through my makeup in return.

He eventually pulled his head away and looked up at me. "What's happening? Are we having dinner?"

I laughed. "No, we're breaking you out. Mr. Connelly agreed to help and Davee is waiting for us. Come on, we have to go."

We wiped our faces, I took Tomas by the hand, and we went out the door. We hid Tomas in the trunk of Connelly's vehicle. They usually only searched vehicles entering the base and our luck held and we were waved through the exit. If the guards noticed Connelly's date had ended early, they didn't comment on it.

I had Connelly drive on manual so he could make some random turns while I looked for tails. I scanned for EM emissions with my diary to check for drone surveillance.

After about three-quarters of a div we arrived at an abandoned farm way out of town. The weathered white farmhouse sat on a small rise that made it easy to spot anyone approaching. Davee had scouted the location after finding it on archived sat images.

It was near full dark when we pulled in behind the house. The only illumination came from a few old solar-powered battery lights on poles. "Davee, we're here," I said as I opened the back kitchen door.

Supervisor Stewart stepped out of the shadows into the pale light that came in through the dusty windows. "Ms. Fields, Mr. Connelly, Tomas," he said. "I'm so glad you made it." He held a small black pistol in his hand. His UN bodyguards stood behind him. "Once the squad is here from your other possible bolt hole, we'll continue this on base."

I was stunned. Stewart always seemed to be a step ahead of me.

"So, what now?" I said, stalling for time. Davee and his contact should be here somewhere. I wished I had my pistol. Instead all I had was my diary.

"Now we wait for your boyfriend and his associate from Freehold intelligence," Stewart said. "After all, Kassie, they are the reason for this, not you, little girl."

"And Tomas?" I said. "He's not part of this. You'll let him go?"

"No, I think I'll send him to Earth with the others. Do you know how much certain people will pay for a Grainnean child to raise as their own? He's young enough to be remade in their image. In a few years he'll be a good, contributing member of civilized society."

"No! You bastard!" Connelly cried, and lunged for Stewart. I hadn't quite forgotten Connelly was there, but I had dismissed him as not important in this fight. I was wrong.

Stewart was caught off guard as well. As the two men grappled for the gun one of Stewart's goons moved in to help him. The other covered both of us. I heard the soft *tink* of breaking window glass and his head exploded in a spray of blood and tissue. The other one stepped back and swung his carbine, and he got shot, too.

"Tomas, down!" I yelled. I couldn't turn to look. I stepped into the tussle as Stewart fired twice. The shots were muffled as the rounds tore into Connelly.

I grabbed Stewart's left arm with my left hand as he pushed Connelly's body away. I dug my extended fingernails in as hard as I could. Stewart turned his pistol towards me and tried to fire.

I punched him in the right eye. A hard, straight jab with my right hand. I held the stylus from my diary as a spike between my fingers. I let all my rage and frustration out in one glorious burst.

"Aaarrgh!" he screamed. He stumbled away, arms flying to his face, the stylus protruding from his bloody orb. It went deep, but not deep enough, not yet. He staggered and landed face down and I jumped on his back. I grabbed his head and slammed his face into the old kitchen floor.

He twisted around, hideously leaking goo. He was stronger than I thought.

Davee shouted, "Look out!" and then BANG! shot him. Blood spattered on me.

Then he said, "Shit, I killed him." Yeah, he had. We had.

I slumped on the floor, exhausted. I heard Tomas vomiting. I needed to comfort him, I needed to check on Connelly, I needed to rest...

The next thing I knew Davee was next to me. He pulled me to him and I could feel his body heat. I felt so cold and started to shake. I heard others bang through the kitchen door. Three people in our uniforms burst in.

At once they pulled us up, patted us down, whispered, "Let's move," and dragged us out at a run. I was thrown into a truck and scrambled to sit up as we rode off.

I woke some time later wrapped in musty blankets on the floor of an abandoned warehouse, or maybe a factory. I wasn't sure and it wasn't important. The uniforms were ours.

I felt someone wiping my face, looked up, and my heart jumped.

Her hair color was different, her eye color was different, and there were new lines on her face. But, it was the face I thought I'd never see again. It was my...

"MOM!"

"Welcome back, honey," she said.

"But, you're dead. They said you were dead," I said through my tears.

"Oh, baby, I know, I know. I'm so sorry."

She continued, "I wasn't on base when it was hit with the kinetics. I was supposed to be there, and the casualties were so high, everyone believed I was dead too. Since no one would be looking for a dead woman I got out with a few others. We've been working."

"Is that when you became a spy?" I asked.

"Honey, my real job was always intelligence. Who do you think recruited Davee?"

I looked at Davee, who was sitting with Tomas next to Mom. "If Mom was your contact all this time, that means... you knew. You knew she was alive and you didn't tell me."

"I'm sorry," he said. "I wanted to, I really did, but I couldn't. You know why."

"Operational security," I said bitterly. I knew what the term meant but I still couldn't believe he'd kept this secret from me.

"What about Dad?" I asked, "Did he know?"

"That I was alive? No. That I was intel? I'm sure he suspected but he never asked. And no, I don't know for sure what's happened to him."

I sat bolt upright. "Supervisor Stewart," I said. "And Connelly."

"We killed Stewart," Davee said. "And Connelly was gone by the time I got to him. We left them both there and set the house on fire. We grabbed Stewart's comm unit first."

"Mom, did you know Stewart was hunting you? Did you know he was using Tomas and me to get to you? Did you know we were bait?"

She didn't answer.

"Mom?"

She looked me right in the eyes. "Yes, but he didn't know we were hunting him too. He was selling Freehold children and had to be stopped. We had to get him outside the perimeter. His comm should have information on where he sent the children."

"Why didn't you shoot him before we got there?"

"We weren't in position. We thought he'd follow you so we were covering the road. You got him, baby. I'm so proud of you. I love you so much."

"I love you too Mom."

Our reunion with Mom was short. She hugged us both, and then she was gone. She's fighting, though. We all are.

Dad is still missing. If he's on the run, we'll find each other, eventually. If the UN has him, that's one more reason to win the war. Freehold forever!

■   ■   ■

Huff #8

Strategic Impacts/Justification for Lethal Force
(1 April 210)

The CAG drafted this letter for me, I added the notes at the bottom.

UNPF OPERATION MIDNIGHT KESTREL

1 Apr 210

MEMORANDUM FOR:
CHAIR OF THE CHIEF OF STAFF
SECRETARY OF THE BUREAU OF MILITARY AFFAIRS
(IN TURN)

FROM: CDR, COMBINED JOINT PEACEKEEPING TASK FORCE
EDEL

SUBJECT: FORMAL REQUEST FOR AUTHORIZATION OF
CJPTF-EDEL FORCES TO INITIATE LETHAL FORCE,
DEPLOY STRATEGIC CAPABILITIES, AND FOR
MODIFICATIONS TO THE STANDING RULES OF
ENGAGEMENT

1. This letter includes my analysis of the changing situation on Grainne Colony, both planetside and system-wide, as well as my best military advice. I have a series of requests that I believe are necessary to achieve the desired endstate of compliance and full reintegration of the so-called "Freehold."

2. First, I must address the strategic impacts of recent setbacks. The short-term loss of Skywheel Three itself has only a minor impact, but the greater risk comes from the damage to Main Operating Base Unity. The loss of hundreds of experienced aviation personnel, and hundreds of millions of credits in primary equipment significantly increases operational risk.

3. With assets retasked to cleanup and reconstruction efforts, my ability to conduct active peacekeeping missions is severely degraded for a minimum of thirty (30) Earth days. RC-Capital has ceased operations

"outside the wire" except for basic security, until damage assessment and casualty collection are completed.

4. Reconstruction will take a minimum of 30 days to restore core services. The increased threat of infectious disease in the damaged zone will strain our medical footprint.

5. The loss of JP6 bears significant consequences for our operations. I urge you to support immediate reconstruction. Without Sol JP6 / Iota Persei JP1, we face adding as much as two Earth weeks for transit, plus the additional delays imparted by coordinating with Novaja Rossiyan and Caledonian Colonial authorities. The loss of a direct Sol–Iota Persei transit route exposes us to critically increased risk.

6. BEST MILITARY ADVICE:

   a. Immediately authorize JP6 reconstruction.

   b. Deploy civil and base engineering brigades to reconstitute MOB Unity.

   c. Replace lost aviation assets and plus-up to 1.75 times original requirement.

   d. Deploy 3.5 brigade combat teams, 1 x Divisional HQ to reconstitute RC-Capital; allow for simultaneous reconstruction and peacekeeping missions.

7. To regain the initiative and expedite compliance, I request the following:

   a. Authorization to initiate lethal force, offensive operations, and lethal joint fires.

   b. Approval to delegate these specific authorities to the Regional Command level.

   c. Combatant command authority for the use of strategic capabilities to include power armor and space-delivered kinetics.

      i. Enclosure A is the coordination guidance developed by my staff and BuMil Joint Staff. All use of strategic capabilities will require dual concurrence by the Chair and myself.

ii. Enclosure B includes the planning caveats and decision trees.

iii. Enclosure C includes an initial target list, starting with [REDACTED].

8. We will make every effort to use nonlethal fires where appropriate to the maximum extent possible, but an ability to hold the insurgency and rebel partisans at lethal risk will change the calculus in-system. I estimate our ability to use nonlethal means will remain above 70% of all encounters.

9. Please see Enclosure D for recommended changes to the standing Rules of Engagement, prepared by my staff Judge Advocate in conjunction with BuMil General Counsel.

10. Enclosures E and F detail budget proposals and legislative initiatives my staff assesses as necessary to better enable us to achieve the administration's policy objectives.

Very Respectfully,
//SIGNED//
JACOB HUFF, GENERAL, UNPF
Commanding, CJPTF-EDEL
(Attch: Encl. A-F)

[Handwritten] *Vlad, Kimbo: you need to get the General Assembly and SecGen on my side for this, I wouldn't ask if I didn't think it absolutely necessary. Send your own team out here to assess the weapons caches and intelligence we're recovering, if you need further proof!*

Proxy War

Larry Correia

"How many murders have you committed?"

He answered without hesitation. "Zero."

"Liar!" the UN inspector shouted.

The last man who had called him a liar to his face, he'd shot dead promptly after. But that had been under the old rules. These were the new rules.

He didn't care for the new rules.

In addition to the bureaucrat conducting the interrogation, and his secretary slash flunky, there were two soldiers inside the interview room. They were supposedly providing security, but were only armed with stun batons. The UN loved its "less" lethals. He'd already thought up several plans to kill everyone in the room, only he wasn't a rebel, or a freedom fighter, or an insurgent, whatever they were called, depending on who was doing the describing. He was a businessman. He only killed people when someone paid him to. Nobody was paying him to kill aardvarks, and his association rep had already told the UN that he intended to cooperate fully.

"Don't deny it, Mr. Murdock. We've got the membership records of this so-called Freehold Professional Duelists Association. You're on it. I can't believe how barbaric this place is that such a thing actually existed. There's at least one recording of you savagely gunning a man down in the street, and others of you fighting people with swords, or even knives!"

"Okay, yeah, that I have done."

Custom required the duel's participants to agree beforehand what methods would be used to settle their grievances. Though his specialty was firearms, as a professional it behooved him to be skilled with all the regular choices. Other members of the association had other areas of expertise. Rich highlanders often hired the proxies who specialized in sword fighting. In Jefferson it was all about the ten paces quick draw. It was actually a very elegant process, but the official conducting the interview was obviously appalled by what he'd seen.

"It was depraved! It was inhumane!"

What a pussy. But Murdock kept that opinion to himself and instead responded politely. "My apologies, sir. You inquired about murders, and I answered truthfully. Though I've taken lives, under the customs of the Freehold of Grainne, I've never committed a murder. Each of those events was entered into willingly by all parties."

The inspector's lip curled upward in a sneer. "Just answer the question. How many people have you killed?"

It was so tempting to make a joke of it, and say none today but it wasn't even lunchtime yet. Murdock resisted the urge, and instead answered, "Five." Which was a complete lie, but five was how many of his duels had been to the death *and* recorded. He figured the UN probably didn't know about the rest. Usually the clients who could afford his services liked to keep things discreet, no recordings, and only the minimal accepted number of witnesses.

But sometimes—in his case five—the client had wanted an example to be made, or maybe the client just really hated the challenger and wanted to be able to watch their demise over and over again. That wasn't his kink, but who was he to judge? The challenged had the right to bring in a proxy to stand in his place. Hiring a professional, and letting people see the inevitable results, sent a message to other potential challengers. *Don't fuck with me.*

"Disgusting." The UN man made a note on his tablet. He snorted. "Five lives pointlessly snuffed out."

It took all of his self-control not to tell him to stick another zero after that five just to be safe. And that was just the fatalities. Most challengers had the sense to yield and apologize when they learned who they were up against. If not, maiming them was usually sufficient to settle things. He really only ever had to kill the prideful.

"It shocks me that dueling was legal on this backwoods colony.

If it was up to me all of you monsters would be held accountable for your crimes against humanity."

Luckily it wasn't up to him, because the FPDA had cut a deal—and paid a lot of bribes—to the occupiers to keep all of its dues paying members out of the UN *reeducation* camps. They would receive immunity for their previous violent activities, and in exchange they would be well-behaved, law-abiding citizens.

"Yes. I feel terribly sorry for my awful behavior." It was really hard to keep a straight face as he said that.

Then the UN prick launched into a giant tirade about how violence never solved anything—ironic considering they'd just invaded the planet—and how there would be severe repercussions for failure to blah blah blah. So even as Murdock was imagining other interesting ways to steal a stun baton and bludgeon all these aardvarks to death, he only nodded along and tried to look contrite.

At the end of the rant, he signed the contract.

"This is bullshit. We were celebrities. We were a big fuckin' deal. We took shit off nobody. Who are these earthlings to strut in here and tell us we can't do our jobs no more?" Bandara was half drunk and all angry, which was a bad combo.

"Relax, man." Murdock looked around the cantina. It was all locals eating tacos. The UN people didn't go outside of their compounds much since the bombings and assassinations had started. Even then there were still plenty of people in Jefferson who would rat on them if Bandara got too spun up and started loudly talking about how easy it would be to cap a bunch of aardvarks.

"No, you relax." Bandara pushed the bottle toward him. "And spare me the bullshit about how you don't drink, 'cause it messes up your robot arm and laser eyeball or what the fuck every science shit."

"Even thirty milliliters, that's about a shot for you illiterate hillbillies, of alcohol can cause up to a one and a half percent degradation in interface time between my central nervous system implants and my gun hand. That could slow my draw nearly a tenth of a second, and linger until it's fully metabolized, which could take a couple of divs—"

"And you never know when a client's gonna call, 'cause some

punk just slapped him with a glove. Look around, *pendejo*. We're unemployed. There ain't no more clients. There ain't gonna be no more clients in a few divs or in a few years. So you might as well get wasted."

"Good point." Murdock grabbed the bottle and poured himself a finger of the murky liquid. "Let's fry some implants."

"Jokes on you. I ain't got none. I'm this good all natural. Well, except for the gene mods and steroids, obviously."

If Bandara considered that natural, Murdock—who had sprung for the best cybernetic enhancements money could buy—was full on supernatural. But Bandara was all about the flash and the show, hired when the client wanted knives and trash talk. Murdock was the cold-blooded son of a bitch hired when they absolutely positively needed to make sure their challenger got put in the ground.

Now they were both unemployed bums. So they drank in silence for a while. Murdock winced when he downed the glass, not only because he wasn't much of a drinker, but because this really was trash. With all the chaos going on nobody could get the good stuff. But trash was appropriate for an unemployed bum, so he poured himself another.

"It's not the same without Dave around," Bandara muttered. "He never missed Taco Tuesday."

"Dave used to be a Blazer. Of course he ran off to join the resistance."

"And that crazy Japanese fucker, what's his face, you know, the one with the samurai sword."

"Kimura," Murdock answered, as he realized it had gotten lonelier around the Association's usual hang outs. "Last I heard he was raiding convoys down south."

Proxies were an odd breed on an already odd world. There were very few of them good enough to actually make a living at this sort of thing, about fifty in the whole system. Joining the Freehold Professional Duelists Association was a prestige thing, so they all knew each other. Occasionally, they ended up facing a friend in a duel, but that was just part of the job. It was nothing personal. In the meantime, they hung out together, because honestly the other members were the only other people crazy enough to get them.

"Fighting against these pathetic, low-gravity, bird-boned chumps, I bet Kim and Dave are stacking corpses."

"To our brave and stupid colleagues and their futile, noble gestures." Murdock lifted his glass in a toast. They clinked them together and downed another shot.

At least the melancholy had gotten Bandara to lower his voice. "I don't know, man. It's tempting. You know, hoist the black flag and start cutting throats. I've never been patriotic or nothing, but I don't like fools telling me what I can and can't do."

"Oh, then you'd love being in the army." Murdock chuckled. "I've done that before. Never again. I'm my own boss now."

"You ain't the boss of nothin'. The UN saw to that. I got into this for the challenge, because I wanted to be the scariest motherfucker in the room, and make all the *chicas* swoon. Now? What? I'm supposed to get a *job*?"

"Trust me, amigo. War isn't like dueling. War is chaos. There's no rhyme or reason to it. You can do everything right and die, or everything wrong and live. You can hone your skills your whole life, and catch a stray bullet from an amateur. You can be a certified badass and step on a mine. What we do? There's order in a duel. There's *rules*. It's just you and your opponent. Its skill and focus, and a moment of perfect clarity, then the better man's still standing."

"That's downright fuckin' poetic, Murdock. What about you? Why'd you start dueling?"

"It paid good. Look, you want to get yourself killed because you're an adrenaline junky and now you're bored, knock yourself out. Me? I'm not a soldier anymore. I was a lousy soldier. I'm a good businessman. While I'm out of business, I'll be a slob and live off my savings. And if it turns out the market's changed permanently, I'll move on. I don't owe these people shit. This isn't my war."

"But you live here."

"I'm not *from* here."

"Then why stick around?" Bandara demanded.

Murdock didn't have a good answer. He shrugged and poured another drink. At this rate his neural interface was going to be scrambled way worse than 1.5 percent. His targeting eye was starting to get a little static around the edges. "What is this shit? Ethanol?"

"I know why, Murdock. You act all cold, like you try to make what we do into some kinda science, but you're no different than kilted Dave painting his face blue and swinging around that big old claymore, or Kim and his mystical bushido bullshit. You're addicted to the fight, man against man, life or death, nothing purer. You're a fucking gladiator. And this is the one place in the whole galaxy where guys like us could not only live, but be *needed*. You're here, because there's nowhere else for the likes of you to go."

In a way, that made sense. And when a lunatic like Bandara started making sense, it was time to call it a night.

It only took a few weeks for the UN to change the rules again.

"What does this mean, illicit gains?" Murdock did his best to keep his voice level and nonthreatening as he held the bank notice up against the window.

Apparently he wasn't nonthreatening enough for squishy UN standards, because the man on the other side of the glass said, "If you don't calm down I'm going to have security remove you from the Processing Center."

The building had once been a bunch of rental offices for various small businesses, but the UN had confiscated it and declared it a *Community Outreach Processing Center*, which was a fancy term for a place the occupied could go to beg their occupiers to step on their necks slightly less hard. He'd been standing in line for a div and a half to file a protest. When they'd finally let him talk to someone, it wasn't even the same inspector from last time. Now he just got some low-level flunky. It wasn't just that they'd invaded his planet and put him out of work, now they'd stolen his money, and they were so damned smug about it too.

"Apologies." Murdock ground his teeth together, then tried again. "All my accounts are frozen because the UN has declared my life savings to be illicit gains."

The official checked his pad. "That appears to be correct. Inspector Hollister issued order fifteen dash three, that declares all colonial assets which came from illegal activities are to be seized. Everything appears to be in order here."

"It wasn't illegal at the time. Those are my credits. I earned them."

The man sniffed. "Apparently in an unapproved manner. We started processing the order yesterday. I've been getting this same complaint all day, mostly from prostitutes." He looked at

Murdock suspiciously, probably wondering why anyone would pay someone with so many ugly scars for sex.

"It was a different kind of whoring." Murdock thought about smashing his artificial fist through the security window, dragging this shit heel through the hole, and demonstrating what an *unapproved manner* really looked like. "Can I talk to Inspector Hollister? That's who went over my immunity agreement with me."

"The inspector is a very important man. He oversees all civilian and refugee integration functions in the city. You'll need to file an appointment request."

He sighed. "How do I do that?"

"I can't access those forms here. You'll need to ask at window 6B."

Window 6B had a line twice as long as the one he'd stood in to get to this useless asshole. And just to be extra insulting, 6B appeared to be the line for pathetic orphans and crying widows. To a man who measured his job performance by the millisecond, that kind of inefficiency offended him. It was almost like these aardvarks were begging for an ass kicking. "You'd better call Hollister right now, and you ask him where the fuck my money is."

Apparently the clerk had an alarm button under his desk, because the next thing Murdock knew several soldiers were approaching to ask if there was a problem. The real problem was that the metal detectors and drone scanners around the center had forced him to leave all his guns at home, but instead he just told them, "No problem. I was just leaving." And he walked out before they could work up the energy to throw him an educational beat down.

When Murdock returned to his luxury high-rise, he discovered that the he couldn't access his apartment either, because the UN had just seized the entire building to house troops. He'd been standing in line and missed the notice, so hadn't even gotten a chance to pack his shit. The tenants' remaining personal items had been stuck into sealed bags, labeled with their flat number, and dumped on the sidewalk. His bag looked like they'd dumped a few drawers of his clothing into it, a few knickknacks, and an inventory list that declared the remainder of his property had been seized once they'd detected the presence of illegal firearms and ammunition, and that if he wanted to file a protest, to go back to the same place he'd already spent the day uselessly waiting in line.

Well shit... who is going to feed my fish?

He stopped in front of the sealed entrance to read the notice one last time. "Great. Now I'm homeless too."

When he said that aloud, one of the UN security drones posted at the door had helpfully printed a ticket for a nearby refugee camp.

At least the UN was efficient at something.

"I hereby call to order this emergency meeting of the Freehold Professional Duelists Association. As the senior ranking member available, I, Alfonse Murdock, will be presiding. We have a quorum of ten members present and one invited guest. We'll skip the reading of the minutes and go right into new business." He looked around at the other proxies who'd agreed to gather in the dusty old warehouse in the middle of the night. "Well?"

"I move that we fucking kill everybody," Bandara said.

"Seconded," proclaimed the duelist known only as the Swede.

"Okay, hang on. We need to be more specific." Murdock wasn't big on Robert's Rules of Order, and the well-spoken types who usually conducted had either gotten themselves thrown in a prison camp, had already joined the rebels, or were probably dead, but Murdock was going to do his best, and they couldn't just kill *everyone.*

"*How* do we want to proceed?"

The duelists kind of shrugged and shuffled their feet at that. They were like guided missiles. Give them a target and it was doomed, but they were pretty much shit without the guidance.

Even though this was a system that tended to attract prickly individualists, the FPDA had been formed after a few messy incidents where duels had spiraled into full on village-burning family blood feuds. The professionals decided that they needed a code of conduct. Competition was good and all, but they needed to be able to work without stepping on each other's dicks. Clients needed to be able to know they were hiring pros, and not just some psychotic asshole with delusions of being a gunslinger. Membership in the association meant that you at least had your shit together. It was a pretty loose organization, but it had kept them busy and well paid... until the stupid UN had arrived.

"First things first. Are we all in agreement that the UN has screwed us over, so that our agreement with them is null and void?" When he asked that, everybody nodded. Even their calmer members looked rather determined to slot some aardvarks.

"If anybody dissents, now's your chance...No? Fine. If you're sticking around, you're complicit."

Nobody got up and left. He figured they wouldn't. There had been a couple of members who he'd thought might be Earth loyalists, so he'd neglected to send them an invite. *Whoops.* The hotheads and true-believing Freeholders had stormed out of the last meeting after the majority of the membership voted to sign the agreement and play nice. So what they had left here were the pragmatists and businessmen, the types who normally wouldn't pick a fight unless there was a good angle in it for them.

Murdock had started thinking of them like a pack of wolves. The same way wolves killed to eat, to these guys violence was just business. Don't mess with them, and they won't bite you. Except for some idiotic reason the UN really enjoyed kicking wolves.

"All right then. We won't waste time debating whether they deserve it or not. So how do we best hurt them without dying in the process?"

He'd known there would be some bickering about how to proceed. They were all really good at hurting people, but it was the getting away with it part that they were ignorant about. A few of the proxies had been military, but none of them had any sort of background in how to wage guerilla warfare. The guys like Kilted Dave had left two months ago, and were probably hiding in the swamps and playing commando right now.

Murdock waited until they were good and frustrated poking holes in each other's stupid ideas before he stepped in again. "Hey!" He really wished he'd had an official gavel or something. "Shut up and listen, assholes. We've got skills, but we need resources, intel, and direction. So I've got someone you need to listen to. Mr. Mattias, the floor is yours."

The former client had been waiting patiently for his turn to speak. He was the only nonmember present, but he was no stranger. As a very rich man who tended to infuriate a lot of people, who was himself not martially skilled whatsoever, he had hired several of the duelists here. Normally, Mattias would be dressed nicely, wearing the latest trends, because he was one of those guys who liked it when just a cursory look at them screamed serious money, but tonight he was dressed humbly, like he should be stacking crates or sweeping floors. It must be difficult for a celebrity to try so hard not to be noticed.

"Hello. Many of you already know me, but I'm Joseph Mattias."

"The designer-shoe guy?" Swede asked incredulously.

"Fashion is where I made my fortune, but I've got a diverse portfolio. At times I've hired Mr. Murdock, Mr. Lamb, Mr. Anwar, and Mr. Bandara."

"Well you sure manage to piss a lot of people off," Swede said. "I didn't know ladies' shoes were so cutthroat."

"I'm also invested in pharmaceuticals, weapon systems, and high-grade military electronics. Because of that I've got a good working relationship with certain individuals who are currently on the occupier's bad side."

"Homeboy's legit. I vouch for him."

"Thank you, Mr. Bandara," he nodded. "But yes, I am a bit opinionated, and that has caused me some trouble over the years. I've got a low tolerance for bullshit. It's provoked a few regrettable confrontations, which is why I've had to make use of services such as yours."

Murdock had to chuckle. Joseph Mattias hired enough proxies that the Association should give him a punch card. *Ten killings and your next duel's free.* He was one of those proud rich guys, who loved big parties, beautiful women, fast ships, and never ever admitting he was wrong. But the reason Mattias had reached out to Murdock again was because he loved his home world something fierce.

"In the past, I've hired you men to settle differences of opinion for me. Right now I've got a very serious difference of opinion with the United Nations."

Murdock's old place had been in the upper levels of one of Jefferson's premier high-rises. He'd worked hard to afford that kind of view, and it angered him to see all the windows covered. But to be fair to the UN troops living here now, they kept the windows closed because the lights attracted snipers.

The maintenance pass card Mattias had hooked him up with had gotten him through the security gate. The scrambler he was wearing kept him from being picked up by the other sensors. The makeup disrupted his profile so the cameras wouldn't match the image they'd taken at Hollister's office. After that he knew his way around the property better than any of the aardvarks occupying the place, so getting to his apartment unseen had been no problem.

There was no one inside, though from the look of things a bunch of them were bunking here. They'd written their names and drawn dicks on his walls. He had many paintings and re-creations of ancient photographs, all of them featuring famous gunfighters of the American Old West period. They'd all been defaced by drawing goofy childish shit like glasses and mustaches over their faces. Despite them disrespectfully trashing the place, Murdock was surprised to see that his Siamese fighting fish was still alive, and somebody had even been keeping the tank clean. He'd stopped to drop in a pinch of food, for old time's sake.

Five. He counted five occupants from the signs.

Though the UN had seized a bunch of his equipment, he'd kept one go-bag stashed in a hidden compartment under the bedroom floor. Sure enough, after they'd found all the stuff sitting in the open, they'd not looked hard enough to find this. Mattias had the hookup for guns, but that was generic crap. Artists preferred to work with familiar tools.

As he was coming out of the bedroom with the bag slung over one shoulder, the door opened and a bunch of UN soldiers came swaggering in like they owned the place. Even though the UN forbade drinking and fraternizing, that rule had never worked on any army in history. From the boozy smell, the disheveled uniforms, and lipstick on their collars, they had clearly been out partying.

There were five of them, laughing and joking. They were all low ranking; because of the sniper menace—almost everybody on this planet could shoot a rifle—the lower floors were safer, and thus claimed by the officers. The soldiers were flopping onto his couches, or heading toward the bathroom, comfy and oblivious.

Murdock waited until the door was closed to muffle the sound before walking out of the shadows. It took a moment before anyone spotted him, and one of them blurted out, "Hey, who the hell are you?"

"I'm the guy who used to own this place."

"What?" They were all pretty high or drunk, so that didn't immediately compute, but Murdock's free hand was empty, so he must not have looked too threatening. "Get the hell out of here!"

"Just one question first, which one of you has been taking care of the fish?"

The soldiers shared a confused glance, and then one of them meekly raised his hand. "I like them. I think they're pretty."

"Okay, cool." Then Murdock killed the other four.

The sound of the bullets impacting their skulls was louder than the suppressed pistol itself. The readout in his eye told him that it had been 0.39 seconds from beginning of draw to first shot. His eye was still showing a glowing line for each flight path. A controlled pair to each head, eight shots clean, no misses, total elapsed time 2.67 seconds.

Murdock frowned. Those split times were unacceptable, and they'd even been bunched up. He was out of practice.

The remaining soldier seemed befuddled, sitting there on the couch. To him it must have looked like Murdock had suddenly waved his sparkling hand across the living room and tossed a handful of firecrackers. But then when he turned his head, and saw his companions' blood and brains all over the carpet, he shrieked. When he looked back, Murdock was standing right in front of him, pistol at his side. The soldier started to shake uncontrollably.

"Please don't kill me. Please don't! I'm just a logistics tech."

"Good for you." Murdock reholstered. "The blue-and-red betta's name is John Wesley Hardin. The dried shrimp pellets are his favorite. Got it?"

After the soldier nodded vigorously in understanding, Murdock clamped his artificial hand around the man's throat and squeezed. It only took a few seconds to choke him unconscious. It would only take a few more to kill him, but then who would take care of Wes?

Murdock took one last look around his pad, then walked out the door. He was going to miss this place. Yet even though the rules had changed once more, it did feel really good to be shooting people again.

This time when Murdock returned to the Community Outreach Processing Center, he didn't bother waiting in line. He'd made his own appointment. The intel from Mattias's spies was spot on, because Inspector Hollister and his security detail arrived exactly when expected.

Joseph Mattias had given them a detailed To Do List. Inspector Hollister hadn't been on that list. Oh no . . . Hollister wasn't one of the targets. The info on Hollister was part of the billionaire's *payment* to the Freehold Professional Duelists Association for services to be rendered today. As in, at this very moment every remaining member of the FPDA in Jefferson was about to take out a UN officer or collaborator who had made Mattias's shit list.

The broke, unemployed, and bitter proxies had drawn lots to see who got to be the lucky one to gank the preachy aardvark who'd dared to kick the wolves. Murdock had won, but only because he'd cheated, having temporarily cranked the feedback on his artificial hand until it was sensitive enough to tell which little piece of folded paper hidden inside the hat had ink on it just from the relative density and vibratory frequency. *Suckers.*

Getting into the center and making it out in one piece would've been difficult, especially since they'd beefed up security. Hollister's living quarters were in an extremely secure compound reserved for diplomats and top-tier functionaries. He was most vulnerable while travelling back and forth, so they used an armored car and varied his schedule. Murdock didn't know who Mattias had on the inside to get a look at the inspector's itinerary, but they were good. That rich bastard really did have a lot of friends.

As the vehicle approached, four soldiers left the security checkpoint at the entrance and walked down the stairs, shooing away pedestrians, until their boss had a clear path to work. It only took a quick glance for Murdock's eye to focus on those four and tag them as targets. To him, the approximate areas of their vital organs and major blood vessels took on a faint glow. The more important, the brighter.

Murdock continued his casual stroll down the sidewalk as the armored car pulled up in front of the steps. It seemed like planting a bomb would've been easier, but there were a lot of civilians around. Despite being an asshole, Mattias was very specific about not hurting innocents. Besides, Murdock was a whole lot more precise than a bomb.

Plus, he had to admit, shooting them would be far more satisfying.

The armored car stopped. All but the driver's door opened. The soldier on the road side got out to help stop traffic. Two more joined the other four on the stairway side. The new arrivals were wearing body armor that his dueling pistols couldn't punch through, so his eye automatically highlighted their most vulnerable points. Murdock tagged them all except for the driver. He didn't have a good angle on him yet.

Inspector Hollister got out of the car, looking smug. He was probably hoping for a long and productive day being a meddlesome dick to regular folks who only wanted to be left alone. Murdock looked forward to crushing his dreams.

Two of the bodyguards seemed alert, heads up, visors actively scanning the crowd for potential threats or magnetic anomalies that might be a gun or an IED. He'd take those two first. The others were punching a clock. Their reactions would be slower. He could take his time with them. Murdock's implants read the change in his brain waves and went to active targeting mode. As he walked along, lines appeared in his vision, stretching between him and each guard, marking the trajectory. Red for a clean shot, orange warning that there would be insufficient penetration to ensure an immediate stop, and blacked out meant that something too solid to shoot through was currently in the way.

It was a lot of information to process, but he was used to it. They were spread out and some of them were rather far away, but Murdock had spent most of his life training to shoot people, and occasionally actually getting them. One of the alert guards turned his visor toward Murdock. From the subtle shift in stance, Murdock knew he'd just been subconsciously made as a threat, the soldier just hadn't processed it yet. He'd been hoping to close the distance but this would have to do.

"Hey, Inspector Hollister."

His hand moved in a flash, scooping the pistol from his belt, and firing the instant it cleared plastic. The guard who'd been paying attention hadn't even time to gather the oxygen to shout a warning before a bullet went through his open mouth to separate his spine from the base of his brain. The soldier in the street had one hand raised to direct traffic, and caught a round through his unarmored armpit which bisected the top of his heart.

By the time the bureaucrat realized someone had called his name and begun to reflexively turn his head, Murdock had killed twice.

Still walking, Murdock shifted slightly and rapid-fire dumped one of the guards on the stairs. Then he hit the next guy. He didn't even pull the manual trigger. That would've taken too long. His brain just activated the electronic firing mechanism as soon as his hand told him the gun was aligned. As the dying soldier stumbled a black line turned red, giving him a clean shot at the next soldier in line, and Murdock put two rounds into him too.

Before Inspector Hollister blinked, Murdock killed three more. The bodyguard closest to Hollister had good reflexes, and started to reach for his charge.

The last soldier on the stairs recognized Murdock as a threat, but all he managed to do was flip the safety off his stickyweb gun before he died poorly. The final bodyguard shoved Hollister, trying futilely to get him to safety. The angle wasn't good. The armor caused most of his targeting lines to go black. So Murdock went to manual override and repeatedly fired at his less protected legs. The bodyguard toppled, still trying to draw his handgun, but as his head turned a red line appeared to his neck, and Murdock's next bullet severed his carotid artery.

As Hollister hit the pavement, Murdock rushed up on the still-open rear door, and repeatedly shot the driver in the back of the head. Blood painted the inside of the windshield.

They were all down. A few of them were still alive, but wouldn't be for long, and none of them were getting enough blood to their brains to pose a threat. Murdock dropped the partially spent mag, and had a new one loaded before the old one hit the ground.

Inspector Hollister looked over at the bodyguard next to him, flat on his back and coughing up gouts of blood, and that was the moment the bureaucrat realized what was happening. All that gunfire had probably been the worst two and a half seconds of Hollister's life.

It was about to get worse.

The inspector realized who he was looking at. "You!"

"I kill people I don't even know for a living. What'd you think I was going to do to someone who personally fucked with my life?"

"You'll pay for this!"

"Eh, maybe." Nobody had sounded the alarm yet, and his dueling pistols were fairly quiet, but there were a whole lot of witnesses now screaming and running for cover. He didn't have long. He probably should've just executed Hollister and gotten it over with, but the bodyguard's pistol was lying on the sidewalk, so Murdock used his boot to slide it toward Hollister.

"What's this?"

"Your only hope." Murdock dropped his dueling pistol back into the holster, and let his jacket cover it.

All his lectures about violence never solving anything aside, Inspector Hollister still grabbed the gun.

Murdock used his flesh-and-blood hand to draw the second dueling pistol from his weak side, and his human eye to aim. He killed the bureaucrat the old-fashioned way. There were no rules anymore, but it still seemed more sporting like that.

Then he walked calmly to the corner, where all the security cameras and sensor feeds had mysteriously gone down, and his promised get-away driver was waiting. He got into the delivery truck and they set out for the next location.

Today was just the beginning. Mattias had given them a really long list.

■　　　■　　　■

Huff #9
Assassin's Guild? [Mid-April 210]

"Sandeep, tell me again..." I stopped for a moment; lately there's an odd echo effect whenever I use this line, and I need the comms people to fix it! Once the echo faded, I started again: "Whose bright idea was it to invade a system with an assassin's guild?" I wasn't angry with Sandeep, but I needed to vent. I squeezed the secure handset so hard, my wrist locked. A souvenir from Mtali: rock shards, a touch of shrapnel, and nerve damage.

I could hear the concern in his voice. "The flask is in the left side pouch on your armored jacket. Behind the emergency beacon. Baldy refreshed it last night."

"Thank you. Did you see the report on the Jefferson attacks? Community Outreach Centers, barracks, banks, a couple of court-houses? It's mostly UN civil government targets; even with our enhanced security and drone coverage, these guys managed several big hits. Intel think it's this 'Professional Duelists' Association.'" They killed some of the Econ section's councilors, including a few of the POLAD's buddies. He's really spooked now. "Ambassador Trudeau is getting panicky, and that's not good for us."

"Sir, I'll be back to Jefferson on the next shuttle. Thank you for the R&R, I can't tell you how much I needed it."

"You get some flight time in?"

"No, sir, the base commander decided to hold a safety down day, something about navigation software issues. However, I played the four-star card to get a shuttle out."

"Get your zipper-suited butt back here in one piece. And tell that CO to get his wing flying, *now*."

"With bells on, sir."

Soft Casualty

Michael Z. Williamson

Jandro Hauer waited in the hot, bright light of Iota Persei for his shuttle to clear for boarding. On his forearm was a medication patch feeding a steady dose of strong tranquilizer. Above that was an IV line from a bottle hanging off his collar. He'd be in orbit in a few hours, and transferred to a starship home. Perhaps then he could calm down.

"Hey, Soldier," someone called. There were eighty or so people at this boarding. He looked toward the voice to see another uniform. A US Marine with a powered prosthesis on his right leg gave a slight wave.

"Hey, Marine," he replied. "Soldier" wasn't strictly accurate for the combined South American Service Contingent, but it was close enough.

"I noticed the meds," the man said, pantomiming at his own arm. "Are you a casualty? If it's okay to ask."

Jefferson was a beautiful city, or at least it had been before the war.

Jandro Hauer looked out from his quarters. This building had once been apartments for the middling wealthy. The enlisted people had a good view, the officers were lower down. That's because the locals occasionally fired a missile. Usually Air Defense intercepted it. Usually. Three floors up there was a hole, and a sealed off area, where one had gotten through and killed two troops. That's why he was inside the window with the lights off, not out on the balcony. He could see the towers of brilliant white clouds rising over the coastal hills just fine from here.

178

Support troops spent a lot of time indoors, not interacting with the planet or its residents. It was safer that way. That, and it meant not having to deal with the bright local light, thin air, vicious fauna.

He still didn't get it. The former colonists were so willing to fight the UN and Earth they'd destroy their own city in the process, which would just guarantee whatever was rebuilt would look like all the other major colonial cities. Being independent had let them develop a unique architecture and style. That wasn't going to last with them reverting to colony status.

It was 1900, but still full light here. The local day was twenty-eight and some odd hours. The UN Forces stuck to Earth's twenty-four-hour clock. That led to some really surreal days where it would be midnight at noon.

A chime at the door indicate his roommate returning. He stepped aside because...

Jason Jardine swiped the lights on.

"Off!" he shouted.

Jason scrabbled with the touch plate.

"Sorry," he said as the room darkened.

"Always check the window first, Jase," he said. Jase was a senior corporal in Finance, but had only been here a week. He was still adapting. It was his first offworld mobilization.

The man nodded. "Yeah."

Some troops even kept the windows opaque 24/7, or 28/10 here. That was safer, but it didn't let them have a view.

"Goddamn, it's a hell of a city," Jardine said, walking over to the window.

"It is. That concentration of wealth thing is pretty dang good, if you're the one with the wealth." He looked around inside.

Troops had scribbled notes, art, tags and names on the walls. There had been decorations. Even though war trophies weren't allowed, there were ways to get stuff out.

Jardine looked where he was looking.

He said, "Just pay some local a few marks to sign it over as something sold to you, and as long as it passes customs, you're fine. The guy you replaced picked up quite a few neat things in town."

"It's that easy?"

"Depends. If they have kids to feed, they'll sell just about anything. You know prostitution was legal here, right?"

"I heard. Not just legal, but unregulated."

"Pretty much. So some of them are still in business, and others are freelance."

Jardine said, "Just wear an all-over polybarrier."

"Not really. Most are actually clean. That was one of things they were very strict on."

"I heard they're cheap, too." Jardine stowed his day pack on a rack by the door.

"I've heard that. Never tried, not planning to. I also hear some of them made a fortune."

"Doing what?"

"Doing rich guys. Apparently when you have a lot of money, you want to spend it."

"Makes sense. Almost like a tax."

"Hah. Good." He hadn't thought of it that way. What would you do if you had all that money? "Heading for chow?"

Jase said, "Nah, I was wondering if we could go out and eat? Into the compound area, I mean. I know there's vendors out there. Do you know much about them?"

"Yeah, why not. I've eaten at several. That will be a change from the chow hall. They're doing lameo chili again anyway." He hated military chili. It wasn't chili with paprika and rice and whatever else they put in to make it international. It was nothing like the chili he'd had when visiting Texas, or that you got in a restaurant back home. He'd also had enough sandwiches lately. He didn't want another bland burger thing.

He took a step, looked down, and said, "Let me change into casuals." He was still wearing a Battle Uniform, even though he never went out on patrol. They had orders to "support the battle-fighters." That meant dressing up like them during the work day.

He went to his room, undressed and tossed the Battle Uniform onto the bed for later. It was a nice room. Most of the furnishings were still there and in good shape. The dresser was real wood of some figured sort. He grabbed a clean Casual Uniform from the top drawer and pulled it on. He was back into the common room in two minutes.

"Let's go," he said to Jase.

Six squares of this area was controlled compound, barricaded off with triple concrete and polyarmor walls. Inside that were military and UN contractors only. Outside that was another four blocks of restricted area, where local contractors took care of nonessential functions. Outside that, chaos.

Though even there, most of the fighting was subtle. It wasn't until you got outside of the metroplex that violence started in earnest. Here, they didn't even need armor. As long as it was stored in their quarters, it was considered "within reach."

They walked the two blocks to the inner perimeter and berm, scanned out through the gate, and entered the Gray Zone. It was patrolled by bots with cameras, and there were a few MPs rolling around in carts. He still wasn't sure how many, but there was usually a cart in sight. He looked both ways and saw one patrol. There were probably a hundred troops in sight, more around the rest of the perimeter.

The local sun was gradually going down. It was late summer, and it was merely hot, not scorching. It reminded him a bit of Rio, except for the thin air and higher gravity. The sky was clearer, though, and this city had a split personality. Most of it continued to function, its business and politics monitored by the Interim Government in this compound and in those two buildings to the south, protected by lots of heavy floater platforms, manned air support and ground-based lasers. Very little got a shot at it these days, but occasional gunfire happened to little effect.

This area was a low-intensity war zone.

To punctuate that, his phone chimed a message.

He looked fast, wondering if there was something inbound, some political change.

It was from Kaela Smith at the MP station.

The screen read, "Jandro, the sniper casualty earlier today. Moritz got shot. Sorry.—Kay."

He didn't even swear, he just wiped the screen.

Jase asked, "Something bad?"

He realized he was tearing up.

"That sniper this morning at the west side? Got Sammy Moritz."

"I'm sorry. Were you close?"

"No, it's just..." He took a deep breath, because this was scary.

"Right after we secured this area and set up for the diplomats and provisional government, they shot some guy at the gate. Just dropped him from a distance and that was all. He got replaced by someone else. They got shot. Moritz was the fifth or sixth person in that duty slot."

"That's sick." Jase apparently hadn't heard about this yet.

"Very. They're not targeting battlefighters or staff. Just people at random, or in this case, not random. It's been six people in about three months in that slot."

"Glad I'm not an MP. At least not that MP."

"It's creepy. I wonder which poor bastard gets it next." He didn't want to think like that, but he couldn't help it. One field unit kept losing cooks. Convoys got disrupted. They needed live drivers because automated ones got waylaid or hijacked. The enemy was outnumbered, but technologically smart and vicious.

He always wondered if they'd come after Logistics someday.

Jase asked, "Can't they rotate around?"

"They do. But the rebels seem to follow the slot, not the location."

"Sheesu."

"These fuckers have no sense of decency. We laughed, it was hilarious, when they abducted Huff, stripped him naked and made him walk back. But if you're a prole, you're likely to just wind up dead."

"Is that why the no fraternizing order?"

He nodded. "Absolutely. Outside the second line, nothing is safe."

"Almost makes me glad to be stuck in here."

"Almost. Would like to actually fight, though. Or support it. Something." He actually wasn't sure about that, but he kept telling himself that.

"Yes, but logistics is what wins wars," Jase said. "And my family's glad I'm safe," he added.

"Hey, at least you're here, doing something." They crossed into the plaza that had been a park of sorts. Much of the greenery was chewed up from troops walking and playing. One of the trees had been used for climbing until the CO stopped it.

Jase nodded. "You're right about that, and so was the captain. These people really don't want us."

He said, "It's resistance to change. In twenty years, their kids will love life and wonder why anyone lived this way." They were told that, and he wanted to believe it.

"I hope so. The poor people must appreciate it."

"So I'm told. I see interviews."

Jase gave him a disgusted look. "Oh, come on, you don't think those are faked."

He sighed. That hadn't come out right in English. "No, not at all. But everyone I've met locally has a couple of different things going. I've also read that civilians will tell occupying forces anything to keep them happy. And I can't imagine a lot of frustrated rich people are shooting at us."

"No, but maybe the people doing the shooting need money badly enough to do it for them. Or are held hostage some other way."

"Or maybe they're just afraid of us from propaganda. Hate isn't rational."

"Yeah. Okay."

Good. Jase didn't like the conspiracy nuts any more than he did. Sure, there were problems back home, but no one started a war just for a political edge. Bribes, manipulated language, economic payoffs, but not wars.

"So what looks good?" he said. There were ten or so little carts and knockdown kiosks offering food.

"Pizza's always good. Or I always like it. But it just doesn't taste right here."

"They grow different grain breeds."

"That must be it. Don't they use real animals, too?"

"Yes, raised out in the open air and then killed."

"That's awful. It's so awful I want to try that, just to stare at people and tell them."

"Hah. It was really trippy the first time. I got used to it. It's just meat. You realize that's in the dining hall too, right?"

"I didn't." Jase looked at him with distrust.

"All food has to be locally sourced. There's just no effective way to bring in that much meat from outsystem, process it in orbit and land it. So we get it here."

"Why don't they tell everyone?"

"It's inspected and approved. There's some sort of BuAg exemption until we can build enough facilities here. So they don't mention the source in case it disturbs people."

"I guess I can see colonies needing that, but once you get to cities," he waved around at the surroundings, "shouldn't you be building vatories?"

"Exactly. So you've already eaten dead stuff, and these people either don't have a choice, or actually like it."

"The chow hall meat is a bit stronger tasting than home,

I guess. Wow. Suffering animals. One more way we're tougher than civilians."

"You can't really brag about it. Someone will call a counselor."

"I know. But part of it is knowing, and part of it is tossing it out there when someone wants to try to measure up."

He nodded. "There is that. I feel sorry for the grunts. You can't boast about being in combat. It's seen as some sort of moral and mental handicap. No wonder they all burn out."

"Six months is a long time. I've been here a week and it's getting old fast."

"So what are you eating?"

"How's the bratwurst?" Jase asked, and pointed at a cart under a broad tree that was warping the plascrete walkway.

"Spicy and greasy. Occasionally there are small bone chips from processing."

"How spicy?"

"Middling. Hot for Europe, medium for Tex."

"Let's do it."

"Looks like he's closing, too. Better run."

They jogged over to the cart, and looked over the menu. It was posted on a scrolling screen in English, Mandarin, Arabic and Russian. Next to the screen was a tag certifying inspection and authorization to be in the Gray Zone.

The cook looked up and nodded.

"You're just in time. What can I get you?"

Jandro said, "I'll take a cheddar brat."

The man nodded. "Got it."

Jase said, "The 'Meatlog.' That sounds suggestive."

"I had one before. It's good. Savory and salty as well as spicy."

"Sure. That's two hundred grams? I'll take two."

The cook, Gustin, per his nametag, flipped three sausages off the grill, said, "That's all I had left. You're in luck," and rolled them around to drain on the rack. Then he rolled each into a bun, and pointed to the condiments. "What would you like?"

Jase considered and pointed. "Lemme get the dark chili mustard, onions, relish and banana peppers."

The man didn't stint on the toppings. Each boat-shaped bun was overflowing.

They paid him in scrip he could exchange later. It was supposed to cut down on black-marketing, but Jandro had heard of so many ways around it. He wasn't really interested in scamming stuff, but it wasn't hard.

He pointed to a bench under another tree. It was made of wooden timbers locally, not extruded.

"I was on Mtali for a while, too, when I was just out of training," he said.

Behind them, the man closed his cart, unfolded the seat and drove off. It was a fueled vehicle, not electric.

"Oh?" Jase asked.

"That was much worse than this place. Here they're opportunistic. There, they were crooked."

"How crooked?"

"We had to open every package, test every delivery, and no local help at all. They'd steal it in front of you, toss it over the fence to a buddy, and insist they never saw it."

"Hah. Lameo."

"Very. It was pathetic. These people are creative at least." And scary. He'd swap that for incompetently dishonest any time.

"The food looks good."

Jase squeezed and stuffed the bread around the contents, angled his face and got a bite. He chewed for a moment, and flared his eyebrows.

"Damn. If all dead animal tastes like this, I could be a convert."

"Hah. Just don't say that around the cultural officers."

"Oh, hell no. But it's different from vat raised. Stronger tasting? Something. Good stuff."

The cheddar brat was good as always, and he tried not to think about dead pig. On the other hand, he'd seen pigs up close. They were pretty nasty creatures.

Jase took another bite and made it disappear.

"Is stuff like this why people stay in? Seeing all parts of the universe?"

"All parts we know about. It does cost a veinful to travel. We get to see the bombed-out ruins. Chicks in New York and Beijing and Nairobi pay good money for that."

He munched the brat. Yes, once you got used to the ugly fact of a dead living being, rather than one raised in a vatory with no head, they were tasty. Did the animal's emotions and life flavor the meat? That was a bit creepy, and a bit taboo.

He bit something hard. There was something in it, probably

a bit of bone. He worked it around and pulled it out with his fingers. It was gray. He wiped it on the boards and kept chewing.

There was another.

"Damn, they need a better butcher. I'm getting bone bits."

Jase took another bite and twitched, then pulled back with a confused look.

"What the..." He reached into the bun, grabbed something and pulled it out. It was a long, gray piece of polymer. It took a moment to recognize it, and then it was instantaneous.

It was a shredded dog tag, and it had been inside a sausage. That meant...

Jase screamed through the entire audio spectrum, then he vomited a meter, gushing and squealing and choking and trying for more.

A moment later it hit Jandro, and he puked and puked and kept puking. He realized he'd blacked out, and was leaning over the table. Then he heaved again. It felt as if he'd emptied his entire tract, and he hoped he had.

Someone nearby asked, "What's wrong, are you all right?"

"Water!" he demanded. "Ohdioswater!"

A bottle was placed in his hand. He cracked the seal, rinsed, spat, rinsed, spat, gargled, and kept going.

Everything blurred out as two people helped him walk to the clinic. There were MPs around, and camera drones. Someone handed him two pills and another bottle of water, and he tried to swallow them, but spat the water out. The pills went with it.

He didn't want to swallow anything.

Someone waved an inhaler under his nose and he passed out.

He woke up in a bed, wrapped in a sheet, and a South Asian woman in casuals sat next to him. The lights were at half. He could tell that he was medicated.

"How are you doing, Alejandro?"

"I feel ill," he said. Very ill. He'd eaten... oh, god.

"I'm Dr. Ramjit from Emotional Health and Wellness. You're safe here."

"I know. I'm just... it was awful. Jase pulled out that tag..."

"What do you think it was?"

"A shredded dog tag."

"The investigators say they're not sure of that."

He sat up and shouted, "*It was a* maldito *dog tag!*" As she recoiled, he added, "Ma'am." If he wasn't careful, he'd wind up in some long term facility.

She reached out and offered a hand. He took it and clutched at it.

She said, "It may have been. If so, it may have been a prank."

"I hope so." Yes, that was entirely likely. Like stripping the general, or the doped sodajuice one time. The locals wanted to find ways to screw with the troops. He hoped that was it.

"Did they get the vendor?"

She hesitated a moment.

"No, and he's not responding to contact."

"I feel okay otherwise. How long am I here?"

"When you feel fit you can leave. We will do trace analysis on the regurgitate. We'll let you know what we find."

He wasn't sure they would. If they said it was clean, would he believe them?

"Can I get something for the stress?"

"Yes. I've prescribed some tranquilizer patches. You're welcome to come talk to us any time, or the chaplains. You're on quarters for tomorrow so you can de-stress."

"Thank you," he said.

He gave it a few minutes, decided he could walk, and signed out. He made his way back to the dorm, and slipped inside.

Jase's room was dark, but the door was open.

"Jase?"

"Yeah."

"How are you?"

"Sick."

The man didn't want to talk more than that.

He went to bed, and the tranquilizer did help him sleep. He woke up twice, hungry, but shook in terror at the thought of food.

He was still awake on and off, and a glance at the wall said it was 0500. The chow hall was open, and he was hungry. He'd slept in casuals, so he wore those down.

He walked into the dining hall, and walked right back out. They had sausage in there, and pans of other meat. He couldn't do it.

He went to the dispenser in the rec room and swiped his hand. He went to select a bag of vegetable chips, and his hand froze. They were local, too.

Perhaps he wasn't hungry yet.

Two hours later he was back in the clinic.

Dr. Ramjit saw him at once.

"Please tell me," he said. "I have to know what you found."

"The sausage contained human flesh," she said evenly.

He'd known it would be bad news, because he couldn't have trusted the good. He closed his eyes and felt dizzy, as if spinning.

"It was only a trace amount," she said. "Probably a piece of muscle tissue. The identag was deliberately placed to draw attention to it. It was intended to be morally horrifying, and it was."

It was intended to be morally horrifying. What she was didn't seem to grasp is that it really was, and what that implied. The troops knew what had happened, and everyone had been eating local food for months. There was no way to be sure how much of it was contaminated with their buddies, and there was no way to be sure how much wasn't.

It was worse than that.

That was the moment Jandro knew there was no line the rebels wouldn't cross. They'd spent a year and a half escalating the moral outrage, humiliation and fear. The executions of the MPs, and this, had been a message.

We will hunt you down relentlessly, remorselessly, tirelessly. Regardless of your power and the damage you inflict, we will violate the sanctity of your mind. We will make you question reality and yourselves. And we will never stop.

He wanted to go home. There was nothing here but hatred, no one to be liberated, no one to be brought into line with modern thought. They were atavists and savages who could not be reasoned with.

The UN Forces alliance had come here to save them from rampant repression. He'd seen some of the poor in images from patrols. Out of the city only a few kilometers, some people lived in shacks without power or plumbing, because it was cheap. No one should be forced to make that "choice." There wasn't even a right to due process. That had to be paid for in cash, in an annual tax that they insisted on calling a "resident's fee," even though it is a tax. Fail to pay, and you had no status.

Yet, when the Forces arrived to help them, dirt poor and super rich alike homogenized into one people, intent only on fighting them.

"Whose tag was it?" he asked.

She blushed and stammered.

"I don't have that information."

"You do," he said. "It was a real person's tag, wasn't it?"

"It was," she nodded, looking queasy herself.

"Who?"

"Binyamin Al-Jabr. The first MP shot at the gate."

His head spun again.

"That's not for release," she said. "At all. But I'd rather you had the truth than a rumor."

It was orchestrated terror. They'd shot the man and taken his body. They'd shot everyone who replaced him in the last three months. The MPs were near rioting in terror. Then they'd chopped him, or parts of him, up and fed them to Jase and Jandro.

He really didn't want to know what muscle they'd used. Nor how many batches they'd made.

"I can't eat," he said, and erupted in tears. His lips trembled as he mouthed, "I have to go home."

"I will arrange it," she said. "I've documented both emotional trauma and post-event trauma. We'll get you home. We've got other people distressed as a result, though of course, none had the direct experience you and Senior Corporal Jardine did."

"I can't eat," he said again. "Please hurry."

Dr. Ramjit seemed compassionate, but someone in the chain didn't believe him. A sergeant from Commissary took him over to the kitchen, to watch the food being prepared. It arrived in ground and cut form, and he watched a steak go from freezer to grill. He could smell it, too, dead meat. But the cooks were all contracted locally, brought in every morning and searched. A couple of them stared at him, then there were a couple of giggles.

"Didn't you see that?"

"See what?" his escort asked.

"They're laughing at me."

"It's fresh steak. Or you can choose a vegetarian option." Though the man looked unsure himself. He kept glancing furtively at Jandro, and at the cooks.

"I . . ." He had no ability to trust them.

The smell caught him. Somewhere there was pork, and he remembered bratwurst, and there it was again. He ran from the kitchen.

They took him back to the clinic and dosed him again. He felt needles, and they said something he didn't follow.

He almost limped, almost staggered back to the dorm, escorted by a medic. He carried a case of Earth-sourced field rations. He had that, and sealed bottles of expensive, imported spring water. That would have to suffice until he left.

Jase wasn't there. He was probably at the clinic, too. He might even be worse off, since he'd gotten the whole dog tag.

That set him reeling again, and he quickly brought up some landscape images from Iguaçu National Park.

Two hours later he stared at the open packets before him. He'd even placed them on a plate and microheated them, so they'd look more like real food.

He couldn't.

He knew it was perfectly safe, packaged on Earth, and was real food, but he couldn't.

Maybe in a day or two.

The door chimed and opened, and Sergeant Second Class Andreo Romero walked in quietly.

"Hey, Jandro."

"Hola."

"Jase is in the Emotional Health Ward. They reassigned me here."

On the one hand, he needed company. On the other, he knew a suicide watch when he saw one.

"How is he doing?"

"Not good. Homb, they officially haven't said anything, but there were witnesses. Everyone knows what happened."

"Did they find the vendor yet?"

"No one knows where he is."

"Not even the other sellers?"

"They say they've never heard of him. They're also gone. No more local carts. All food is going to process through the dining hall now, for safety."

It might well be. But Jandro couldn't eat it. He pushed back from the table and left the food there.

"Is Jase coming back?" he asked.

Andreo shook his head. "No, he's pretty much sedated and prioritied to return home. He took it pretty hard."

"I took it pretty hard."

There was awkward silence for several moments.

"Well, if you need anything, I'm here. They say you're on extended quarters until tomorrow, then you're on days."

"Days" didn't really mean much here, since each shift would be four-plus hours out of synch with the local clock. It was a gesture, though.

Andreo said, "The cooks are all going to be offworld contractors, too. Pricey. We put in a RFQ already, and have some interim workers from BuState and elsewhere. The chow hall is going to be substandard for a while, but that's better than..." He faded off, and shivered.

Jandro nodded. Lots of people had eaten from the local vendors.

Andreo asked, "Can I finish that ration if you're not going to?"

"Sure."

At least someone could eat it.

That local night, another MP was shot. Officially they were told counterfire had demolished the sniper's hide, along with a chunk of that building, but he didn't think it would matter.

He twitched all night, between wakefulness and dozing. The next morning, he was ravenous. He opened another field ration, and managed two bites before nausea caused him to curl up.

It's from Earth. It's vatory-raised chicken. There's eggs and vegetables. It's guaranteed safe.

Maybe lunch.

He walked into the Logistics compound, into the bay, and got greeted.

"Hey, Jandro. Good to see you back."

"*Danke,*" he said. Johann Meffert was German.

He had materiel to process. Three huge cargotainers sat in the bay, pending sort. This shipment was ammunition, spare parts, tools, generators and nuclear powerpacks for them. He had units and their transport chains on cue, with quantities needed. Those always exceeded quantity available. He broke them down by percentage, then applied the urgency codes to adjust the amounts. Once the captain signed off, the loader operators would dispense it to be tied down and depart for the forward bases.

He ignored Meffert's periodic stares. Everyone was doing it.

"Ready for review, Captain," he said into his mic.

He sat back and stretched for a moment. It did feel good to do something productive.

"Looks good so far, Jandro. But those KPAKs need sorted, too."

He looked at his screen. He'd missed four pallets of field rations.

"It's not my fault!" he shouted at the bay. "I didn't plan to eat him, I didn't want to eat him, and I didn't put him in the food!"

He stood up and walked out, back to the clinic.

"You really must try to eat something," Dr. Ramjit said. "Vegetables should be fine. I've switched to that myself. It's perfectly understandable that you don't trust the meat."

He sat in a reclined chair, surrounded by trickling fountains, soft images, and with a therapy dog for company. It responded to his scratches with a thumping tail.

"They're from on planet," he said. Had they urinated on the plants? Grown them in poison? Fertilized the ground with dead troops?

"How are you managing with field rations?" she asked.

"Better," he said. "I've eaten part of one."

Her frown was earnest. "That's not enough for three days. You've already lost weight."

"I know," he said. "But I can't. I just . . . can't." He hoped she understood.

"It's not just the food," he continued. "It's this place. All of it. I can't be around people like this. The cooks were giggling. Our people stare at me. They get the gossip. They all know. Jase has already gone. Please send me, too."

"I'll try," she said. Her frown came across as pitying. He didn't want that, either.

He untangled from the chair and dog and left in silence, though she said, "Good luck, Alejandro. You have our wishes."

As he entered his room, his phone pinged a message. He swiped it.

"Alejandro, you are scheduled to depart in fifteen days. The clinic will fit you with a nutrient IV to help you in the interim."

"Yes," he said to the Marine. "I'm a casualty."

"Good luck with it, then. I'm sorry, at first I'd figured you were a base monkey. They don't know what the point is like."

"No, most of them don't," he agreed. He looked around at the other people on the rotation. Some were military, some UN bureau staff, some contractors. They might know what had happened, but they had no idea what it felt like. Thankfully, none of them recognized him.

The Marine said, "But I saw that," pointing at the IV. "I hope you're recovering?"

"Yes. It shouldn't take long. Good luck with the leg."

"Thanks. They say three months."

He boarded the ship and found his launch couch. The shuttle was well used, smelling of people, disinfectant and musty military bags. He settled in and closed his eyes, not wanting to talk to anyone. They bantered and joked and sounded cheerful to be leaving. He wasn't cheerful, only relieved.

When they sealed up, pressure increased to Earth normal. He breathed deeply.

The acceleration and engine roar took a faint edge off his nerves. Soon. Off this nightmarish hellhole and home.

The tranks worked. He had a scrip for more, and a note that said he should not be questioned about them. Dr. Ramjit had said that wasn't unusual for some of the Special Unit troops, and even some of the infantry. "The ship infirmary should be able to refill you without problems," she'd said. "Especially as we've put out a bulletin about personnel generally suffering stress disorders. We haven't said why."

They even helped with launch sickness. He felt blissfully fine, not nauseous.

He zoned through nothing until the intercom interrupted him.

"Passengers, we are in orbit, and will dock directly with the *Wabash*. Departure for Earth will be only a couple of hours. Final loading is taking place now."

Good. He eyed the tube on his arm. He could have them unplug this, and he could eat real, solid food from safe, quality-inspected producers on Earth.

Well, he'd have to start with baby food. Fifteen days of the tube had wiped out his GI tract. He'd have to rebuild it. That would be fine. And he'd never touch a sausage again.

He unlatched when the screen said to, and waited impatiently. He wasn't bad in emgee, knowing how to drag himself along the couches and guide cable. Several passengers didn't seem to know how, and some of them were even military.

Shortly, he was in the gangtube, creeping along behind the Marine and a couple of contractors rotating out.

There was a small port to his right, looking aft along the length of the ship. He looked out and saw the open framework of an orbital supply shuttle detach a cargotainer from the ship's cargo lock, rotate and attach another in its place.

He flinched, and nausea and dizziness poured into him again.

The cargotainer was marked "Hughes Commissary Services, Jefferson, Freehold of Grainne."

He fumbled with his kit, slapped three patches on his arm, and almost bit his tongue off holding back a scream.

■   ■   ■

Spider's Web
Part 6

An epidemic raged. Isibéal was among those who developed something that presented initially as a cold and then a severe respiratory infection. It progressed into an aggressive pneumonia in the most vulnerable populations. Infants were given priority on the ventilators, while doctors scrambled to keep them alive. Isibéal coded twice, and Moyra could only watch helplessly while the doctors revived her. Supplies were running scarce, and this infection resisted all of the standard treatments.

Within just a few days of the first news reports about the cold-and-pneumonia, the UN started sharing that *their* doctors and medics had a cure, but every ill individual had to travel to Unity to receive it. One of the doctors at the small hospital Isibéal was at even attempted to travel to Unity himself to get information or treatment to save his infant patients, and was rebuffed. He came back livid. The UN insisted every sick individual had to be "accounted for" in order to receive treatment, and it didn't matter if they were in critical condition. To Moyra, this sounded...questionable. Highly questionable. She was not alone in that determination.

Most curiously, the UN troops showed zero signs of it, and the first complaints from the field had shown up after the UN's "census takers" had made rounds. Occasionally working from Isibéal's bedside, Moyra combed through all of the information she could, trying to determine if or what immunization was necessary to shield her own people from this, or if there was some kind of chemical counteragent. Oddly, she was coming up empty-handed. She tasked Jenkins to assist her, pulling him from his other information ferreting.

Unity's reconstruction was finally completed. Moyra Kelly watched complaints fly back and forth between commanders and staff about it being attacked as soon as a building would go up. The local food trucks idea was down, but the decrease in their ability to import supplies directly from Earth meant they were still dependent on local contractors. DalesOP ensured this weakness was well exploited.

ALERT: EFFECTIVE IMMEDIATELY!
All UN personnel are to eat only within the
approved UN dining facilities until further notice.

Moyra read that one aloud, in the safe house's command room.

Sally, the handler on shift, snorted. "But we have people running their approved dining facilities. How's that going to help?"

Moyra shrugged. "Perhaps they think they can better guard their supply lines that way."

"They haven't caught on to the issues with shipping yet?"

"I hope when a shipment of pigs shows up at Earth marked for funeral honors, someone gets the clue that something's up." Moyra snorted. "They've been slow on the uptake, and willing to blame it on 'transposition' errors."

Sally paused. "Do I want to know what is planned for the deceased?"

"Based on the preferences I've seen at the café, probably sage."

Huff #10
"Winning" [May 210]

This morning, I went to a dignified transfer event. With Jump Point 6 still out of commission, we can't spare the ships to transport casualties home immediately. We have to wait until we have enough to "make the trip worth it," as the bean counters say.

I wish I could show the locals what goes on in these ceremonies. Right now we're just the enemy, *aardvarks*. I want to show them we're sons, daughters, parents, siblings, who value and respect our lost comrades. We mourn their loss and celebrate their lives, just like they do. I believe if we can get more of them to see our humanity, they'll begin to understand our mission to help them. Additionally, Earth needs to see these pictures, and families need the ceremonies. Earth does not need the gory details, because we need Earth not to waver on us now.

After this particular engagement, we had six unaccounted for. Well, not completely, our forces did find a few pieces. A hand, a foot, a pile of intestine chunks, just enough to run DNA for positive IDs, but it doesn't do well for recruitment to send troops home in doggy bags. We'll likely never find the rest of the bodies. We've learned to check our food sources, but so far nothing this time. I almost hope the wild animals got to them before the rebels.

The vehicles file onto the airfield at MOB Unity in a longer line than I ever want to see again. Six teams of six guards in their best dress uniforms, complete with pristine white gloves, ascots, and blue dress helmets, line up to receive their trooper.

I stand and walk to the loading ramp. Sandeep follows closely. We render honors the same, since we both descend from British Imperial / Commonwealth traditions. I salute and silently say each name as they're boarded. I notice that one casket seems off, that of Sergeant Palmisciano. He was just over two meters tall, but in a medium casket, for someone roughly 1.75 meters. He could be out of order, or it could indicate how little was left to bury, but I made a note to have my staff double-check the personnel and transport records after the ceremony. I suppose it really doesn't matter what's in the box—no crew on earth will ever open it for the family—it's who the box represents.

The vertol lifts away and the honor guards hold their salute. I drop mine as the aircraft rises above the clouds. At least our people, uniformed people, receive the dignity of these events. Not so much the civservs or contractors. Civserv casualties are so bad that the POLAD split town last week, and I've received no word on a replacement.

Jefferson, the Delph', and all the main COBs are turning into ghost towns, because the nonmilitary personnel are leaving in droves. Civserv and contractors always outnumber uniforms in these kind of places, by two, three, or even more to one. I can't really blame them. The treatment they get from the rebels is disgustingly evil.

The worst was the contract interrogator; we found him strapped to a table, clothing gone, eyes still wide open in terror. They'd dosed him with an MDMA derivative to heighten physical sensations. Then they started removing his skin, in sheets, beginning at his penis. They literally flayed him alive from the dick outward. This was the only report that ever made me vomit. It was so awful, I made sure that no electronic copy exists. I had all of the physical copies burned. I'm still not sure who I feel worse for: him, or the young man they dosed with paralytics and forced to watch. Contractor morale plummeted as they don't have the same legal protections that we do, and they make very convenient scapegoats when things turn out badly. They also behave much worse. It's a rigged game, and it's having an effect.

[*Note: Time stamp "NEXT DAY"*]

I was right to suspect something about the transfer ceremony. The personnel network, we know for a fact, is compromised, and has been for some time. Personnel records, rosters, duty-status reports, casualty reports, are, in the ancient vernacular, FUBAR. This means we can't be completely sure exactly who we sent home on that transport. I called to my executive assistant, SSG Phillips, outside my office.

"Yes, sir?"

"Get me a secure line to Captain Barton on the *Liberty*. Private communication."

"Right away, sir."

I'm glad they found this kid. He seems bright and professional.

I hope this planet doesn't eat him alive. About a seg later, he comes back. "Sir, Captain Barton for you."

"Thank you." I grab my handset. "Captain, are you alone?"

"Yes, sir."

"Good, because this conversation is need-to-know, do you understand?"

He seemed confused but agreed without hesitation.

"Captain, we've discovered some discrepancies within the personnel system. In short, it's possible you may not be transporting who you think you are. What I need you to do, is examine the bodies."

"Sir, those caskets have been sealed since they left the prep station. They were in secure storage awaiting transport and their escorts haven't reported any unusual activity."

"I understand that. Unseal them and do it anyway. I want DNA scans, a full forensic scope. Take old-school fingerprints if you have to. We need to be sure who we're burying."

"We'll get right on it. I'll send you the results as soon as we have them."

"Thank you, Captain. Out."

I get back to work for a div when SSG Phillips buzzes me. *"Sir, Captain Barton on the secured line for you."*

I open the screen again. "Captain Barton, you have news already?"

"Well, sir, DNA tests weren't exactly necessary. We opened the first casket, the one marked for Sergeant Second Class Palmisciano, and . . . we found a pig."

Did I hear that right? "Say again?"

"A pig, sir. I don't know how, I don't know when, but all six bodies were replaced with pigs."

Pigs. Goddamn pigs. Bodies who knows where. I will need to order whole carcasses only for the commissary, so we know we're getting actual animals.

It was too late to order the transport to return, so I did the only thing I could: I ordered the caskets resealed, quickly thanked Captain Barton, and put a gag order on his crew. No one else could know about this. Beyond the investigation into this incident, the question remained in my mind: Was this just the rebels fucking with us, or were they escalating?

FNG

Kacey Ezell

Sergeant First Class Taryn Morello, UNPF, looked up from her breakfast with a scowl as the lieutenant called her name. She unfolded her 190cm-tall body from the metal trestle table and stood up as the young officer approached.

"Morello," the lieutenant said, not meeting her steely blue eyes. "I've got a new partner for you. He'll meet you at the armory."

"Sir . . ." Taryn said lowly, dismay in her voice. "You're not seriously—"

"I've got no one else I can assign him to, Taryn. He's been here three days, and the other squads have all had trouble with him." The officer still refused to meet her eyes, a tiny bit of cowardice which Taryn resented, but for which she could not blame him.

"What kind of trouble?"

"Apparently he's kind of a ladies' man . . . or thinks he is anyway. You can handle that. No one else will take him."

"Well, I don't want him either," she said, shaking her head hard enough that her long blonde braid flipped over her shoulder to hang down the back of her uniform. She sighed and began twisting it up into a bun low at the back of her skull. "Morgern was a friend of mine, and Al-Jabr didn't last five minutes. Schaeffer, Ang, Moritz . . ."

"We're not putting you guys on the front gate," the lieutenant said. "You have a reputation as a good NCO who controls her troops and follows orders. So follow your orders and keep this one alive."

He did look up at her then, and the pleading in his eyes got to her.

"Yes, sir," Taryn muttered.

The lieutenant paused, waiting as if for her salute. She just stared down at him, using her looming height and musculature to her advantage. Sure enough, he spat a low curse under his breath and turned away.

A small victory, perhaps, but Taryn was taking all that she could get these days, here on this godforsaken planet.

"Sergeant Morello, this is Private Chun—"

"I don't care," Morello said, glaring at the armorer. "Just give me my weapon."

"Well," Chun said, drawing the word out. He was a good decimeter shorter than Taryn, and had an accent that placed him as someone who'd grown up in the northeast New York-Baltimore-DC megalopolis. He had a handsome face with features that spoke of his Asian heritage, and a well-muscled physique. He leaned insouciantly against the wall, body armor open in front, holding his helmet by the chinstrap and swinging it while he grinned up at her. "Nice to meet you, too, Sergeant. You're quite the woman, aren't you?"

"Shut up, Fucking New Guy," Taryn muttered, barely giving him a second thought. She took the weapon from the armorer, checked it, then slung it and turned and walked away without another word. Chun pumped his legs to fall in beside her as they headed down the tree-lined sidewalk toward the perimeter of the headquarters region.

"Hey, why so surly? I'm just trying to be friendly," Chun said. His voice had a distinctly unpleasant wheedling quality to it, and he dropped a half step behind her as they walked. Taryn gave a mental sigh and slowed down, forcing him to keep pace with her. Chun blatantly looked at her butt before meeting her eyes with an unrepentant grin. Taryn just stared at him with her "we are not amused" face. He simply laughed and backed up, showing his palms in momentary surrender.

Satisfied, Taryn turned and continued walking toward the back gate.

Unfortunately for her, Chun took her disinterest as a challenge. He continued to drop hints and innuendos at every opportunity. He seemed basically competent at his job, but no one else would associate with him, which left Taryn as the sole target of his annoying attentions. The worst part was that as she continued to not fall for his increasingly obvious ploys, he started to get mean.

"What's the matter, Sergeant? You don't like men?" Chun asked a couple of days later, injecting a sneer into his tone. They were walking back from another stint. "I bet I could change your mind..."

Taryn stopped abruptly and turned to face him, using her size to loom down over him.

"You need to shut up," she said.

"What if I don't wanna? What if I wanna whisper sweet nothings in your ear until you beg for my cock?"

Taryn snorted, then despite herself, started to laugh.

"Unlikely," she said, "considering I've got a perfectly decent cock of my own."

Chun blinked, startled. "Wait...what?"

"I'm demitrans, asshole. I was born with a cock, but I'm a girl. And trust me, I'm betting mine's bigger than yours. Proportionality and all. So shut your mouth and fasten your damn body armor back up until we get to the armory."

"It's too damn hot, and we're done with our shift, anyway," Chun said. "So, are you gay, then?"

Taryn sighed and grabbed the helmet from his fingers, then plunked it down on his head hard enough to make him yelp like a little kid.

"Yes," she said. "I like girls, not that it's any of your business. That's why I kept my male junk intact. Now, if we're done discussing what's in my pants, you might want to remember that we're in an active combat zone. The last two FNGs before you bought it due to sniper fire."

"What are you, my mother?" Chun asked, bowing up, despite being several inches shorter than she. Taryn had had enough. She let out a sigh, then moved. She grabbed him by the open lapels of his body armor and slammed his back up against the nearest tree. Leaves shuddered and fell around them, and his head rocked back and impacted the wood hard enough that Taryn was glad she'd put his helmet back on.

"Look," she said lowly, speaking very close to his face. "I don't know who you are or where you came from before. I don't know what your problem is. I genuinely don't care. All I know is that the last new guy we got was killed within five minutes of getting to his post. He was shot by a sniper that our guys still haven't found. So. Keep. Your. Body. Armor. On."

Chun gave her a look of such naked loathing that she wondered if she'd have to watch her back around him from now on. But when she stepped back, he obediently reached down and closed up the front of his armor.

"Good," she said. "Now, if you're ready—"

Crack.

Taryn flinched and looked up, wondering if she'd broken a tree branch with her violence and was in danger of getting beaned by a falling stick. So it came as a surprise to her when the obnoxious Chun leaned toward her, as if he were going in for a hug.

Only he wasn't leaning, he was slumping.

Taryn reached out to catch him, and stumbled from the awkwardness of the weight.

"Chun?" she said, trying to turn him and get a look at his face.

His eyes didn't look angry anymore. They were more surprised, as if he hadn't expected his lower face to disappear into a red ruin . . .

Oh God.

"MEDIC!" Taryn shouted, as the new guy's blood sprayed over her hands and face and her perfectly fastened body armor.

They raised the force-protection posture again. Full battle rattle anywhere inside the HQ compound. They hired local nationals to build a screening fence around the perimeter out of concrete T-walls and stationed jammers at intervals along the top. Taryn and the rest of her military police company increased patrols and varied routes and times, and it seemed to work for a little while. There were reports of at least two data breaches, as if they didn't already know, given the body count of newbies.

Until a few weeks later, when they got another new replacement in.

"Sergeant First Class Morello? I was told to ask for you."

The young woman couldn't have looked more different from Chun if she'd tried. Her posture and body language as she approached Taryn in the squad room was diffident, almost flinching. She wasn't tiny, but she carried herself like she expected to be hit. With her light-brown hair and big dark-lashed eyes, she looked like a mouse brought to life.

"Who told you to ask for me?" Taryn asked, her voice wary.

"Lieutenant Jamesin," the young woman said. "My name is Private Alix Montgomery. I'm ne—"

"Motherfucker," Taryn swore, closing her eyes and letting her head drop back. She didn't really believe in a god or gods, but had she done so, now would have been a great time to pray for patience.

"I'm sorry," Montgomery said, misery flooding her tone.

"Don't apologize," Taryn snapped. She lifted her head and looked Private Alix Montgomery in the eyes. "How old are you?"

"I'm twenty-one, ma'am."

"Don't call me ma'am!"

"I'm sorry, I—"

"Stop apologizing! Where did they get you, a damn nursery school?"

"No...I—" To Taryn's horror, Montgomery's big brown eyes began to gloss over with a sheen of tears.

"You've got to be kidding me," Taryn muttered, and pushed past the girl before she began to blubber in earnest. "Lieutenant!"

She marched past her fellow MPs, most of whom turned aside and only watched covertly as she charged up to the lieutenant's office. Despite the "open-door policy" upon which they'd been briefed, his door was shut tight. Taryn banged her fist on the door and leaned over to peer in the window.

"Lieutenant!" Taryn shouted. "I need to talk to you!"

Lieutenant Jamesin jumped at the sound of her voice and picked up his comm handset, as if he had been in the middle of a conversation. Taryn felt her face heat up as rage boiled within her, and she kicked the bottom of the door.

"I'm not taking on another FNG!" she shouted. "I'm not!"

The lieutenant turned his chair around, still pretending to speak into his handset. Taryn kicked the door one more time and watched as the booming sound made him jump in his chair. But he didn't get up.

"Fuck!" she said, and turned on her heel to walk out, pushing past the miserable-looking mouse-faced girl with tears in her eyes.

"Stay close to me," Taryn growled. "And don't go outside."

"But how are we supposed to do our jo—"

"Shut up."

Taryn heard the girl draw in a shaky breath, but she didn't say anything else. A burst of regret dampened the edges of the rage that burned within the sergeant's mind. It really wasn't the girl's fault, after all. It was just that the lieutenant was such a shit, making her mentor another newbie. Chun had been a piece of work, with his stupid, possibly transphobic machismo, but he hadn't deserved to die like that. Would little mouse-girl here be next?

Not if Taryn could help it.

She led them along interior corridors from the squad room back to the barracks. No one would be in the bay at this time of day. She walked inside and kicked the door shut behind them. Then she stopped and took a deep breath before turning and looking Private Alix Montgomery in the eye.

"Look," Taryn said, fighting not to cross her arms over her chest. "I'm sorry I barked at you. It doesn't really have anything to do with you at all, all right?"

"All right," Montgomery said, her voice barely a whisper. Her bottom lip trembled, and she looked like she was still on the verge of tears, but she hadn't run away, so that was something.

"It's just that my last newbie got shot right in front of me. There were four others before that. These colonists, man, I tell you. They're batshit crazy, and what's worse, they like it that way. The work crews that came in to build the T-walls? They kept asking us about why we didn't have any youngsters around. Like they knew what had happened and were laughing at us."

Montgomery's eyes went wide. "Really?" she whispered.

"Yeah. So here's what we're going to do. I'm going to take you the long way, through the buildings, to SE...Social Equality, remember? You were briefed about them in basic."

"Oh," Montgomery said, "right."

"Yeah. You tell them I hit on you, okay? Make some shit up, as nasty as you can. They won't mess with me too much because of my rank and time, but it might be enough to get you transferred to a different unit."

"But..."

"Trust me, Montgomery, you don't want to be here."

"It's just that..."

"Hell, you can just tell them about my outburst earlier, and that'll probably be enough, if you sell it."

"I'm not very good at selling stuff..."

Taryn took a slow breath and forced the rage back down again.

"Well," she said, allowing her voice to drop down to the lower parts of her register. "I suggest you *get* good at it, if you want to stay alive. You hear me?"

"Yes si—I mean ma'a—I mean..."

"Don't worry about it, Montgomery. Just follow me."

Social Equality was located in a converted hotel suite in the high-rise that faced their current location. A small park, part of the hotel grounds, sat between the two buildings. It should have been safe, since the courtyard, as the officers called it, was surrounded on all sides by UN-occupied buildings. But Chun hadn't even made it to the back gate, so Taryn was taking no chances.

She led Montgomery down an interior stairwell all the way to the basement level of the main billeting building. Their footsteps clanged on the metal-edged risers, and the sound echoed in the concrete space, so Taryn didn't hear it at first.

"Ma'am... Sergeant? Are you... are you laughing at me?" Montgomery asked, her breath coming quickly. She had yet to adjust to Grainne's higher gravity, she was that new.

"What?" Taryn said, stopping so suddenly that Montgomery bounced right into her. Taryn stumbled down one more step, but caught herself on the handrail and held up a hand. "Be quiet for a minute."

Montgomery closed her mouth. She kept breathing heavily through her nose, but the difference was enough to let Taryn hear it: distant and tinny, like it was coming from a small speaker far away... but it was there.

Laughter.

"Is that what you heard?" Taryn asked.

Montgomery nodded, her eyes wide enough that white shone all around her huge dark irises.

"It's probably just somebody watching a comedy vid in one of the offices next to the stairwell," Taryn said.

"They must have it up pretty loud for us to hear it through a cinderblock wall," Montgomery replied, her voice just as soft and diffident as ever.

"Let's just go," Taryn said, starting down the stairs again.

She ignored the cold shiver of doubt that slithered down the back of her spine.

❖   ❖   ❖

The laughter followed them intermittently all the way down to the basement level. From there, Taryn led Montgomery into a low-ceilinged service tunnel that connected the MP's chow hall to the loading dock on the north side of the building.

"Hold up here," Taryn said, motioning to Montgomery to step to the side. "Let me make sure it's clear."

Montgomery frowned, then nodded and backed up against the wall. Taryn leaned out and checked. As she had remembered, the loading dock opened onto a ramp onto an alleyway a little over ten meters wide.

"I'll go first," Taryn said. "See that duraplast door opposite us, over there? I'll get it open, and when I say, you run flat out as fast as you can for the door. Don't go straight there, either. I want you to zigzag like your life depends on it, okay? Just like in training."

"Okay," Montgomery said, sounding breathless.

"Like your life depends on it," Taryn said one more time. Then she hustled out onto the loading dock and ran to the edge, leaping off and careening across the open space to hit the brick wall on the other side. She rolled right and ducked into the alcove that held the door. It was locked, but she had a key, thanks to having to do security sweeps.

She got the door unlocked, then looked up toward the loading dock. Montgomery's pale, anxious face seemed to float in the yawning doorway. Taryn took a deep breath, then motioned her forward.

"Go!" she yelled.

Montgomery darted out and tried to make the leap off the loading dock like Taryn had done. But instead of running out her landing, she tripped and fell flat on her face.

"Get up!" Taryn bellowed. "If I let this door go, it'll lock! Get up and keep moving!"

Montgomery scrabbled in the dirt, her hands and knees slipping as she fought to get up. Taryn heard the *whizz-crack* of gunfire, and saw the dirt jump less than half a meter from the hapless girl's head.

"Montgomery!" Taryn screamed, "Get Up! Move!"

The mousy girl got her feet under her and began to hobble, crouched over, toward Taryn. Other troops in the area scattered and shouted. Taryn fumbled at her personal comm, and called,

"This is Morello, I'm engaged on the north end of the compound, between buildings 1532 and 1534! Small arms. I need eyes in the sky immediately," she said, just as three more shots cracked out, raising a line of dirt right behind Montgomery's heels...as if they were chasing her.

Or taunting her.

Taryn reached out and grabbed hold of Montgomery's outstretched arm and threw herself into the relative safety of the doorway. She landed hard on her ass, Montgomery's smaller frame impacting her chest and knocking her down.

"Get off," Taryn said, shoving the girl. Montgomery was making gasping, hiccupping sounds as she slid to the floor next to Taryn. At their feet, the heavy door slammed shut, and a line of dents appeared, punching their way up the center of the door with the cracking *thunk* of bullets hitting duraplast.

Taryn took a moment and closed her eyes, letting her head fall backward. How the hell had they known? Montgomery couldn't have been exposed for more than a minute or two, even with her tumble. Where were these bastards watching them from?

"S-sergeant?" Montgomery said, her voice weepy.

"Yeah, Montgomery, I'm all right. Are you?" Taryn said, sitting up with a grunt and looking around. They were in another utility hallway, but her memory had served her well. She knew how to get to SE from here.

"Y-yes. I think so. W-were they shooting at us?"

Oh, to be so young and stupid.

"Yeah, kid. They were shooting at us. Well...shooting at you, anyway," Taryn said. She rolled her body over to her hands and knees, then used the wall to help her get up. Full battle rattle was heavy, and heavier still on godforsaken Grainne. As she stood, more MPs began pounding down the hallway toward the door they'd come in through. Taryn grabbed Montgomery's arm and hauled her up and out of the way.

"Morello?" one of the arriving MPs asked. Borani, her counterpart in this sector.

"Yeah," she said. "We were engaged right outside that door. Shots came in from a higher angle, so either an elevated position or a drone. I'm not sure which."

"We'll figure it out," he said. "What were you doing here?"

"Taking the private to SE," Taryn said with a grimace. The

guy pursed his lips, then frowned and pressed his fingertips to his earpiece. When he looked up, his grimace had changed to a grin.

"Good news," he said. "It was a drone. One of ours went up and shot it down from above. They just announced it on the 'net. Good work...and good luck with SE."

"Thanks," Taryn said, and grabbed Montgomery's arm to turn and march her down the hallway. Drone kill or no drone kill, she was getting this mousy girl the hell out of here.

"Wh-why would they be shooting at me?" Montgomery asked, her voice squeaking on the last word. She looked completely forlorn, her huge eyes wide and waterlogged.

"Because you're new, kid," Taryn said, letting her hand drop as they walked. "Remember I told you they killed the last two new guys we got? It's like it's some twisted game for these psychopaths."

"B-but I didn't *do* anything," Montgomery whispered.

"Sure you did. You came here."

"I thought we were here to help these people."

"Yeah, well. Like I said, they're psychopaths. They don't want our help. They just want us dead."

"Me, dead." Montgomery said in a whisper. Taryn didn't bother to reply.

She was right, after all.

The utility corridor led beneath the north wing of the old hotel, below the conference rooms and fitness center that now served the UNPF brass. Once they reached the ninety degree bend in the building, Taryn knew that they had entered what had been the main part of the hotel.

Just a short elevator ride left and they were home free.

"Sergeant Morello?" Montgomery said as they whizzed up to the twenty-second floor. They had the elevator to themselves, and her little voice echoed weirdly in the hollow box.

"What?" Taryn asked, keeping her eyes fixed on the display above the door, willing the numbers to tick up faster. *Twelve, thirteen...*

"I-I just wanted to say...thank you—"

"Don't thank me," Taryn growled. *Sixteen, seventeen...come on, damn it, go faster!*

"But you saved my life," Montgomery said, her voice barely a whisper.

"It's just my job," Taryn said. She darted a glance over at the girl huddled in the opposite corner of the elevator. Montgomery looked like she wanted to say more, but the chime dinged, and the floor gave a soft jolt. They had arrived on twenty-two.

She felt a tiny fraction of the knotted tension in her shoulders and neck ease as they stepped out into the carpeted hallway. A couple of admin pukes walked by, their expressions slightly condescending about troops in armor, and slightly relieved, probably at not having to wear it.

A sign on the wall directed them to the right, and three doors down, another sign informed them that they'd found the Social Equality office.

"Go ahead," Taryn said, reaching back and giving Montgomery a little push toward the door. "Just knock and tell them that you want to file a complaint."

"But I—"

"Trust me, it's the quickest way to get you out of here."

"But you haven't been—"

"Damnit, Montgomery," Taryn said, feeling shoulders clench up again. "I didn't drag you all the way here just so you could sing my praises and stay. If you stay, you'll die, got it? Just knock on the door, tell them you want to file a complaint, and they'll take it from here. I promise, I won't get anything more than a slap on the wrist."

The girl looked thoroughly miserable, but then, that was nothing new. But she stepped up toward the door as Taryn moved to the side, where she'd be out of view of the SE personnel inside.

Montgomery knocked. Taryn heard the door open.

"Hi," Montgomery said. "I-uh . . . want to make a complaint?" She lifted her voice at the end, as if it were a question rather than a statement, and turned miserable eyes to look at Taryn.

"Is someone there with you?" Taryn heard the male voice of the SE troop. "Why don't you come inside?"

Crash!

Crack!

The back of Montgomery's head blossomed open like a flower in a time-lapse vid. Thick red splattered all over the textured wallpaper. A high, incessant ringing echoed in her ears as she watched Montgomery's body crumple to the floor. Somewhere far away, a man's screams tried and failed to pierce through the sound.

She turned to look into the hotel alcove doorway. Oh. The screaming man wasn't far away. He was right there, on the floor, hands over his ears as he crouched amid the broken glass from the picture window behind him.

The picture window that had an amazing panoramic view of Jefferson City, spoiled only by the small drone that hovered not ten meters outside the broken glass—but just outside the perimeter of the HQ compound.

"Shut up," Taryn said. Maybe it was the tinnitus, but her voice came distant as well. Distant and detached . . . exactly how she felt. She glanced down at Montgomery's mousy little corpse and stepped over her to enter the SE office. She felt, rather than heard, glass crunching under her boots as she approached the window.

Once again, the sound of laughter trickled in over the ringing in her ears.

To her left, a table sat next to the entryway. A rectangular glass vase held dead flowers there. Taryn reached out, grasped the vase in her right hand and hurtled it with all her strength at that hovering, laughing drone. The heavy glass hit right on one of its four stabilizing fans, and the thing began to spiral down twenty-two stories to the concrete below.

But she could still hear the laughter.

Taryn ended up in the clinic, being treated for shock and temporary hearing loss. The UNPF doc prescribed a few days rest and a course of nanites for her ears.

He didn't or couldn't or wouldn't do anything about the mental images. Every time Taryn closed her eyes, she saw the back of Montgomery's head opening up like the petals of a flower. It made it difficult to sleep. It was enough for Taryn to wish the docs had given her some heavy painkillers to knock her out.

It was enough to drive her to drink.

"I thought you didn't like hard liquor," Thorvald Okeke, their supply sergeant and general "guy who can get stuff" said when she turned up in his barracks room with her request. Okeke's ice-blue eyes held a look of concern, and a frown creased his coffee-colored features.

"Ordinarily, I don't," Taryn said, gruffly. Too gruffly, perhaps. Okeke was a friend, and he seemed to be genuinely concerned. "Do you have something or not?"

"I can get it," Okeke said slowly. "But you know too much of that stuff can fuck with your brain, right?"

"Yeah, I know," Taryn said. "But damnit, T, if I don't get some sleep soon..."

"Nightmares?"

"Memories. Laughter. I can't stop hearing it..."

Okeke let out a heavy sigh and stood up off his bed.

"C'mere, girl," he said, holding out his arms. "Bring it in."

"T, I don't want—"

"Bring it in or no liquor."

"Fuck," Taryn said, shaking her head. But she stepped forward into her friend's embrace. Okeke was a couple inches taller than she, so she rested her forehead against his collarbone and closed her dry eyes.

"It's okay, you know," Okeke said, his chest rumbling as he spoke. "You can cry if you need to. It's healthy."

"I know," Taryn whispered. "But I can't. I've tried. I'm just numb."

"Shit," Okeke breathed. "Okay. Well, I'm here when you can, girl. You know that."

Taryn nodded against his shoulder.

"All right," he said, squeezing her one last time before dropping his massive arms from around her body and stepping back. "I've got something special for you, because I like you. But you have to promise to take it easy, this stuff is no joke."

"What is it?" she asked.

"Some shit the locals call 'Blacque.' It's illegal, so don't be caught with it, but it will fuck you up right. Just a half shot, okay? That should be enough to put you to sleep." He walked around behind his bunk and opened up the standard-issue wall-locker that they got as NCOs. His had a false back, apparently, because he opened this up and pulled out a flat bottle with a faintly blue-tinged black liquid inside.

"Thanks," Taryn said. "How much do I owe you?"

"Shut the hell up," Okeke said. "You just get some sleep and feel better. Remember I'm here."

"Thanks, brother," Taryn said.

"Anytime."

The local stuff worked as promised. That night, Taryn took a half shot before lying down to sleep. She closed her eyes and woke

up the next morning feeling rather better rested, even if her mouth
did taste like an excavated sewer. For once, though, there was no
barely heard laughter, which was nice.

She was still on medically prescribed rest, so she got up, hit
the gym, and was actually feeling slightly optimistic as she headed
to the chow hall, her hair still wet from her shower.

"Hey, Sergeant," one of her guys greeted her as she grabbed
her tray. She gave him a small smile and filed through the line.

"Sergeant," another one of her MPs said when she finished
loading up and stepped out toward the tables. "We're sitting over
here if you want to join us."

"Sure," Taryn said, her optimism growing. This was like old
times, before . . .

Well. She didn't want to think about before what. So she
focused on carrying her tray over to the table and finding an
open spot. The MPs shifted to make room, and soon she was
seated amongst her people, snorting a soft laugh as someone
made an off-color joke.

About midway through her food, though, Taryn noticed
something.

"Who is that?" she asked, gesturing with her fork at a lone
individual sitting at the far end of the table. He appeared to be
male, of medium height and build, with blond hair. He sat quietly
eating, with a look of frustration or anger on his face.

"Ah . . . that's the new guy," the woman seated to Taryn's right
said. "He arrived this morning."

"He looks experienced," Taryn said.

"Yeah, command got him from Base Solidarity near Westport.
He's a first-class problem child."

Now, Taryn knew what she should do. She was a sergeant
first class, and esprit-de-corps was her job. She should ream her
MPs asses for isolating the new guy, then she should go over and
loudly and publicly invite him to join them. Maybe he could be
shaped up into a good troop.

It's what a good NCO would do.

But she couldn't. She just couldn't make herself do it.

"I'm done," she said abruptly, standing up and stepping back
over the trestle bench. Someone in the chow hall laughed, the sound
ringing out through the crowd to wrap around Taryn's throat and
squeeze. She grabbed her tray and half ran to dump it in the return

window. She used too much force, causing a rattling crash from her dishes and flatware falling. That meant that behind the window, someone else would have to clean up her mess.

It would have mattered to a good NCO.

But it didn't matter to Taryn. In that moment, all she wanted was to get back to her room, and take another shot of that local oblivion, to shut out the sound of that mocking laughter. It had to be easier than watching another newbie die.

To everyone's relief, nothing happened for the next couple of weeks.

Taryn came back from her medical furlough and found that the new guy had been assigned to another NCO's squad. That made her life much easier, since she had no intention of interacting with him at all. Somewhere deep in the recesses of her mind, she hoped that maybe *she'd* been the trigger. That the insurgent assholes were watching her and targeting their newcomers by virtue of her proximity. So maybe, if she stayed away, the new guy would be safe.

Plus, he really was a jerk, as it turned out. Taryn overheard her fellow NCO ripping the dude up one side and down the other one morning after breakfast, and the guy had the gall to talk back. He was a bit antiauthority, it seemed. He actually walked off duty.

But then, she had a few days before.

Not that it surprised her in the least. Word must have gotten up the chain about their problems keeping newbies alive, so it stood to reason that their unit would now become a dumping ground for problem children. It sucked, because it would further decrease their company's effectiveness . . . but she had to admit that it was an elegant, if cynical, way of making a shitty situation somewhat useful.

This place was a shithole that ruined everyone.

Bloody hell, but she hated herself for even thinking that way. Her sudden culpability slammed her in the face with almost physical force. No wonder the new guy—she still didn't even know his name—was being a jerk. No one had talked to him since his arrival. He was being completely ostracized, and he likely had no idea why. As the ranking NCO, it was up to her to set the example . . . and she hadn't.

"Come on, Morello," she muttered to herself as she watched the new guy's NCO stomp away. "Time to put on your big-girl panties and get the job done. After all, it's been two weeks, and this guy's been on the gate multiple times. Maybe someone rolled that asshole sniper up in one of the last patrols or something. That would be awesome."

With this pep talk bolstering her confidence, Taryn pushed back the edge of the headache she had from too much of the local liquor the night before and got up to follow the new guy as he headed back to a seat in the corner. He'd tried to sit with the others when he first arrived, she knew, but he must have gotten tired of everyone getting up and leaving him alone at the table.

"Hey," she said as she approached. He sat shoveling a bowl of lumpy cereal into his mouth and didn't look up. Taryn pursed her lips and looked around to see her usual tablemates all watching her with wide eyes. She waved a hand at them, beckoning them to come closer. They looked at each other, then slowly started to obey. She moved to sit down opposite the new guy, bending so that he could hardly miss her.

"I said hello," she said.

"I heard you," he replied, looking up for the first time. Sure enough, anger and hurt simmered in his eyes. "I just figured there wasn't no way in hell you were talking to me, Sergeant."

"Yeah," she said. "Well, I was. I'm Sergeant First Class Taryn Morello."

"I know who you are."

"What's your name?"

"Why do you care?"

Taryn took a deep breath and reminded herself that she deserved this. Her squad started to cluster around, and she pointed at the benches to indicate that they should sit.

"This is Jim, and Beckett, and Amare, and Irina, and Fadel," she said, pointing at each one. They murmured hello or gave a nod, or otherwise acknowledged his presence, which had the new guy staring at them in disbelief.

"Okay, what the fuck is this?" he asked, pushing his bowl back away from himself. "I've been here for over two full weeks, and you guys all act like I don't exist. Now, all of a sudden, you want to be buddy buddy?"

Taryn sighed. "Yeah," she said. "Basically."

"That's fucked up. That's beyond fucked up."

"Yeah," she said again. "It is. Just listen, okay? You're the fourth FNG we've gotten in the last month. The last three individuals to fill your spot didn't last more than a day before they were killed. Mostly sniper shots, though one was a drone kill. It's always the new guys, never any of us vets. That's why no one talked to you. We didn't know how long you would last."

The new guy stared at her, his mouth slightly open, for a long, uncomfortable moment. He blinked, then looked around her at the men and woman she'd introduced. Amare gave a grave nod.

"But you're not assigned to me," Taryn went on. "And it's been two weeks, so we're thinking that maybe they got the guy, or that they were specifically watching to see if I took supervision of a new troop, or something. Anyway. After this long we thought . . . well . . . screw it."

The new guy closed his mouth with a snap, then shook his head and shrugged.

"Well," he said slowly. "I can't say that it's any less fucked up . . . but . . . hell, I'm glad you're here now. I'm Andris." He stood up and offered his hand. Taryn shook it, and just like that, the spell broke. The others crowded around, introducing themselves, shaking the man's hand, laughing and talking loudly as they finally, finally, felt free to welcome a new brother to the group.

For the first time since Montgomery's death, Taryn felt the dark pressure in her chest ease just a little. The maelstrom of emotions that continually raged inside her skull quieted just a bit, just enough to let her feel true, genuine pleasure when she saw Andris's dour expression turn to a brilliant smile.

Most of the group had finished eating before Taryn walked over to Andris, so they just hung around while she finished her meal. Someone had invited Andris to join the group for their usual basketball game over in the big gym in the other building. He'd accepted, happily, and the group fell into its usual trash-talking routine as they cleaned up and headed out of the chow hall.

The sidewalk to the other building ran through a group of trees, which was all to the good as far as Taryn was concerned. It kept them free of sightlines from outside the compound, and made an attack by drones far less likely. Plus, it was pretty. This hell planet had so much wrong with it, but the flora was worth looking at, for sure.

They set out on the path, under the spreading leaves, accompanied by the chirping and chittering of birdsong. Someone said something funny, and Andris tilted his head back and laughed.

And so did the tree next to him.

The tree didn't laugh, of course, it just seemed that way. Taryn froze for just a second, staring up into the crisscrossing branches and the wide, tangled leaves that blotted out the aching blue of the Grainne sky. Laughter filtered down from those leaves. Laughter that sent ice running through her veins.

"Andris, get down!" Taryn screamed. "Cover Andris!" She suited actions to words and leapt forward, using her greater mass to tackle the new guy and throw him to the ground. Laughter erupted from all around, as if the birds had quit singing and started cackling at Taryn and her troops while they looked helplessly around for the threat.

"Sergeant, what—" Andris asked, his voice muffled by the way Taryn kept his face pressed into the dirt.

"Shhh. They're watching us, laughing. It's gotta be their drones. Their damn drones! But you don't want me, do you fuckers?" she went from whispering to Andris to screaming at the trees, flattening as much of her body over the man's prone form as possible. "I'm right here! Shoot me... but no! You just want our new guys! Well you can't fucking have him!"

The laughter intensified, and the other members of her squad looked around with wide, frightened eyes. There had been other people enjoying the park, too. From her vantage point, Taryn could see a few of them running away from the commotion. Shouts in the distance told her that backup was coming. She hoped they got there in time.

"Taryn..." Irina said.

"They musta bugged the trees," Taryn said, "They've been watching us for weeks."

"Clever," the trees said, and began repeating it over and over. "Clever, clever!"

They repeated the word for several seconds, and then abruptly stopped. Taryn held her breath for a moment longer, then let it out slowly.

"All right," she said, "This is what we're going to do. You guys gather around. I'm going to get up, and then we'll keep Andris surrounded. Andris, you'll have to crouch low, but as long as we shield you, you should be safe. This is a game to these guys, they only want you, not any of us. Otherwise they would have shot me already. Does that make sense?"

She shifted her weight, preparatory to getting up off of him. He didn't respond.

"Andris?" she said again.

"Taryn," Irina said, her voice soft and scared, "Look."

The female MP pointed at her new friend's face, which had gone darkly purple in color. Taryn pushed off of his body and bent to look closer. A thin line of blood ran from Andris's nose and mouth.

He had no pulse.

"Look at this," Beckett said, sounding sick. He bent down and flipped one of the wide leaves over, exposing what looked like a child's model of a tracked vehicle. Only this one was fitted with a long needle that glinted in the light that filtered beneath the trees.

"They got him while we were staring at the trees," Taryn whispered. "It was an ambush all along! The gardeners, or the construction workers... or someone... Damn it!" She pushed up to her feet and shoved her way through the ring of her horrified troops.

"Sergeant—!" Beckett called after her. She ignored him and just marched back to her room to crawl into the bottle.

The UNPF cut down the pretty trees and tore up all the grass in the courtyard park. Not that it mattered. The next new guy fell victim to another drone attack within forty-eight hours of arrival. Ten days after him, the next chick was found with her throat slit in the women's locker room.

After that, Taryn lost track. She finished that first bottle and coerced Okeke into giving her another. She stopped showing up for duty, reasoning in her drunken state that maybe if she never showed up, the insurgents would stop killing the newbies.

It didn't work.

The next two dudes were both sniper or drone kills while on duty. Crazy shots, from what she heard, that would have been near impossible for most people to make. Taryn figured the insurgents must have had cameras in the squad rooms, too, and recommended new force-protection guidelines had all MPs masked up to hide their identity. Then she specifically pushed to have a couple of guys come sweep her quarters for bugs.

"Sergeant, you gotta come back," Beckett begged. "The whole place is falling apart without you. People are suspicious of one another, everyone's scared."

"Can't come back," Taryn said, fighting back the urge to let out a huge belch. "Tracking me."

"I don't think so," Amare said, shaking his head in the negative. "They got the last two new guys, even while you were 'on leave,'" he said, using finger quotes.

"But I can't do the right thing," Taryn snarled at her friends. "Can't be a good NCO, because the newbies will die. Can't ostracize them, because that's not being a good NCO. So if I'm not going to be a good NCO, I'm going to get drunk."

"You're already drunk," Beckett said, his voice pleading. "Come on, Sergeant—"

"Forget it, Beck," Amare said. "I told you. She's useless. They got her too. You heard her talking about the laughter... Your room is clean, Sergeant Morello. At least, we can't find any of your damn bugs. Enjoy your leave, until the captain finds out, anyway."

Taryn knew she should have said something to him, but the truth was, it was just too damn hard. So she lifted her bottle to her lips and took another drink.

Taryn sat up straight in her bed, sweat drenched, head pounding. Her ears rang with the memory of mocking laughter...

Wait.

No, that was real laughter.

She tried to get up and tangled her feet in the blankets, sending her sprawling on the cold floor of her quarters. Nausea rose within her, and she had to hold very still and breathe slowly while she fought it down.

Careful, Taryn, she told herself. *Crap, when was the last time we ate anything?*

She didn't have an answer to that, but since dry heaving was worse than throwing up, she took the time to regain control before getting slowly to her unsteady feet.

The laughter beckoned her forward, like the tantalizing glimpse of a lover's smile disappearing around a corner. She followed the sound toward her bathroom and slapped on the light above the mirror.

And stopped, transfixed, at the face that stared back at her.

She hadn't been taking proper care of herself, and it showed. She'd lost weight, leaving her face haggard and square. Her prominent jawline made her look like a man. Her eyes squinted through pouchy, heavy bags. Her skin looked sallow and unhealthy, and her hair was so much ratted straw.

"Fuck," she breathed, barely recognizing herself.

The laughter stopped, then started up again. Louder.

"Oh," she said, scowling at her reflection. "Was that funny?"

The laughter stopped then.

"Guess not," she said, then bent to splash water on her face.

"*No,*" a voice issued from somewhere overhead. Maybe in her light fixtures? "*It's not really funny. You were a good NCO once, Sergeant Morello.*"

"Maybe," she said, leaning on her forearms over the sink. She reached up and turned the water off. "Maybe I was once."

"*You were. It has been an honor to watch you lead your young men and women through some difficult circumstances.*"

"'*Some difficult circumstances*'?" she asked. Now the laughter crept into her own tone. "I guess you could call it that. You killed my newbies out from under me. I watched them die one by one!"

"*Yes. We are at war.*"

"You're telling me," Taryn said. "I should really get cleaned up and go back to work, or they're going to court-martial me eventually."

"*Sooner than that. Proceedings have begun.*"

"Well, fuck. That sucks. Guess my family back home won't get my pay after all."

"*We could help you with that, Taryn.*"

"What?"

"*You have a window.*"

Taryn straightened and looked at herself in the mirror again.

"If I do this," she said slowly. "Will you stop?"

"*No,*" the electronic voice answered. "*We are still at war.*"

"But I will be at peace."

"*If that is what you believe.*"

Taryn didn't know what she believed. But she knew her mom could really use the benefits that would be paid out on her death.

She also knew that the bottle just wasn't cutting it anymore. No matter how drunk she stayed, she still heard the crack of gunshots, the mocking laughter. She still saw the light dying in Chun's eyes, in Montgomery's face, in Andris's eyes.

More than anything else, she just wanted it to stop. And the local drink she'd nicknamed Oblivion couldn't do the job any longer.

Sergeant Taryn Morello squared her shoulders and pushed off the sink of her bathroom vanity. She turned without another word and walked through her pigsty of a room to the window that had been boarded up in accordance with the force-protection directives. She flung the curtains wide and slipped her fingers around the edge of the impact-resistant plastic board.

Then she leaned back, every muscle in her tall frame straining as she slowly pulled the board back away from the window frame. One by one, the adhesive dots holding it in place popped and failed. The board cracked and bent with a sound like a rifle shot, and with one last great wrench, Taryn pulled half of the board free.

She let it fall down beside her as the late spring night air rushed in. It smelled sweet and wet, like the local vegetation. It made her head spin.

"Good night, Sergeant Morello," the voice said from somewhere in her room behind her. *"You were a valiant enemy."*

She thought she saw a thin, spiraling trail of smoke, invisible but for the reflection of the streetlights below, start to snake its way toward her.

"Fuck off," she said, and stepped out to meet it.

Huff #11
PSYOP [May 210]

Morale on the ground is firmly in the shitter.

My J6 is barely scratching the surface of just how utterly the rebels have penetrated and compromised our networks. We purge sensitive information as we find it, but entire units have been doxxed, including their dependents. We're finding publicly posted vids of insurgent drone and security camera footage including an office bombing, and the disturbing instance of a seasoned MP NCO's suicide—with full audio.

I spoke at a conference of my senior enlisted leaders today, and by all accounts, the new ones are terrified and the old hats are pissed. Suicides are up across the force. Leaders at all levels are preaching resiliency and every counselor we have is working overtime, but it's bad. So many of these troops, just kids really, are so inexperienced that they simply lack the instincts and coping skills to deal with this kind of psychological onslaught.

Centuries of research show how suicides tend to cluster in military units; once one goes, more follow. One suicide report referenced a 30-year-old father hearing a child crying for her daddy in the middle of the night. Another was the 19-year-old daughter of a recently deceased single mother back on Earth. She reported hearing a woman humming a lullaby. Seasoned officers aren't immune either. The shelter commander who marshaled the survivors after the Skywheel attack, and went with the first damage assessment party to the flight line? She committed suicide this morning. We've taken every member of that party we could find under medical hold for behavioral health.

These "cognitive targeting vectors," as the J2 calls them, are things easily culled from compromised personnel files, open social media, electronic communications, and the unauthorized personal devices the troops brazenly use. Devices they hook up to unauthorized accounts and transmission stations. The real killer is the sheer number of troops dealing under the table with the locals for contraband entertainment—vids, modified VR players, and stacks of unlicensed porn. Now, add in cheap transmission time and data to send messages home nonstop... and it's all compromised, recorded, and weaponized. Idiot troops eagerly buying the rope that's hanging them.

As a result, the rebels have infiltrated the whole unclassified government, military, commercial, and media datanet ecosystem. Payroll, promotions, orders, maps, everything might be doctored. Emphasis on "might," because so far, only a few artifacts are confirmed, but it's enough that we trust practically nothing without third-party verification. This slows everything down. Frankly, those systems have been screwed up for so long that no one even noticed until forensics started investigating.

The drones though—that's just sick. Our people are using tunnels to get to work, let alone avoid harassing fire and intel collection. I mentioned the MP NCO. This woman was groomed; they deliberately broke a good, decent human being by making sure every cherry troop under her died, but made sure she lived, without a scratch. They had her so perfectly targeted, they knew exactly what to do. Her room was bugged. The kind of thing one would think they'd save for someone like me, they did to a nobody NCO.

The rebels might win this, but at what cost? Is it really worth it to them? Someday, everything they've done, all the petty cruelties, and the big ones, will come back to haunt them. If we can't escape what we've done, right or wrong, then neither should they. Eventually, they'll pay too.

Spider's Web
Part 7

A notification from DalesOP came through. He'd been tied up on a particular PsyOps target round the clock for weeks, while Damocles and Moyra managed the other tasks. It was uncharacteristically terse, just requesting her to respond.

:: Dal? :: Moyra replied. :: You rang? ::

:: I seem to have promised my target we'd be sure her family got taken care of. ::

:: Is it over? ::

:: Except the mopping. ::

Oh dear. Moyra felt that asking for details would make it harder on her friend. :: We'll do what we can to make good on your promise. I'll get the database adjusted. ::

:: Thanks. ::

Moyra personally made the changes to one Sergeant First Class Taryn Morello's records, taking petty satisfaction at removing a bureaucrat's whining about Morello's performance toward the end. Fourteen effective NCOs had been selected for special targeting; Morello resisted the longest. Only one NCO had sufficient family connections and money to get called back to Earth after the second incident with an underling.

This war was hard on the families of the UN troops, and Moyra felt pity for the damage they were inflicting. Grainne *needed* the outcry back on Earth, from the pigs in the caskets to bureaucrats being assassinated in gruesome ways, to force *them* to force the bureaucrats into ending this pointless, bloody, stupid, ego-wanking war. It had been sold on Earth as an easy task. It had to be made clear that it was costing lives, sanity, and suffering.

But it was even harder on the families of Grainne.

Isibéal made a slow, painful recovery. DalesOP took nearly as long to recover from what he'd done to Morello, but he was able to return to command team tasks. Slightly freed, Moyra turned her attention to looking for more weaknesses.

Codger Command

Mike Massa

"Vicky, that aardvark is looking at your ass again!"

Victoria automatically controlled her impulse to look over her shoulder, and instead continued to walk towards the only other resident present. Betty was poolside, draped languorously across a blue waterproof chaise lounge. Her voluptuous friend thoroughly filled an otherwise modest one-piece, and she flashed a bright grin from beneath her oversize sunglasses, proof against the late morning Iolight.

Victoria quickly stuck her tongue out, earning a nose wrinkle in return from the unrepentantly smiling blonde.

"Keep that shit up, dear heart, and I'll let the air out of the tires on your old-lady scooter," Victoria said, shrugging her pool bag off and dropping it onto the lounger adjacent to her friend. She shot a quick glance across the pool, where her quarry, the much younger khaki-clad Earth colonel, was ostentatiously studying his paper.

"Was he really?" she continued more softly, strategically bending over to rummage in her things.

"Oh, I wasn't making it up," Betty replied quietly. "I don't think Colonel Jones-Durand's a tit man since he's been ignoring these for the last twenty divs." She shook her ample bosom enough to make her point.

Victoria carefully didn't look over her shoulder. Some men could be influenced by the fulfillment of their desires, others by denying them. The mostly friendly colonel of the UN research station seemed to belong in the latter group...and had a thing for older women. Months ago the UN had "requisitioned" Victoria's special retirement home, located high in the Dragontooth Range. Within days most of the residents had departed the mountaintop campus, leaving only those who, as far as the UN knew, had nowhere else to go. Victoria had managed to retain only three effectives, besides herself.

For values of the word "effective."

It had fallen to her to try the oldest gambit of all, despite her age. Even with all that modern medicine could offer, from persistent medical nanos to dermal therapy, stem-cell treatments to high-tech organ replacement, a lifetime of Grainne's slightly higher gravity eventually caught up with everyone, including Operatives, Freehold's clandestine special warfare force.

Her workout routine, sheer stubbornness and a ruthless diet had kept her figure trim enough to attract Jones-Durand. Of course, his predilection helped, and he hadn't guessed her age to within a decade, yet.

"Do I smell chlorine again?" Vicky asked, sniffing the pool hall air experimentally.

"Bert bombed the pool, something about the Earthers and their bad hygiene overloading the regular filters. It's gonna be hell on your dye job," Betty said, squinting across the pool. "Hey, he peeked again. Definitely an ass man."

"Well, I've been dressing to give him the occasional opportunity to appreciate it," Victoria said, scuffling her sandals off before reaching for her swim cap. "Speaking of asses, did you get any word on the you-know-what about the additional arrivals?"

"Don't know much," replied Betty, lowering her voice to a murmur. The notoriously bad acoustics of the natatorium could only be trusted so far. Caution was in order, since they relied utterly on the covert comms network that Bert, their resident retired Special Projects troop, had found. The Freehold military had hidden an encrypted signal in the entertainment broadcasts, piggybacking on apparent interference. Its existence was one of the most closely held secrets that the Freehold had left.

Courtesy of her addiction to Meijian flash-dramas, which had the added benefit of being utterly boring to everyone else, Betty had the most unmonitored access and had become their de facto comms officer.

"I've haven't been able to get anything in days, but the newbies are replacing their unexpected attrition," Betty said. "They're down four in the last month, counting that Earther they found wrapped in firethorn last week."

They shared a brief, fierce grin.

"I *just can't imagine* where he might have gotten the idea that there was some undiscovered enzyme in that plant," Victoria replied. "Hmm. I wonder if any of those scientists will use Frank's insect repellent."

The warming weather produced a bumper crop of blood-hungry native and imported Earth insects, and the Earthers were suffering disproportionately. Another retiree, this one a former intelligence officer, had offered them an effective repellent based on *local* materials.

"All they said is that the 'varks were gonna bump up security, which they've done," Betty said, referring to the HQ message. "We're supposed to keep our ears spread for more intel."

"Well, at least they know who the go-to girl is for spreading," Victoria said, replying in an equally low tone as she stretched out her lean legs, ostensibly examining her pedicure. She noted a furtive rustle of paper from their observer across the pool.

"Bitch!" her friend replied with twinkling eyes.

"Whore!" Victoria answered, completing their rote formula.

Accompanied by a "hubba hubba!" from the peanut gallery, she strode lithely to the edge and smoothly dove in.

Strenuous pool workouts were among the remaining outlets for an aging Freehold special-warfare veteran. Victoria could push her pace, keeping her heart rate at nearly her old unaugmented best. Like any retired Operative, she was no longer *officially* issued the supplements which allowed her body to synthesize the range of chemicals in her onboard pharmacope, but she retained all the skills accumulated over a lifetime of service.

Victoria settled into a strong rhythm. Her arms and back pulled her cleanly through the water while reducing extraneous motion and splashing. Beneath her, the pool shifted from a transparent blue to a darker color as she crossed the five-meter section under the diving platform, and then back again. Completely in the zone, time seemed to pause as she shuttled between the ends of the fifty-meter pool, her thoughts mercifully free of the ceaseless churning turmoil that had begun since the start of the Earth invasion of her planet, her home and her Goddess-damned retirement.

Her peripheral vision picked up a flicker of motion as she approached a flip turn, abruptly pulling Victoria from her reverie. She rested a hand on the scratchy nonskid of the pool edge, to discover it was neatly bracketed between the toes of a pair of shiny black boots.

She looked up the length of sharply creased khaki trousers to see the unctuous smile of another Earth officer. This one was the female half of the new UN security officer's personal attack dogs. From her regulation brush cut to her lean physique, Lieutenant Porter was a near copy of her superior officer, right down to the sneer.

"Ma'am, your pardon," Porter said, smirking. "I'm sorry to interrupt your swim. I understand from my mother how important it is for senior citizens to exercise."

Being yanked out of her exercise trance did ugly things to Victoria's mood. Her chest still heaving, she fought against her urge to snatch the young officer by the ankle and drag her into the deep end.

I'll show you a godsdamned senior citizen.

"Major Horvat has called a meeting of the remaining residents to discuss additional security precautions," the sable-haired bitch went on, extending a white towel toward the pool edge. "I'm afraid that he requires all residents to muster in the common hall as soon as possible."

Ignoring the offered towel, Victoria glanced around to see Betty already packing and the Earth officer missing. She awarded the lieutenant a curt nod before wordlessly launching herself off the pool wall again.

She intended to finish her current lap.

You couldn't let the Earth pigs feel like they had complete control, especially when, for the moment, they rather did.

Major Horvat tapped the lectern impatiently.

Upon arrival, he'd done the basics: sweeping the campus for weapons, explosives or unauthorized communications equipment. He'd confiscated an impressive number of guns, including several military-issue weapons illegal for civilians on his own planet. He'd installed cameras, sniffers and microphones. Just keeping his charges safe from the local environment was hard enough. Willful stupidity, like wandering into the coils of a carnivorous plant, was a new twist. Days ago, one of the scientists imported from Earth had decided on a lunchtime solo hike and then waited too long to activate his emergency beacon. Horvat's team had found him an hour later, unconscious and wrapped in a semimobile, thorned vine endemic to the region. Bleeding from hundreds of puncture wounds, his discolored body had already begun bloating in reaction to the alien toxins. The biologist might never awaken; the surgeon suspected brain damage due to anaphylactic shock.

Meanwhile, Horvat was still expected to keep the rest of the science boffins out of trouble. The colonel nominally in charge of this circus was nearly no help at all. Jones "We have an obligation to show them the human face of the UN" Durand was much too soft to impose proper order on the UN personnel, let alone on the retirees who were still allowed to remain.

The commanding officer had even cautioned him against harassing the elderly residents who had nowhere else to go. Never mind that a little pressure would go a long way toward convincing them to live elsewhere and make Horvat's job much easier.

Fuming, the major waited for the last of the retirees to arrive and scanned the already seated Earth contingent.

The new arrivals filled in the chairs on their side and spread across the aisle to the residents' section. An additional fifteen UN neuroscientists and nanobiologists had arrived with scant warning. There was plenty of room in the common area since the overwhelming majority of the former residents of this home had been taken in by families immediately after the long overdue UN occupation of Grainne. The latest batch of visitors were accompanied by additional security, which he'd immediately absorbed into his existing force. The mission warranted the improvements.

Not that the local residents were much threat.

He watched one of the gray-haired retirees wheel himself inside, internally wincing at the man's disfiguring double leg amputation. The newcomer slid into an open space at the end of row, and patted the arm of another seated old man. That one alternated between gently rocking himself and rubbing his scarred, black head. The bald rocker was almost lost inside his baggy denim overalls. Horvat checked his clipboard for these two.

Garcia, Franklin E. Fifty-six Grainne years old, nearly eighty-five Standard. No known family, indigent, employed as handyman to offset cost of residency. Lost his legs in an industrial accident.

Jackson, Bartholomew A. Seventy-nine Standard. No known family. Also indigent. Grainne military veteran. Pool cleaner, when he wasn't curled into a corner, sucking his thumb. He had a full complement of limbs, but courtesy of a long-ago accident, the man was labeled as differently abled, shorthand for the label that Horvat applied privately; retard.

Both of them had been shuffled off, tucked out of sight and largely ignored.

Horvath grimaced.

It was exactly that sort of situation that Earth's superior economic and social systems were designed to prevent. Despite the good intentions of the UN administrators who were attempting to bring modern social statism to this benighted backwater, the resistance to Earth's lawful occupation continued to mount. Cost projections known only to the brass and Security were far outstripped by the actual bill.

Next to the simpleton was a chair-free space filled by a mobility scooter, occupied by a grandmotherly type with blonde hair streaked with gray and a figure that was over-generous, if anything.

White, Elizabeth A. Seventy-two Standard. Widow. Retired, PhD in botany. Another charity case, she "worked" in the retirement home's greenhouse, tending a truck garden and some Earth plants that didn't do well in Grainne's highly variable climate and thinner atmosphere. Her knowledge might be of some use, if one could overlook her slatternly manners.

The wooden door to the conference room nearly slammed open as another Grainnean strode in, wearing a bright blue jumpsuit and track shoes. This one was a troublemaker whose apparent hobby was the creation of incessant and acerbic complaints. She submitted near daily screeds about security restrictions, invasion of privacy allegations and damage to her precious landscaping from the UN armored vehicles and wheeled transport.

Yeah, he knew her name alright.

He flicked his eyes back down to his list anyway.

Steinberg, Victoria C. Allegedly sixty-nine Standard, which statistic clashed with her quick stride and bright eyes. Also a widow—lucky husband to have escaped that sharp tongue. Former professor of economics, she'd been flagged due to her interstellar travel, resulting from her guest lectures on New Caledonia,

Alsace and NovRos. Like the other remaining residents, she didn't appear to have any living relatives that could take her in. She'd been employed as the recreation coordinator, according to the records pulled off the administrative computers.

That last was credible given her athleticism, rare among Earth-side retirees. Porter had reported that Steinberg had stalled at the pool. Horvat narrowed his eyes, filing that away for later.

"Thanks for saving me a spot, Fred," Victoria said, squeezing past his wheelchair.

"Nice of you to make it," he answered grudgingly. "Now that you're *finally* here, the Senior Citizen Squad is fully assembled."

She'd persuaded him to seem as debilitated as possible so prior to the arrival of the UN, Frank had cached his fully customized and synchronized prosthetic legs off campus, and now they, along with almost all their weapons, were out of reach. His irritation with the wheelchair took the form of cheap shots at their collective superannuated status and by derivation, her little cell. Technical know-how or not, he was still exasperating.

"Hey, boss!" Bert tittered very quietly, still rocking himself. "Polyp Patrol is standing by!"

"Shut up, Bert!" Victoria whispered, slipping past Betty's travel chair and plunking down in the empty spot. "You're only supposed to pretend to be a moron. What did I miss?"

Unlike Sara and Bill, the two remaining retirees who actually had no living family and genuinely suffered from dementia, Bert was perfectly lucid. His humor was, if anything, even more lowbrow and darker than Fred's. That was consistent with every other Explosive Ordnance tech she'd ever known, retired or not.

"Nah, he hasn't even warmed up yet," Betty answered her, her aluminum knitting needles quietly clicking over her latest project. "Of course, if you wanted to be less conspicuous, you might try a lower-profile entrance, sweetlin'."

"When faced with rudeness, step on their toes until they apologize," Victoria replied acerbically. "Speaking of which, wasn't this stupid meeting supposed to have started already?"

A glance at the time displayed on his wristcom prompted Horvat to begin, though there were still a couple missing retirees. The commander and several other UN officers were also tardy.

Meanwhile, he didn't have all day.

"Welcome, all!" he said, projecting his voice. "Thank you for being *on time*. We've called this meeting to provide a follow-up to the incident last week, where Dr. Buckley was seriously injured as a result of getting tangled a thicket of"—he consulted his notes—"firethorn. Unfortunately, he remains in a coma. Due to the seriousness of his case, we're reevaluating our safety procedures to address the serious risks from local fauna and flora. This will require new precautions to keep us safe in the face of the hostile planet-side environment."

He ignored the stir on the UN side of the room as well as the eye-rolling on the other and pressed on.

"Effective immediately, there will be a two-person rule for any movement beyond the gardens and exercise patio," Horvat said sternly, disregarding the rising mutters. "Further, both permanent UN staff and short-term visitors will check out a comm from Security, maintain it on their person at all times, and leave the settings configured to auto-burst location to the Security and Operations center. A list of off-limits locations will be posted in the refectory. All personnel, including the remaining retired residents, are responsible for conforming."

"That's outrageous!" complained Steinberg, standing up. "This location for the retirement and therapy center was selected precisely because it was safe! The only people at risk are you Earthers who are overdue to understand that they shouldn't climb crumbling shale cliffs, drink unfiltered water and oughtn't touch unrecognized local plants!"

"I'm not finished, Mrs. Steinberg," Horvat said tightly. What was really overdue was instilling a little discipline around here, but no, Jones-Durand required kindness and respect for the retirees. "The east wing has been requisitioned for the new arrivals that you see here. It will be henceforth off-limits to all nonessential personnel and local residents. All interaction between the UN personnel and Grainne residents will be limited to common areas, such as this meeting room."

"That's where our private quarters are, you imbecile!" offered the grandmother in the motor chair. "How am I supposed to move my things from this chair?"

Grumbles from retirees backed her up and Horvat noted uneasy glances among the Earth scientists.

"I will arrange assistance to relocate you to different quarters," the major said through clenched teeth.

"I don't need your meat hooks pawing through my panties, young man!"

Laughter rose from both sides of the aisle this time, and Horvat strangled the polished wood along the raised edges of his podium, throttling his anger.

"Silence!" he said loudly enough to be heard over minor commotion. "These rules are for your own protection. Let me assure of severe penalti—"

"Major, thank you for your attention to duty," Colonel Jones-Durand said from the rear of the room, where he'd suddenly materialized. "Perhaps you could join me and Dr. Phillipi for a short meeting in the corridor."

"Sir—" the security officer began to protest.

"*Now*, Major." the colonel said with a smile that didn't reach his eyes. "If you please. Lieutenant Porter can address the routine issues in the meantime."

Horvat paused, gauging the colonel's intent, before silently waving his deputy up to the front. After a brief pause, Porter began the standard orientation briefing while the two officers slipped down the carpeted side aisle to the door, trailed by the doughy scientist in charge of the new tech section.

Outside, Jones-Durand spun on his heel and faced the other two. Horvat refrained from sneering at his putative boss's carefully styled hair, perfect, whitened teeth or his tailored garrison uniform, complete with Sam Browne belt and baby-blue cravat.

"Major, in simplest terms, we're here for the duration," the colonel stated, looking directly into Horvat's eyes. "Securing this location is important, but neither threatening aging grandparents nor attempting to muscle our own technical experts into compliance will support out long-term mission."

"Sir, my mission is security, not showing the flag," Horvat said flatly, keeping his hands tightly clenched behind his back. He jerked his head towards Phillipi. "Or coddling this bunch. You know their mission as well as I do, and I intend to support it with my full strength. However, I report directly to the Security commander in orbit."

"*Our* mission, Major," the colonel said, stepping a bit closer. "Indeed, *the* mission, is to pacify this planet and return it to full integration with the UN. That's why the doctor and his staff are here. To work quietly and securely on nonlethal alternatives that can accelerate our operations. Rousting retirees, or dramatically altering the routine will just irritate the rebels and draw attention to our operations here, exactly when we need to be invisible. Find a way to keep us secure, commensurate with our strategic mission or I will find your replacement. And I report directly to General Huff, who commands the entire system. Are we clear?"

After a brief hesitation, Horvat nodded stiffly. However, that wasn't enough for the CO.

"Further, we will discuss how we can use these older, retired residents as a test case," Jones-Durand said, warming to his subject. "This generation may have closer, more positive ties to Earth. If we can win them over, we may have part of the strategy to reduce the use of coercive force against the very population that we're trying to absorb."

The security officer very carefully did not snort. The only places that the UN had made significant headway in pacifying this crazy planet had been where overwhelming military force was used, usually at great cost to both sides. The entire planet was homicidal, and armed. Jones-Durand was crazy if he thought he could win a "hearts-and-minds" campaign just because the retirees left behind were old and used up. No matter who he was flirting with.

Horvat forced another nod.

"Perhaps I can think of some sort of social exchange in order to ease the tensions of the necessary move of some of the residents from their current accommodations," Horvat said, smoothing over the tension.

"Thank you, Major," Jones-Durand said. "Now, to my office. The first wave of product was released for use a few days ago and we're about to start shipping the next generation of nanites. Dr. Phillipi here has more ideas on the next steps."

Despite his PhD, Captain William "call me Bill" Jiankui was much younger than his fellows and was often relegated to the neuroscientific equivalent of scut work by the oh-so-esteemed Dr. Phillipi. He was young enough to still pay attention to exercise, and despite the extra effort required to overcome both Grainne's higher gravity and the two thousand meters of elevation of the resort, he was determined to get his run in. Buckley's stupidity had meant finding a new running partner. Fortunately, Jiankui had previously made sorta-friends with the otherwise intimidating Lieutenant Porter. As usual, she was kicking his butt on their first lap around the property.

His footsteps crunched in the gravel, mirroring the lighter tread of his running mate.

"Keeping busy these days?" he asked, trying to distract her.

"It's pretty boring, actually," Porter replied, swiftly leading him down the gravel running path toward the wooded half of the property. "Except for the importance of the research that your team is working on, there really isn't much call for security here, except keeping you guys from killing yourselves by getting poisoned by the local plants."

"Why did Buckley go out there in the first place?" Jiankui asked, huffing with exertion.

"Don't know," the security lieutenant answered. "We boxed up all his personal effects and sent them along to HQ in Jefferson. Nothing else to do. Say, what's that smell? Some weird body spray?"

"Um, no," Jiankui replied, trying to sustain his breathing rhythm. "The bugs have gotten worse so I got some insect repellent off one of the residents, the old guy in the wheelchair. It's pretty effective so far, works better than our issue shit."

"Well, he must have distilled it from ass-crack sweat," Porter said, accelerating even more, no doubt to punish him for having the foresight to avoid being bitten. "Try to catch me before I reach the tree line."

Porter had the advantage of being lighter, and let's face it, in better shape, what with being ex-infantry and not a neurobiology specialist. Jiankui watched her legs flash as she sped ahead on the gravel path, leading him between two large trees and into the darkly shaded area under the tree canopy that covered this part of the estate. The thick vegetation drank in all sound but her footsteps, crunching ahead of him. Stung at being outperformed by a woman, he pushed through his discomfort. His own footfalls sounded more quickly. He'd been training much harder recently and it showed as he began to gain ground. He felt a second wind, and heartened, he picked up the pace even more, really digging into the path, further narrowing her lead.

She heard his footsteps and glanced over her shoulder with a smile. Her eyes widened and she cursed.

"Fuck!"

Then she really began to sprint, which seemed like a bit of an overreaction to being overta—

Jiankui's thoughts were interrupted by a rushing sound, more felt than heard, and then a sudden stabbing weight that punctured his neck and head.

"I'll put every one of them into the ground!" Victoria said, her voice climbing in volume with every syllable. "I will kill—"

"Keep your voice down!" Betty said sharply. "Softly, softly now, Vicky. I know. My children and grandbabies are out there too. Now we know why there hasn't been any mail for weeks. They were prepping this, this filth."

"What's going on?" asked Frank, as he rolled into the shared sitting room that adjoined their new sleeping quarters. "Why the hubbub?"

"This!" Vicky thrust the flimsy at him. "Betty was finally able to use the entertainment unit alone and pulled this off the message queue. It's days old, dammit. The UN is using bioweapons on civilians in order to get outlying areas under compliance and compel a census."

"Respiratory infections which have turned pneumonic in some populations, aerosol-dispersed virus causing open lesions in mucous membranes, vision damage, swollen airways, and occasionally 'hemorrhagic in susceptible populations.'" Frank read aloud, skimming the report. "What the f—"

"Keep going."

"Potentially lethal to persons under two or over sixty without treatment," he finished. "Counteragent 'still in development.' Those dogfuckers."

Victoria replied, her lips compressed into a flat line. "Fetch Bert. We've got to start planning."

Horvat looked down at the deceased, waving his hand at the strong stench of musk coming off Jiankui's body.

It had taken several hours to track the blood trail from the site of the initial attack on the running path. They'd found where the predator had stashed what was left of its meal, no doubt planning on finishing later. The captain looked left and right, partially blinded by the very bright tactical lights of his armed and armored team. The damned thing was probably watching them even now.

Porter cradled an assault rifle, her lean white face composed despite her narrow escape.

"Sir, we're better off conducting an examination of the remains back at the clinic," she said, scanning the blackness that surrounded them. "I recommend against leaving a team here all night."

The Grainne wilderness was largely untamed, including the bits close to habitation. Even the locals stayed out of the woods at night, for the most part.

"Well, at least cause of death is straightforward," Horvat replied, looking at the naked body. The yellow and red spine was plainly visible in the scooped-out abdomen and one forearm was missing. Jiankui's head and, well, his haunches appeared intact but very reddened, almost abraded. The security captain wrinkled his nose in distaste at the strong smell coming off the body.

"Insect repellent," said Porter, noticing his grimace. "Rank stuff, smells even stronger now."

"Baugh, what, did he bathe in it?" Horvat said, waving his hand in front of his face. "Get samples of everything in situ, then bag and tag the body for transport. We'll get our science lads to perform an assay for anything useful. Half of this ecology is still undocumented. I've got to report to Jones-Durand. We've got that damned get-together tomorrow."

"This is a perfect place for the reception!" Dr. Phillipi bubbled happily to his escort. "I had no idea that the botanical garden was so extensive, Dr. White!"

The steamy, humid air in the greenhouse was making him perspire a bit and he patted his brow with a monogrammed handkerchief. The narrow paths, edged with flinty volcanic stone, forced Phillipi to follow his hostess in her travel chair. The hulking myrmidon assigned by the overbearing security officer brought up the rear.

"I keep telling you to call me Betty, Carlo," the white-haired retiree said, rolling alongside him in her scooter. "Nobody has called me doctor since I was young enough to have grad students. Now I spend as much time knitting as I do tending these beauties."

She gestured around them at the riot of carefully tended plants. "It's a labor of love and a memory of home."

"I don't specialize in botany, but I can appreciate how this exquisite collection, Doct— I mean, Betty." Phillipi couldn't believe the breadth of the specimens in what he'd assumed was a hobbyist greenhouse. He leaned over to read the little name tags on the specimens. "I've never seen a better example of a Grainne Callista vine! And this is an *Amorphophallus titanum*? From Earth? The blending of plants from both planets is the perfect backdrop for the reception."

"Well, I love botany in general," Betty said. "I've tried to curate representative Earth specimens, from the Amazon basin to the Pacific Rim. I love my planet, but our heritage is important too."

"I couldn't agree more," Phillipi said striding to the next cluster of plantings. He trailed one hand down the vines covered with thick, waxy green leaves. They girdled a mature Grainne tree that stretched nearly to the roof, ten meters overhead. He read the tags on the container. "Blue maple and...Chondrodendron? This pairing is another example of two species that are mutually intertwined."

"Just so," the woman replied, studying the degree to which the vine had wrapped the trunk, scarring the bark. Phillipi saw her frown for a moment before she shook her head and forced a bright smile. "Oh you poor thing, look at your perspiration! There's a water fountain at the entrance. Why don't you ask your escort to fetch us some, I'm thirsty too."

"Yes, quite," the preoccupied scientist said, examining another plant. He gestured distractedly towards the front of the space, hidden by the dense plantings. "You there, find some glasses and bring us some water."

Mr. Monobrow looked skeptically at the pair before shrugging and turning away.

"As a fellow scientist, I can appreciate how our planets need to cooperate," White said, glancing at the retreating back of the guard. "But I don't really understand the exact nature of your research."

"Well, there are some sensitive bits," Phillipi said cautiously. He was coming to appreciate the local botanist, but technically there was a war on. "The military aspect, you understand. My entire mission is to find ways to reduce the violence of this unpleasant and unnecessary conflict."

"How can you do that?"

"I'm interested in nonlethal options," Phillipi replied. "Halting or deferring confrontation before it becomes deadly."

"Are you making progress?" his escort said, restarting her chair down the path towards the rear of the greenhouse.

"Actually yes, were steadily improving our . . . well, our project," Phillipi said with growing enthusiasm. "We're finding new alle . . . err, new ways to reduce the capacity for violence. But, my dear, I'm afra—"

"Carlo, it's just me, who am I going to tell up here?"

Pompous, egotistical, self-important puffwad, Betty thought as she emphatically keyed the greenhouse office terminal for Vicky's private room. *Doughy little twatwaffle with a comb-over needs an overdose of—*

"*What's up?*" Vicky answered on the first ring. "*When's my fitting?*"

"No time now," Betty said tersely. "I just finished talking to the aardvark scientist, Phillipi. I didn't get a lot, but I got the confirmation that we needed."

"*And?*"

"They're making the shit here," Betty said. "The research is backed up in orbit but there's copies of all the work locally. Best of all, the antiviral is onsite."

"*Holy crap, that's exactly what we needed!*" Vicky exclaimed happily.

"We can—"

"Betty, behind you!" Vicky's face contorted in alarm and Betty jerked her head around to see the scowling military goon that had escorted Phillipi. The security man loomed in the office doorway that she'd left open in her haste.

There was no way that he hadn't heard everything.

Forrest didn't much care for this duty, but so far it still beat getting sniped and bombed and rocketed and poisoned by the freaking animals that claimed this planet. Three squares, keeping track of a bunch of fidgety scientists and a handful of old folks was light work, even if none of them properly respected him. Take that fat-ass Phillipi, for example. First he'd sent Forrest off for water as though he were a servant, and then he'd dropped his "special" handkerchief somewhere in that sweatbox of a green-house. Naturally, he'd peremptorily ordered Forrest to find it.

The security sergeant had a sudden rush of blood to the head and decided to ask the old fat lady that had escorted Phillipi if she had a lost and found, or something. The cool relief of the air conditioning in the little office was wiped away by the conversa-tion she was having on the terminal.

As soon as he heard her talking about counter-nanos and research it was obvious she'd gotten information out of the foolish scientist. That meant she had a date with Major Horvat and his pet attack bitch, Porter. Forrest was proud of his muscles, which had enabled him to mostly shrug off the higher gravity that affected so many of his comrades. It was the work of a moment to pluck the lardo from her motorized chair and start dragging her to see his boss.

"You over-muscled oaf, let go!" the old lady said. "This instant!"

"Afraid not, ma'am," Forrest said, tugging her toward the door.

"Well, then at least let me bring my purse!"

"Afraid not, ma'am," he repeated but even as he spoke, the wriggly bitch twisted and lunged for her handbag, spilling fuzzy multicolored balls of yarn.

He sighed, made a long arm, and grabbed her left wrist hard enough to make her gasp. He started towing her hefty frame into the greenhouse, and the humidity immediately restarted his sweat. He squeezed the bones in her forearm just out of spite, eliciting a second gasp.

"You're coming with me, now, and if you want to complain, you can tell Major Horvat all about the conversation that you were just having," Forrest said, knowing that it wouldn't do her a lick of good. "Maybe he won't care, and you can get right back to your stupid plants, but I wouldn't count on it. So we're going. Now."

"Well, fine!" the biddy huffed. "At least let me walk with dignity!"

Forrest kept his grip, but it would be easier to let her walk instead of actually towing her all the way to the main building. He kept her skinny arm in his grasp, but allowed her to gather her feet beneath her, sling her purse strap over one shoulder and smooth her dress one-handed.

He gave a her a little tug. She nodded and he began to walk to the front of the greenhouse, staying to one side of the path so that she could keep up. His mind was already leaping ahead to the consequences of his catch. *Promotion? R&R? Hell, would they send him back to Earth?*

His daydreaming was interrupted by a blurred motion towards his head. His flinch wasn't enough to entirely avoid the blow and he registered a sharp stabbing sensation on his neck. He jerked his captive's wrist hard and, wheeling, reflexively raised his left hand to strike her. She'd already fallen, breaking his grip in the process. The old lady looked up, terrified, clutching a bloody knitting needle in one hand.

He touched a hand to his neck and looked down, and sure as shit there was bright red blood, mercifully a small amount, smeared over his palm. The crazy bitch had just tried to punch his ticket! With a fucking *knitting* needle! His rage built and he stepped forward to kick the improvised weapon out of her hand. Somehow, his leg felt sluggish and he stumbled instead, coming to rest across the flagstones that lined the path. He caught himself awkwardly with his left hand, since his right arm had also decided disregard his orders.

Forrest half rolled to his left, feeling a wave of warmth and dizziness wash over him. He heard scrabbling sounds, and the old biddy came into his field of view, laboriously climbing from her knees all the way to her feet.

He tried to sit up but only managed a sort of convulsive twitch. His breathing was shallow and the dizziness was more profound. Could it be blood loss? The itsy-bitsy hole, a scratch really, that she'd made in his hide was only bleeding a little bit.

The woman bent over him, clutching a fist-sized flagstone in hand. Her wide eyes were partially obscured by her stringy gray-blonde hair.

"You insufferable Earthers invade my home, and never bother to learn what I keep here?" she huffed. "All these are just stupid plants to you? Ha! Feel warm? A little short of breath are we? Can't move? That's called curare, you dumb bastard. If you don't find a good friend who will start breathing for you, you're going to suffocate, because my poison is going to finish paralyzing your diaphragm in a minute or two. But you know what?"

Her hand dipped towards his face, but he couldn't even move his eyes to follow the motion. A searing pain scorched its way along the side of his neck and he felt a gush of some hot liquid paint his shoulder and arm.

"I've just severed your carotid artery, you son of a bitch," she finished, straightening all the way up. "So in my professional opinion, you're going to die from lack of circulation before you get around to feeling the lack of respiration."

The light coming through the greenhouse roof was very bright, and it blurred in the tears that sprang in Forrest's eyes.

Horvat shook his head and then looked back down at his draft report.

Buckley had never woken up. Instead, his heart stopped and declined to be restarted.

Buckley, then Jiankui and now Forrest. Two invaluable scientists and now one of the very specialists intended to protect them. Three fatalities in what was supposed to be a sleepy little retirement home.

Horvat just could not buy it and his superior in Jefferson wasn't going to either. And yet there were no connections between any of the three that Horvat could see. He'd responded in person to the latest death, pounding along behind the security team that responded to the frantic emergency call from the greenhouse. It had been called in by the older of the two retiree females, White. She'd been out of her chair, kneeling on the blood-stained white gravel, red to the elbows, trying to put pressure on a neck wound, even though Forrest had already stopped bleeding by that point.

The preliminary investigation couldn't come up with anything better than "freakish accident." A stumble in high gravity and a fall that gashed the security noncom's neck open, opening his carotid artery. It was preposterous. The only other theory was even more ridiculous. It required the unarmed pensioner, who could barely stand on her own, to have overpowered his trained and equipped man, all without sustaining any injury herself.

He'd have to send the report up and await developments.

Just outside the foyer that led to the reception, Vicky glanced down at what the shimmering green dress was doing to her ... developments. It was interesting.

Against her better judgment, she'd allowed Betty a free hand with wardrobe suggestions for the UN reception. Betty had decided to employ the style that Victoria immediately named "Slut

Mode." The discussion became quite spirited and Betty called for reinforcements from the Retired Regiment.

"The goal's to get the data out!" had gone Victoria's argument. "If we don't do that, nothing else matters. And I can't do that while missing half, hell three-quarters of my clothes! I haven't needed to be this obvious since, well, forever!"

"Sweetie, it has been forever," summed up the consensus reply from the other three. "Also, the entire plan relies on you getting one of the officers alone long enough to, ah, acquire the biometric data. Then you've got to make it to the lab without arousing suspicion and then you've got to get the data to the lounge. As soon as you do that, we pop the surprise and then drive out of here. All of that means looking like anything but a Freeholder trying to be sneaky."

Her capitulation had led directly to the iridescent, strapless gown that now sheathed her. Victoria's daily workouts had kept the flab quotient to a minimum and a piece of shape-wear elastic stiff enough to double as armor against light pistol rounds was compressing her stomach against her spine.

Of course, it was also doing wonderful things for her butt. Not to mention the twelve-centimeter heels that left her perched on her toes. Or the slit all the way to her thigh. So, yeah, it was the opposite of sneaky.

"It looks fine, Vic," Frank had offered during the first fitting, which all four had used as an opportunity to coordinate. "Just be glad that these idiots are going ahead with the party, otherwise we'd be boned. How about next time you two leave off getting all murdery until after we've done the important bits?"

"Screw you, Frank, it isn't your ass literally hanging in the breeze!"

"Stop bitching. Besides, sooner or later they're gonna figure out that the incidents are connected and then we're screwed," Bert had opined. "Just be grateful that you're not courting vertigo from rocking yourself five divs a day. I happen to think that it looks very professional."

"A professional what?" Vicky had answered before turning to her impromptu seamstress. "The way you're fitting this, you're planning to keep a percentage on anything I make on my back."

"Mmppph," was the extent of Betty's reply, through mouthful of pins. Followed by, "Think of it this way, Vicky: Jones-Durand will be too fixated on your figure to notice that we're going to rip off his lab, kill his scientists and murder him. Does that help?"

Victoria could get behind that, so she'd stopped wiggling and focused on the op.

Betty's instincts hadn't been wrong.

When Victoria glided up to greet Colonel Jones-Durand and Phillipi, their struggle to keep their eyes fixed above her shoulders was evident. The hunger on the little rotund scientist's face would've been alarming if he hadn't been part of her plan.

"Mrs. Steinberg, you look lovely," Jones-Durand said, with a smile that was only a millimeter shy of becoming a leer. "And your suggestion to hold the party in the sports complex was perfect. I confess that the ornamentation far exceeded what I expected."

His eyes performed a textbook up-down pass of her form.

"Thank my friend Bert," Victoria answered, gesturing toward a table at the edge of the room where the slight man rocked himself back and forth. "It's a big night for him—despite his disability, he loves parties and decorations."

Bert had been busy during the unsupervised night.

Dimmed wall sconces lit the natatorium, supplemented by Gealachlight, which shone through the transparent roof. Floating on the pool were floral wreaths which each held real anachronisms, clusters of actual candles. Their cheerful flames reflected distractingly on Victoria's sequined gown and the several hundred gaily colored balloons which clustered against the ceiling.

"Indeed, madam," the colonel said, bowing over her hand. "I'm pleased that all the remaining residents elected to press ahead with our get-together despite the recent unhappiness. If we can find common ground here, it augurs well for peace between our planets."

Victoria murmured something pleasant in return as he turned to introduce her around the group. The round of introductions slowly expanded from other officers to the even broader circle of scientists. Betty rolled up to be introduced, shortly followed by Frank. With the increase in the little circle, it hadn't required much effort to cut her quarry out of the cluster, and herd him upstairs.

"You know, Colonel," she said over her shoulder as she climbed the steps, "The vista from the resort's viewing platform can be breathtaking, and it's quite private."

"Well, my dear," Jones-Durand said, his gaze flickering between her face and her swaying hips. "I don't see how it can compete with your charms. But if you insist, I'll give it a chance."

As Victoria led him upward, she reflected for a moment that what she'd planned wasn't fair at all. During the ruthless selection process to join Special Warfare, she'd learned that fair fights were for fools. Winning was what counted. That's why she'd stayed in shape all these years. That's why she'd never decommissioned her pharmacope.

"Oh, I'm all about chances, Colonel," Victoria replied as they stepped on the landing together. She carefully reached past him for the door, brushing her chest against him as she turned the lock. "Surely you'll allow me a chance to persuade you."

"Please, call me Herbert," Jones-Durand said, sliding an arm around her waist with a grin. "What sort of chance did you have in mind?"

"A chance for my homeland to remain free," Victoria said. "And I just know that you're going to *see* it my way."

Jones-Durand's suggestive smile froze, warring with sudden confusion.

With a quick mental command, she activated her Boost.

Horvat kept one eye on the security vid monitors while casually flipping through a sheaf of operations summaries. The war might actually be tipping in Earth's favor. The nanite weapons had dramatically reduced partisan activity. There had been a greater number of fatalities among civilians than hoped, but some breakage had been expected.

A chime, accompanied by a blinking red light, alerted him to the arrival of priority message traffic. He lowered shiny black boots from his desk and leaned over to tap the pad on his inbox. The icon for encrypted security traffic appeared. That was redundant since the UN comms system itself was secure, but it did keep serve to keep information compartmented. He removed the digital key from his dangling security pass and unlocked the message.

The forensics on the accidents had come back from Jefferson at last. He scanned the screen and gasped. He punched for a flimsy while rereading the details with something akin to growing panic.

Buckley's diary? Jefferson ops had found notes that the legless handyman had suggested firethorn as a source of an indigenous salve.

Jiankui's insect repellent? Synthesized pheromones, traced to the "retard" poolboy, mimicking the sexual secretions of rippers, large predators endemic throughout Grainne's wilderness.

And lastly, Forrest? Traces of a Terran poison commonly called curare, made from a climbing vine. Possibly from the goddamned greenhouse woman in her goddamned travel chair.

Horvat was well trained, and therefore he didn't actually reel in shock, though he felt an icy sensation descend his spine as he considered the ramifications. At least three of retirees were actually murderers or direct accomplices. Murderers who at this moment were circulating with the entire, irreplaceable cadre of scientists making the war-winning bioweapons.

He slapped the emergency alert, grabbed his personal carbine and headed for the door, shouting into his comm.

Lying behind an armored door, the biolab had been protected by extensive physical security, including seismic and thermal sensors. Entry had required simultaneous presentation of passwords and a retina scan. She had both.

Learning the password had required her to use a variety of persuasion somewhat different than Jones-Durand had expected. Next to her impatiently tapping, red-enameled fingernails, Durand's eyes rested in a small polymer bag.

Inside the deserted biolab, security was limited to elementary safeguards that did little more than enforce quality control. Victoria immediately slotted Fred's prepackaged infiltration software. The rapidly scrolling list of files cascaded down the terminal, reflected in her hungry eyes. The mole programs sneered at these rudimentary protections, and rapidly began siphoning files.

Even as she worked, the others would be at the reception, socializing with as many of the UN scientists as they could, keeping them in place. As soon as she signaled them that the data was out, they'd excuse themselves and epoxy the fire doors. Bert's "special" was a straightforward gas bomb that would fill the swim hall with chlorine gas in sufficient concentration to liquefy unprotected lungs in less than a seg. At least that was the plan.

As soon as the data-stick was loaded, she'd head for the entertainment unit and—

A whooping alarm rang throughout the lab, accompanied by a blinking red strobe.

Deep in conversation with Dr. Phillipi, Betty lifted her head minutely when she heard the muted alarm sound. All the scientists seemed oblivious, but Betty watched Lieutenant Porter first jerk upright before lifting a wristcom to her face. The security lieutenant answered the call, obviously receiving information. As Betty watched, the UN officer pivoted her head and stared right at the Freeholder in her scooter.

Mutual recognition of the emergency's origin was instantaneous.

There wasn't going to be enough time to seal the room and trap the scientists inside, Betty realized. Three unarmed retirees weren't going to be a significant impediment to thirty panicked Earthers, never mind the armed security bitch. Even if they released the chlorine from its hiding place in the pool filter, the researchers would still escape. She looked to Frank, still in his hated chair. He scanned the room and then met her eyes, nodding once. They both glanced at Bert, who'd stopped rocking, and instead stood perfectly still, one hand on the pool filter assembly.

One of the contradictions of explosive ordnance disposal was that the EOD technicians responsible for defusing explosive devices also liked making big booms themselves. And all good EOD techs believed in backups. Bert had prepared a doozy, hoping that he wouldn't need it. Chlorine wasn't just a lethal toxin, but a powerful oxidizer as well. Mixed with a modest amount of fuel, such as the hydrogen that he'd used to fill the thousand or so aluminized balloons in the room, and a source of ignition, he'd improvised a weak fuel-air explosive device. Naturally, even a modest example of this sort in confined space would have spectacular effects, if you overlooked the little problem of survival...

He looked wide-eyed at both Frank and Betty, and reached into his pocket where he'd hidden the remote.

"Your attention, please!" Porter yelled, cutting across the party talk. "Attention!" Betty glanced back over to see that the bristling security lieutenant had drawn her pistol and was aiming it at Betty. There was exactly no more time.

C'mon Bert. Just do it. Do it!

Betty closed her eyes, thought of her grandchildren, and smiled.

✧   ✧   ✧

The call with Porter dropped just as Horvat, still running toward the reception, registered the mushy but overwhelmingly loud *whoosh-slam* of a very close explosion. Instead of a single sharp detonation, the report lasted longer and trailed off unevenly. His building shook as the explosion propagated from the adjacent structure. The deafening blast rocked him but he wasn't prepared for the view when he stepped outside to survey the blast site.

"Medic!" Horvat yelled, clamping the closest victim's spurting forearm in reflex. He turned and yelled again to one of the first responders. The security officer crouched closer, belatedly recognizing Phillipi's charred features. "Doctor, can you hear me? Don't move, we'll take care of you!"

Phillipi wasn't altogether present. His lips moved but no sound emerged. Horvat leaned in to decipher the faint mumble.

"The-colonel," Phillipi whispered faintly. "Steinberg-took-the—"

His bloodshot eyes rolled back and Horvath screamed again for a medic.

Steinberg was alive.

Doing what?

His comm went off again.

As soon as the klaxon alerted her, Victoria checked the status of her file recovery. The instant it was complete, she ran to the door, ditching everything but her purse gun, a little nine-shot Miyako. Unfortunately, the armored door was locked and failed to respond to the lab-side controls.

Funny thing about security lockouts—they also lock you in.

Victoria immediately inventoried the room for a way out. The lab had replaced the old dispensary and the four-bed medical suite. Unfortunately, the Earthers had lined the walls and overhead with lightweight security panels, which would yield only to specialized cutting tools. No windows, no ventilation apertures larger than ten centimeters in any dimension, no additional weapons but what she could improvise. Eventually, that door was going to open and she'd doubted that her rescuers would be friendly. Getting the data out was still the priority—her escape secondary. She glanced around and got busy.

Horvat stood outside the lab's armored door and tapped on the terminal. The logs clearly showed that Jones-Durand had entered just prior to the bombing, and hadn't yet left. This was curious, since his mutilated body had been found in the overlook attached to the pool complex. Garcia, White and Jackson were accounted for—he'd personally stepped on each one. Porter was dead as well, identifiable only by her issue sidearm. Phillipi and a few others were stabilized, awaiting transport.

That meant that the remaining rebel was inside, no doubt trapped with her stolen information. Behind him, their weapons aimed floorward, a team of eight assault troopers were stacked along the wall, anonymous behind their reflective face shields. Behind them were two medics, whose white-and-red tabards clashed with the soldiers' camouflage. Horvat wanted that bitch alive and singing, if remotely possible. Steinberg wasn't going to have any poison or pet rippers inside to help her, and even if she did, it wouldn't be enough.

His career was finished, but first he'd peel that *puta* like a grape, and squeeze every answer out of her.

"Stand by," he ordered the assault lead. "Remember, alive if possible."

His comm buzzed.

"Sir, we're getting urgent requests from Delph' and Jefferson as well as the system command about our messages," the comms tech in the operation center said. *"They're ordering you to stop transmitting immediately."*

"Transmitting? What are we transmitting?"

"Sir, we've been pushing large amounts of data across every UN subnet there is, from logistics to research to tactical to command staff. It's all unencrypted research files, petabytes of it."

"Cut it!"

"Major, I can't do that from here!" the tech complained. *"The lab and the ops center are set up to be able to communicate independently, even during emergencies."*

He dropped the comm and spun to the team lead.

"Initiate, do it, now!"

Victoria had left the terminal with her messages queued to loop and resend to every unclassified UN military recipient in the system. The system wouldn't allow her to message any non-UN addresses, but she was reasonably confident that there would be a leak somewhere. If Freehold intel couldn't take advantage of that, it was out of her hands. In the meantime, several of their scientists were dead.

Sometime very soon that door was going to open. Probably as soon as they figured out what she'd done.

She looked down at her gown ruefully. What she wouldn't give for her old set of blacks, the skintight monomolecular-woven unitard that Black Ops wore in vacuum. Victoria suppressed a sigh. Operatives didn't moan about fairness, they improvised and attacked all out.

They were taking their time out there.

Victoria thought about her lovers and her surviving grandson who was still loose, fighting with the irregulars somewhere. The entire stay-behind idea had been coordinated with him. Victoria took a last deep breath, watching the steady light of the door terminal. She thought of the best memory she could, when she was a little girl, and her father had taken her on her first hunt. The pine smell of the forest, the chill wind that ruffled her hair. Her father's strong, cheerful face. When she was small, he would throw her up into the air, floating, floating.

She caught herself woolgathering and mentally kicked herself. Mission first.

She crouched behind a table, the little Miyako held in a firm two-handed grip. The taped handle of the club that she'd improvised from the chromed, tubular steel of an equipment stand was braced against the drawer.

Any moment now.

The door terminal flickered and she Boosted for the last time. The same old rush flooded across her, and her vision briefly quivered before attaining a diamond focus. She could feel the cool linoleum of the elevated floor under her bare feet. Keeping the gun in one hand, she covered both ears, exhaled and left her mouth open. A pair of oversized lab glasses protected her closed eyes.

A fraction of a second later, the actinic glare of stun grenades shone through her closed eyelids. The stuttering blasts of the paired grenades battered her small frame, but even before the echo faded, Victoria opened her eyes, leaned sideways and pre-aimed on the opening hatch.

The first assaulter was still clearing the doorway, riding the swinging door. Her augmentation allowed her to precisely calculate how long she had before his slowly rising gun muzzle would threaten her. Victoria's first two rounds only starred his faceplate before the next round punched through and he dropped bonelessly to the floor. She moved on to the second and third figures, servicing targets with machinelike precision until the Miyako's striker clicked on an empty, smoking chamber. The number-four man stumbled across the bodies but navigated the doorway in time to meet Victoria's charge.

Her club took him across the neck, compressing the vagus nerve and instantly stunning him. She pulled him sideways as a shield and dropped the club before operating the retention mechanism on his pistol holster. As the fifth trooper entered, automatically clearing in the direction opposite the preceding man, she rotated the appropriated gun upward, point shooting the new target in the armpit even as she raised the weapon all the way up, getting a proper sight picture. Number six managed to clear the door, stumbling only a little. At point-blank range, they traded shots. His punched through the frontal armor of her human shield, but failed to exit. Her pistol rounds found his throat. The now-dead weight of her shield pushed her back further as number seven entered, pivoted and started to fire while some pessimist outside donated an electroshock grenade.

She fell backward, simultaneously trying to draw her legs up as high as possible while still shooting. The grenade went off and without a ground, she took a jolt on her exposed gun arm, numbing her hand almost to uselessness.

Deafened and half-blinded, Victoria still kicked off the floor, and swarmed the staggering trooper. Panicked, he spun nearly one hundred and eighty degrees and emptied his magazine. He managed to shoot her low in the abdomen, and the fiery stab of pain brought tears to her eyes as she fell heavily to the floor. She looked up to see yet another trooper crumple just inside the doorway, having absorbed several of his mate's rounds. Screaming from the hall accompanied a wave of nausea that would have dropped her if she hadn't already been on one knee somehow.

She rolled over and automatically delivered security rounds to the head of the man who'd shot her. She crawled toward her next target to scrabble for any weapon she could find, trailing her unresponsive legs behind her.

A hard kick lifted Victoria from her victim and shattered several ribs.

Yelling finally overcame the crashing whine of tinnitus that had sung since the very first grenade exploded.

"Who the goddamn hell are you? Who are you, you fucking *puta*?"

She tried to roll over onto her back but another kick stole her breath, like a knife to the chest. She fisted her hands together, clutching her prize and tried to roll into a fetal ball. The floor was slick with her blood and each kick skidded her a few centimeters, accompanied by little huff of effort from her attacker, audible over the siren song of tinnitus. She registered each blow, but despite the intense pain, it felt almost like she was watching her end, observing from an arm's distance.

Horvat stooped over her, slapping one side of her face and screaming. She saw a medic standing behind him, arms flapping uselessly.

Victoria glanced upward and saw his face contorted with enraged yelling. The cords on her questioner's neck stood out. Her strength seemed to have fled and she reached up with one heavy arm. She tried to speak, but nothing seemed to come out.

"Who the fuck are you, Steinberg? Who sent you?"

Horvat had really lost it. He knelt over her, trying to slap her sensible, forehand and backhand.

"Okay, okay," she said, gently laying a hand on his chest in supplication, making him pause. "I'll tell you."

He paused, one hand arrested in mid-swing.

"Codger Command got you a present."

"Present?" Horvat said, squinting in incomprehension. "Codger Command?"

With the last of her augmented strength, she pulled him so that they were chest to chest. She relaxed the fist that she'd used to conceal the appropriated microgrenade, letting the spoon fly with an unmusical *ting*.

"Even retired, Freehold Special Warfare says *fuck you*." Victoria breathed into his reddening face as his hands uselessly scrabbled at the iron-hard muscles of her arm.

Horvat's eyes widened in understanding, but aided by her native planet's higher gravity, she clutched him to her in an inescapable embrace.

She never relaxed her grip.

Floating. .

Oblivion.

Huff #12
Nano Data Leaked! [Late May 210]

I'm on the *London* for a few days. The command ship usually stays in orbit, mostly unescorted. The near-planet environment around Grainne is incredibly secure. The Spacy has locked down things down so tight, even Baldy relaxes, slightly. I'm here for a briefing on Grainne stealth ships and supply smuggling, since J2 and S2 are rightly obsessed with finding FMS *Force*. I knew we shouldn't have taken out so much of the system architecture. There are still too many dead zones.

First though, I have some executive reading time. It's just me, Sandeep, and CAG. The top report is a "redline" with Herbert Jones-Durand's signature block on it, perhaps a breakthrough? This should be over a classified network. He's a bit of a hound, but he's got a mature outlook on this conflict. I wish I had more like him. Now, his charge, Dr. Philippi, has me barely convinced about these viruses as it is, so this had better be about making them safer and...

The screen flickers, and pages fly by. That picture, are those KIDS? Fuck me, this is bad. "Sandeep! Cancel the brief. I need a conference call with key staff in five minutes. They're here or on the line, or they're fired!" As he runs out, I watch the transmission from the research facility—why is this on an unclassified account? Was it sent to every damn UN address in the registry? A fucking party? Are you joking? Page after page of data flooding every mailbox in the system. These are the crown jewels. "Higher deaths than expected of the young, elderly, and other vulnerable populations"?

I hear shouts outside the DV lounge.

I yell at the CAG, "Get the J6 to shut this off and purge it!" Too little, too late, but we had to start damage control. Finally, a stoppage. We must have started jamming.

Now, reports of additional explosions inside the lab, casualties. Top scientists, soldiers, one of my best colonels, all dead. The research station is completely destroyed. Some scientists survived, but they won't be useful any time soon. Losing all that data is bad enough, but the worst part is the comm burst went system-wide, which means they know everything, or they're about to. This will get out of control, and we'll be lucky to live through it. We thought they were savage before, there's no telling what kind of retaliation will come next.

"CAG, start drafting a message for SecMil. Direct from me to him." If I go down over this, I'm taking some SecGen and BuMil potentates with me.

Spider's Web
Part 8

:: Hesp...I need you to look at something, :: Jenkins messaged to Moyra.

:: OK? ::

:: I found...this...on a segment of the network we can't see a lot into. I am not comfortable with what I think it's saying. :: He shared the text.

Moyra read it over. :: ...I...are those INFECTIONS they're offering to cure ENGINEERED VIRUSES? ::

:: I was so hoping you weren't going to read what I was reading into it. "Non-lethal," my ass. ::

:: Get me every scrap of that file and related information you can. Immediately. Top priority. ::

:: Already on it. Looks like the buggie was already released, because I found it when some of the text conversations I snagged were bragging about how many had shown signs already. ::

:: Signs? ::

Jenkins gave her a rundown of the symptoms, and she recognized the "eczematous epidermal infection" from what the medical staff and field teams were reporting.

:: Fuck. Track down whatever they're giving their troops for protection. That's first, and then everything else on it. ::

:: Got it. Are there any other resources available to help me track this one? I don't want to miss anything. ::

She bit her lip. So far, keeping Jenkins slow and small, passing on tidbits that Kozlov could make use of, helped keep Jenkins's activities under the radar. They operated in completely different ways.

:: I'll help, for now. ::

:: Hesp! You're already overloaded. ::

:: I'll deal with that. Just tap me in. ::

He grumbled, but tossed her the data dumps he had so far. She directed him to pull *everything* he could possibly find, and gave him a specialized storage spot for *that* data. She set to work on building her AI searches and flags for the data.

She relayed information to Damocles about where this "research" was taking place. Information from Naumann filtered back, with ways to confirm a few individuals there. Naumann considered those resources to be "highly competent."

Moyra directed resources toward attempting to get those individuals connected in, to get out whatever information they could get their hands on. The segment was disconnected enough that they couldn't quite bridge it. Only a few messages made it in, and none made it out. Moyra was set to have handlers direct a "freelancer" team to the site, when her AI filters caught the data flooding the standard UN network. Among the precious information: the structure of the virus and the effective treatment. Moyra got that to Naumann's people immediately to work on production, but there were no guarantees.

Reading the related correspondence, it quickly became apparent that *this* little project was only running with partial UN oversight and approval. Among the justifications, "there's no active military," "the resistance is just delaying the inevitable," and "they're not organized." They also bragged that they'd gotten away with pretending the pneumonic and skin-lesion infections were "nonlethal" to the brass. "Exterminating these savages," said one message, "brings such joy to my soul."

Moyra ensured the most scandalous, incriminating, unredacted correspondence made its way to not just a Sister Station, but a regular news station. She concealed her own identity, claiming to be a horrified UN civilian support staff, whistle-blowing. The staffer in question was deceased within a day, but neither side claimed responsibility for the death. Skylight helpfully ensured the resulting broadcast made it into the info packet for jump point dispatch. Enough data spilled across the UN network that every UN troop knew, including the medical staff, while the official position remained "lies and slander."

It might not officially be a war crime *yet,* but the UN was actively, functionally *insane* if the brass somehow believed that biowarfare was the least bit acceptable. Every single person in all of settled space needed to know *that.*

Damocles relayed that, while Naumann would have "appreciated being kept in the loop," he agreed that the damage from releasing that information outweighed the risks posed to their operation. Damocles just snickered when Moyra went off about "not everything being about war, how DARE THEY."

The remains of the retirement village were reviewed by drone, and the devastation laid straight on the feet of the UN forces who occupied the facility. The Sister Stations, soon followed by the regular broadcasts, pointed out for those still ambivalent about the occupation that the UN was willing to murder babies and the elderly.

As a secondary effect, Resistance recruitment again increased, while every UN-associated individual with any skill, connection, or ability to perform obscene sexual favors found ways off planet. In some ways, the war turned even more brutal. Those without such capabilities could not be considered the moral, honorable, or functional cream of the crop. Thuggery increased in the cities, while reports from the field indicated the troops were desperate.

Moyra's handler teams reported that their disconnected elements were struggling, as more of the supply depots were discovered by aerial reconnaissance. Moyra directed Kozlov to return to hijacking the convoys if at all possible.

Buffalo Fifteen

Brad R. Torgersen

"Campos!" shouted the balding, older man with the Fu Manchu moustache.

Matthew Campos, formerly of the Greater Los Angeles Medium Security Correctional Facility, stopped pushing his broom, and wiped the sleeve of his coverall across his forehead. There had been a time when Campos thought summers in LA hot, but then he'd come to Grainne—and discovered a whole new meaning for the word. Summers here were half again as long, too. So were winters. Midautumn here was still as hot as LA in midsummer.

"Boss," Matt said, tipping his wide-brimmed sun hat to the gentleman stomping across the depot's gravel yard. Sergeant Megsley looked to be at least ten kilos and fifteen Earth years past his prime. But if anyone knew the depot like the back of his hand, it was the Yard Dog.

"Save sweeping the loading dock," Megsley commanded, looking up at Campos. Megsley's own t-shirt was soaked through at the pits of his arms, and at the collar. He wore a floppy boonie-style hat with his rank sewn into the fabric. His uniform pants were cut off at the knees—against regulation—and his lower legs were covered by high khaki socks descending into the tops of a pair of very battered Freehold military boots.

"But Senior Sergeant Crock—" Matt began.

"No time now for facility maintenance," Megsley said, cutting Campos off. "Just got the news of UN armed patrols forty kilometers southeast."

"What does that have to do with us?" Matt asked, feeling beads of perspiration run down his muscular back to pool at his coverall's waistband.

"If they're that close," Megsley said, "it means they're looking for us. Something's tipped them to the depot's existence. Either orbital reconnaissance, or a clue they found closer to the city."

Matt shifted his gaze from the Yard Dog's sunglasses, to the sky overhead. Things were still fairly quiet. Thus far, the United Nations invasion of Grainne hadn't touched their remote little piece of the planet. As one of ten indentured prisoners detailed to perform janitorial services at this Freehold auxiliary arms depot, Matt didn't really have much to say about the war. He'd come to Grainne hoping to get away from a life lived much too close to the bone, and off the streets of an Earth city which typically ground up and spat out young men like him. Except, taking the street out of the man hadn't been quite as simple.

He frowned.

"Guess you all gotta move," he said matter-of-factly.

"We all?" Megsley said, laughing harshly. "You think *you're* just gonna stay put?"

"Job's to keep up the depot," Matt said. "Anything else doesn't concern me."

"Like hell," Megsley said, his hands braced on his hips. "As long as Captain Dean holds your contract slip between his fingers, you belong to us. Doesn't matter now what you were first told you'd be doing on this detail. That was before the war started."

"Not a soldier," Matt said, tapping his sternum with the end of the broom handle.

"You think *I'm* a soldier?" Megsley said. "I ain't fired a weapon at a living human being the entire time I've been in. You know me, I do this job all the time anyway. Just in a civilian capacity. War's made me put my stripes on. For a change."

"Still not my fight," Matt said, feeling himself begin to get angry.

"Don't matter none if you think it's your fight, son," the Yard Dog said. "UN has made it *everybody's* fight. Yours. Mine. All of us. Or did you forget that you were lucky to get *away* from Earth, when the getting was good?"

Matt didn't say anything. Megsley had a point. Back on Earth, Campos's options were few. His record made it impossible to return without facing the same dead ends which made a new start on Grainne seem so attractive in the first place. Assuming he was captured, what would the UN do with him? Where would he go? Did he dare trust his fate to a world government which callously disregarded the individual futures of so many of Matt's jailed or dead friends back in LA?

"Now," the Yard Dog said, "we've got to get the trucks ready to roll. We can't evacuate everything. But we can get the vital stuff up on the road. You're one of two people on the detention detail I trained to run the forklifts. You still feel comfortable working that piece?"

Matt thought about it. Then shrugged.

"Beats standing around with my thumb up my ass," he said.

"Atta boy," the Yard Dog said, clapping his hands together.

Captain Prassert Dean drew a breath between his teeth, and pushed it out again. From his window in the mezzanine office in the old mine, over the depot yard, he could see Sergeant Megsley and his two specialists mustering the prisoner detail. There were plenty of flatbeds on site to serve, but not nearly enough tractors to haul even half of them, and even fewer drivers for the tractors. The Freehold had not prepared for the war to come to Dean's depot. He was incredibly short-handed, even with people like Private Paine pressed into service. She'd been kicked out of Recruit Training two years before. Not that it mattered now. Everybody who could do *anything* even a little bit military was being pressed into service, regardless of their readiness or qualifications. Force Support Branch was intended for the sick, lame and antiquated who really weren't suited to be military but still wanted to serve. They filled roles other nations' militaries used civil service for. They were not actually expected to be combatants.

That had changed. The depot had already scrammed once, from the city to this remote abandoned mine that just might look like nothing interesting to satellite recon.

"Sir, we need you," reminded Senior Sergeant Crock, who stood in Dean's doorway.

"Right," the captain said, turning and walking quickly toward the exit. He followed the senior sergeant across the threshold, then stopped, and turned around. The office wasn't much. As a part-timer, Dean himself rarely saw it. He'd only brought a couple of items from home. And a fine layer of dust coated all but the frequently used surfaces. He was suddenly struck by the notion that he might not ever see his office again.

"Sir," the senior sergeant said softly at Dean's side.

"Sorry, coming," the captain said, and walked with his senior noncommissioned officer to the makeshift crisis center where the depot's evacuation was being planned on the fly. Where for six months they received and distributed a host of Freehold military consumables—bullets, missiles, fuel, rations—to those elements still fighting, now they were deciding what was vital to keep, and what could be abandoned.

"It's a crapshoot," said Warrant Leader Elton, the only one under Dean's command who had any experience with the United Nations military. He didn't know much about her, other than that she'd emigrated from Earth after her retirement. She walked with a limp, and her hastily appointed Freehold rank—slapped on, shortly after she'd arrived in civilian clothing, eager to help—was purely for utility.

"What does that mean?" Dean asked her.

"We take all of a few things, or a little bit of everything. Doesn't much matter. We're leaving the lion's share for the wolves."

"Then what do you suggest, Warrant?" Senior Sergeant Crock asked.

The older woman—silver hair, cropped short, with lines around her eyes—chewed her bottom lip.

"If it were up to me," she said, "I'd prioritize field rations and small arms ammunition."

Dean looked to Crock, feeling the urgent need for a sure answer. Crock was one of the few of them who'd done time in the regular Freehold force. He'd have stayed retired except for the war. Now, out of shape and showing it—with his beer belly—Crock was being expected to put his experience to work for a Reserve commanding officer twenty years Crock's junior.

Crock nodded his head. "I'm with Warrant."

"And the rest of it?" Dean asked.

"We blow it up," Crock said, his eyes not leaving those of the captain.

"What?" Warrant Elton blurted, looking up from her comm.

"We put only what's necessary on the flatbeds," Crock said, "then move 'em out. Leave some of the high-yield missiles—with the big warheads—in the mine. Surround the missiles with what's left of the ammunition and fuel. Along with any other parts and equipment we don't want the UN to have, and we det-rig it."

"We don't have a demolitions expert," Dean said.

"You don't have to be an expert," Crock replied. "Just somebody who knows how to sync the warheads electronically. Set a laser trip across the depot entry. The second the UN rolls through, *boom*. It's a bad day for them."

"Or a bad day for some of your own," Elton said.

Both Dean and the senior sergeant raised eyebrows at her.

"Sorry, *our* own," she corrected herself. "We're still not sure we won't be coming back here in a few days. And if not us, then someone else from the Freehold."

"Maybe," the senior sergeant said. "Ma'am, if you truly have a better idea, now's the time."

Warrant Elton went back to chewing her lower lip.

"I just *hate* the idea of wasting it," she confessed. "The Freehold *needs* what we have here. All of it. The UNPF won't want it, other than to keep it out of Freehold hands. For us, this stuff is priceless. For them? No."

"And the moment we put up resistance, trying to keep it, that will make us a magnet for their sweep-and-destroy missions," Crock said.

Dean saw Private Paine out of the corner of his eye. The young woman looked scared, and was hunched over her computer, trying to keep a line open to the broader Freehold improvised communications network. It all piggybacked on entertainment broadcasts, but only at certain times for certain durations. They didn't yet have an ephemeris and had to monitor constantly. They'd learned of the threat to the depot when a Freehold aerial scout flew past the depot hell bent for leather and alerted them to the peril. Paine's face was pale, and she looked just a little bit sick to her stomach. Which reminded Dean of how he himself felt.

Nothing in his young life had sufficiently prepared him for this. A native of Grainne, he'd always thought of Earth and the United Nations as remote concerns. Not once had he or his parents ever worried about the potential threat, and Dean himself had gone into the Freehold military auxiliary branch purely to satisfy his father's insistence that the family—Freeholders from the beginning—keep up its end. Never had he seriously considered the possibility of an actual fight coming to Grainne in his lifetime. And now that the fight was here...

"We go with the senior's idea," the captain said.

Warrant Elton's face darkened.

"I don't like it any more than you do, Warrant, but we don't do the Freehold any favors just letting all of these assets fall into enemy hands. If we had days to prepare and move everything, I would. But we don't, so we can't."

"Yessir," Elton said, frowning deeply.

"How soon to set it up?" Dean asked the senior sergeant.

"My part's easy. I can sync the warheads now. As soon as Yard Dog's guys have the flatbeds loaded and ready to roll, we can start the actual evac. We'll need the loaders to stay back and work while the flatbeds get staged on the highway. Once the loaders finish their jobs, we pull those operators and put them in the tractors up on the hardpan, while I get the laser trip system set, and then we go."

"And when the UN sends air assets to scout us out, ahead of their column?" Warrant Elton asked.

"We try to beat that," Dean said very seriously.

Matt Campos didn't understand the decision-making process for what got loaded, and what stayed. Half the time, when he had a pallet lifted and ready, either the Yard Dog or one of the Yard Dog's corporals was telling him to put it back down again. The cab of the scavenged forklift was sweltering, the AC burned out. If they'd had more time, he'd have unlatched and removed the bubble that formed a rain barrier over the driver's seat. But that would take time, and the Yard Dog was in a veritable tizzy trying to cat-herd all the other coverall-clothed punitive detail, not to mention the cluster of soldiers.

It was the picture of organized chaos.

"Down!" shouted Corporal Pulver, whose t-shirt was sweat-soaked to his waist. He wore a safety-yellow hard hat, and matching work gloves.

Campos gusted air out of his puffed cheeks, and put the pallet he'd just lifted back onto the gravel with a crunch.

"That's the third time I've dropped this load," Campos shouted back, leaning out of the bubble's open side window.

"If you'd picked up the pallet I told you to in the first place, we wouldn't be having a problem!" Corporal Pulver shot back.

Matt felt a retort boil on the tip of his tongue, but held it. Unlike some of the other Grainne natives, Pulver was from the barrios of Earth, just like Matt himself. Perhaps a bit younger than Matt, the corporal had the upper body of a weightlifter, and an attitude to match. He'd also come in with the transported "refugees" two years before, and managed to impress a recruiter enough to get into Force Support. To Pulver, the punishment detail was not even on the same level as some of the fresh privates who were scurrying about. Pulver regarded the indentured prisoners as scum, and typically treated them as such, with a balled fist to back up his intentions.

Sergeant Megsley strode into the picture. He and Pulver carried on an animated conversation for several seconds, then Corporal Pulver was shaking his head, and pantomiming for Matt to put his tines back under the pallet he'd just been ordered to drop.

Matt allowed himself a small smile, wiped his eyes of sweat, and proceeded with the maneuver. In the weeks since he'd been assigned to the depot, he'd gotten fairly good at running the forklift. A job which Matt knew technically should not have been entrusted to any of the prisoners. But the Yard Dog hadn't seemed to care. He'd only had eyes for people he thought smart enough, and capable with heavy equipment.

The pallet, contents unknown to Matt, went over to one of the many flatbeds pre-staged along one side of the depot's yard. Matt gently worked the forklift's controls, lifting the pallet up until it was level and ready to be placed onto the flatbed's surface, then settled the pallet, and backed the forklift, turning rapidly away, while another loader approached with another pallet.

Suddenly, the sky buzzed angrily.

A craft zoomed overhead, circled once, and then disappeared back the way it had come.

All of the Freehold military personnel gaped, then looked at each other with panic in their eyes.

"What is it?" Matt yelled, again out of his bubble's side window.

"Spotter," Corporal Pulver hollered. "Remotely piloted vehicle. Now they for sure know we're here, and what we're doing."

Matt felt a sinking sensation hit his stomach, but the work continued. This time, nobody was picky about which pallets he loaded. The instant they were shoved out of the mine, one of the forklifts grabbed it, and drove it to a waiting flatbed. The drivers hooked up while the loading was ongoing, safety be damned. They then hauled the loaded trailers into line and sat at the controls, twitchy about a likely air attack.

✧   ✧   ✧

"Damned crazy to be doing this without air support," muttered Warrant Elton as she followed Captain Dean out of the depot. They'd each gathered helmets and armor, along with carbines and pistols, and were hastily trying to pull it all on—heavy, chafing, awkward—while the command group fast-walked toward the two armored GUVs which waited on the yard gravel.

"We're not completely without air defense," Dean noted, aiming a finger at the cupolas on the roofs of each of the tactical vehicles. Each was equipped with twin M23 15mm heavy machine guns. In a pinch, those could be directed skyward. Each also had a four-block launcher of short-range AA missiles.

"When's the last time those privates trained on or fired those weapons?" Elton asked.

Dean stared at the young Freehold residents—barely older than teenagers—sitting in the cupolas. They too looked uncomfortable and encumbered by their helmets and armor. They glanced this way and that, as if unsure of themselves, or what to do.

"I honestly don't know," the captain admitted.

"Every one of my soldiers is prepared to do their best," Senior Sergeant Crock snapped.

Private Paine emphasized this point by tripping and dropping the portable comm and radio pack which she'd clutched to her chest with the rest of her gear. The lot of it spilled across the gravel, while she cursed furiously, and snatched it up quickly, checking to be sure she hadn't damaged it.

Senior Sergeant Crock struggled to get his armor buckled. He was too fat for the size issued to him. After huffing and puffing repeatedly, he shook his head in disgust, and gave up trying. Now the front and back flapped freely, joined only at the shoulders.

Warrant Elton closed her eyes and made a motion across her torso which Dean vaguely recognized as something one of the Christian sects did when it seemed like nothing save a higher power might help you.

Dean realized he'd never been closer to wishing he believed in a higher power. His parents had been scoffers, or so they proudly said. And in his short life he'd never given any church of any type much thought. But now that he eyed his vulnerable collection of personnel—none of them tested in combat—he was struck by how absurd the whole thing was. They called themselves soldiers, but in actuality they were mechanics, computer specialists, logistics analysts, warehouse managers, supply clerks, heavy-equipment operators, and in the case of people like Private Paine, former rejects who'd never even gotten out of training. Or, as with the senior sergeant, old men who were in no shape to fight, activated for the duration of the UN's invasion.

"Captain?" Elton asked.

Dean suddenly realized he'd stopped ten meters short of the GUVs, his armor half-buckled, helmet still dangling by one hand, and his sidearm rattling loose in its unsecured holster. His command group turned to look at him, and in that instant, he felt an overwhelming urge to drop everything and run straight out of the depot yard, across the highway, and just . . . keep on going. Forget about it. The whole evacuation. Who was he to lead these people? To think that he had what it took to order men and women to die?

"Sir?" asked the senior sergeant, looking almost comical with his belly pushing his unbuckled armor away from his body at an odd angle.

Dean's moment of panic passed, as quickly as it had come.

"Fire 'em up," he ordered.

The two tactical vehicles growled to life.

Matt Campos had never ridden in a convoy. There were twenty tractors joined to twenty flatbeds, each flatbed festooned with an odd assortment of pallets, and each pallet containing ammunition or consumables. They were staged side by side on the highway—which had seen precious little civilian or military traffic since the war's beginning—with the tractors all idling like so many gargantuan bumblebees buzzing. Out of the window of the cab Matt sat in, he could see one of the depot's troops monkeying with something down at one corner of the mine entrance, while the senior sergeant messed with something else at the opposite corner. Per the plan, a motley pile of high-explosive rockets, ordnance, and fuel cans had been hastily built in the mine's entrance.

"What happens now?" Matt asked the tractor's driver.

"Assuming the UN isn't smart enough to spot the laser-tripping system," the woman said—she was older, and had needed help up into the tractor cab on account of her bum leg—"when somebody walks across that invisible line, the pile explodes."

"Will that snuff the UN force coming at us?" he asked.

"Some, possibly." the woman said. "But it ought to flatten the mine itself. And give 'em a bloody nose for their effort. To the victor go no spoils."

"What's that mean?"

"They don't get to put their hands on any Freehold goodies," she said.

Matt nodded his head, and looked out the opposite window, up into the still-bright sky. It was just past midday. Other than the overflight by the small UN drone, nothing had crossed their way. Not Freehold. Not anything. And though Matt had asked several times, nobody seemed to have a clear idea where exactly it was they were going. Just that the convoy would depart as soon as Senior Sergeant Crock was finished with his work.

The tractor's driver gripped her controls with tendons standing out on the backs of her liver-spotted hands.

"Could have stayed in Topeka," she muttered.

"Huh?" Matt said, startled. "That's Kansas, right?"

"I'm from there," she said. "What's it to you, prisoner?"

"Matt Campos," he introduced himself. "Los Angeles, California."

The woman grunted. "Never did like Los Angeles."

"Same here," Matt said, grinning suddenly. He put out his hand, reflexively.

"Chrissy Elton," she said, shaking firmly. "But you can call me Warrant."

"You don't wear a uniform like the others," Matt said.

"Didn't have time to get fitted out," she replied. "I figured they would need all the experienced help they can get. And I was right. Even if I'm not Freehold official."

"You're not UN military, are you?"

"Used to be, kid. Used to be."

"Why did you come to Grainne, then?"

The old woman dipped her chin to her chest, collecting her thoughts.

"Because I'd finally had enough of home. Just like you, I assume. Too many stupid people, making and enforcing too many stupid rules. 'Enough rules to choke an elephant,' my grandfather liked to say. And it wasn't even as bad in his time. Not like now. So, I bailed out. Spent my pension to get here. Left it all, to try to come here and see if I couldn't live out my retirement in a place which offered me genuine freedom."

"We're free back home," Matt said reflexively.

"Bullshit," Elton declared. "I used to think that, too. But it's wrong. What we have back home... is just enough comfort to keep people from rioting. And enough fear of the authorities, that we still hate jail more than we hate being told what to do. How to live. How to eat. Getting the air conditioning turned off in the depths of summer, and the heat turned off in the middle of winter. Because the goddamned government wants to save resources. While the goddamned suits fly around the globe, enjoying their climate-controlled, security-cordoned lives."

Matt grunted. "They told us in school to be thankful."

"Well, that makes you and I a couple of ingrates, then, doesn't it?" she said, cracking a small smile at her driving partner.

Matt laughed in spite of himself.

Her expression turned serious.

"What brought *you* here, kid?"

"Nowhere else to go," he said, also turning serious. "Most of my friends were like me. In and out of prison. And once a man has a rap sheet... well, Grainne and the Freehold had this refugee thing going, we were told."

"Aaaaaand you wound up right back in the clink," Elton surmised, amused, with her eyebrow raised.

"Life here... is different than I thought," Matt admitted, thinking as much as he was talking. "Back home, a lot of shit's provided. It sucks, but it's not nothing. Here? You have to *work* for everything you get. Even though—as you say—there's fewer rules."

"So, you managed to break some of those rules anyway," she said.

"Yeah."

The older woman just nodded her head, and went back to staring out the front window of the tractor cab.

Matt cleared his throat, then said, "What's an old lady know about drivin' one of these things?"

"First job I ever did for the UN," Elton said. "Their tractors are different, and it's been more than a little while since I got behind the controls of something this big. But it'll come to me as we roll."

Matt laughed, but half because he was suddenly nervous.

With one GUV up front, and one to the rear, Captain Dean's now-mobile depot rolled out. They'd had no success summoning additional assets, since the whole of the Freehold was actively engaged repelling UN forces at points both near and far. Dean himself had orders to bring his convoy to such-and-such coordinates, where he would rendezvous with a Lieutenant Comte, who would also be bringing her convoy, plus one additional train of vehicles, all in an effort to consolidate and move the sum total of ammunition and consumables to where the fight most badly needed them. From this point forward, Dean knew, there would be no letup. Having prepared for war, and hearing about it happening all around him for months, he would now be *in* the war continually. There would be no getting out of it until the United Nations was sent back to Earth, broken. Or the UN broke the Freehold. Whichever came first.

Dean wondered what it would be like to become a prisoner of war. As with so much else that was happening to him, he'd never given the matter serious thought. History showed that being a POW was a hit-or-miss proposition. Depending on what rules your enemy thought to abide by, you could get an experience not too dissimilar to initial-entry training, with regimented captivity and uniform discipline, or you could—at the other end of the spectrum—expect torture and death. Or death *by* torture if you were especially unlucky.

What the UN might try to wring out of a lowly logistics captain, caught on the road with minimal defense, he couldn't guess.

It was a rattling shock to hear the weaponeer in the top cupola shouting down into the car, "The depot just went up! The depot just went up!"

A few seconds later, the thunderclap of the explosion—with compression wave—passed over them. *Whump!* Like getting mildly punched in the chest. At several kilometers distance, no less.

Dean unbuckled himself and unlatched his armored window, then swung it aside. He shoved his head and one shoulder out to have a look.

The mushroom-shaped cloud that rose into the sky was a hellish specter of black soot mixed with dust, and the boil of sooty flame beneath. Even at this distance, it rose greatly into the air, shifting and dispersing as the gentle breeze caught it.

Bringing himself back inside the vehicle, Dean heard the driver, a young corporal whose name he didn't remember, remark, "We're in it now."

Indeed, they were.

How much the destruction of the depot and any attendant UN vehicles and personnel with it would slow the UN down was impossible to estimate. Dean imagined that if it had been his recon element checking on a suspected resupply point, and *he* lost people and vehicles to a booby trap, he'd spare no expense attempting to immediately locate and punish those responsible.

The young driver didn't need to be told to pick up his pace. He dialed the GUV's sprint up to the limit that the tractors and their flatbeds could handle.

On his little tactical control system in the vehicle commander's seat, Dean saw the whole convoy gradually dispersing in an ever-longer column of vehicles. Instead of side-by-side, they were now rolling single file with a healthy gap between each of them. With the highway being two lanes wide in one direction, the left lane would be kept open for passing, in case any of the vehicles became disabled and the rest of the convoy had to navigate the blockage.

"This is Alpha," Dean said in his helmet's mic, "how we looking in the back, Bravo?"

"Bravo reporting clear for now, sir," said a female voice. *"But I am not sure how long that's going to last."*

"No matter what happens," he ordered, "stay with the tail. If we lose anyone, we keep moving. But protect the tail of the convoy."

"Yessir," came the truck commander's reply.

Dean peered over his seat, at Private Paine.

"Any luck getting comms with surrounding strategic forces?"

"I'm trying, sir," the young woman said.

"Don't stop until you can raise somebody. Doesn't matter who they are. If they're Freehold, and they're armed, and they have wheels, we can link up with them. Or they can link up with us."

"Roger, sir," Paine said, and continued to focus her attention on the comms pack in her lap, its screen shining up into her freckled face.

Dean wasn't old enough yet to be her father, but she was much too young to be in battle, he thought.

The convoy rolled onward for a good ten segs, occasionally passing the burned-out hulks of what appeared to have formerly been Freehold tactical vehicles.

"Senior Sergeant, you seeing this?" the captain asked over the convoy net.

"*Yes, sir,*" said Crock, from the cab of one of the tractors. At the last moment he had elected to drive, since he—and the warrant, and several others—possessed at least minimum necessary familiarity with the partially automated tractor controls.

"What happened to them?" Dean asked.

"*Probably Freehold ground armor scouts, checking to see how far UN forces had pushed. They got surprised by UN gunships looking for targets. Let's hope that the convoy itself doesn't run into any of that. Drones are one thing. Gunships are something else. Or, if you want to be an optimist, let's hope we get found by Freehold gunships looking to escort us. Any word on that, from our comms kid in the back with you?*"

Dean just peered back at Private Paine, who continued to frown.

Three aircraft streaked overhead so fast, and so low, Matt never got a look at them. Only the roar of their exhausts could be heard inside the tractor cab.

Warrant Elton cursed vigorously.

"Not Freehold?" Matt guessed, feeling sweat spring out instantly on his palms.

"Didn't sound like it," she said. "Sound like Avatars to me. UN interceptors."

"What will they do?" Matt asked, his heart hammering.

"Depends on if it's just more drone spotters, or craft fitted out to deal damage. Either way, we know they're tracking us now. Enough to be interested in what we are, or where we're going. Tighten up your harness and be ready for some crazy driving. I'm going to manual."

Matt watched as she disengaged the autodrive, and took full command of the tractor. The vehicle's speed dropped, then picked back up again vigorously as she tested the brake, the accelerator, and the steering. The trailer swayed from side to side before Elton settled on a pace and course matching the flatbed some two hundred meters ahead. It was sufficient spacing that they would theoretically not be hit like pins in a bowling alley. But as Matt imagined one of the trucks in the convoy going up in a ball of fire, the highway suddenly seemed much too narrow.

The three aircraft again streaked overhead, but were this time followed by yet another sound of hurtling machinery: throatier, with a bit more rumble to it. That craft too was gone in a flash, while the cab's audio came alive with the sound of hoots and cheers from the Freehold military personnel across the convoy.

"Buffalo Fifteen calling Alpha," Elton said, breaking comms.

"Alpha, go ahead Fifteen," replied Captain Dean's voice.

"Was that what it seemed like?" she asked.

"Affirmative," Dean said. *"Three of yours—errr, I mean, three of theirs—being pursued by one of ours. The one that's ours appeared to be up-armed. So, the skies aren't owned by the UN. Let's hope ours keeps theirs off our backs. We're still having a real devil of a time establishing comms with the outside world right now. Suspect a lot of UN jamming operations going on, trying to disrupt local comms."*

"Roger, Alpha," Elton acknowledged.

"Charlie Mike," Dean replied, then closed the conversation.

"What does that mean?" Matt asked.

"Continue the mission, kid," Elton told him.

Matt squirmed in his harness, and tried to keep calm. If Elton was rattled at all, it didn't show in the way she handled the tractor. Her reflexes were firm and cool, her eyes scanning the road ahead very methodically.

She glanced at the dark control panel in front of him.

"You got any experience on big rigs, kid?" she asked.

"None," he said.

"Well, in case something goes wrong, there's no better time to learn."

"Wait a minute—" Matt began to protest, but his control panel suddenly came alive, as did the manual set of controls.

"I'm gonna talk you through it," she said. "One step at a time. You got anything better to do?"

Matt realized he did not.

Captain Dean never saw the first two flatbeds lost. He merely heard the screaming on the convoy net, followed by the shriek of the UN gunship which had done the deed. On his tactical display, Buffalo Six and Buffalo Seven turned bright red, while the blue sigils for all of the tractor-trailers behind began to swerve and dodge wildly. Some of them had to cut out pretty far onto the margin of the highway before regaining traction on the hardpan.

"Alpha to convoy," Dean called, "Talk to me!"

"Six and Seven went up," replied Sergeant Megsley, who was

both operator and truck commander for Buffalo Eight. *"Looked like missiles to me. Almost caught me and Buffalo Nine, too. We managed to evade. Hopefully everyone else did too."*

"Alpha, acknowledge," Dean replied. "Increase spacing to three hundred meters."

"Roger," came the multiple replies.

There wasn't time to ask who had been in the two tractors which got hit. That would come later. Assuming there *was* a later.

"Alpha and Beta gunners, this is yours!" Dean commanded. "Go hot, but do *not* fire until you're positive you've got good target acquisition."

Just then, the guns in the cupola above Dean's head erupted with a stutter. Blasts of flame burst momentarily over their heads, above the front hood of the GUV. The sound was deafening, despite the protection afford by his helmet. He resisted the urge to slap his hands over his ears, and pushed his face against the windscreen, hoping to get a look at whatever it was his truck gunner was aiming at.

Dean saw nothing.

"Goddammit, I told you *not* to fire without good target acquisition!" he yelled.

"S-s-sorry, sir!" the gunner said over the vehicle net. *"You said go hot!"*

"Not with your goddamned thumb on the firing stud!" Dean yelled.

"C-copy, sir. Won't happen again, sir."

Dean resisted the urge to reach up, unlatch the gunner from his harness, and drag the young man down out of the cupola. His sudden rage over a stupid and potentially deadly mistake was then tempered by the realization that had he been as young and frightened as the man above him, he might have made the same error. All of this was new to all of them. They were making it up as they went along. No situational training exercise, this mad convoy across the continent.

The shrieking UN gunship passed again, only much farther away.

"Grazing cannon hits," said a voice on the convoy net. *"Buffalo Fourteen."*

"Oh my God!" hollered an unfamiliar voice.

"Buffalo Fourteen, are you disabled?" Dean asked.

"Nossir," came the reply. *"But I think Buffalo Fifteen has a problem."*

The tactical display showed Buffalo Fifteen beginning to weave.

"Talk to me, Buffalo Fifteen!" Dean commanded.

"*She's dead!*" screamed the new voice.

"Who is this? Give a proper situational report!"

"*Shot through the neck! Oh God, blood everywhere!*"

"Steady, Buffalo Fifteen. What is your tractor *status*, over?"

"*Uhhhh...autodrive is reengaged. I am trying to...Jesus Christ, she's gone. Never knew what hit her.*"

"Warrant Leader Elton?" Dean asked, hearing his voice squeak on the last syllable.

"*Yes!*" the man said, clearly horrified.

"*Co-driver, are you capable of assuming command of that tractor?*" came the reassuring voice of Senior Sergeant Crock.

"*Uhhhh...I...uhhhh...*"

"*Hey, Matt, this is the Yard Dog,*" said the voice of Sergeant Megsley.

"*Yah,*" the lone driver replied. "*I hear you, Yard Dog.*"

"*Just sit tight for a second, and get your head right, please.*"

Dean was amazed at how calm Sergeant Megsley sounded. Almost too calm. But his voice on the convoy net seemed to have the desired effect. After a couple of seconds, the lone driver—now impromptu truck commander—of Buffalo Fifteen came back on.

"*Uhhhh, the tractor seems okay. Everything's green. Shell smashed through the main driver's side of the window and killed Warrant Elton. But nothing else has been damaged. Uhhhh, I'm leaving the autodrive on for now. Keeping my distance from Buffalo Fourteen after we had to swerve around Six and Seven.*"

"*That's mighty good, Fifteen,*" Megsley said. "*Matt, you just keep cool in that tractor cab, and everything's gonna be fine. Stick to the rest of us, and we'll make it through this.*"

"*Sir!*" interrupted the Alpha gunner. "*Acquiring target as it crosses us for another strafe!*"

"Tell me you've got missile lock," Dean asked.

"*Uhhh, not...uhhhh...yes.*"

"Then launch, keep it in the reticle and start shooting, dammit!"

Once again the guns on the roof blazed forth, hurtling tongues of flame at a forty-five-degree angle to the road. In the midst of the burst, odd shrieking bangs announced a missile pair launching. Countermass debris cracked against the roof. An instant, intense smell of spent propellants filled Dean's nostrils. He watched intently out the window in the direction the cupola was facing, until he thought he saw a dark shape manifest. It sparkled briefly, and the road ahead—along with the dirt to either side of the road—fountained with the shell impacts of the UN gunship's autocannon.

But the gunner in the cupola must have done something right, because the UN gunship never pulled out of its shallow dive. It continued overhead and shot past the convoy, auguring in at a phenomenal speed. The fireball was tremendous, if somewhat distant, and for a brief moment Dean's terror-filled heart swelled with triumphant joy.

"Alpha, this is Beta," said the truck commander's voice on the convoy comms. Matt was startled out of his stupor by the sound. He'd not paid any attention to the crash of the UN gunship, nor the convoy-wide cheers which had followed. His whole world was a tractor cab filled with coppery-smelling blood, and an old woman's dead body slumped at his side.

"Copy you, Beta. Go ahead," said the voice of Captain Dean.

"We've got company on the highway, sir. Doesn't look like Freehold, and they're moving up on us fast. Expect to be overtaken inside of nine zero seconds."

"Copy that, Beta. Same as before: Do not fire until you have a positive target lock. Be damned sure that's not Freehold you're shooting at, when you shoot. Understood?"

"Roger, sir."

Matt just stared at the green icons on the tractor's autodrive control panel. He didn't dare touch any of the controls, spattered as they had become. He just folded his hands under his arms and tried to get control of the spinning feeling in his chest. He'd seen people get hurt before. Even badly. That was just LA. But he'd never been right next to a woman—calmly telling him about the intricacies of multishift variance from axle to axle—when that woman was essentially drive-byed with a shell the size of his wrist. It had only taken a grazing hit to almost completely take her whole head off, and now that head bobbed lifelessly against her chest with every bump or turn in the highway. Air rushing through the gaping hole behind him was a constant reminder.

"Yard Dog to Campos," said a familiar voice.

Matt keyed his mic.

"Yah," he croaked.

"*You gonna make it, partner?*"

"I...I don't know," Matt admitted.

"*I wish to hell I'd shown you around these things,*" Sergeant Megsley said.

"Warrant..."—he couldn't remember her name right now, first or last—"was kinda giving me tips," Matt said.

"*Well listen, things are probably gonna get real messy here quick, so what I want you to do is just ease your feet and hands into the right position, so that you can steer and brake—not a ton different from the forklift, if I think about it—and get ready to turn off that autodrive. Your only directive is to keep that rig rolling, you hear?*"

"Uhhhhh," Matt said.

"*Come on back again, please,*" said Megsley's calm and reassuring drawl.

"Copy, Yard Dog."

"*Okey doke,*" said the voice.

"*Engaging!*" yelled the voice of the young female truck commander in Beta.

Matt didn't think about her. He only did what he'd been told to do. Ignoring the coppery, sticky blood spotting the controls, he slowly got his mind and hands wrapped around his vehicle—his, for the rest of whenever—so that he eventually snapped off the autodrive, and watched as the lights went to yellow. Ahead, the convoy kept moving. They had at this point come out of the flatlands and were rolling directly into a range of hills. Matt hadn't been on Grainne long enough to know the geography. But seeing those hills was comforting. If he could just get his truck deeper into those hills, everything would be okay. That was his only goal. Get into the hills, in one piece.

Grasping the control handles more confidently, Matt applied a bit of pressure to the accelerator, and felt the tractor surge ahead. He'd let a lot of distance come between himself and Buffalo Fourteen. Much more than the requisite three hundred meters. He rapidly ate up that distance as the shouting of combat to the rear filled his ears. But the noise gradually faded until Matt heard nothing but the sound of his own heart beating. A rhythmic, potent sound. So that there was only the highway streaming past, and the hills ahead, with another flatbed in front of him.

✧   ✧   ✧

"Dammit," Captain Dean spat, listening to the hollering from Beta. Whatever had come up on the convoy, it was wreaking havoc in their rear. Two more flatbeds, Buffalo Twenty and Buffalo Nineteen, were lost, and a third would soon follow. The new vehicles were UN ILAWAVs. They mounted a small cannon each and might have infantry aboard. They were engined and armored in ways none of Dean's vehicles could match. So while Beta was doing its best to keep itself between those and the remaining flatbeds, the UN chasers could weave and bob as they pleased.

"Put us over one lane, and drop us back," Dean ordered.

"But, sir—" said the driver.

"Do it!" he said again. "We're clear ahead, but Beta's outnumbered, and the UN is eating our lunch!"

The driver jerked left, then let off the accelerator.

"Weaponeer!" Dean said, pounding a fist on the roof.

"*Weaponeer ready!*" came the young man's reply on the net.

It didn't take long before the convoy was whizzing past them.

And suddenly Alpha was in the fray. Out of his own armored window, Dean could see Beta gamely trying to maneuver and block. Buffalo Eighteen was lost, leaving Buffalo Seventeen wide open, with Buffalo Sixteen and the already-hurt Buffalo Fifteen bringing up the convoy's rear. Beta, meanwhile, appeared to have taken some glancing damage, but the tactical vehicle's armor held. The UN combat vehicles were much faster, but the weapons in their own turrets didn't appear to match the heavier guns of Alpha or Beta. In fact, two appeared to mount nonlethal projectors. Just the same, the cupolas for Alpha and Beta could not traverse nor elevate with nearly the agility of the UN attackers. So, it was just a matter of time before the United Nations vehicles—numbering three, and very nimble—picked off Beta, and began to chew their way back up the convoy proper.

Alpha's gunner opened up, only this time the big automatic was belching death to the rear. The motors on the cupola whined as the gunner tried to adjust fire, but it was slow going. Back, and forth. Back, and forth.

The loud *pang-pang-pang-pang* of shots hitting steel, rang through Alpha.

The gunner's body slumped overhead.

Dean shouted for a response, and when he got none, he unbuckled his own harness, turned, unlatched the gunner, and pulled the boy—bleeding profusely—down into the vehicle, then

pushed him into Private Paine's lap. Hoping she'd know what
to do next, Dean wormed his way up into the cupola and was
presented with weapons controls.

Air whistled in Dean's helmet as he grasped the handles,
uneasily slewing the cupola this way and that, trying to get a
feel for the thing. The erratic bursts from his weapon did little
more than chew up both soil and roadway, as the ILAWAVs
buzzed along, occasionally taking their own shots at both Buffalo
Seventeen, and Alpha and Beta alike.

When Buffalo Seventeen at last gave up the ghost, jackknifing
across the road, both Alpha and Beta swung out and around the
conflagration, then closed back again. But not before the three
UN vehicles zipped ahead, and were firing directly into Buffalo
Sixteen unimpeded.

Dean screamed, and slewed his cupola.

Matt Campos could still only hear his heartbeat. But in the
left-side views from his tractor's cameras, he saw the blocky, dark
shapes of the UN combat vehicles racing up the length of the
convoy, their weapons firing directly into Buffalo Sixteen. With
Alpha and Beta hopelessly outmatched—unable to accelerate in
time—it would only take the UN vehicles moments to reach the
middle of the column, and then the head of the column. Where
they could pen the entire convoy in, and crush it at will.

Matt jerked the manual controls so that Buffalo Fifteen swung
out of position and into the passing lane, where it blocked the
vehicles' path. Then he let up off the accelerator and touched the
brake, enough to send himself lurching against his harness. He
ignored the gore seated next to him, and felt the sudden thuds as two
of the three UN scouts slammed violently into the back of Buffalo
Fifteen's flatbed. Several red icons began to flash on the controls,
indicating damage to the hauler. But a rear camera check showed
smashed pieces of two UN vehicles spinning down the highway.

Buffalo Sixteen slipped effortlessly by, the driver looking panicked, and Matt saw the single square shape of the final scout
chasing. But only for a brief instant.

Two rockets fired at almost point-blank range spat from the
cupola of Alpha.

The UN vehicle ceased to exist.

✧   ✧   ✧

When at last the convoy came to a stop, Captain Dean found the prisoner laborer being helped down from Buffalo Fifteen's blood-soaked cab. The young man's face was pale, despite his complexion, and his eyes had a distant look in them, almost as if seeing through stone. Now surrounded by friendly Freehold forces, the remnants of the Reserve depot, fourteen flatbeds surviving out of twenty total, could rest easier for a while.

"Hell of a move," Dean said to Buffalo Fifteen's co-driver. Dean wiped a crusty hand at his face, which felt flecked with dried blood to the same degree as the prisoner's. "I'd say you helped save the entire convoy from disaster."

Sergeant Megsley was keeping the young prisoner upright, with a protective arm around his shoulder.

"He's kinda shocked out, sir," the Yard Dog said. "Give him the evening to recover."

"No, wait," Matt said, patting a shaking hand on Yard Dog's arm. Megsley let him go.

Dean and the prisoner stood face to face.

"Warrant Elton said something," Matt mused. "She told me she left everything behind, her whole life, on Earth, just to come here and have a chance to be *free*. I'm not sure I cared much about what that means, before today. But *she* cared. And, I'd really like . . . I'd like to *honor* that, see?"

"How so?" the captain asked.

"This morning I told Yard Dog this war wasn't my business. I mean, I'm just part of the prison detail. Not a soldier. But now? . . . I think I've changed my mind."

Dean stared for a few seconds, then reflexively stuck out his hand.

"Mine too," he said, and took the prisoner's hand in a firm shake. "When this is all over, I have a feeling the Freehold will be waiving the remainder of your sentence. At least if Sergeant Megsley and myself have anything to say about it. Go get some chow, soldier."

"Appreciate it, sir," the co-driver said. Then he stumbled over to one of the bivouacs where a bunk and a hot meal awaited.

Huff #13
Reservists and Cowboys [June 210]

One of the trickiest things with this place is the number of part-time and retiree soldiers who mobilized just as we hit Grainne in detail. I'm impressed at how quickly and efficiently they managed it, and at the quality of personnel. When I stayed in the CIC aboard *London* after my latest press brief, I viewed targeting pod footage from a strike on a reserve convoy expediting down a highway—about twenty flatbeds, such a beautiful target! From the way Sandeep cheered, you'd think it was a football match. Then, one of the Avatars ate some missiles. Sandeep didn't cheer much after that. This convoy came from a supply depot, and, unfortunately, the reservists boobytrapped it—no spoils for us this time.

I'm not happy about the exchange ratio—we only took out six—granted, they were widely spaced and moving breakneck, but we should have done better. The convoy managed to break contact, and we lost them. We still don't have enough aerial reconnaissance planetside yet.

I am not impressed.

Starhome

Michael Z. Williamson

One didn't have to be involved in a war to suffer, nor even in line of fire. Collateral economic damage could destroy just as easily.

First Minister Jackson Bates looked over the smallest nation in space. From the window of his tower, he could view the entire territory of Starhome up above him. Centrifugal gravity meant the planetoid was "up," but he was used to it. It was a rock roughly a kilometer in diameter, tunneled through for habitat space, with its rotation adjusted to provide centrifugal G.

The window was part of a structure had once been Jump Point Control for Earth's JP1. As orbits and jumplines shifted, and as technology advanced relentlessly on, it became cost-ineffective to use the station, and it was too small and antiquated for modern shipping. A new one was built, and this one "abandoned to space."

When the UNPF made that final assignation, his grandfather took a small ship with just enough supplies to let him occupy and declare it private territory. The tower became the family home and offices, and the control center for their business.

Agencies on Earth panicked, and there'd actually been a threat of military occupation. The UN courts had ruled the abandonment made it salvage, and the Bateses' occupation was that salvage. The family owned a hollowed-out planetoid of passages and compartments, and could do with it as they wished.

At once, the bureaus of Earth protested. BuSpace, BuMil, BuCommerce all took their shots. If they hadn't been so busy fighting each other, they'd have wiped out Starhome a century ago.

The family's entire livelihood was fringe, marginal and unglamorous. Actual smuggling would have made them a valid threat to be attacked. They were information brokers, dealing with untraceable data that was useful to someone, encoded heavily and carried through the jump point directly. Eventually, legitimate cargo transshipment began, since their docking rates were cheaper, just enough for the additional flight time to be offset for certain classes of ship. Tramp freighters came by, and finally a couple of fleets contracted gate space.

All of which had evaporated when the war with the Freehold of Grainne started. The UN bit down hard on tramp freighters, anything with a Freehold registry, and then started more in-depth monitoring of every jump point it could access directly or by treaty.

The last ship had docked a month before. Little was moving, and what was tended toward huge corporate ships who wouldn't waste time on Starhome. What were docking fees to them?

For now, Starhome had food and oxygen. When it ran low, they'd be forced to pay for direct delivery at extreme cost, or ultimately abandon the station and return to Earth. There'd already been inquiries from the UNPF to that effect, offering "rescue."

Jackson Bates wasn't going to do that. He might go as far as Jupiter's moons. He wouldn't step foot on Earth again if he could avoid it.

His phone chimed.

"Yes?" he answered. All forty-three staff and family knew who he was.

Engineer Paul Rofert said, *"Sir, if you're not busy, I need to show you something at the dock tube."*

"On my way," he said.

Starhome's docking system was a long gang tube with docking locks protruding. It was axial, so ships had to be balanced with each other or counterweights. It was "mostly" axial. Over a couple of centuries, drift happened. That was a known issue, and he hoped that wasn't the problem now.

It took three minutes to run a trolley car down the tower, to the axis, and along it. He knew every centimeter of the route, every passage and compartment. Those had once been quarters for visiting VIPs, when just visiting a station was novel. That had been rec space, and still was, officially. There weren't enough people to make proper use of the gym, so some of the equipment had been relocated over there, to what was once commo gear for jump control. Now everything was aging in either vacuum or atmosphere, a century or more out of date and quaint at best. But, it was his home. Apart from four years in college in Georgia, this was the only place he'd ever lived. There was room enough for hundreds.

Rofert was waiting at the hub before the dock tube, which was still empty.

Jackson's executive, Nicol Cante was with him. He unstrapped from the car and shoved over in the near-zero G.

"Chief," Jackson greeted and shook hands. Rofert was tall, black with gray hair, and had worked for the family for three generations. He knew every bolt and fissure in the place.

"Sir," Rofert said with a nod and a firm shake back. "I hate to deliver more bad news, but..."

"Go ahead." It wasn't as if things could get much worse.

"The axis drift is worse than we'd anticipated. It has precessed enough the tube can't be considered axial anymore. We'll need to adjust rotation."

"Can our attitude jets do it?"

"No, we'll need external mounts and a lot of delta V over several days to avoid lateral stresses. And it has to be done soon or feedback oscillations will rip the dock apart."

"Then I guess we're out of business," he replied. He was surprised at how easily he said it. Apparently, he'd known the outcome and just been waiting for the cue. "We can't afford that."

Rofert said, "Sorry, sir."

He sighed. He was glad his father wasn't here to see that. They'd lasted two generations as an Independent Territory. Now they were done.

"I'm Jackson, Paul. We're friends even when the news is bad."

He continued, "My personal craft can take twenty if we have to. That will be the last one out. See what transport you can arrange, Nicol. Call Space Guard if you must, but I'd prefer we leave with dignity."

She swiped at her notepad. "On it, Chief. When should we plan for it?"

"Part of me wants to get it over with, and part wants to hold out until the bitter end. Use your judgment."

"Got it."

Her judgment was exceptional. She had degrees in physics and finance. She'd offer him a grid of windows, costs and movements and guide him through the decision. That ability was why he'd hired her. No doubt she'd find other employment, but he felt he was cheating her by asking her to plan her own evacuation.

He'd sounded depressed and defeated. She'd been calm and solid.

Nicol's suggested schedule meant they'd start leaving in a week. There was one in-system charter willing to haul most of the staff at that time, and that would clean out much of the available credit. They were that deep in the hole. The command staff would go with him, as would a demolition crew, who'd strip cables, metals, food, anything aboard that could be salvaged. It would either go aboard, or in a planned orbit. Mass and material were commodities in space. At least with that and the proceeds from selling his boat he'd be able to reestablish on Titan, or if he had to, on Earth, somewhere reasonably still free. Chile, perhaps. Sulawan. New Doggerland.

He still wouldn't be in space then though, nor independent.

Nothing had docked this week, either. Nothing was going to, even if they could have. The dock and davits were silent, the workers helping tear out nonessential materials for recovery. What had been the old gym was now a pile of iron and aluminum for reuse, for the little value it held. The hatches were sealed, the oxygen recovered to stretch what was used in the working space.

His phone chimed, breaking his musing and his mood.

"What?" he answered.

"Inbound vessel, sir. Very stealthy. And it came from out and forward, not from the point."

He realized it was Astrogator Marie Duval in Docking Control. His estranged daughter-in-law by the son of his estranged wife. They were both back on Earth, just not the type for space. Marie had stayed.

A vessel? Not from the point?

"Human?" he asked as he started swimming that way, grabbing a loop on the cable that wound endlessly between hub and DC, as a cheap elevator.

She said, *"Yes, it seems to be. Forceline propulsion, but tiny."*

"Phase drive for interstellar, then?"

She replied, *"No indication of that, no."*

"I'm on my way across," he said. Centrifugal G increased as he was pulled outward.

He needed to see it. He fidgeted until he arrived, pulled himself through the hatch, and looked at the monitors.

There it was, tiny and dark.

Marie said, "I tightbeamed them, sir. No response. Should I try laser?"

"Go ahead. How far are they?"

"Six light-seconds. We saw them about six and a half."

That was close. No one had seen them until now?

A minute later she said, "Laser response, sir."

The audio said, *"We are a private ship, offering trade."*

Jackson responded with, "Approaching ship, be aware our docking facilities are compromised and unsafe. You cannot dock directly. Who are you and what are you offering?"

"We will avoid the dock tube. Please stand by for our arrival."

He shrugged. "Well, they're human, and talking. I can't imagine anyone wants to hijack this place."

Duval said, "That is a warship, though, sir."

"Based on the stealth?"

She nodded. "Yes, sir. It's stealthed stupid. No one tries to stay hidden in space without a reason."

"You're correct, but we can't do much. Prepare to zip a request to Space Guard if we have to."

"It's already queued, sir. The ship will be here in under an hour. Space Guard is at least four hours away after we call."

"Understood. I'll wait here for any updates." They could call him, but he wanted to show his support, and it would be faster if he could see screens directly. He made himself some coffee and found the cookie stash. The chairs were good, this being one of the few places with decent G levels. They were half a century old, repaired multiple times to avoid excess costs.

It was definitely a human ship, and it maneuvered in slowly. It had to have been en route at low thrust for a long time, or the energy signature would have shown.

It had no markings, no IFF. Active radar and other scans showed almost nothing, just bare ghosts. It was a hole in space as far as sensors were concerned.

It moved in almost to contact, then opened a hatch, deployed a line, and tethered to the base of the dock assembly. Three figures came out in V-suits, entered the maintenance lock and cycled through.

Jackson and Nicol had time to get placed to greet whomever it was, and four security personnel stood at angles with shotguns. "Stood" in near-zero G by hooking to stanchions. It didn't seem there'd be need, but there was no proof there wouldn't be.

It was cold in the terminal. There was no reason to heat it, with no ships inbound.

The lock unlatched and swung. The three inside were young-ish, fit, definitely human, and unarmed. They doffed helmets.

The woman in front said, "Greetings. First Minister Bates? I'm pleased to meet you and apologize for the circumstances. I'm Dr. Hazel Donahey. This is Dr. Andrew Tyson and Assistant True Hively."

"Doctor," he agreed and shook hands. "This is my executive, Dr. Nicol Cante." If they were going to use titles, so was he.

He asked, "What can I do for you?"

Dr. Donahey said, "We need a research base for stellar and deep-space observations. You have a habitat that's unfortunately rather quiet, but that suits our needs." She didn't look threatening, and certainly could be an academic. Space-short hair, no jewelry, no wasted movement.

He didn't want to accuse them of being vultures, but he didn't have a great bargaining position.

He said, "It is quiet, and I wish it wasn't. I regret that I don't even have functional facilities anymore."

Donahey said, "Our budget isn't large, but is underwritten, and we can provide a certain amount of oxygen, food and power beyond our own needs. We'll also have available people with technical training to assist in overhaul."

So what did they want?

"You said you need observations?" He gestured for them to follow. There was no imminent threat, and there were frames at the edge of the bay.

She spoke as they pulled themselves along. "Yes. Sol is unique in many ways, still including the elusive intelligent life. There are several competing theories on stellar development. Then, drive research is notably concerned with terminal effects around jump points. The deep space, but still heliospace is critical, and again, this is a very convenient place to operate from."

Nicol asked, "Why not just use a leased liner? And who do you represent?" She draped across a frame with the casual sprawl of someone who had spent years in space.

"Liners have tremendous operating costs. We're from Brandt's research arm. We are strictly private."

He said, "And we're supposed to overlook that Brandt is based in Grainne, the UN has occupied your system, and you're magically here near a jump point for 'observations'?"

Donahey shrugged and tucked into the frame, as did her assistants. "Science is about knowledge, sir. This is a project we've worked on for a long time. I can make the data files available if you wish. We were using a remote site in Salin, but there's a significant difference in stellar environments between a K3 and a G2 star."

He hung from one stanchion, just to have some sort of base. He noted Nicol wasn't in the same orientation as the rest. She liked to get angled views on things to spot discrepancies.

On the one hand, he wanted to believe them. On the other, they had a stealth ship, probably military. On the other, he really owed nothing to Earth at this point. They'd tried everything they could to kill his family's dream. On the other, there was a difference between not owing Earth and assisting possible espionage. On yet another hand, he needed operating cash even if he was shutting down, and food and oxy would close out two costs on his accounts.

"Let's go to my office," he said.

They were experienced spacers. They followed easily in low and no G. Everyone was quiet on the trolley, and he was embarrassed at the worn, out-of-date seating. He was glad to get to his office. That wasn't more than a decade out of date, and it had enough G.

He offered his restroom so they could change into shipsuits and shlippers instead of V-suits and grips.

When they came back in coveralls, he asked, "May I get you anything? Hard or soft."

"Hot tea with lemon would be very nice," Dr. Donahey said. "Two."

"Three, please."

He nodded. Even a short EVA could be cold out here. Then,

the terminal wasn't kept warm, relying on waste heat from equipment to heat it. The equipment wasn't in use.

"Tea all around, and drinks later, please, Frank," he said to his grandson, the Factotum On Duty. That was a fancy title for "gopher." Though they did more than just gophering.

His title of First Minister was a fancy way of saying "owner." It just gave a political spin. In reality, his leadership was smaller than any but the tiniest rural villages on Earth. But the volume of nothing he commanded...

"You do understand I'm nervous, with the war on," he said.

Donahey said, "Understandable. If you prefer, we can negotiate with Earth and occupy after you leave. The only problem is it would take several months to get approval, but since we're a recognized research institute, there's no real problem. And of course, you wouldn't be benefitting."

Yeah, there was that. Everyone had plans for the station, when he was forced to abandon it. It made him stubborn.

Frank brought back the tea, and he took the moment it was being served to signal to Nicol, who asked, "So what do you think of Carnahan's hypothesis on jump point eddy currents during the reset phase?"

Donahey said, "That's more Andy's area."

Andrew Tyson said, "Bluntly, the man's deluding himself. Those currents occurred twice, during a specific combination of ship and point, and similar but far smaller effects were identified with the same class ship in an earlier generation of the same point mechanism. It's purely an artifact of circumstance, not a general effect. But that is the sort of thing we want to test."

Nicol nodded and asked, "What was the delta X on that ship?"

"Well, it was forceline propulsion, so the delta X was almost entirely within the hull. Induction field harmonics are more important, and it was under a k-value of six."

"Fair enough," Nicol said. "So you at least understand physics. Would you mind if I observed your findings?"

"By all means," Donahey said. "We'd want an NDA for discretion, but you're quite welcome to observe the process."

Jackson caught her signal back.

So, they were legitimate, just here in odd circumstances.

"What do you need and what are you offering?"

She said, "We'd need lodging for ourselves, there are twelve, and boat crews as they come through. We'd need access to two divergent points—the end of the dock assembly, and the antipodean point on the outside. We'll be occasionally pulling a lot of power from your reactor. We'll make up the mass."

"And what do we get?"

"Oxygen, food, fuel, metals and organics. Everything a small habitat needs, since we need it functional too. We assumed occupancy and support for a hundred."

Jackson thought about asking for money, too, but that really was a generous offer. It was twice current crewing level, so should last a bit. He hated being forced to take it, though.

"Our docking gantry is no longer axial, and in danger of catastrophic failure from oscillations," he admitted.

The three looked at each other and seemed to swap expressions.

True Hively said, "I should be able to coordinate that. It's a significant amount of reaction mass and maneuvering engine, though."

Donahey said, "We'd consider that our top offer."

Really, it was fair, in that Starhome would remain functional for as long as this took, and docking facilities would be back online.

It wasn't fair in that it only prolonged the inevitable.

Since he'd be returning to Earth's economy even on Titan, and taxed again, he wondered what kind of write off he could get for donating the rock to them.

"How long is the project?"

Donahey said, "Our current funding allows seventeen months."

"Deal," he said.

It gave everyone seventeen more months of employment and distance from Earth. He'd have to keep paying them from shrinking capital, but he wouldn't have to turn them out.

Donahey said, "Then we'll return to our ship, and arrange to move into your ante section, as you called it. Thank you very much for your hospitality. And you, Dr. Cante."

Right after the visitors were escorted out, he got notice of an incoming transmission from Space Guard. It was an offer to evacuate his people now, pending acceptance of...

"Nicol, do we have some sort of demand from the UN?"

"It just came in," she said. "Apparently these idiots can't even coordinate their own memos."

"What is it?"

"It's a salvage price offer to buy you out and relocate us."

"Bastards."

He took a moment to calm himself, and said, "I wonder if Prescot will pick up my request. It seems like the scavengers aren't even waiting for us to die."

The scientists and crew started moving stuff at once. They had supplies for themselves, crates of technical gear. They took accommodations in the other privately owned lodging Starhome had already sealed off, and brought it back online themselves. Their ship transferred reactor fuel cells.

They double sealed the passages to that section by physically locking airtight hatches. They requested no one approach the ante pole during outside maintenance, either.

"We can do that for you," True Hively said. "Our sensors are easily disrupted."

A week later, a freighter arrived with cargo pods of oxygen, food and attitude engines. It was good to look out his office ports and see a ship again. Even only one ship. It approached in a long arc to dockside only, which was costly in fuel.

"I don't like it," Nicol said.

Jackson said, "It's all from Govannon, and all properly marked. Legitimately purchased."

"Yes, and I suppose they may have phase drive to explain how they came in the back way. You haven't asked about that."

"I haven't," he agreed. "I wanted to see if the deal was real, and if it would help. We have a year and a half to hope things turn around, or to withdraw in stages."

She said, "I'm still bothered by a heavily stealthed boat from deep space, and the lack of advance notice. So is Marie. They really don't want to be seen."

"Their credentials checked out with Brandt, didn't they?"

"They did," she admitted. "Then I messaged my friend Travis in R&D over there. He's never heard of them. Corporate says they're legit. Operations isn't aware."

"I suppose it was classified research."

She said, "And if so, it was for Grainne...who we are now at war with."

"We are? Earth is. We're neutral."

She said, firmly, "Boss, neutral status goes away if you aid a hostile power."

"Have they done anything illicit?"

"No. They really are making solar observations, but you real-ize they could be tracking ships, habitats, commo and anything else as well, right? They're in-system, with shaky credentials and sensors that can image fireflies in Iowa from here."

Jackson was enjoying really good French bread, baked by his staff using wheat that came in aboard the researchers' supply ship.

He checked off points. "Grainne's jump point with Earth is down. No one is going to let them jump warships around. They had phase drive of course, since Brandt is located there, but only a few ships. They can't stage an attack here, they no longer exist as an independent system. Even if these people are spying, it's not going to do any good."

Nicol said, "I more wonder if they contracted to NovRos or even the Prescots. The UN is building infrastructure everywhere against other independence movements. The Colonial Alliance can't do anything the UN doesn't want to allow. It's more likely corporate or political espionage than military."

"Exactly."

She said, "Either way, we'd still wind up in jail for life for helping. Even if they've locked us out of our own habitat, we can't claim we didn't know."

"Do you want out?" he asked. This was important.

She shook her head. "No, Boss, I'll stay. I'm curious. I just wanted to make sure you realized the risks."

"Always," he said.

She said, "At least I have work again, monitoring our guests. They pass down the axis daily and are making observations. I'd sure like to see their other end, though."

"Have they furnished the data for you to review?" he asked.

"They have. It's too detailed and esoteric for my skill set, but looks real, and even if I understood it, I'm holding with the NDA unless it's relevant to our safety."

"Well done, thank you."

He couldn't run the place without her.

The next ship was a week later, with more supplies and more personnel. They graciously offered other upgrades, those spon-sored by Prescot Deep Space in Govannon. It irritated Jackson more. Prescot had refused a previous deal, hadn't responded to his new one, but were willing to send stuff if someone else paid for it. That defined his status.

The station rumbled with the low hum of reaction engines nudging it back into alignment as built, with a promise that the docks could reopen in less than two weeks. Assuming, of course, there were any other ships.

Dr. Donahey visited his office every two or three days. She was on the schedule for today.

"Good morning, Jackson," she said on arriving. He'd been clear he was not "Sir" or "First Minister."

"Good morning, Hazel." He pointed to the tea.

"Thank you," she said and took a cup. "I just came back from the sensors at the end of the docking tube, and checked with True on my way. Did you see your terminal should be online next week?"

"I did," he said. "I appreciate it greatly, even if we never get to use it. At least we won't be abandoning the place."

"I like it," she said. "It's old, but has character. Have you thought of asking Prescot if they could use it?"

"I have. They're not interested."

"That's odd," she said. "I thought they'd find it useful, especially as they built it originally."

She seemed bothered.

He asked, "Can you tell me about your project? I'm an educated layman."

She took a deep breath and said, "Well, we're working on several. In my case, we're watching the chromosphere currents and variable fluctuations of the Sun, and running hefty simulations backward on how it was at the time life first evolved, and the varying radiation there would have been. That's to see if any of it might be significant to stages of the evolution of life. So far, we've found lots of habitable planets to terraform, a handful with their own life, and few that have any advanced organisms. Any number of factors could affect it. So I'm a physicist, dealing with life scientists. Mine is all 'how?'; theirs is all 'what if?'"

"What cycles are you tracking?" he asked, and had some tea. That was an expensive import here, too.

"Milankovitch, Rujuwa, the neutrino flux variation, several others."

"Interesting. Are you religious at all, Hazel?"

She shook her head. "Not at all, but I would enjoy exploring outside influence on it all, if there was any way to determine its existence. Are you?"

"No, but I often wonder."

"That seems to be human nature and how the supernatural came to be created. Humans recognized a pattern, couldn't find a reason for it, so created one."

"How is Andy doing on his projects?"

"He has a lot of people building processors and setting sensors. Still. What he's looking for is very subtle, and it's annoying having to work around it. That's why we sealed the entire ante third of the station."

"Yeah, I signed off on that, after a lengthy tour. As much as I want to help, being locked out of my own home is a tough call." He also had Paul using an abandoned conduit to check on them. The engineer reported everything good.

"It affects my observations, too, but even though I'm nominally in charge, both Prescot and Brandt want his data. So I have to make do."

"What do I need to know about anything upcoming?" he asked.

"Well, once you can operate again, Andy has a clear zone we really need kept free of trajectories, if you can manage it at all. He's very firm on this, but of course, it's your station. Keeping in mind if his team pulls out we have to renegotiate our terms." She seemed embarrassed. "There's another large pod train coming in with additional gear, stocks for you, and a few more personnel."

"Understood. As long as Operations has it, I have no problem. It's not as if it's an astrogation hazard. One other question, if I may."

"Go ahead."

"Why did you arrive in what's essentially a stealth military vessel from deep space?"

She made a face.

"Andy's work, again. They were explicit that we not disrupt space any more than critical so we had a clean baseline for examining forcelines and other structures. We were towed around by a tug, and he made them detach further out than I was comfortable with. The boat is secured against as much leakage as possible. It's basically the equivalent of a clean room. You notice the supply vessels only come in from the docking pole vector."

"So am I even going to be able to resume docking ops, then?"
She looked really embarrassed.

"Yes. Andy will be very unhappy, but at that point, he has to
make do. We've accommodated as much as we can. That decision's up to me, and that's why I'm in charge even though his
research has priority."

"Administration and politics," he said, feeling empathy for her.

"Exactly. Thanks for the tea. Shall I check in on Friday?"

"That should be fine."

He didn't bring up that Brandt wasn't clear on their status.
He'd save that a bit longer.

After she left, he called Rofert.

"I have a favor for next week," he said.

"Yes, Boss?"

"Can one of your inspection tugs make an orbit around the
station?"

*"Not an orbit per se, in any reasonable time, but we have
enough juice in one to pull a loop, yes."*

"Thanks, I'll get with you."

He thought about contacting Space Guard and reporting on
events, but he was officially a neutral nation. Contacting them
put him more under Earth's thumb and less in the independent
category. As curious as he was, he was still a head of state. If
Earth stepped in, even the courts might revoke his status.

They were demanding a response to their previous offer, too.
The UN Bureau of Space Development understood he controlled
a station, etc., and were pleased to extend an offer of salvage cost
for the low-use asset, etc., in lieu of further action to assess a
bunch of issues that could result in fines.

He needed something soon or they were just going to show
up and drag him to Earth.

Could Govannon or Brandt run some public ships here and
put up a pretense of interest?

He called back. "Paul, and Nicol, we need to have a meeting
on this."

Rofert replied, *"On my way."*

Nicol said, "Right here." She stepped through from her office.

With everyone seated in G, and something stronger than tea
to drink, he opened the discussion.

"The UN, Earth specifically, is trying to hurry us into

abandonment. They don't seem to be willing to wait, and they're pestering us. Govannon hasn't expressed interest, but is happy to support a Brandt operation here. We've got speculation that Grainne, if they remain this 'Freehold,' is interested. I need input."

Paul Rofert sipped whisky and said, "Prescot has plenty of resources and might like a remote maintenance facility. You and I have discussed this. If that offer wasn't good then, it doesn't mean it might not be good again soon. They value privacy, too."

Nicol said, "The problem is, they have everything they need on their side. On our side, Frontier Station isn't presently doing enough business to get in the way of maintenance docking, and they have lease agreements for dock space."

"And Grainne?" he asked.

Paul twisted his mouth.

"That all depends on them surviving a war and remaining independent."

"Yes," Jackson said. "The same applies to us. We're smaller, and even more readily occupied. But I don't want to throw in with what may be the losing side."

"Will almost certainly be," Nicol said. "They don't have the infrastructure to fight for long. The UN, meaning Earth, is stupidly focusing on the planet more than on space resources, but still, they can't do it."

Paul said, "The guests are straightforward to deal with. But the scientists can't speak for the government, and what government they had is in hiding."

Nicol said, "That still may have been a warship they were in. It was probably repurposed, but I still don't trust them."

"Why not?" he asked.

"Business as usual, oh, and by the way, can we set up clandestinely with you, right next to our enemy? I don't like it."

"Any more word on their bona fides?"

She said, "The scientists have written peer-reviewed papers and appear to be legitimate, but I'd be hard pressed to say they have the seniority for a mission like this."

"Meaning?"

She said, "Meaning they could have been hired as a front."

Paul said, "Possibly they were the only ones available?"

She shook her head. "You'd still send them, but someone with more field time would be in charge."

Jackson said, "The issue is, this is our only income at present, and while it covers some essentials, we're not making any money. I'm paying everyone out of company capital. I can't do that for long. So we still come down to, do we close shop now, hold out until this science mission runs out and hope something comes along, or do something else?"

Nicol said, "You've been honest with everyone about when it might roll over us. Don't worry about that."

"But I do," he said. "Stringing it out isn't fair and doesn't make sense, unless we have a good chance of succeeding."

She said, "I suppose I should be honest and admit I sent my resumé to Prescot for any relevant position."

"I don't blame you," he said. He didn't, but damn, if she didn't see an out, and he didn't, it was all over. "I guess in that case, when you get an acceptance, I take that as the turning point and close up."

Paul sat very still and said, "I'll remain until the end. There's nothing for me on Earth."

Jackson remembered that Rofert had been in space since his family died in a "pacification" conflict. All cultures were equal on Earth. But occasionally a culture was deemed troublesome and "reintegrated."

He looked at his engineer and lifelong friend. The man had been working here before he was born. "You will ride with me, and we'll go to Titan. And I guess I know what I have to do. Nicol, tell everyone we'll resume departure plans. Paul, your people will need to stay. And I still want to make that survey. Call it nostalgia."

"Understood."

"Got it."

The incoming ship did have a lot more supplies, and more personnel.

It was getting very suspicious. What did a group of researchers need with so many technical assistants? Yes, they'd helped do a lot of equipment overhaul, even to the point of surface treatments and duct cleaning. But why?

If they wanted a hostile takeover, this was a slow way about it, and what point would it serve? If tramp freighters didn't need his station, no larger group would. Few corporations had the funds to waste, and those would have just offered to buy him out and grant him a bunch of favors. The actual governments just wanted to ignore him or exercise eminent domain.

He was going to make that orbit, and Andy's research be damned.

Later that day, Jackson realized he needed a new V-suit. He hadn't gained much weight, but a decade had changed his shape. This one pinched and rubbed. It would last the trip, though.

Rofert personally flew him. They had to inspect the docking array anyway. They ungrappled and slowly accelerated out from the axis.

Pointing to the dock through the port, Rofert said, "It's aligned within very close tolerances, about point five mils."

"Impressive," he said. The visitors' work was honest, no matter what else was going on.

"Now aft and ante," Rofert said.

They overshot the dock while decelerating, got a good scan of the outer terminal and beacon, then slowly moved back. There were workers in the pools of illumination on the scaffolding, some his, more of them visitors. There were over fifty of them now, and it made no sense.

"Let's see what the sneaky bastards are up to," Rofert said as they reached relative zero and started moving back. "Control, Engineer One stating intent to change trajectory and proceed ante for scheduled observation."

"Engineer One, Control confirms, proceed."

The docking pylon, then the melted regolith moved a hundred meters below, punctuated with ports and structures of the lodge, of old construction locks and the control tower and his residence. It really was a tiny station, and a tiny nation. It couldn't be relevant to anyone, and long term it was doomed anyway.

There was nothing significant visible as they passed the irregular lump that marked the arbitrary equator, but then...

"Holy crap," he muttered. "Did you see all this, Paul?"

The entire ante polar region had been built. There were scaffolds, gantries, three docked tugs he could see in addition to the regular boat. There were a lot more than a hundred personnel here, too, because he could see close to that many swarming around building stuff.

In one way or another, it was a hostile takeover.

Then everything went black.

Rofert said, "I'm afraid I did, sir."

"'Sir'? Are we down to that, then?"

Sweat suddenly burst from him. It was a sellout, and it was hostile. Paul had been in on whatever it was.

"We're not low on power," Paul said. "We've been disrupted." He pulled out a rescue light and started flashing it, just as something obscured the view.

It was a stealth boat, bay open, maneuvering to intercept.

"Paul... this was not cool. Not at all."

"Hold on, please, sir. You need to see this." He sounded earnest and urgent.

The invading force, because that's what it was, had turned the rear third of his castle into a combat operations center. He'd seen what he needed to.

He kept quiet, because his life might depend on not irritating anyone. He'd let them have the rock, as long as they let his people go, even if it meant detention for a while first.

Detention, at least, would still be in space. Arguably better than being "free" on Earth.

Whomever was in the boat was cautious and careful. It was long minutes before they were ensconced in the bay. It closed, blacker inside than out, the stars and station disappearing.

There were bumps, and lights came back on. Hanging off the davit holding them were several armed troops.

The one in front waved for attention and spoke through a contact mic. *"Mister Bates and Mister Rofert, if you will please open and disembark, the atmosphere is safe."*

Rofert looked at him, shrugged and unlatched the hatch port.

They were allowed to maneuver to the forward end of the bay, where the actual deck was, and tie to stanchions. The bay was pressurized and the others unmasked, so Jackson did, too.

The nearest man said, "We apologize for the circumstances. We'd hoped to delay this a bit longer." He looked Hawaiian in ancestry. And broad. About fifty. His accent was from the Grainne Freehold Halo.

Jackson replied, "I'm sorry to have hindered your war."

From the other, "Who said anything about war?"

"It's obvious you're from Grainne and using my home as at

least an intel base. It's already set up for that, and I don't have any way to stop you." He should be furious. He'd had suspicions and at this point, it didn't change the outcome of losing his livelihood. Both sides could die, for all he cared. And Paul...had obviously seen this in his conduit crawl, and why hadn't Jackson insisted on going along, too?

He turned, "Paul? Why?"

Paul said, "Sir, I know you don't want to abandon your home. Earth would kill you whether intentionally or not. I promised your father I'd maintain it and keep it. This is the only outlet we have, for now."

The officer said, "We intend no violence against you."

He asked, "Do you intend violence against Earth?"

The man responded, "At present, we are gathering scientific information."

"That doesn't answer my question."

"How many questions about the data you transfer have you answered? Or even asked?"

That was valid. He knew much of the data they handled was questionable, if not outright illicit. This, though, pushed the envelope of plausible deniability.

He said, "I acted in good faith. Even though your presentation was questionable."

The man said, "You acted in your own self-interest. You still can. The scientists are doing so."

"So you're funding them?"

"They're funded by Brandt and Prescot, as they said. We're furnishing labor and transport."

He'd accuse them of being cheap, but he knew what charter transport would cost.

The man added, "We're also providing your supplies, at present."

There was the offer. "What do you require me to do?"

"Nothing at all. Just tell no one. We'll continue to cover your operating costs, and we hope the war will end shortly. At that point, you resume being a private exchange and transshipment point."

He believed that was true and honest. He wasn't sure it was something the man could realistically promise.

He replied, "So I have to choose which side I take, in a war I didn't want any part of."

"I guess that's up to you," his counterpart said. "When a landslide starts, the pebbles don't get a vote. The war has started, but the hostilities haven't reached here yet. You not only get a vote, you must vote."

He could be their ally, or their prisoner. Either way, Earth would regard him as hostile and treat him accordingly. They'd wanted Starhome back from the moment his father claimed it.

"I'd have to tell my exec," he warned.

The man nodded. "Yes, just face to face. No transmissions, and none of the inside staff."

It wasn't as if he could call anyone. If he managed to get a message to Earth, even if they believed it, they'd destroy everything his family had, and likely charge him anyway.

Earth had attacked a small nation with a lot of resources because it offered political leverage against others. They in turn had occupied his home because it offered leverage back.

"I wanted to be neutral," he said.

Very seriously, the man said, "So did we, sir."

The parallel was ironic.

Jackson said, "I have nothing to lose. At the same time, I have nothing to gain. What bargaining position do you have, sir?"

The big officer flexed as he moved. It wasn't intimidation. He was just that big with muscle. He pulled out a flask, took a swig, and offered it.

"Silver Birch. Some consider it our finest liquor."

It was informal, but they were in a cargo bay, on a deck surrounded by loading equipment. He accepted with a nod, took a drink, and damn, that was smooth. Notes of exotic fruit, ice and something like pine. He'd heard of it, but even the head of state of a rock couldn't afford such imports.

"Very nice," he said.

The officer said, "For now, I can increase cash payments somewhat, to cover our 'maintenance facility.' And I assure you only noncombatant craft will dock here for the duration. That's to our benefit and yours. If you'll tell me what you need for payroll and other overhead, I can approve it."

That was a significant shift. However, if he was selling out, he wasn't going to sell out cheap.

He asked, "What if I am attacked by the UN forces?"

"We'd be attacked as well, in that case."

"Yes, but what is my status?" he prompted.

"At that point, you are an engaged ally, and we'd do our best to defend you as well. Since we'd need the facilities for retreat and repair at that point."

Jackson said, "I'll have my exec draft that as a formal agreement, if you don't mind, holding you to tenant status." He wanted his people drafting the agreement on his terms.

"Fair," the man agreed.

Yes, but . . . "And after the war, then what?"

"What do you want?"

"First refusal on docking rights for any Freehold-flagged freighter."

The officer shook his head. "That would be impossible to enforce, given our legal system."

"What instead, then?"

The man said, "We can strongly recommend that our vessels use your services. If you've studied our culture, we're very big on social connections and support of friends."

"Well and good," Jackson said. "But I need something stronger than recommendations."

The man sat and thought for a moment, and Jackson let him. He looked around. The other personnel were still on alert, ready to react to orders. He figured this guy was the officer in charge of the project.

Finally, the man said, "I can guarantee ten years of baseline support of your operation at its present size. Expansion is up to you."

That did it. He was subsidized and beholden, but still independent. They hadn't taken, hadn't threatened, and hadn't tried to buy him out. They respected his sovereignty and circumstances.

First Minister Bates addressed the foreign officer officially. "Reluctantly, and under protest, I accept this pending signature, and offer you continued sanctuary, with the expectation that my people will be given proper treatment as both noncombatants and nonparticipants in our agreement."

"Then, sir," the man said, extending his hand, "You have my word as a Freehold officer."

He shook, and wasn't sure what to say next. He turned to Paul and said, "Whether we live or die, Paul, it will be here, in our home."

His friend grinned back. "That's the only way it should be, sir."

The Danegeld
Part 2

After smuggler-turned-transport *Graci*'s third drop to the UN's northern base in Darkwood Hills, Ananda Romdee was impressed by how her husband Cal had the UN grunts all but cheering their arrival, slipping in treats and losing a hand or two of poker at critical points, everything so friendly even Hank, still the angriest of their crew, nearly dropped his guard on those runs. It had all become routine enough to make Ana itchy. With this new batch, the frisson of the unknown client bled back through, a push of energy that made her poke at the soldiers despite knowing better.

"Need help loading?" For reasons both inane (arcane procedure) and, she admitted begrudgingly, practical (potential for bombs and sabotage) the soldiers were required to examine the goods on the ground before stocking their transports, rather than having the hauler load directly from the ship to their trucks.

Cal was good, but not that good. Ana guessed it'd be at least one more delivery, maybe two, before Norris would allow such a breach, no matter how often he glanced into the woods. The jumpier these soldiers got, the more she considered ways to make it worse.

Not her finest trait.

Tico gestured last load, and she rocked back on her heels, looking over the soldiers chatting with Cal. Just a handful more months of this, and they could stop this dance, get back to work.

"Everything in order, Sergeant?"

"Manifest checks out." His tone had less bite in it. Didn't make her want to hit him any less.

"We'll be on our way, then."

"More deliveries to make?" The question was almost human—more actual question than jibe.

"Orders," she answered, lifting a shoulder. Goddess, she was tired of UN orders.

"These ones probably have a bead on some good liquor," Cal offered as the gangplank clunked and the lock cycled closed behind them. Every moving part of the lander made too much noise, to distract from how smoothly the ragged craft moved. "Smelled it on that ensign, and I don't think it's any of ours."

"Can you even help yourself, charming these yahoos?" Despite her real exasperation, Ana's amusement bled through. "Need to have them all in your pocket?"

"Hank's good at electronic seals and manifest wanking, but even he's not perfect. If they like us, they trust us, then they miss the little slips. Foolproof."

"Foolproof," she echoed doubtfully, with the slightest of eye rolls. "Goddess, I love you, you idiot."

"But you don't like me." He leaned over for a kiss before sauntering out of the cargo hold to the front, leaving her to laugh with Tico. "What would you do without me?" he called back over his shoulder, not waiting for the answer.

"Spend less time with the UN," she muttered.

"Your lips to the goddess's ears," Tico replied fervently, turning to stow his gear.

Hank popped back out of the pilot's cabin as Cal settled himself inside, glowering and rubbing his bare scalp, and Ana tensed again. "Tico, take us up? I'll strap in with Hank back here for this one."

"Up up, or sideways?" They'd dared a few small side trips, with logs that reported worse fuel usage than their "shitty" lander actually burned covering their tracks.

"Cal wasn't that charming—these boys'll keep line of sight on us, and it's not worth skimming orbit or having them see something they shouldn't. Use that pilot cert and take us back to the *Graci*." When Tico had cleared out and pulled the door shut, she turned to Hank.

"Cubbies are full." He strapped in without looking at her, movements too jerky for a man who spent more time in space than not. For such a big man, he never took up so much space as when he was mad. "And the UN can win this, Ana. They're everywhere. We're tough, but we're not a fuckton of ships and debilitating resources tough."

"We're traders, not fighters."

"We're smugglers, and the UN knows it. So let's do what we do. Cubbies are full, let's unfill them. We got the nanos from our last NovRos run, we got a shit ton of UN gear, and you know we got contacts on the other side of Greendoor who can run a blockade."

Silence carried them through the thrust of lift-off and the

worst of the burn, Ana's thoughts racing with the shuttle. Of course the UN could win this. They wouldn't have committed so much if they couldn't—she'd been fooling herself to pretend otherwise. Took the risk for the shiny reward that she would never be able to enjoy. If the UN won, didn't matter who had Graciela's islands, because they'd all be UN drones who maybe got to live on an island, if the UN didn't "reallocate" their resources. If the UN lost, they were the assholes who'd worked for the UN. They'd fucked themselves, and she'd known it the whole time. This never would have happened when Graciela—

"I have that stock of hunting gear from when our last NovRos gangster got murdered and we had no one to trade weapons to," she said when they'd cleared into free fall. "It's back home, but one of the kids could get their hands on it. Nothing fancy—"

"We don't need military grade." Hank knew her well enough to understand her decision buried in that answer. "Anything that can kill a ripper can kill a fucking aardvark."

"Who are we offloading to? Everyone knows we've been gelding the fucking Danes." She heard the mistake as she said it, and both of their resulting laughs edged bitter.

"Not yet," Hank said fervently. "But let's stop paying them, and start gelding them for real, Captain."

"Here's a thing." Ana stepped back from the crates and shook the manifest to catch Hank's attention. "Come see."

It took bare moments for Hank to see what she saw, and he grunted, glancing between the packs of gear and the manifest the skywheel had left with their UN load.

"Extra cases of comms." He circled the next crate. "Extra boots. Tools that aren't on the list."

"Skywheel getting careless?"

"Maybe we got someone else's shipment. You want to tell them?" His half smile indicated he knew her answer.

"I want to get it to the ground. Let's still skim the usual, and put the gravy to good use."

"I'll work on the repackaging. Be nice to have a challenge."

"Make it look like we have a second delivery, just in case we get stopped before we have a chance to unload. I'd never say no to free goods, but we're out of space to hide it in the shuttle, and I don't want to keep it on the *Graci* with Sam alone on board."

She left him there to work. The lander couldn't detach from the *Graci* while they remained docked with the skywheel, because of raggedy mechanical issues that were purely invented, and she had a call to make.

Seb answered, *"Hey MamAna."* Graciela's kids had always been content to call her Auntie, except Seb. The middle son had invented the name when he'd been nothing but a toddler, and kept it alive ever since. She wasn't sure if that's what gave her a pang, or the ragged edge of his voice that so perfectly complemented the bags under his eyes.

"Seb. They feeding you, boy?"

"The hunting's good enough. I miss you, MamAna. Will I see you soon?" The lag of communications was short enough to make no difference, and if anyone at the UN decided to listen in they'd hear nothing of interest. Ana and her family had never needed a code to get things done.

"I wish we could get home, but at best we'll get to wave over Jefferson on our next trip. You know this boat's more likely to shake apart on a trip than go on joyrides. No matter how much I'd like to stretch out on your mama's old hammock."

"She loved that thing." Seb blinked once, registering that Graciela had never lounged on a hammock a day in her life, but Ana had a favorite hammock, and a cache built underneath it. *"Maybe I'll go rock on it for the both of you."*

"Do that. I'll collect my toll next time we're in the same place."

"You always do." The exhaustion in his voice bled through, though he summoned a convincing smile. *"Tell Pops to keep you out of trouble."*

"Sebastian Goderitch, you know very well it's the other way around."

"Never mind—I'll tell Sam to keep an eye on the both of you. Besos."

She cut the connection before he could see the tears collecting in her eyes. She forced the moisture away, considering the plan. They'd meet outside of Jefferson, which was enough on the way to their next UN drop that fuel and orbital insertion wouldn't raise any eyebrows. Sammy had talked her brother into believing in them, and the cache of older hunting rifles he was about to secure would help. It panged her to give up that whole shipment without a payment—damn NovRos thugs, getting killed before they could complete deals—but if they wanted to get goods to Freeholders opposing the UN, after months of working for the UN...she was too proud to call it penance, but it was at the least an investment on further trade.

Maybe a little bit of penance, too.

Ana pulled up the subroutine Hank had built years back, keeping a surface of activity on the computer that anyone looking in would see while she went about other business. With that executed, she accessed the fuel logs to tweak performance reports, justify their slow speed, and hide all excursions. She skewed a few internal heat readings, making it look like the shuttle had faulty shielding, which gave them reason to go slow once they hit atmosphere.

While she should really go back and help Hank finish tweaking the weights, actual and recorded, of each delivery, she sat and stared at her computer instead. Pushing away thoughts of Graciela, of Sammy and Seb and their siblings as toddling babies. Of Cal laughing without bitterness in his smile.

"Fuck." She shoved back and stood. Time to get to work.

They ran silent and without their transponder, routine these last months. But once the curve of Grainne blocked any line of sight, a ragged section of the ungainly lander slid open and a large aerodynamic bucket of cleverness boosted off, continuing on their original trajectory. The drone mimicked the lander's false heat readings and sluggish speed, and the actual shuttle accelerated away, cooler and far faster than should be possible given everything it communicated.

"Gilligan away," Tico confirmed, switching and clicking all the things needing to be switched and clicked.

"Feels good to be free," Ana said, shifting in her seat to poke Cal when he didn't reply.

Before Skywheel Three blew, they'd received packages with coordinates taped between boxes. Weeks of slowing the lander just enough to let goods drop off the back into an approximate space, hoping it was for Freehold but preserving plausible deniability. And now, finally, an actual meet with Seb, knowledge they were finally doing right. Using all their old tricks to do so.

"You know you missed this."

"Gilligan almost got us killed on NovRos." He kept his head

back in its brace, eyes closed, though the gravity had returned to normal.

"That was an unlucky break. We're close enough to ground that there's enough traffic to blend us, and no one's looking. We'll be down and back up to grab Gill before anyone notices. Tico?"

"We're clear, landing in ten. Smooth as mush. No one's in our spot."

The lander—less ungainly with a large chunk missing—settled against the curve of a cliff as though it had been built there. Beyond the encroaching forest, the land around them remained utterly empty.

They were on time, so the lack of a welcoming party spiked Ana's adrenaline. Had Seb been found out? Had they been found out? All those drops had been a trap, and now they'd pay the price. The UN had given them bait, they'd run with it, and now fighters were chasing them down even as she realized it, and—

"Cap." Hank's voice interrupted her spiral, just ahead of his face poking into the pilot's cabin from the cargo hold. "You taking point? Someone's waving a tree a little too regular to be wind."

"Go ahead," Cal said, taking his time unbuckling. "Seb always liked you better."

She took a breath, shook her head, and touched Cal's shoulder as she walked by. He'd wanted to charge significantly more for the goods they were about to furnish to the resistance, but she figured he still held a grudge from Seb going military instead of joining their old crew. It couldn't all be profit, not if they were going to make a real go of this.

The walk through the lander and into the open air set her heart racing again. Of course they'd be caught just as she'd started to make it right. Seb must have been on their watchlist. The UN would take them, then their whole planet, and she'd never see the bullet—

"MamAna!" Seb, dressed for hunting, stepped out of the forest and made his way toward her. A small group materialized behind him, melting out of the shadows and dragging something that might have been a carcass. To any casual observer, they were a group of Freeholders out to get some food.

Most of the tension bled from Ana as they approached, the sound of Hank's and Tico's safeties re-engaging behind her settling her pulse.

"I picked up some friends. We were going to be more cautious, but Sammy was convincing, and your drops were appreciated." His eyes remained steady on her face as he got close enough to speak quietly.

"Seb." The longing to hug him pressed on her, doubled by the relief that everything that fell off the back of their shuttle had gone to good use. She forced herself to hold out her hands instead of throwing himself at her. He squeezed them briefly, glancing over her shoulder to nod at the crew behind her.

She tried not to look at the people with her wife's son, attempting to show she was no threat to them. "You look—"

"Ragged, I know. Like this lander. Did you chew it into that shape?"

"How long have you been out here?"

"Months. About as long as you've been running for the UN." The point landed hard, and she nodded, stepping back.

"You don't have time for chitchat, son, coming all this way, and neither do we." Cal appeared between Tico and Hank, giving his son the once over as he sauntered down the plank. "You want to come in and load up the tarp?" Unlike Ana, he cast an appraising look over the handful of people accompanying Seb, and whistled low. "Military?"

"Something like that. Those boots were a help, Captain." The largest of the men stared Cal down, aiming his words at Ana. "Which of you has the good aim?"

"We have some practice," Ana said, losing the thread of the conversation when a dappled head and body emerged from the woods behind them, pausing long enough to be seen before lazily disappearing. Leopard? Then these men were...

"Pops." Seb's voice had roughened, and it pulled her back to the matter at hand. "Let's be efficient. The guns went a long way, sorry you lost the profit on that. I'm sure someone on NovRos or Alsace is real sad not to have them."

Cal stepped back and turned his head to stare at his remaining wife, and Ana, still thinking about leopards in the woods, managed not to react. She probably should have told him she'd bargained the old rifles and civilian ammunition stock away for nothing but the chance to barely sell more goods. Poor Cal—none of the profit he'd hoped to reap on the black market would hit his account this run.

"You have nanos?" One of the cloaked figures asked, holding his position.

"We had some from our last run to NovRos. There's more on the ship—"

"We'll take as much of it as you can get," the man under the cloak interrupted her. "Can you get more?"

"Maybe. The Greendoor jump point is locked pretty tight, but we know some people." Ana tilted her head slightly, running the next steps they'd need and knowing better than to overpromise.

Cal grunted. "We know some people who will charge us half an island for nanos during a fight."

"Get us the materials, then. The key ingredients—I have a list. We have people who can help if you can take the runs." The man eased his hood back, meeting Ana's eyes rather than Cal's.

"They'll still charge—" Cal moved forward, trying to pull the attention back to himself.

"We'll pay." Seb cut his father off with more heat than the other man had had for Ana. "Nanos today, and what else? We can get more ambitious next time."

Ana, with the *Graci* full and countless UN jobs ahead of her, took a moment for a small internal celebration. There would be a next time, and this group, leopard handlers, had connections. This was going to work, as long as nothing went wrong.

Force Majeure
Part 4

Back at Station
Late Autumn 210

Force was again docked to the secret starbase with no name. A name wasn't really necessary, since there was only the one that anyone knew of, and no one could speak of it. Any crew going aboard referred to it as "The Base," much as the one they'd built in-system was "The Rock."

Yates was in personal conference with Colonel Sansing, who was de facto commander in chief. There was also a commander in chief on the ground—Assault Commander Naumann, out of 3rd Mobile Assault Regiment, possibly one in the Halo, and hypothetically one more with other surviving ships. As the UN had near-complete control of all communication, it was unlikely they'd ever properly coordinate. They had to do what they could.

Sansing had been a major he'd barely heard of, other than through a couple of papers. In person, she was dark haired, fit, and damn, that was a lot of quals on her uniform—Space, Space Warfare, Space Pilot, Space Command, Ground, Blazer, Mobile Assault, Small Arms, Unarmed Combat, Combat Medical, Vacuum Operations. She wasn't unattractive, but wasn't remarkable. Then she had that pedigree. And an Apache tribal symbol tattooed on her left arm, below the rolled sleeve.

The conference room was a bare rectangle of steel, since they had plenty of it, with very basic chairs. There was enough rotational G to hold everything, and a light fixture. That for a conference among commanding officers. None of them needed amenities, but the lack of them was a reminder how badly off they were.

They had their own comms on the table. There was food and water.

Sansing started the discussion very directly. "The first matter is a status report on what we do have. Ships, ground forces, and in fact, some intel elements."

Everyone paid attention at that, and there were mutters.

She read from the notes, "Some of our civilian tech geeks, mostly volunteers from the electronic-espionage industry, are able to get brief messages out from time to time, which are timestamped and relayed ship to ship. The last we have are from ten days ago. It's an execrable way to fight a war, but it's better than nothing."

"They've been vetted?" asked Kacito.

Sansing nodded and said, "As best we can. They have furnished intel that let one element hit a UN component hard. There's documentation from another source confirming they've hacked automated supply convoys and redirected them. They're screwing with schedules, manning docs, supply manifests, security protocols."

"Excellent. So we're positive it isn't a ruse?"

"Captain DeFries?"

Bethany DeFries had an intel sig on her coverall. She was tall, seemed relaxed and sounded very confident.

"There are ways to authenticate a source. We've done our best. They seem to have an element in each major city, and one in Breakout Habitat, and possibly on Skywheel Two and even in the now-UN facility on Gealach. They've been reliable, they cross ID so we know they're secure on each signal. Naumann vouches for them."

"I'll accept that judgment of course. Glad to have them."

She said, "Very much so. It makes this a war rather than just scattered unrest."

Sansing said, "Captain Yates, we need you here to refit *Malahayati* again and provide a full weapons loadout. Then, bring everyone else back up to capacity and fit. Can you let us know your fuel capacity and margins?"

"Yes, I have that information. We're as full as we can get, and I hope it's enough."

"Excellent. Then, as mentioned, you're going in-system, and we have contacts for you. You will coordinate with them, and whatever craft are available, to provide equipment to the surface combatants. It appears to be a combination of a stealth boat, a vetted civilian smuggler running parallel UN deliveries on contract, with 'errors' in lading and additional mass for our elements. We can get some down via skywheel."

"Impressive. Not efficient, but avoids any single point failure."

DeFries brought up a summary chart and said, "They're

putting up a hell of a fight on the surface, too. There's near total noncompliance, and then there's massive resistance and sabotage, especially against support elements. The UN's direct combatants are being ignored, while the convoys and logistics are getting hammered."

That was something. Yates asked, "That is good news. Do we know what our elements need?"

She replied, "I'd prefer not to guess. If we're wrong, it's wasted mass-energy. How fast can you configure to build in-system?"

Karanov twisted her mouth. "That depends what they need. We'll do what we can. I can have everyone ready to full-shift for the first few days to make sure it's a good delivery. In the meantime, we can convert refined material into some base stocks—alloys, compounds."

Yates continued, "I assume we don't have support and will be relying on stealth?"

Sansing nodded. "I'm afraid so. You'll be respectably far out, with craft transferring through The Rock. You will be an independent command. If you are discovered"—*more like "when,"* he thought—"you are authorized to surrender if it is your best option, scuttle and evacuate, flee to wherever you can. Just do your damndest to deliver what you can and don't let them secure the ship and resources."

"We'll give it our best."

Updating the other ships was straightforward, except for *Malahayati*—nicknamed "*Hate*." She was a mess. Reactor and drive damage, physical damage to the hull from near misses, missiles expended, proper fuel literally down to grams, material used as reactor mass and apparently jettisoned to improve performance. On the other hand, she'd taken out a major mobilization space base, three ships, and seven boats that they knew of, and scattered her four pursuers across Sol system, hindering their operations for weeks. There was credible intel that several other UN ships were now inbound to reinforce Sol and Earth against another attack—that being the second one actually in the home system, and far more lethal than the first. The Earth-based government was scared at how it had not been a simple pacification. They were used to nationalist fronts with little actual military or logistics, and had apparently assumed the same for the Freehold.

I am pleased we can disabuse you of that notion, he thought with welcome schadenfreude.

It did boost his morale and he made sure it was disseminated. They'd lost one ship. They'd destroyed four of the enemy's, harassed all the Earth home fleet, and terrified the rest. It was the first war in interstellar space, and the UN spacers now knew they could die. *Hate* and *Mad Jack* had lived up to their names.

It took a solid week, ten divs a day, to bring *Hate* up to function. Really, she needed a professional dock and another month, but at least she was combat worthy again. Her reactor was near standard, her drive slightly above, her weapons and support at least were over spec. She'd never pull maneuvers like that again, though. There was structural wear and damage.

The repairs would have to do. There was no time.

Grappled to Carrier *Matahourua*, nicknamed "*The Canoe*," they pushed off as they had before. As they departed, Yates wondered who'd built out the base. It was bare, but adequate. There was weeks' worth of work in the structure. At what point had someone decided or ordered it built? And who had transported the materials? Any freighter could have done so, or either *Energy* or *Power*, the other factory ships.

He'd probably never know.

Huff #14
Lethal Force Revisited [June 210]

This conversation was not going well. The councilor was incredulous: "You fought us tooth and nail to get permission for lethal weaponry, and now you want to take it back?"

I always change my tone and diction when talking to the political class; they have a different vocabulary, a different cant. It pays to know and throw it back at them. "No, just restrict it per the law. Which is a horrible compromise to have to make, but it wasn't my doing."

"Mind your words, General."

"I am not criticizing the administration. The existing Laws of Armed Conflict—Hague, Geneva, the Mars Protocols—restrict lethal force when fighting declared combatants. They're showing up in standardized uniforms with standardized weapons. No one knows how, yet, but they are. The catch is they only have lethal weapons, so while we're forced to use nonlethal, they're not. I'm acknowledging that laws passed centuries ago are a hindrance to us."

"Exactly. They're no longer relevant, and we're prepared to show the rebels have access to nonlethal tactics and weapons, but refuse to use them."

I remained skeptical, but played along. "If you win that decision, I'll be pleased to proceed. My concern is that regardless of intentions, the courts might decline to accept that definition, and I am the responsible party. Especially since I was not informed of massive failures in the 'nonlethal' bioweapons that were supposed to be a harassment tactic, not kill children and leave the survivors with gaping sores."

"We don't have time for legal niceties."

No, *you* don't have time for legal niceties. "I don't have the luxury of ignoring them. My tasking is specific."

"These orders come from—"

"My tasking is specific, in writing, from the Military Bureau, from the Executive Branch of the United Nations. Is the SecGen issuing the order? Or SecMil?"

"No, it's—"

"Then I must respectfully decline such an order without written approval. It's my signature and I will make damn sure any operations carried out are within the letter of UN regulations."

"It will not help your career to be so pedantic. Especially as you've previously worked around orders you found, shall we say, inconvenient?"

This asshole really thought he had me. "I'll retire as a general, unless you think you can attach any operational decisions to me when the MilBu's own IGs were involved in most of them." At this point, dropping my retirement packet started sounding more conducive to long-term survival.

"Does that mean you're afraid to fight?"

"That means I'm more afraid of the enemy's *actual* hit teams than any hypothetical ones you might have. Remember, we've invaded a system that practically boasted of having an assassin's guild. One of those monsters is running around disemboweling bureaucrats with a goddamn sword! On the whole, this campaign is almost as stupid as starting a land war in Asia. I hope you know enough history to understand that analogy."

Force Majeure
Part 5

Matahourua with *Force* attached precipitated far out in the Freehold system. If the coordinates were correct, and there was no reason to believe otherwise, they were several light-minutes from the hidden base, far out beyond the inner system, distant from the jump points. For an in-system craft, they were days away from Grainne or most of the habitats.

They unshackled, *Matahourua* nudged her maneuvering engines and cleared the location, as *Force* reset for in-system navigation and her own power. A div later, *Matahourua* phased back out.

Yates felt very cold. They were far enough out from the inner system to make locating and matching them very unlikely. They had a fuel margin that would let them reach a capture orbit around Iota Persei in an emergency, with nothing left. It would take weeks to do that. They were as far out as one could get without actually being lost.

And they were dependent upon that carrier to recover them, unless they could arrange for anyone to bring fuel and supplies out to them. The UN might recover them as prisoners, or pretend not to hear them and wait for them to die.

They had a coded signal for a specific point in space at a specific time. The point was easy to locate. Time would be close enough, but was based on clock calculations, since they weren't close enough to zero against known baselines.

They transmitted, "Contact, do you receive and acknowledge?" and waited.

Long divs and segs went by.

Eventually Mati reported, "We have a beam, sir."

A male voice said, *"Hello, contact. We are told you have supplies. Our authorization code is 'Because I said so.'"*

He still grinned at the simplicity of that code.

He replied personally, "Hello, contact. We do have supplies. 'Go to your room.'"

Normal spaceside duty continued, and he got dinner. It would probably be a while before there was an answer. He went off-shift with his usual order to contact him if needed.

He went to the common mess, got in line, declined a spacer's offer to let him forward—that was reserved for crew on critical duty, and he held himself to the reg—and got a tray full of vat beef stew.

He'd thought about recreation every evening, either some sort of video or some handcrafting. As usual, he woke with his head on the desk, never having managed to open a file, and rolled into his bunk for the rest of the night.

Next morning he checked the log as he was debriefed. The transport had replied during the second watch. Third Officer Alito took the reply.

The approaching boat asked, *"What do you have?"*

Alito had replied, *"Segala sesuatu."* Indonesian for "Everything."

He was in time to hear the reply, *"Shit. Hold on. We're coming. Can you fuel us for return?"*

For now, they could. "Yes. Send us your fantasy list. We'll do what we can."

The boat's reply also included a slow load of needed supplies. He forwarded that to Tirza so she could get the deck crew to work.

The coded reply itself was, *"Will do."*

The Fabrication Section started on the list of requests. It looked like a full infantry loadout. Weapons, ammo, rockets, optics, radios, orienteering gear, boots, body armor, toothbrushes, packs. Easy stuff they could produce by the bale. A separate listing wanted V-suits in standard sizes, and tools. The complication remained *Force's* fuel, food, and the need to not waste material on containers. Transfer Logistics came up with a method of surrounding fragile gear with softer components, reinforced with weapons and frames, bound with a web of lashing cord, with minimal actual packing material.

Three days later, Farana reported, "Sir, faint signs of something. Must be one of our stealth boats."

"Understood. Confirm and bring them in."

Three divs later, Boat 4J17 shackled alongside the secondary-hold hatch. They were carrying an external pod buried in black-body foam.

Yates watched remotely as Karanov met the boat commander, Warrant Leader Costlow.

"*Permission to come aboard, ma'am.*"

"*Open access granted to your crew, Warrant. On behalf of Captain Yates and myself, welcome.*"

Yates spoke, "I'm remoted in. Welcome. We're ready to load you and adapt as needed."

The pilot acknowledged, "*Thank you both. I've brought a meeting gift.*"

"*Oh?*"

He sounded proud as he rattled off, "*Twenty-two tonnes of refined iron, forty-seven of tanked hydrocarbons, one of rare earths, and twelve of recyclable polymer shreds.*"

"*We'll take it.*"

Yates took the audio and transcription while eating an apple for breakfast. The fresh supplies weren't going to last long; he may as well enjoy them while he could.

Tirza told Costlow, "*We've got your first load ready. Is it just you?*"

"*There should be three other boats at present. We're detouring through The Rock to deliver fuel to them and some of what was on the list. Then we go in-system. Whatever we can bring back, we will. I didn't mention the polymer shreds were salvaged crate wrapping from the UN. We also delivered fifty UN weapons and some sundries due to a 'manifest error.'*"

Yates put in, "How are you fueling at the other end?"

Costlow replied, "*Siphoned from UN safe margins. Also, there's a couple of double-agent smugglers who haul UN cargo. When the BoL doesn't match the contents, they lose the overage. We recover it.*"

Karanov flared her brows and said, "*Without anyone else seeing it? That's impressive.*"

"*They send a coded message, and we have really good sensors. Our biggest risk is that we radiate effectively nothing when buttoned up. Anyone looking our way sees a hole in space.*"

Yates commented, "Well, good luck. We'll be maintaining this orbit, so effectively stationary."

"*Yup. We'll come looking.*"

Karanov slapped Costlow's shoulder and said, "*Then let's get you loaded.*"

With a more detailed list of what was needed, *Force*'s crew went on maximum shift time.

The factory decks were running at capacity and then some.

Crew borrowed from engineering, services, support, and even medical were handling the grunt labor tasks, much of the semiskilled work, and even some of the mission specialties. Every fabricator of every kind was running nonstop—cutting, milling, welding, printing, distilling, combining, extruding, stitching. Despite heavy scrubbing, the atmosphere grew thick with alkenes, propellants, metal oxides, polymer fumes. The machines hummed, buzzed, zapped and hissed. Crew hurried about at safe walking speed, but as fast as that walk could be made.

The entire ship was on a ten-div rotating cycle, working at theoretical combat max capacity fabricating weapons, ammo, stitching backpacks, boots, uniforms—Freehold Residents' Provisional Forces would now be a uniformed and official combat element. Yates had figured out what wrench that was going to toss into the UN mix.

Outward in the cargo deck, finished products were crated in the bare minimum padding to keep them as bundles. Every bit of packaging used polymer that would not be available for other products.

While awaiting the second craft, Yates took a command tour below. The crew had orders to ignore his presence and continue with duty.

He went aft to cargo handling and worked forward.

Cargo was taking the finished bundles and attaching slings and air jets for transfer across. Even in emgee, a mass that size needed assistance to move.

He pulled forward into Transfer Logistics and oriented his feet. From here forward was rotating for minimal pseudogravity. It really made operations work much better. The crew assembled the goods into the complex bundles he'd only seen at a distance. Up close, the geometry was brilliant. Whoever devised that deserved a decoration.

That bundle contained uniform blouses in three standard sizes. Next to it were rucksacks. One entire load was ammunition, for the pallet of carbines next to it. There was the bundle of boots, socks and some toothbrushes.

Toothbrushes. The UN had apparently shut down the factories for noncompliance with environmental regs, hadn't gotten them back up, and couldn't import enough. They'd taken over a star system with absolutely no idea what that entailed.

They were actual brushes, not sonic or hydro. But for troops without any, that would hopefully be a benefit.

He walked to the Fabrication Section and watched a tech build boots. The sole and parts of the sides were molded over a tough ballistic fabric. A manipulator punched holes and inserted fastenings.

"How are they arranging sizes, Tech?" he asked.

The man turned, nodded in courtesy, and said, "Sir, we're doing standard sizes in two centimeter increments, bell curved for adults aged ten and up. This style tightens enough that socks or wrappings will let people operate without too much slop."

"Five sizes then?"

"Yes, sir. That's all. The optimum we can manage."

"Excellent. Please carry on."

"Thank you, sir. Good day to you."

Further forward, Base Materials turned raw elements into alloys, processed chemicals and ingredients, and those into sheets, plates, tubes and blocks. Ahead of that were the spacers on dollies pulling chunks that the cargo crew cut or drew from the holds. Raw material here, finished combat supplies aft, bundled and ready for transport.

4J17 loaded fast, fueled simultaneously, and departed. Within segs they were invisible against the background, even knowing where they were.

Spider's Web
Part 9

Sebastian from Team 5 contacted Moyra Kelly on the emergency channel, just as she was about to start handing over comms to DalesOP. :: Need to nuke all devices for Freelancers B53. ::

:: Done. What happened? :: Moyra replied.

:: Captured, possibly all dead. Devices were collected, but there was an active connection back here when the attack started. We heard it. ::

:: You are ordered to move operations to the next assigned safe house, immediately. ::

:: Already in progress, :: he responded.

:: Good. Stay low, :: Moyra cautioned. She pinged Salamander. :: Need you to kill ALL comms using App ID 3Z98UK. Nuke the applications, force a failover for the devices not tied to the attached hardware IDs. :: She sent the list of IDs.

:: In progress, :: Salamander confirmed.

Moyra could only hope that the devices were remotely fried fast enough to prevent data preservation and subsequent targeting.

Moyra's intelligence and communications network expanded, and with it, the risks. In an attempt to mitigate the risks, each team of handlers was installed near one of the safe houses Naumann's team had left or built for a similar purpose. The "houses" varied in appearance, but all came with critical necessities.

Such as the autodestruction system warning, alerting for Team 5, which woke Moyra from a sound sleep and left her scrambling to her console.

She keyed open the surveillance feed for Team 5's base of operations. Her monitors filled with the various views. UN soldiers surrounded the building, and internal cameras showed them dispersing. Sebastian, Sarah, and Max had barricaded the doors, and were in the process of ensuring the equipment was slagged. A digital readout counted down the trigger for the explosives.

"Get out, you fools," she hissed under her breath, despite the futility.

6.

The doors of the room shuddered as presumably the invaders attempted to breach the barricade. Moyra fumbled for the comm, trying to toggle it open.

5. 4.

Defiant and scared, the three gripped hands. Max hugged Sarah to him.

3.

"I'm sorry." It was stupid, but what else was there to say? They glanced at the camera, and Max nodded.

2. 1.

The explosions didn't immediately cut the feeds. Moyra... watched, comm off, for as long as they stayed available, muffling her sobs. She couldn't leave them alone.

Her team hadn't suffered as much as she feared, and she couldn't give a flying fuck about the UN's people.

Once she composed herself, she alerted Damocles and DalesOP. :: I need a complete analysis on how the team was detected. Find *everything*. We have to do better, and we need to know ASAP if any other handler sites are compromised. Redistribute freelancers to handlers as appropriate. ::

:: Working on the distribution logic now, :: DalesOP replied.

:: It's time for drones, :: she added.

:: Hesp...are you sure? :: Damocles asked.

:: I just watched three of my people sacrifice themselves. I'm completely fucking sure. ::

:: They don't know how compromised they are, yet, :: Damocles said.

:: We have to blow that away at some point. If this was an isolated detection, something not known higher up, having the drones go AWOL and hostile may provide some cover for the explosion. Maybe even get blamed on the UN. ::

:: Naumann expresses his condolences, and agrees with your logic. ::

Don't fucking care what he thinks, that dogfucker. Rational thought kept her grief-rage from replying, but she certainly thought it.

She woke Kozlov. :: It's time. I want Convoy 6503 and associated drones, headed to Delph', hijacked and slaughtered. Send it to the nearest friendly element. Initiate the drone vacation plan as well. ::

:: Peterson? That's ... aggressive. What happened? ::

She told him.

:: Fuck me. How the hell? ::

:: I don't know. That's my next task. Be careful. All of your people, be careful. ::

:: You got it. And we're off to target practice. ::

Moyra hadn't practiced enough with the drone controls herself to participate, but she had a split feed off Kozlov's video and audio feeds. More than ten operators were switched to the task, and Moyra listened in while each confirmed selection and contact with a support drone. The screen split into various camera views, with controlled drones and the convoy's main camera marked with icons. Moyra pulled that feed over to the largest display she had at her disposal. She separated out the secondary driver's helmet cam and audio for a single view.

"*All drones accounted for; cutover available at command. Convoy 6503's controls are active but not enabled. Number Six, please confirm go,*" Kozlov said.

"This is Number Six," Moyra confirmed. "If all devices are under our control, I confirm go."

Kozlov gave the order.

The drones immediately broke formation, and turned on the convoy. The convoy itself yanked hard turns in an alternating pattern in an attempt to throw the occupants off balance.

Moyra's view jerked and an audible thump indicated the driver's helmet made contact with a wall.

"*What the ever loving fuck just happened?*" the driver—she— yelled. The camera panned back across the windshield as a drone zipped past, strafing fire on the vehicle in front. "*GARCIA, WHAT THE HELL IS HAPPENING WITH THE DRONES?*"

The gunner shouted from behind her. "*Fuck if I know, McCarty! My controls are dead, I can't issue any overrides. I have video—oh fuck, the drones are shooting our people. Smith's down!*"

The vehicle started backing up. The camera jostled as McCarty scrambled. "*Get out, get out!*"

"*Fuck that! We're safest in here!*"

"*It's going to ram the vehicle in front of us! GET OUT.*"

"*We get out, we DIE.*"

An audible explosion rocked the camera view. Moyra glanced at her screens, and saw the sixth vehicle back had rammed into the side of the fifth, and damaged the power pack. McCarty's camera view shook, like the driver was clearing her head from another impact, and the hatch opened. Her gunner shouted, *"Don't!"* but the camera showed McCarty jumping out and to the ground. She sprinted for the tree line, screamed, and toppled. The camera went dead.

"Drones, clear the vehicles of remaining crew," Kozlov ordered. A couple of drones were lost in the process, as the holdouts fought back. *"Vehicles appear to be clear."*

"Destroy any vehicles that are too disabled to move. Proceed to the provided destination," Moyra replied.

"Confirmed." Kozlov paused. *"Initiating takeover commands for all other active drones now. AI instructions disseminated. Should start homing in on the UN transponders now."*

"Good job," Moyra replied.

For you, Sebastian, Sarah, Max. For you.

Three days later, every awake drone on Grainne actively remained under Moyra and her team's control. UN forces struggled to respond with functional countermeasures, while their own tactics escalated.

Previously dormant drones were activated, with mixed success for the UN. The troops, however, were disinclined to trust the drones any further than they could throw them. Several units apparently did throw them, immediately followed by gunfire to ensure the drones couldn't shoot *them.*

But, so far, the remaining handler teams continued undetected.

Near as could be determined, the same UN unit that breached the safe house had found the activated communications channel, and worked back from there. The only data Moyra's team could find was a few offhand comments about how they'd have something to show the brass later. Piecemealed data from local cameras showed a physical stakeout and questioning of uncooperative locals.

The handler team communication distribution logic had previously routed freelancers to the nearest handler team, in the interests of decreasing communications lag. To minimize the ability of a single unit to make that connection, the distribution logic scrambled that slightly.

Handler teams were also physically shifted around again, and cautioned to use physical security measures, including varying the routes taken to the safe houses.

While the primary purpose for the drone takeover was, of course, pure war, other uses were also possible. Moyra approved hounding the bastards in any way feasible.

:: Hey, we still have the other UN feeds? :: DalesOP messaged.

:: Yeah. Why? :: Moyra replied.

:: I've got a little side project to farm out to the forum trolls I know. They're bored. ::

:: The professional shit-stirrers? What now? ::

:: I need to get them some video feeds from Unity and blast addresses for the UN. They're planning on imaging a bunch of penises into it, just enough background the UN has to review the images to see if it provides useful intel. ::

:: ...That almost makes up for the "tit pic" messages. Almost. ::

Huff #15

Unsolicited [Early September 210]

"Oh, bloody hell!" I yelled out loud, which caused several of the ops and intel analysts to pop their heads up like stupid meer-kats and stare before disappearing again. I'm not one given to unprofessional outbursts, at least, I wasn't before this tour began.

We have incredible advantages. We have vast resources, the greatest scientific minds, and the most gifted engineers in human-settled space. The rebels are clever, creative and gifted themselves, but we outclass them in every way. We *should* already have this planet fully compliant. At the very least, we should have a clear, reliable intel picture. We've raised human-machine teaming with drones to an art form. They react faster, one operator can control many at once, we arm them. They make security quicker, easier, and they don't violate General Order No. 1.

But what do we *actually* have? Hijacked drones, dozens of dead troops, and hundreds of "dick pics," which I just happened to get a full sample of. Also anuses and horribly diseased vulvas.

The field commanders will know we can no longer trust our own equipment. If we're going to get anything useful done here, we're going to have to do it the old-fashioned way, with boots on the ground. A lot more boots. A lot more problems.

"Go to Grainne," they said. "It'll be good for your career," they said.

Survival

Justin Watson

The Mountains North of Delph'
2nd Platoon, Bravo Company 1-87 Infantry

The sky above the tall evergreens turned purple-gray in Grainne's predawn, casting the forest in a dreamy half-light, just enough to make the naked eye the superior option over night optics. In the distance to the east, Rhys noted a herd of Old-Earth Elk dipping their heads to drink from a crystalline blue pond. The scene might have been a sylvan idyll if it weren't for the rumble of his Assault Vehicle's engine as it trundled in between the trees. Rhys had a great view of the scenery from the turret of his ILAWAV or "Eel," as the troops affectionately dubbed them due to their slender shape and curved hull. Even the frigid mountain breeze that buffeted his face and caused his nose hairs to freeze together like tiny, frosty spider webs didn't bother Rhys. Too bad all he could hear was engine noise and radio traffic, all he could smell was hydraulic fluid and unwashed bodies.

Even Alaska isn't this wild. Sergeant First Class Rhys Harlingen thought of his hometown of Fairbanks back on Earth, now a shining metropolis compared to its frontier origins. *Not anymore. It's so gorgeous. Too bad all the locals want to kill us.*

The trees were getting thicker. Rhys guessed they had less than a kilometer before the platoon had to dismount, leave the vehicles in a temporary patrol base, and continue on foot. He rocked easily with the wheeled APC as it rolled over a small stream bed. Looking left and right, he saw that the three other Eels in his platoon were maintaining relative position well enough.

327

Formations were always more of a suggestion than a hard and fast rule in close terrain like this.

Rhys's Eel crested a small rise in the forest and he saw a clearing with six wood-frame buildings.

"All Blacksheep Two elements, halt." Rhys held down the transmit button on his helmet-borne commo suite. "Blacksheep Two-Six, are you seeing what I'm seeing?"

His platoon leader, Lieutenant Lang, responded immediately.

"*Roger, Two-Seven,*" she said. "*That hamlet isn't on the map. Do you see any movement in or around it, over?*"

Rhys scanned with bare eyes, then flipped his radio frequency to intercom to talk to the gunner in his own Eel.

"Hensley, do you have anything on the gunsight?"

The turret rotated left to right and back again with a hydraulic hum as Hensley scanned the collection of buildings. The Eel's sensor package was top notch. Granted the rebels had figured out various ways to spoof sonic, IR, and thermal, but it was still a useful platform.

"*I've got multiple signatures on sonic and thermal, three to five per building, about twenty-five total,*" Hensley said, his voice betraying his New Jersey roots. "*Can't see any weapons, but that don't mean nothing.*"

"I gotcha Hensley," Rhys said, then flipped back to the platoon net. "Two-Six, Two-Seven, we're seeing twenty-five signatures, no weapons spotted, yet."

"*Roger, Two-Seven,*" Lang acknowledged. "*That's what we've got as well, Two-Two, Two-Three, what do you see?*"

The squad leaders riding in the other two vehicles' observations were identical to Lang's and Rhys's.

"*All right, let's call it up to Blacksheep Six,*" Lang said. "*Then I'll take 1st and 2nd Squads to check out the hamlet while you overwatch with the rest of the platoon.*"

"Ma'am, why don't I take the patrol," Rhys started.

"*Because if I get my head blown off, you'll have a better chance of saving the rest of the platoon, Two-Seven,*" she said. "*Besides, it's my job. Don't worry, I'll take the Ears.*"

Rhys looked to his left over at his platoon leader's Eel. Its back ramp was down and he saw the petite figure of Lieutenant Lang flanked by her radio operator on one side and a man hauling a light machine gun on the other.

Her radio operator wore the Mobile Operational Utility Sensor, which consisted of an extra module attached to the long-range commo suite in his assault pack and a helmet with two lightweight, circular sensor dishes affixed side by side atop it. They didn't have the range or resolution of the Eel's suite, but they'd have exactly the perspective the operator had, up close.

It was something he both loved and hated about his platoon leader; she was very self-aware as to her place in life. She understood that having platoon leaders at all was largely a means by which to blood officers for company command, that the NCOs could run the platoon quite effectively without her. She also understood that unless she got out into the mud with her people, she would never earn their respect or develop the tactical sense she needed to be a good officer. Thus she listened to Rhys on just about everything, right up to the point he tried to convince her not to take a risk to herself.

Rhys didn't think he was being overprotective because Lang was female, at least not consciously. He just knew that unlike too many of the young lieutenants he'd seen in his fifteen years of service, Lang had a chance of being a decent officer.

Nothing for it.

"Alright, Suarez," he said to his driver. "Follow the tree line around west of the village. Two-One, Two-Two, Two-Three, follow us."

Picking their way through the trees to get a good firing position took some time. Finally they had all four Eels in position and 3rd and Weapons Squads on their bellies observing the town, weapons readied.

"Two-Six, overwatch is set," Rhys reported.

"Roger, Two-Seven," Lang replied, her voice betraying excitement. *"We're stepping off."*

Rhys slid down into the hull of the Eel. Their attached Forward Observer team, Corporal Crabbe and his sensor operator, Lutzen, were on one side bench, the platoon medics were on the other.

"Okay, Hensley, you and Suarez have got the Eel," he said, then he turned his attention to the medics and artillerymen. "You four: with me."

Rhys set up the two medics well behind 3rd Squad. Then he and the two forward observers joined the machine-gun team near the edge of the wood line with a clear view of the tiny settlement.

Planting his elbows on the not-pine-needle-coated forest floor to comfortably support his rifle, he scanned the windows of the buildings through his rifle's combat optics for any sign of movement, flipping back and forth between black-white thermal, IR, visual light magnification and composite settings. Lang and nineteen of their troops advanced across an open field toward the collection of single story buildings.

"*Sergeant,*" Hensley's voice was in his ear, his agitation audible even through the tinny distortion. "*Signatures are disappearing; looks like they're going downstairs but I can't read them in their basements.*"

Oh, fuck—

Rhys shouted into his mic.

"Two-Six, get down!"

The words had no sooner left his mouth than a hail of fire erupted from the hamlet; not from the first floor windows as they'd expected, but from slits where a normal residence might have a cellar window. Except all the buildings had cellar windows on every side, and the building facades were perfectly positioned to create interlocking fields of fire across the entire clearing.

They built a whole fucking village just to ambush us, Rhys realized even as a burst of machine-gun fire took great chunks out of the tree trunk next to him with a bone-rattling THWACK-THWACK-THWACK. *Weaponized STDs, drone hacks, that poor bastard they fed to his buddies down in Jefferson, and now this. This horseshit would be cartoonish if it weren't so effective.*

"Return fire," Rhys yelled into the comm. "Aim for the foundations of the buildings."

Rhys's Eel lumbered forward like some great metal beast and began to belch fire from its autocannon as Hensley went about systematically dismantling the building nearest them. The basso thudding chorus of the four Eels laying into the town silenced the enemy's fire for a moment.

But only for a moment; over the thunder of the Eels' auto-cannons and the staccato rattle of the rifles and machine guns, Rhys heard a higher pitch CLANK-BOOM, and saw Eel Two-Two engulfed in flame.

"Eels, pull back," he shouted into the comm. "Pull back to the last hill we crossed and start engaging via berm drill."

"*They've got antitank missiles?*" Staff Sergeant Quinn, 3rd Squad Leader, asked over the platoon net.

"Negative, those are recoilless rifles," Rhys said.

It wasn't really good news. While they didn't have the range of missiles, recoilless rifles were good for close terrain like this. Their warheads were insufficient for the frontal armor on a main battle tank, but his Eels were no more tanks than a bobcat is a tiger.

Another shot punched a hole in the back ramp of Rhys's own vehicle with a metallic screech, but to his relief there was no secondary explosion and the vehicle kept rolling back through the woods, out of range of the enemy's antitank fire.

Rhys looked at the rapidly deteriorating tree trunks around him, and south to where 1st and 2nd Squads still lay completely pinned in the open with nowhere to go. If enemy reinforcements arrived before the rest of Blacksheep Company, they could easily lose half the platoon in ten minutes.

From behind, Rhys heard short but earthshaking bursts of fire from the Eels' autocannons. They were answered with the higher-pitched report of the enemy's recoilless rifles. The unguided rounds weren't terribly accurate at that range, but it was enough to keep the Eels honest, having to duck back behind the terrain between volleys rather than standing and pouring fire into the buildings. The insurgents in those basements were apparently brave enough to stand to their firing slits even with occasional bursts of high explosive 20mm going off around them.

"Blacksheep Six, this is Blacksheep Two-Seven," Rhys called for the company commander and was answered immediately by Captain Schultz's cornbelt rasp.

"This is Six, I'm monitoring your net," Schultz said. "I'm with 1st Platoon and we're one hour away, air support is thirty minutes out."

"Sir, that's not going to work. What about the company mortars?" Rhys asked.

"*Won't be in range for another thirty minutes,*" Schultz's distorted voice answered. "*And if those basements are withstanding direct 20mm, our mortars may not be enough.*"

"I was thinking white phosphorous for obscuration." *And to set their buildings on fire and hopefully roast them alive.* "To give 1st and 2nd Squads a chance to get to cover."

"*Sergeant, what about the howitzers at Forward Base Blair?*" Crabbe's voice broke in on the net. "*They could reach us with rocket-assisted rounds.*"

"Good idea, Crabbe." Rhys nodded. "Sir, can you get us the artillery?"

"Will do, Two-Seven, have Crabbe switch over to the battalion Fires net."

His part in the conversation over for the moment, Rhys went back to the platoon's immediate situation. Crawling back and forth between fire teams, Rhys refined the platoon's sectors of fire on the fly, reminding the riflemen to conserve ammunition and wait for good shots, let the machine guns do the suppression work. Adjustments made, he got on the horn to see about the rest of his platoon.

"Two-One, this is Two-Seven, how you holding, Abe?" said Rhys.

"Like shit, Two-Seven," Abraham answered immediately. *"Total four dead including the LT, five wounded, I'm down to ten effectives."*

"Roger, stay where you are and stay low, we're bringing in artillery," Rhys said.

"Whenever you're ready, Two-Seven, we're not objecting."

Crabbe raised his voice just as Rhys signed off with Abraham.

"Sergeant, we got a problem," Crabbe shouted over the din of the heavy machine-gun fire. Rhys closed the gap to him in two long strides.

"What is it, Crabbe?" Rhys asked. "I know we're not out of range. They've got four howitzers on Blair, less than one hundred kilometers away."

"They do," Crabbe said a bit too quickly. "But this dickhead in the Fire Direction Center"—Crabbe pointed to his headset as if it were the offending dickhead—"says that without an officer on scene we have to have a fucking general sign off on the fire mission to use lethals, much less special munitions."

"What the fuck?" Rhys said. He flipped channels and spoke.

"Thunder Main, this is Blacksheep Two-Seven," he said, not bothering to hide the anger in his tone. "The reason you are talking to me instead of an officer is because my platoon leader got her head blown off. If we can't get those penetrator munitions, either enemy reinforcements will show up and kill us all *or* the majority of the enemy will slip away while the bunkers keep us pinned, either way we are going to fail our mission if you don't fucking fire it."

"Blacksheep Two-Seven, this is Thunder Main," a young, nasal male voice answered him. *"My hands are tied, guidance from Division is clear—"*

"God DAMN it, Thunder," Rhys shouted, feeling frustration and fear close around his heart like an iron-mailed hand. "We need a silver-bullet mission right goddamn now and if you won't give us one you better pray I die out here."

"*I'm an officer you can't talk to me that way—*"

"*Thunder, this is Summit Six,*" a smooth, modulated voice cut through the artillery officer's retort. "*Process the fire mission as requested on my authority. Immediately.*"

Rhys recognized his battalion commander's voice and felt the hand constricting his heart loosen now that the Old Man was involved.

"*Sir, I'm sorry,*" the younger officer said, a plaintive note in his voice. "*You can't override, without an officer on site to do a proper collateral damage estimate—*"

"*Lieutenant, I'm coming to your Operations Center,*" Summit Six said, and an unmistakable edge of menace tinted his cultured tone. "*It will take me about five minutes to get there. If your guns aren't firing by the time I arrive you are going to be the collateral damage. Summit Six, out.*"

Less than sixty seconds later, Crabbe was back on the Fires Net working out the details of the fire mission.

"... okay, roger, time of flight seventy-two seconds. Our PRF code is Seven-Three-Niner," Crabbe said into his mic. "Roger that, logged. Make sure you give us the splash-call right on time; I'll only be lasing ten seconds before impact... Okay, let's do this. Fire Target Number Alpha-Bravo One-Zero-One-Niner."

For a moment Rhys focused on what his forward observer was doing despite the continuing firefight before them. Infantry was, of course, the most important and best branch of the Army, but he had to admit the artillery had some pretty cool tricks.

Crabbe was behind his designator but he didn't press the button yet. To minimize detection he'd wait until the last few seconds of the round's descending ballistic path to lase.

"*Shot, over,*" Crabbe's radio announced.

"Shot, out," Crabbe acknowledged. He began to count down the seconds by tens. "Sixty seconds... Fifty seconds... Forty..."

They were too far away from Forward Base Blair to hear the actual report of the cannon, but at around the thirty second mark, Rhys heard the freight train shriek of the round on its final approach.

Looking south, Rhys caught the flash of the first rocket and could just make out the black dot dropping through the air toward the bunkers. The seventy-five-kilo shell was audible even over the sound of the heavy machine guns pounding away.

"Splash, over."

"Splash, out," Crabbe said, depressing the button on his designator. "Lasing."

The outer case of the shell split apart one thousand meters above the target revealing a silvery core of pure tungsten, a millisecond later the second rocket assist fired with a bright flash and an audible boom. This rocket drove the tungsten rod into the roof of the bunker at nearly six hundred meters per second.

The thunder crack of the round shattering the bunker was earsplitting, the resulting concussive wave powerful enough that Rhys felt it roll his guts from almost four hundred meters away. He looked over to see Crabbe's freckled face split in a wide, gleefully malignant grin. Even in the middle of combat, Rhys found himself grinning back.

"Nice work, Crabbe. Let's do it again."

By the time Captain Schultz reached them with the rest of Blacksheep Company, there was nothing left to do but count corpses, treat the wounded, and collect intel off the crispy and dismembered remains of the rebels. Once that work was done, Rhys stood outside the one remaining structure left in the artificial hamlet, waiting to talk to his superiors.

They had repurposed the only standing building as the company aid station. Rhys had been unsurprised to find nothing but concrete floors inside the walls. This structure and all the others had only been empty facades to conceal the concrete bunkers the insurgents had dug.

"Shitty day, Sergeant Harlingen," Captain Schultz, a tall rangy man said in his corn-belt rasp as he walked up to Rhys. Rhys was unsurprised to see that his company commander was flanked by the battalion commander and battalion sergeant major.

Lieutenant Colonel Wesley Antoine was similar in build to Schultz, tall and lean, but had dark red-brown skin, exceedingly handsome features and graying hair. As he closed the distance, Rhys could see his hazel eyes sweeping back and forth, measuring everything from the positions Blacksheep Company occupied in the woods to the ruins of the town.

Behind him marched Sergeant Major John Matthew Taumoepeau.

Taumoepeau was the same height as his commander, but nearly twice as broad, a solid wall of Tongan muscle. The sergeant major's mahogany-cast features were hard edged and blunt, and he might as well have been an automaton summoned from the bones of the earth for all the emotion they betrayed.

Rhys stiffened but did not come to attention or salute when Schultz, Antoine and Taumoepeau joined them in front of the bodies. For a moment, all four men stood in silence, allowing a few seconds for grief.

"Alright, tell me what happened," Antoine said. His modulated, deep southern voice was tinged with weariness.

Schultz gave the overview and then turned it over to Rhys, who gave Colonel Antoine a complete blow-by-blow of the engagement. Antoine listened intently, rarely interrupting, for twenty minutes while Rhys recounted the whole battle.

"That's about it, sir," Rhys finished. "I should have insisted on taking the dismounted element."

"Bullshit, Sergeant," Antoine said. "I'm sad we lost Lang too, she had a lot of potential, but she was right where she was supposed to be and so were you and so were Mahoney, Mazeres, Rodriguez and Gilbert."

It wasn't lost on Rhys that Antoine didn't need to be reminded of the names of the dead. He never did. Rhys had managed through determination and shameless finagling of the personnel system to stay in 1-87th Infantry under Wes Antoine's command for more than eight years. Even given that longevity in the unit, he wasn't sure why Antoine hadn't been either promoted or forced to retire or at least ousted from his battalion command. There were rumors that his family was well connected, but wanted him to stay away from the family business, but Rhys didn't know how true they were.

"Yes, sir," Rhys said.

"Enemy killed in action?" Taumoepeau said.

"Six confirmed," Schultz said. "Enough pieces and parts for one or two more. Eight to five is still a shitty exchange rate, sir. Especially given that we know they had at least thirty motherfuckers in the hamlet. Two thirds of their force got away."

He continued, "Sir, I'd like to recommend Sergeant Harlingen and Corporal Crabbe for Gallant Action Awards with V. Without their efforts, it's likely we would have lost the whole damn platoon."

"Sir, I don't want a medal—" Rhys protested.

"Shut up, Harlingen." The sergeant major spoke up for the first time, his deep voice monotone and unyielding.

"Indeed," Antoine said, his fingers drumming on the buttstock of his Mod96A1 which was slung across his chest. "Here's what we'll do, Schultz, write up the narratives, I'll forward them both as Superior Action medals. They will, of course, get downgraded to Gallant Action, the medals you actually deserve."

Rhys frowned, but said nothing further knowing he would be overridden. Besides, Crabbe was a good troop and a decoration for valor would help his career along.

"I see that sour expression, Harlingen," Antoine said, a note of levity entering his tone. "You may not care but every time we hang a medal on one of you heroes, a *deserved* medal mind you, it deepens the legacy of the battalion, not just for us but for those who come after us."

Sir, the fact that you can say shit like that unironically is the only reason I'm still in uniform.

Unable to think of any other response, he simply said, "Climb to Glory, sir."

"To the Top, Sergeant," Antoine said, completing the unit motto. "Gentlemen, you can go about your business. I'm going to have a word with the troops who were wounded."

Taumoepeau spoke up again.

"Just a reminder, sir, we've only got an hour. The RC-D inspector general will be at Blair this afternoon," He said. Harlingen's brain automatically translated RC-D to Regional Command-Delphtonopolisburg. If they were sending an IG, which these days was basically a politically-correct term for inquisitor…

Oh, goddamn it.

"Fuck the IG," Antoine said. "I'm with my men."

"Sir, she can cause problems," Taumoepeau said. "Especially since we just circumvented RC-D guidance on the use of lethal and precision-guided munitions."

Rhys felt his stomach lurch, and Schultz immediately echoed his feelings aloud.

"Sir, if we've got you in trouble, I'm sorry," Schultz said.

Antoine whirled on the younger officer, his right index finger thrusting at Captain Schultz's chest.

"No, Captain, *I* protect *you* from bullshit, not the other way around," he said. "And Sergeant Major, I do not intend to rush away to kiss the IG's ass. She can look through our laundry all she likes, everything we have done has been justified by military necessity. I'm going to go talk to my men as long as I damn well please."

Without another word, Antoine stormed away, threw open the door to the aid station and stepped inside. Taumoepeau watched his commander disappear inside the structure. Then he turned to Rhys and Captain Schultz.

"Gentlemen, while I agree with our commander's stance regarding the righteousness of our conduct," he said. "I think he's being optimistic about how the IG will see matters, and how RC-D will react to her report."

Captain Schultz nodded.

"Yes, Sergeant Major," he said. "What do you suggest?"

"Well, to quote one of my favorite movies, sometimes honesty needs a little plus, sometimes fate needs a little push..."

Forward Base Blair
1-87 Infantry HQ

Even in the twenty-sixth century, some things still were better with ink on paper. In this case, Wes Antoine did not mind the burden of paperwork attendant unto his office as he signed off on the posthumous awards for Lang and her men, as well as the Superior Action Award recommendations for Crabbe and Harlingen.

People like this are the only reason I'm still in uniform.

A knock on his door brought Wes back to the present and the unpleasant business at hand. His head came up out of his hands, he took a deep breath and assumed a relaxed-but-alert posture in his chair.

"Enter," Wes said.

The woman who stepped through Wes's office door was surprisingly attractive. He placed her in her early forties with all the bearing a woman her age should have and more. Her figure was discernible even in baggy battle dress uniform and Wes had to force himself to keep contact with her sea-green eyes, which didn't help much as they were lovely as well.

You are fifty years old, not some hot-blooded lieutenant, Wes reminded himself firmly. *And pretty or not she* is *the enemy.*

"Sir, Colonel Madison Kornberg to see you," Taumoepeau announced.

"Thank you, Sergeant Major," Wes said. He stood and came around his desk, extending a hand which Kornberg took with a firm grip.

"Colonel Kornberg," he said. "I'm Wes Antoine. Welcome to Forward Base Blair."

"Thank you, Colonel," she said; her Standard English accent complimented her sharp demeanor and rigid posture perfectly. "I know the presence of an Inspector General is never a comfortable experience, but I do hope we can work through this investigation as efficiently as possible."

"Of course," Wes said, waving to a chair in front of his desk. "Please have a seat. Forgive my bluntness, but if you don't mind, I'd like to know the specific concerns that led General Parvati to dispatch you to our backwoods outpost."

Kornberg sat primly in the proffered chair, hands folded on her lap, and regarded Wes levelly.

"There are a number of irregularities in your command that have come to General Parvati's attention," she said, her voice cool. "You have the highest lethal munitions expenditure rates of any battalion-sized element in RC-D according to your own ammunition reports, and you are usually late with those reports. You have, on multiple occasions, *creatively interpreted* guidance on the use of lethal munitions. Your investigations into lethal incidents have been woefully lacking in depth and documentation and sometimes even flippant in tone. We have reports that your troops regularly deviate from the theater-approved equipment load-outs for patrols. You and many of your officers and NCOs are accused of using gendered speech and other bigoted expressions in verbal communications and finally there was the latest incident when you threatened a junior officer with bodily harm to coerce him into ignoring RC-D guidance regarding mandatory collateral-damage estimates."

Wes was silent for a long moment, formulating verbal defenses for each of her charges, but then he realized arguments would be wasted this early in the game. Instead, he gave Kornberg his most winning smile.

"Well, of course it sounds bad when you say it like that," he replied.

Wes was rewarded with a small laugh of amusement and disbelief from Kornberg.

"I'm afraid it does, Colonel," she said. "General Parvati is considering your relief."

Wes nodded, schooling his features from flirtatious to very-serious/much-concern.

"I understand," Wes said. "But I'm confident you'll find that all my actions, as well as those of the men under my command, have been justified by military necessity."

"What I don't understand, Colonel," she said. "Is why your methods are so different here than they were on Mtali. I've read the unit histories and a large percentage of your after-action reviews from that campaign. I know you were not shy about direct methods there, either, but you seemed to employ softer options when possible. Why haven't you attempted such tactics here?"

That... was a disturbingly intelligent question.

"Two primary reasons, Colonel," he said, holding up index and middle finger. "One, my battlespace here is largely rural. On Mtali I had several city neighborhoods. Civil-military operations get less mileage out here in the sticks."

Kornberg nodded.

"Still, there are local villages, if you could turn them to our cause the way you gained the cooperation of the local police on Mtali, would that not increase your intelligence gathering potential, if not your combat power?" she asked.

"It would, but that brings us to reason number two. At the risk of using bigoted speech," Wes said. "On Mtali, the culture was primarily Islamic. Most of my people are from North America and Mtali was almost entirely alien to them, thus I was never overly concerned at my men identifying too closely with the locals.

"Grainne, on the other hand, is very nearly a platonic expression of American Rugged Individualism, and they even speak the same language we do. Certainly, American nationalism has been dampened over the course of the last several centuries in favor of the welfare state and transnational progress, but rugged frontiersmen and their hardy, beautiful women are memes that run deep in our culture even still. I fear that were I to allow the level of interface between my troops and the rebels that I did on Mtali I would be inviting mass desertion."

"Your troops' loyalty is that fragile?" Kornberg said with a raised eyebrow.

"You may judge my troops' loyalty for yourself, Colonel," Wes said, allowing an edge of frost into his normally smooth baritone. "We've arranged transport for you to join Bravo Company at Patrol Base Lang up north."

The Mountains North of Delph'
Patrol Base Lang, Bravo Company 1-87 Infantry

Rhys heard the vertol's engines and resisted the urge to look up, knowing that human faces were easier to pick up than the tops of helmets. The fieldcraft was mere habit, though. Rhys had a good idea that it wasn't an enemy vertol, or at least not an *insurgent* vertol. Sure enough, it flared out and landed in the clearing south of the hamlet.

He didn't go to see who it was. Getting his platoon situated properly was the first priority, even over the clandestine mission Sergeant Major Taumoepeau and Captain Schultz had cooked up.

Unfortunately, the new arrival found him. A few minutes later, a runner from Captain Schultz summoned him back to the command post, and when he got there, Colonel Antoine and Captain Schultz were standing with a middle-aged female colonel.

"Ma'am," he said, saluting crisply, on purpose. The woman answered with only a wry smile.

"I may be a REMF, Sergeant Harlingen," she said, her English-accented voice holding more irony than malice. "But even I know that it is customary to eschew saluting in field conditions."

"Customary, but not in accordance with service regulations, ma'am," Rhys said, unapologetically. "I would hate to be found violating regs by the regional IG herself."

Antoine snorted, and Schultz turned a laugh into a cough. The English colonel smiled thinly at him.

"You may find that I'm more comfortable with necessary deviations from regulation than you'd expect," she said with just a touch of asperity. "Especially when they keep me alive."

"That's good to hear, ma'am," Rhys said, finally dropping his salute.

"Sergeant, Colonel Kornberg will be with Blacksheep Company for a week," Antoine said. "In order to more fully render her report, she'll accompany your platoon on patrols. Captain Schultz has already briefed her on our interdiction mission out here. Furthermore, we have established that while you and your troops will render proper courtesy, Colonel Kornberg is an observer with no command authority in the field. She will accompany you on mission, but she will not be considered a member of the chain of command, is that clear?"

Thank God for small favors.

"Yes, sir." Rhys nodded. "Respectfully, may I suggest that you get some sleep, ma'am? Our first patrol steps off in five hours, and we'll have a lot of ground to cover."

"Of course, Sergeant," she said. "Show me where I'll be out of the way."

Rhys, who was travelling between the lead squad and second squad in the order of march, stopped about halfway to the summit and looked back on the rest of his platoon. They were making decent progress up the rocky slope. They were under heavier load than usual, so Rhys had purposefully moderated their pace. Still, it was a hell of a climb, and they were doing well. Even their guest.

Cold as it was up here at altitude, crushing as the gravity was on Grainne, Rhys had to admit Colonel Kornberg was more of a trooper than he'd expected. Even as the straps of the ruck dug cruelly into her shoulders ("See, ma'am, the approved packing list, just like it says in the RC-D Standard Operating Procedure"), and with the unfamiliar and awkward burden of a Mod96 in her hands ("Well, ma'am, if you wanna walk around without a rifle you can, but the rebels might take it to mean you're someone worth shooting first"), she was keeping up, albeit at great and obvious cost.

He saw that as she was huffing for breath, Private First Class Ericsdottir was marching alongside her, clearly keeping up a cheerful, if one-sided dialogue. He purposefully waited until the duo passed him to hear what she was saying to Colonel Kornberg.

"So, ma'am," Ericsdottir was saying. "If we fail this inspection will ya send us home in disgrace?"

"Not how it works, soldier," Kornberg puffed in between gasps for air, her eyes returning to the rocks under foot so she didn't fall flat on her face. "No one's going anywhere until we've got the rebels under control."

"That's right, Ericsdottir," Sergeant Abraham's back-alley Bostonian accent cut through the conversation. "Only way out is through. So quit bothering the colonel."

"Oh, of course, Sergeant," Ericsdottir said brightly, then turned her eyes back to Kornberg. "The rumors about 1-87 are bullshit anyway, ma'am. I mean Sergeant Abraham there would never call anyone a syphilitic twat-waffle, or address his squad as leaky douche-canoes on a regular basis. We're a very sensitive and woke unit."

Kornberg chuckled softly in between gasps of breath.

Is that a real sense of humor, or is she just drawing more information out of my people?

"Sergeant Abraham," Rhys said, raising his voice enough to startle Ericsdottir, who had been so busy pestering Kornberg she hadn't noticed her platoon sergeant marching a few feet behind her. "Call a short halt before the summit. Rotate by teams into the center of the perimeter to have Doc check feet."

Rhys hung close enough to see when it was Kornberg's turn to check in with Doc. There were some definite blisters forming on the backs of her heels and the pads of her big toes, but not a whole hell of a lot she could do about it. She strung the damp socks off the back of her ruck as she saw the veterans doing and rummaged around for a dry pair.

Someone stopped her with a "Wait, ma'am." Rhys saw it was Crabbe, his forward observer. He was holding out a yellow tube.

"Here," he said. "Put this powder in your socks before you put them on and it'll help wick the moisture and avoid blisters."

She gave the man a tired smile as she accepted the tube and glanced at his nametape.

"Thank you, Corporal Crabbe," she said.

"You're welcome," he replied. The ginger boy smiled shyly and turned to walk away.

Ericsdottir, lacing up her own boots a few meters away, coughed something into her hand that sounded suspiciously like, "Kiss ass."

"Nasty cough there, Ericsdottir," Kornberg said. "Perhaps you should get the medic to look at it."

"Oh, no, ma'am, just had some water go down the wrong pipe," Ericsdottir replied, smirking.

"Really? Because it sounds suspiciously like an inflammation of the twat-waffle," Kornberg said sweetly.

Crabbe and Abraham laughed heartily, Ericsdottir looked chagrined and even Rhys gave a ghost of a smile.

"Alright, alright, get your shit on," Rhys said. "If you've all got enough air to laugh, we can keep moving."

✧   ✧   ✧

The rest of second platoon's two-day patrol was uneventful, as Rhys had known it would be. Like a herd of elephants, a full platoon of infantry was too small to go unnoticed and too large for the rebels to engage lightly. Burdened with all the bullshit from the SOP in their packs, they'd had no chance of reaching the remote mountain summits in time to check out any of the leads turned up by aerial or orbital recon.

The first ploy was complete, and Rhys hoped it had its intended effect since it required Kornberg learn from direct experience and draw the proper conclusions about the absurdity of one-size-fits-all solutions, with the pain in her back and shoulders as the teachers, rather than outright deceiving her. Phase II of the operation was much riskier.

"We have everything in place," Schultz told him as his platoon's vehicles were pulling out of their turret defilade and into column formation pointed north. "As soon as your platoon hits the Eight-Six Northing on Route Blue, all hell will break loose. We've got a shit ton of pyrotechnics, four captured enemy machine guns rigged to fire unmanned, and of course, enough bodies to make it look real for battle-damage assessment afterward."

"You know, sir," Rhys said. "I'm pretty sure using enemy cadavers like that is actually a war crime."

"Yeah, it is," Schultz said, unconcerned. "But given that the fuckers are fucking chopping up our people and feeding them to us, literally, I'm not going to get all choked up about it."

"Okay, fair point," Rhys admitted.

"How do you think she took the first phase?" Schultz asked.

"I think maybe the message got through, sir," Rhys said. "Honestly, I feel kind of bad. She was obviously sucking gas the whole way, but she didn't bitch or moan. She did her best, was friendly to the troops. She even got Ericsdottir with a zinger, and if anything could make me like a REMF officer…" Rhys shrugged eloquently.

Schultz nodded understanding.

"I get it, Sergeant, but don't forget the first rule of dealing with the Inspector General," he said, his voice rasping harder than usual.

"What's that, sir?"

"You don't like the fucking IG," he said. "But the IG *loves* fucking you."

✧   ✧   ✧

"All set, ma'am?" Rhys said. Madison Kornberg was in her body armor and helmet, leaning against the hull of B21, Lieutenant Lang's old Eel, now Rhys's since his had been hulled by a recoilless rifle.

"Yes, Sergeant," she said, rapping the hull of the Eel with the knuckles of her left hand. "I do hope that this means we're not on another hanging nature walk?"

Rhys picked up on the fatigue in her voice and the slippage of her accent to something a little less proper with dropped h's. "Hanging," had come out a little more like, "'angin'," "hope," like, "'ope."

"Not most of the way, no, ma'am," Rhys said. "We suspect we've located a logistical node in a town about thirty kilometers north of here. We'll drive up to about a kilometer before we dismount. Since contact is likely, we're taking an extra Eel with a squad we borrowed from 1st Platoon and the company mortar-carrier Eel."

"Okay then, Sergeant," she said, hoisting her pack. "I'll be in the vehicle when you're ready."

With that she climbed into the back of the Eel; at a nod from Rhys, Hensley hit the button and the back hatch lifted up and sealed with a hydraulic hiss. With it almost dark outside, and now inside the hull of an armored vehicle, Colonel Kornberg wouldn't have a chance to see that the fourth vehicle in the column had a hole through its back hatch and belly, and that the sixth was towing a burnt out hulk of an Eel with their vehicle data plates conveniently swapped with whole and hale vehicles back at Patrol Base Lang.

THWOOM. The pyro detonating inside of the hulks of B24 and B22 shook Rhys in his commander's hatch.

"Contact right," Rhys announced over the platoon net. "All Blacksheep elements, turn into the ambush and engage."

Every vehicle turned right and started advancing through the woods toward the hilltop where Captain Schultz's detail had set the phony enemy fighting positions.

The position erupted in fire as the rigged machine guns started firing blanks, and arty simulators started igniting both at the enemy "position," and from random hidey holes throughout the forest between the platoon and the alleged enemy strongpoint.

It was enough to get Rhys's blood going, and he knew it was all for show. He thought he probably had a good shot at convincing Kornberg, too.

"Hensley, you got them?" Rhys asked over the intercom.

"Roger, sergeant, weapons free?" Hensley asked, his Jersey accent betraying his excitement. Hensley loved servicing targets with the Eel's autocannon, even when they were notional.

"Light 'em up," Rhys said. The hull shook as Hensley depressed the trigger, letting fly a burst of 25mm.

"Shit," Hensley said as the glowing tracers fell short of the summit of the hill. *"I can't elevate high enough to hit them."*

All around them, glowing streams of autocannon fire impacted short of the fictional enemy position; just as Schultz and Rhys had planned.

"Blacksheep Elements, execute Case Purple," Rhys said. Each squad leader acknowledged the call. If Kornberg asked, Purple was the battle drill for react to contact. In reality, it was the brevity code to let B24's driver know it was time to set off the pyro in the back of his vehicle and run like hell.

THWOOM.

"Aw, shit, Two-Seven," Abraham's voice came over the radio. *"We just lost the mortar carrier."*

"Damn it, can't anyone range those motherfuckers?" Rhys said. A chorus of negatives answered him.

"All Blacksheep elements, dismount, and engage the hilltop with small arms," Rhys said, sliding back down into the Eel's hull. "We'll have to do this the hard way."

As the ramp dropped, Kornberg looked at him aghast.

"We're going out there?" she said, her voice cracking on the last syllable.

"Ma'am, until we can get those antitank weapons suppressed, it's safer out there than it is in here," Rhys said and put a hand on her arm to haul her out of the vehicle. "Now come on."

If the show had been convincing inside the hull, it was magnificent in the pitch-black woods. Muzzle bursts flashed from the hilltop and arty simulators detonated willy-nilly amongst the trees. Rhys wondered absently if the battalion would have any pyrotechnics left after this production.

Kornberg stumbled along behind him, kicking every root, stumbling over every rock with a string of profanity, half of it unintelligible to his American ears. Deciding she was stressed enough and he didn't really want to lose her before the finale, he pulled her down on her belly next to Crabbe who was shouldering his designator to make it steadier. They were close enough to want to ensure accuracy.

2nd Platoon was engaging the hilltop with every dismounted weapon system available in a cacophony of rifles, machine guns and grenade launchers, but since the machine guns atop the hill were being fired by automated timers with no emotions, their attempts at suppression failed according to plan.

A tree branch cracked and then shattered less than a foot over his head. Rhys felt a rain of wood chips hitting his helmet and heard the repeated *crack-thweet-tunk* of a machine-gun burst tearing into the trunk.

What the fuck?! Did Schultz put fucking live rounds in the machine guns?

"EVERYONE GET THE FUCK DOWN," he screamed. "THOSE ARE LIVE ROUNDS!!"

Madison thought, *What the fuck? Of course they're live rounds.*

Her night-vision monocle was filled with bright green-white flashes. Madison pressed herself into the evergreen-needle-coated forest floor as the impact of bullets chipped bark off the trees, sent up tiny fountains of mud and grass and filled the air with the horrible sound of angry hornets. More than anything it was that awful, alien sound that made her bowels feel like water.

Harlingen was lying on the ground as well, shouting into his radio.

"Abort Case Purple, I say again, abort Case Purple," he said. "Weapons hold, I've got no thermals on the position. They hijacked the automated firing systems, we can't suppress them so don't mark your positions. All vehicles, see if you can angle for a shot from further down the valley... YES, I'M FUCKING SERIOUS!"

"Sergeant, what the bloody hell is going on?" Madison shouted over the steady drumbeat of heavy machine-gun fire coming in on them.

"Ma'am, follow me," said Harlingen, and began crawling on knees and elbows toward a collection of large rocks a few meters away. With no better ideas, Madison followed him, coating her uniform in mud and grass as they slithered across the ground.

Once they were behind the marginally improved cover, Harlingen turned over on his back and looked at her and a third soldier who crawled up to join them. Only now that the other man was mere feet away from her in the darkness did Madison realize it was the nice ginger boy who had given her foot powder during yesterday's patrol.

"Crabbe, work up a mission on that hill," Harlingen said. "Ma'am, I need your help."

Madison looked at him, confused but trying to appear composed.

"What can I do?" she asked.

"We need artillery on that hill," Harlingen said. "Policy hasn't changed and I don't think the artillery is going to let us bully past them again. I need you to clear the mission on our end."

Madison stared a moment. This was the moment of truth, he was asking her to risk her career to save lives. Enemy fire continued to tear at the landscape around her, this was what the line animals lived with, the conditions under which they had to make their decisions.

"Ma'am, we've been lucky so far," Harlingen said, sidling closer, pressing his face right next to hers on the forest floor. "But if we don't silence that strongpoint, we're going to start losing people."

As if on cue, she heard someone scream, then the age-old cry of, "MEDIC!!"

Exhaling, Madison nodded.

"Very well then," she said. "Just tell me what to say."

Crabbe gave her the channel for Field Artillery FDC and she switched over.

"Thunder this is Colonel Madison Kornberg, the RC-D IG," she said, her voice mechanical with the rote phrasing. "I confirm that probable collateral damage for this fire mission is minimal and justified by military necessity, over."

"Ma'am, this Thunder Three," a confused voice answered. *"As an inspector general I don't know that you have the authority to clear—"*

As the artillery officer on the other end of the line spoke, Madison felt rage bubbling up from some primal place inside her.

We're out here getting shot at and you're worried about niceties like whether I'm the right kind of colonel?

"Listen here, ya stoopid cunt," she shouted into the hand mic. "Unless ya want to spend the rest of the war in a cell with a bag o'er yer head and power cables on yer cock, you'll fire the fookin' mission, all right?"

Crabbe's freckled face split in a wide grin and Madison could hear Harlingen's laughter even over the sustained gunfire.

"How was that, then?" she asked, handing the mic back to Crabbe.

"Out-fucking-standing, ma'am," Harlingen said, meaning every word.

Crabbe handled the rest of the fire mission with professional excellence, bringing in the rod from God down onto the hilltop. The impact of the rocket-assisted tungsten projectile lifted Kornberg off the ground, but also put a smile on her face. The "enemy strong point" fell silent, followed a few seconds later by 2nd Platoon's weapons.

"Ma'am, I'm going to clear the objective, I want you stay here with Corporal Crabbe," Harlingen said, a melancholy note in his tone. "When I get back, I'll be happy to answer any questions you may have about the day Lieutenant Lang died."

Madison's face grew solemn.

"Thank you, Sergeant Harlingen," she said. "But I'm not sure it will be necessary anymore. I think I get it."

Rhys gave her a melancholy smile.

"Thank you, ma'am."

It was the same story as usual on the hilltop. Rhys saw two mangled torsos and at least one leg that wasn't attached to either. Rhys called it three enemy KIA and knew in his heart it wasn't doing dick to stop the insurgency. The sun was creeping up on the horizon, coloring the mountain sky in brilliant oranges and pinks by the time Rhys made it back down the hillside to his platoon. When he did he found Colonel Kornberg staring at B24's burnt-out hull.

Aw, shit.

"Ma'am, we're getting ready to move out," Rhys said.

"Right," she said. Her face was pale and drawn, her sea-green eyes troubled. "Crabbe told me we didn't lose anyone last night, is that true?"

"Yes, ma'am," he said. "We do have three wounded, but no one took a direct hit from any of those heavies, thanks to you."

"Right," she said again, she stared at the burnt-out hulk. "No one was even wounded when this—"

She waved a hand at the vehicle.

"No, ma'am," Rhys said, and sweat started to accumulate at his collar despite the cold mountain morning air. "They had a few seconds before the fuel and ammo ignited, thank God they all managed to get out."

"That's good," Kornberg said, and when she turned to face him, her eyes were no longer troubled, just clear and cold. "Sergeant Harlingen, why did you feel the need to tell your men the enemy was firing live rounds, was it not obvious?"

"Uh, ma'am, you would think that, but communications were a mess today and I had to make sure everyone got the word, especially the new arrivals."

"I expect we'll be returning to FOB Blair today?" Kornberg's voice could've cut glass when she spoke.

"Uh, yes, ma'am."

"Good. I need to talk to Colonel Antoine."

Oh, fuck, she knows . . . we have to warn the Old Man . . .

Forward Base Blair
1-87 Infantry HQ

Madison Kornberg glared at Antoine as he approached her outside the mess facility. She refused to share a meal with him, and he didn't want to have this conversation at his headquarters, so they met in a quiet corner of the FOB. That was fine with her; as far as she was concerned she was merely serving notice of his impending prosecution. It wasn't going to be a long conversation.

"Colonel Kornberg," he said, his urbane southern accent grating on her nerves. "I owe you a very deep apology."

"Oh, I'm afraid I'm not accepting apologies this evening, Colonel," Madison said. "I will take a few careers, though. I could've been killed because of their stupid prank. Three of your men *were* wounded."

Antoine frowned and she was glad to see *some* crack in his composure. The man had been so confident, so assured that he could flout whatever rules he wanted and call it military necessity because he was a good tactician and well connected.

Surprise, asshole, no one gets away with this kind of shit forever.

"Some of my people did go entirely too far," Antoine said. "I'm not defending their actions, but they did what they did in an effort to protect the unit. They couldn't have foreseen that the enemy would get to their position in time to hack the system and change out the blank cartridges for live ammunition."

"Harlingen and Schultz intentionally deceived a commissioned officer in the prosecution of her duties in time of war," she said. "I can spare the rest of your men, but they don't walk. They are directly responsible for two men with more holes in their body than biology intended."

"That's not why you're angry," Antoine said.

"It's not is it?"

"No, you're not angry because the line soldiers lied to head-quarters or even that some of us got hurt, you've seen that too often to let it get to you," Antoine said. "You're mad because your comrades lied to *you* and manipulated *you*. You, personally, not the office of the Inspector General."

"Oh, they're my comrades now, are they?" Madison spat.

"Yes, they are," Antoine insisted. "Because while they may have tried to manufacture a battle for your benefit, your reaction to it wasn't anything less than real. The minute you prioritized protecting the men over your own career, the second you told that FA weenie to fire the mission or end the war with an electrode up his pee hole, you became one of us and we became a part of you. Only then you found out we'd betrayed you."

"Yes, you did," Madison snapped, stepping across the gravel, getting right into his face. "You lied and cheated to cover your ass, and all this brotherhood-of-war shite doesn't change that."

"I didn't—" Antoine shut his mouth over that sentence.

"You didn't what?" Madison said.

"It doesn't matter," Antoine said, but Madison had conducted too many interrogations, and Antoine wasn't a great liar.

Fuck me, he didn't. His men put on this great fucking theater on his behalf and didn't tell him.

"It does, Colonel," she said. "It does matter. Your actual life might depend on it."

"My life is nothing compared to the unit," Antoine said. "And I think if you're honest with yourself, if you look past your hurt feelings, you know exactly what I'm talking about."

"How are we supposed to win a war with soldiers who lie to their superiors?"

"Oh, that's an easy one," Antoine said. "We're not."

"What the fuck is that supposed to mean?" she asked.

"Look at it objectively for a second," Wes said, waving a hand. "Given our limited reach up here, I suspect they have further reserves of material and personnel we haven't seen yet. But most of all, the rebels are fanatical and intelligent. They've hacked our convoys, disabled infrastructure that hurts them, too, developed their own intel net. Rather than join our society, they fight knowing they'll die. Our will is not equal to theirs, and so we will lose this war eventually."

"If we're not going to win, why are you and your men fighting so hard?"

"Because our battalion will outlive this war," Antoine said, his spine stiffening unconsciously. "Even in defeat our legacy will remain honorable, a unit that did its duty to the best of its ability despite an impossible situation. And perhaps someday there will exist a better civilization for the 1st Battalion of the 87th Infantry to serve, one that will allow them to fight for a just victory. When that day comes, our spirits will march with them. Your spirit, Madison, will march with them."

The night was suddenly quiet. Madison felt Antoine's words rolling over her like a benediction.

"Wes," Madison said, but then words failed her, and her mouth worked soundlessly. She took a deep breath, and coughed. "You would've made one hell of a preacher."

Antoine's charming smile was back in place.

"My Granny Alette wanted me to go to seminary, actually," he said.

"Don't doubt it," Madison said.

"Look, I wouldn't blame if you wanted to dick-punch the lot of us," Antoine said. "But I'm begging you for clemency for my men. Don't ruin them for good. They were stupid, but desperation can make even the best people stupid. And I think you can see why they were desperate to try and keep 1-87 the way it is."

Madison opened her mouth but a high-pitched wail interrupted her; the incoming indirect-fire alarm.

"GET DOWN!" Antoine yelled, tackling her to the ground. Even as they hit the gravel she felt a wave of overpressure wash over her, heard a loud POP, followed by a ringing noise, and felt warmth spreading down her pantleg.

Did I piss myself?

Madison felt strong hands turn her over, feeling at her, not in a groping way, but in a clinical way. She heard a voice calling her name as if from the other end of a long metal funnel, followed by a cry of, "MEDIC!"

As her vision cleared, she was able to make out Antoine's face over hers. He was cutting and ripping her pants off.

"Why, Colonel Antoine, I didn't know you cared," she said with a hysterical giggle.

"Quiet, Madison," Antoine said, and held a folded piece of

her torn uniform near her mouth. "Bite down, I have to apply a tourniquet and it's going to hurt."

Madison took his advice and was glad she did so, as he cinched a strap down right where her leg met her hip joint. She nearly bit through the thick cloth.

"It's okay," Antoine said after he'd tightened it to a cruel degree. "You're going to be alright."

"Thanks for that," Madison said, sleepily. "I think I'm going to have to pass out now."

"Madison, don't go to sleep, no, stay with me... Medic... MEDIC!"

Her first thought was that her mouth was terribly dry and she smelled copper and bleach, but that otherwise she felt fine. Well, not fine, she felt weak as a kitten and sore everywhere, but for some reason those facts didn't seem to bother her. Then it occurred to Madison that she had to be alive, her current state was too good for hell, not good enough yet for heaven.

She opened her eyes. She was in a hospital bed with her leg strapped down and an IV stuck in her right arm. There were five men around her. Four she recognized: Antoine and his minions Taumoepeau, Schultz and Harlingen. She assumed the fifth was a doctor.

Madison tried to speak, but all that came out was a croak. Sergeant Harlingen heard her first and rushed to her side. Retrieving a glass of water, he held it gently to her lips, as if tending his own sick mother.

"Ma'am, we're so glad you're awake," he said.

Madison coughed.

"What? Afraid your con would go to waste?"

The wounded expression on Harlingen's face actually touched some part of her.

"Oh, forget it, Sergeant," she said. "We're all alive. No bodies no foul, as you Yanks say."

"No, ma'am," Schultz spoke up. "What we did was wrong. We have no excuse."

All four men were looking at her with such genuine concern, and there was, she realized, so much painkiller flowing through her veins, that she felt tears welling up.

The doctor said, "Really, gentlemen, if you're going to upset the patient, I'm going to have to ask you to leave."

Antoine was chuckling as he turned to leave with the rest.

"Wes, wait," she said. He stopped, turning to face her.

She waited until the others had left. As the door swung open and closed, she saw Crabbe's freckled features and several dozen other familiar faces, craning around, trying to get a look into the battalion aid station.

"Another bit o' theater?" she asked, nodding her chin to the door. "All the lads and lasses coming to check up on Colonel Korny?"

"Actually, they're calling you Colonel Maddie now," Antoine said. "And you can question each of them to see how genuine they are when the drugs wear off."

"Ach, I hate that name," she said.

"But you don't hate them," he said.

Madison didn't address that.

"You saved my life," she said, instead.

"I did."

"If I'd bled out, you and your men would've been safe."

"My reputation for violence aside," Antoine said, "I don't hand out death sentences to cover my ass. Or even to protect my men from the consequences of their actions."

Madison nodded. That was the answer she expected.

"Besides," Antoine continued. "You're one of us."

This time the tears wouldn't be stopped. It had been a fuck-all of a day.

"Oh, fuck ya, Wes," she said between sobs. "You've got your stay of execution. I could never destroy such a beautiful anachronism as you anyway."

"I knew that." Wes smiled at her again, but with no polish, nor devil-may-care luster, just genuine warmth. "I just wanted you to know you've got a home with us, even when you're not here. We might be a bunch of 'anging wankers, but now we're your 'anging wankers."

■　　■　　■

Huff #16
Artillery ROE [September 210]

"Sandeep, what's this report? An ambush and artillery ROE?" I tasked the staff to review and tag reports to help justify ROE changes. Especially anything involving authorizations for lethal fires, air, and artillery.

"Yes, sir. I tagged this one, got it from a war college chum. Maddie works in the IG here. The first ambush, on its own, is nothing to get terribly excited about, other than the discouraging exchange ratio between us and the insurgents, however there were delays in getting artillery support, and…"

"Hold on. What do you mean 'discouraging'?" Sandeep took his time, picking words carefully but truthfully. That's one of the things about him I respect; he doesn't bullshit me.

"The initial report estimated the OPFOR at twenty-five. The platoon sergeant on the ground insists upwards of thirty. The rebels had a bunker system built under a village facade, very well designed. Excellent interlocking fields of fire, perfect for ambushing dismounts. This supports the intel assessments that surviving Grainne regulars and SOF are reorganizing. Of course I'm not infantry, just a Sentinel driver, but I understand tactics. Over the course of the fight, we lost five KIA, at least four more wounded, one Eel a catastrophic loss, another damaged, and for all our efforts, we got only eight of them. The rest successfully evaded."

I skimmed the report. "We're lucky they only had recoilless rifles. If they had missiles, that platoon would have been completely fucked. Those bunkers do look good. I wonder how long that took to set up? Heh, 'threatened bodily harm to the fire direction center OIC.' Cute." Then, I noticed a bit about the second engagement. "Hacked perimeter security defenses? That's not the first time, unfortunately." Something else to yell at the '6 and the '2 about. Ah, another artillery fire clearance problem. That's enough of that.

"What do you know about General Parvati?" I could see Sandeep searching for the diplomatic answer. He wouldn't lie, but being a gentleman and a professional, he wouldn't disrespect a senior officer outright.

"I only worked for him briefly, but in that time, I found his command style left, shall we say, something to be desired."

"So, he's a prick and no one likes him. Got it. Is he effective? Can he get the job done?"

"It's not my place to say."

"Would you use words like 'inflexible,' 'hide-bound,' maybe even 'toxic'?"

"Perhaps 'a bit lacking in imagination.'"

"Should I fire him?"

"Expeditiously, sir."

Spider's Web
Part 10

:: Northcaps ambushed! :: reported Handler D20Crit, an old gamer friend of Hespera's, but recruited by TripleShot. :: Reporting UN has new drones up, and they're taking heavy fire. Supplies are being destroyed now. They're not going to make it out. ::

:: Dam, :: Moyra tagged him, :: can Northcaps get support? They were ambushed just after collecting supplies. ::

:: Negative. We have nothing in range. Arty's been re-sited; we can't risk the aerials yet. ::

"Shit," Moyra muttered aloud, swapping to Kozlov. :: I have reports of a unit under ambush, with new UN drones. Do we have any intel on new units? Any overrides? ::

:: Not yet, :: Kozlov replied. :: Nothing's shown up on manifests for new equipment of that nature, or on the primary network. ::

:: Get looking, then. They slipped it in past our filters somehow, somewhere. :: She swapped back over to D20Crit. :: Attempting to locate resources to help, but not located any yet. Updates? ::

:: I think they're about to be captured. I just heard the order to smash all personal devices, and I've got no signals from them. ::

:: Fuck. :: Moyra swapped back to Damocles. :: Northcaps are down. May be captured, possibly killed. Devices destroyed. :: She didn't wait for a response, switching to Salamander. :: App ID J8392R assumed compromised. Device IDs attached for those to blacklist. Initiate rolling blackout procedure. ::

Salamander acknowledged the command, and Moyra flipped back over to Damocles. :: Northcaps maybe lost along with supplies, :: he reported. :: Low level drones are en route. ::

Video feed showed a small crater. Supplies definitely destroyed, but it was still unknown if personnel were as well. However, no visible UN vehicles remained near the vicinity, nor were there any obvious bodies.

"Bring it lower," Moyra told the drone controller over voice.

"*Yes, sir,*" she acknowledged. The video feed drifted down and closer.

"See that camouflaged bit over toward the left? That's not ours. Check it out." The view moved closer and circled around the item. "That's...different. Does that look like a drone fragment to you?"

"I think so, sir. Should I attempt to collect it?"

"If your unit has enough range and power to bring it back, please. Less likely to set off any booby traps than sending in personnel."

The drone got close enough to pick up the partial drone, and lift it up and clear. Moyra gave the operator coordinates to take it to, far enough away from any active field units but close enough for retrieval. It may still have a functional tracker located in the device, left as bait to find other locations.

She created an AI monitor to review network traffic indicating any awareness of the damaged drone's movement. After several days, she ordered a passing unit to pick it up and drop it off with Charles, the restaurant owner, now located near his wife's family and otherwise a noncombatant. He could not fight, but he could function as a drop point for information and the occasional UN contraband item.

The fragment landed in the hands of Kozlov's team, who made short work of extracting available information from it.

:: We have control of the new generation of drones, :: Kozlov messaged within a week. :: Drone controllers have been upgraded with access switches to enable takeover capabilities, but the changes are sufficient that we haven't been able to make that a seamless switch on the neural controller side. We're working on it. ::

:: Good. How's the smart gun project? :: Moyra replied.

:: There are still a few models resisting other methods, but I would estimate 75–80% penetration on average. The heavy weaponry is the most consistently compromised. ::

:: How confident are you in being able to bring the compromised items offline to manual control only? ::

:: Command scripting is ready and waiting. As long as UN C&C has the capability of communicating to take over control remotely, we have the ability to nuke the processors. Not all of the devices have a manual fail-open design. Those ones won't operate at all. ::

Moyra smirked slightly. *Even better.* :: Estimated time to do it? ::

:: Variable on device's connection, but the majority will shut down within, call it, nine divs. Most of them just need the execution command; the code's already waiting. ::

:: I suspect we will be using that soon. ::

:: Understood. I'll see if we can't get a few more stragglers, then. ::

She loved working with professionals.

Is That A Fire?

Philip Wohlrab

"Well, shit, that worked out worse than expected," muttered Senior Sergeant Felix Tolstoy. His green eyes, the color of summer grass, watched the last bit of flaming wreckage float back to earth. That wreckage just moments before had been the last of his militia team and their air lorry. Felix's face was twisted in a mask of frustration and anger, for he had put months into training Team Charlie.

"Yeah, though come on Felix, what did you expect from those guys?" This came from a big beefy man with prematurely snow-white hair except for streaks of black going past his ears.

"I expected that they wouldn't have got themselves killed so fast, Gerhardt," snarled back Felix.

For his part Senior Sergeant Gerhardt von Mauersteine just raised his hands placatingly. The two were partners in the Free-hold of Grainne's 3rd Special Warfare Regiment, with long service together. Their current rotation had been Blazer training on Grainne when the UN forces struck. Falling back into an old mission given special forces throughout the centuries, they were tasked with train-ing indigenous forces in successful guerilla warfare. Their unit had been fairly successful, perhaps too successful given the amount of force that had just been used against it.

WHAM WHAM WHAM

The two men moved fluidly through the bush, as they avoided incoming enemy mortar fire. The fire was sporadic, and seem-ingly laid down as if probing for a response. It soon eased up.

"I don't think the UN has an actual fix on us, Felix"—Gerhardt had to pause to breathe in a great sucking breath as he continued to run—"and let us both be thankful for that, I like living, and there are some ladies that would be awfully upset with me, were I to die on them!"

"Small comfort," panted back Felix, though Gerhardt's quip did cause him to crack a smile momentarily.

The two men pushed deeper into the bush. Once free and clear of the UN patrols, Felix broke out their comms system to report in to higher. Using an existing special warfare code, he made a succinct, but brief report. The chance that the UN would pick up on the transmission was small, but if one wanted to live to retirement one didn't take chances where anything like electronic emissions were concerned. Once done he stowed his gear and they beat feet out of the area.

Four divs later Felix made a quick check for response. Once powered up, he saw they had a coded response.

"Message from HQ," announced Felix.

"Well, what does it say?" asked a slightly exasperated Gerhardt. He was not over losing the team that they had spent the last several months with. It hurt and hurt badly. They'd been good guys and girls. Aranak, Hawley, short little King-Smith...

"We are to move back to staging area Kilo, from there we are going to be taken to our next team. We are to embed with a group known as the Congregation of Our New Lord."

"What the hell is that?" replied Felix, his voice having risen sharply with the group name.

"Fundies way out in the boonies, like so far out I don't think they would have noticed an invasion unless it poked its nose in where they are."

"Great, fundamentalists," was Felix's only response. *Maybe I won't fail them as badly as I failed my last team.*

Rehoboth, Hinterlands District

"...and that about sums up where ours and their forces stand right now," finished Senior Sergeant Felix Tolstoy.

Felix had stood more or less at parade rest, arms crossed behind his back with feet shoulder width apart, as he had laid out events since the UN forces had come to Grainne. His camouflage uniform was worn looking but neat, and he had removed his beret and tucked it under an epaulette when he had come into the chapel. Likewise had Gerhardt, as the two were trained to be courteous to local customs.

"So, let me get this straight, you guys are getting your butts kicked and you want our help in attacking the blue bellies?" drawled someone from the congregation.

Felix didn't quite sigh. *You have to win them over to your side, not antagonize them. Besides, with your track record would you jump up and immediately volunteer to join up?* Felix was still struggling to answer his own internal question when he heard someone else speak up.

The craggy-featured Elder known as Saul, who was the leader of the Congregation of Our New Lord, intoned, "That's enough Brother Hiram. These gentlemen have asked us for our help, and though they may be outsiders from Jefferson, at least they leave us alone. Most of you don't remember what it was like before we came to Grainne, and I only remember because I took care of Elder Mason in the last years of his life. Elder Mason would speak of the time of persecution in Idaho on Old Earth. How the busybodies put their noses in where they didn't belong. The blue bellies are never going to leave us alone to live our faith the way we see it. They will want to take our children for their schools and teach them apostasy."

Felix winced when Elder Saul had called them outsiders. *So much for us all being Freeholders against the UN. Still,* he reflected, *it does appear that these people are going to help.* Felix was about to open his mouth to reply when Elder Saul continued to speak.

"Brothers Jed and Hiram, I want you both to take the two Senior Sergeants here over to the garage and arms room. Fill them in on what equipment we already have and get details on what they can do for us. Senior Sergeant Tolstoy, will that be acceptable?"

"Uh yes, yes, sir," Felix replied. "That would be acceptable. We would also like an opportunity to train with some of your people before we go operational."

"I understand, Senior Sergeant, I think we can arrange that. My people aren't without some training, for the Lord tells us to be prepared, but the Lord also says to take help where you can get it." With that last exchange, Elder Saul's craggy features broke out into a toothy grin.

Felix stood in a long, low building that looked like it used to be a dairy barn. He was impressed and said so to the two Brothers of the Congregation. He wasn't sure quite what he had expected to see when he walked through the doors of the barn, but it certainly wasn't the neatly lined-up rows of ground vehicles, weapons racks, and even some light artillery pieces. He whistled softly as he walked down the line of vehicles. *Elder Saul wasn't kidding when he said his Lord told him to be prepared*, mused Felix.

"We have our farming vehicles which you saw outside, but we got these after Elder Saul was on Mtali," said Brother Jed as he gestured at four GenDyn Bogtrotter pickup trucks that were clearly modified extensively.

"Wait, did you say Elder Saul was on Mtali?" asked Felix turning away from the Bogtrotters to look at Brother Jed.

"Yes, he was there with a 'relief' organization." At the word *relief* Jed made air quotes with his hands. "The Lord commands we be ready to fight the last battle. Elder Saul signed on with a group to get training and skills to bring back to the rest of us. When he returned, we pooled our resources, and when we have enough, we buy a little bit more hardware."

"If I wasn't a believer in Mars, I think I could find your church interesting," grunted Gerhardt in a wry tone.

"Well, I will pray God will reach you and find common ground," offered Brother Hiram.

Felix shot glances at both Gerhardt and the little wiry man at that. Hiram had been mostly quiet while Jed was showing them around the barn.

"Right," drawled out Felix. Looking back to Brother Jed he continued, "What kind of ordnance do you have for those pack howitzers?"

"What, those pony guns? Just high explosive, we have about a hundred rounds for each of the four guns. In addition to those we have a pair of dual autocannons that can be mounted to the back of the trucks, we have about four thousand rounds for each of those. One thing you may find an interest in, Senior Sergeant, is these rocket racks we were tinkering with. It was something Elder Saul saw on Mtali, real low-tech things but they are cheap to make, and we can remote fire them."

"How heavy are they?" inquired Felix.

"Oh, not heavy at all, we can transport them with the mules. The launch frame is only about twenty-three kilos, and each rocket is only four and a half kilos. Each frame can fire six rockets."

"Hmmmm, that gives me several ideas..." mused Felix.

Two Weeks Later
Forward Operating Base Pat Quinlan

The UN troops making up the complement of the brigade assigned to FOB Pat Quinlan were primarily from Ireland. Most of them were military police or some sort of support troop, with no armor or artillery on hand. It was assumed by UN Ground Command that if such support was needed that the commander of FOB Pat Quinlan could call for them. Besides, it wasn't as if there was anyone living this far out in the bush except for a few farming communities, and all of them had been compliant with UN visits. So, it came as a nasty surprise one day when the base was rocketed.

"INCOMING, INCOMING, INCOMING," wailed the loud speakers around the base. Unfortunately for the UN troops at FOB Pat Quinlan there was no automated defense system to engage the rockets as they came in, the base being deemed too remote to need it.

Several earth-shattering booms later the UN troops crawled out of bunkers or other holes they had gone to ground in to assess the damage. Several of the housing units were on fire, and the chow hall had collapsed after taking a direct hit. Worse, so had the storage unit for all the fresh food.

"Do we have a bearing and location from where those rockets came from?" screamed Colonel Patrick Ready.

"Yes sir, it came from the forest line eight klicks to the north," replied a UN sensor tech.

"Captain Second Class Powers, take the Badgers and go find the bastards that fired those rockets. Lethal force is not authorized, do you understand me?"

"Sir? But they have inflicted casualties on us," stammered back a confused Powers. Command had finally taken gloves off a few weeks before.

"Captain, first, we are here to help these people develop. It is our duty to teach them, and we can't do that if they are dead. Second, they are uniformed combatants. We must fight by civilized rules."

"Yes sir," replied a chastened Captain Powers.

Six tedious hours later of moving through brush and trees, the UN troops finally found where the rockets had been fired from.

Sitting in a clearing were three frames that appeared to be the source of the rockets based on the scorch marks on them and on the ground. Looking around, the captain and his men found no marks or tracks where vehicles had been, however they did find some evidence that large animals had been in the area but soon lost the tracks when they came upon a large deep creek.

"The colonel isn't going to like this, sir," said a sergeant.

"No, no he isn't," replied Captain Powers.

Three Weeks Later
FOB Pat Quinlan

Colonel Patrick Ready was losing his composure. Previously, Command had ordered him to use a new nonlethal biological weapon that flew in the face of his initial mission orders and now the rocket attacks on the FOB that were seemingly at random over the last three weeks. Worse, his small intelligence section couldn't discern a pattern from the attacks, as they came from all points of the compass around his base and at random times. Satellite tracking hadn't shown any unusual activity at any of the local farming communities, and patrols sent to them found nothing out of the ordinary. Worse, the satellites were increasingly unreliable. Command wasn't saying why, but Ready surmised that maybe the war wasn't going as well as Command said it was.

"INCOMING, INCOMING, INCOMING."

"Match bearing and roll the patrol, maybe we can catch them this time," ordered Colonel Ready.

Captain Second Class Powers was certain they weren't going to find anything this time either. They had rolled out fourteen times after these rocket attacks and found nothing. The rockets were being fired off cheap racks with an attached timer. All the rebels seemed to have the strength to do was shoot harassing fire, and it wasn't like they were even doing much damage anymore. The FOB wasn't particularly large, but most of the times the seemingly unguided rockets managed to land outside the FOB or in the open areas. Still, one thing they managed to consistently hit were the gym, the chow hall, and the Morale and Recreation building. The troopers were less pissed about the casualties than they were about not getting hot chow or being able to do anything except play tablet games.

"All right sergeant, let's see if we find something on this wild goose chase."

Felix Tolstoy and Gerhardt von Mauersteine were aficionados of Ancient Rome: their beliefs in service were derived from the story of Cincinnatus, their religious beliefs were derived from what they knew of the cults of Mithras and Mars, and their gear had a somewhat Romanesque appearance. Felix, preferring a shorter blade, carried a gladius, while Gerhardt carried a spatha as part of his kit, and both had taken a bit of license to adapt a Roman eagle into their armor.

Which made working with the Congregation of Our New Lord a bit of a challenge for them. While the men of the Congregation had taken to heart the lessons that they taught on matters tactical, their religious beliefs demanded daily communal prayers and it was clear that they didn't like having outsiders present during them. For their part Felix and Gerhardt tried to make themselves scarce during those times, but the men of the Congregation insisted on them even in the field. Felix was a strict stoic in the mold of Cato the Censor, while Gerhardt adopted a live-and-let-live attitude, and it was because of this, that the men of the Congregation had warmed up to Gerhardt more than they had Felix. But both men were ready to kill someone after the long grating weeks. And now they had their chance.

The two, along with a contingent of the Congregation, had laid an ambush in for the UN patrol sent to find the source of the rockets. Both men had donned their full armor and gear for this action, while the Congregation had all put on a pattern of camouflage that allowed them to melt into the bush in this part of Grainne.

Felix looked over to the Congregation troops and snorted out of pure wry amusement. *Leave it to mankind to cross the stars, but still rely on horses and mules,* he thought. Gerhardt noting his amusement asked a question as to its source, but Felix merely waved it away as he turned to listen to Elder Saul's instructions to his men.

"When the blue bellies dismount to examine the work we left them we will strike," intoned Elder Saul.

"Yes, Elder," replied the twenty men of the Congregation, each sitting astride a horse. Cross-country horse racing was the unofficial sport in this part of the Hinterlands, and when combined with shooting from horses it had become a lively sport. In addition to the men on horseback the Congregation had brought along two of their pack howitzers. The youngest men of the Congregation manned those, including Elder Saul's oldest boy Cyrus. They all wore camouflage blouses with a chest patch marked CONL. The blouses, along with extra boots, standard carbines and ammo, had been dropped off by a passing farm truck. Two of the village women embroidered the unit ID with their machines.

"Cyrus, make sure of your targets; when I give you the command, I want your gun to take the vehicle at the rear of the UN convoy. Brother Ezekiel, your gun will take the front Badger. After that destroy the other three as they become a threat and support our charge, do you understand me, boys?"

The boys all replied their understanding and ensured that their guns were laid in. The UN troops were dismounting from their vehicles and in a disorganized mob were moving toward where the rocket racks had been laid in a large pasture near one of the few roads in the region. As they neared the racks...

Captain Powers was confused, and something in the back of his mind was nagging at him, but he couldn't place it. It was the first time that the rocket racks had been left near a road.

"I don't like this, Sergeant, this isn't like the rebels," he muttered to his senior noncom. *I should have the troops dispersed more, but I doubt they would listen to me.*

He and the rest of his men were bunching up near the racks when things went to hell very quickly for them.

Powers's first indication that his afternoon was ruined was finding himself lying on the ground, with no memory of how he got there. Worse, his nose was bloodied, and his mouth full of loose teeth. He pushed himself off the ground, and it was only then that he registered the heat. He was horrified to see that three of his Badgers were fully engulfed in flames. Looking back around he saw a sight he thought impossible. Men were charging toward him on horseback from the distant tree line.

"This is Captain Powers, Colonel, we are being charged by men on horseback!" Powers yelled into his helmet-mounted comm system, panic causing his voice to rise in pitch as he did so. It hadn't even occurred to him to fire his rifle.

"Powers, what did you say? Did you say horseback?" asked an incredulous Colonel Ready over the comms, *"Dammit, Powers, answer me!"*

Felix rode the horse long enough to get him across the field; surprisingly few of the UN troopers were firing, and those that were seemed to be firing some kind of nonlethal weapon system. *Their stupid policies and lack of discipline work for us*, thought Felix. As he neared the closest UN troopers, he shot one with his rifle, managing to wing him. He wasn't a particularly good shot from horseback, and he rolled off the horse going to ground. Felix watched in some amazement as the Congregation men cut down several of the UN peacekeepers with their ancient carbines fired from horseback.

Felix shot another UN trooper and then drew his gladius and strode toward what appeared to be the UN officer. The man was gabbling into his comms, and only before Felix was on top of him did he swing his weapon up. Felix contemptuously batted it aside with the gladius and then kicked the man down and raised his gladius to strike. The peacekeeper raised his hands, possibly to surrender, possibly to ward off the blow but Felix didn't care.

"This is for Team Charlie!"

With that Felix slammed his gladius down into the officer's upper chest, driving the point of the sword between where the armor sealed and the man's neck. The officer bore down under the weight and sudden pain, hands shooting up to grasp the blade as it drove deep into him. The man let out a gurgling scream and died. Felix used his boot to help pry the sword free from the dead UN Captain 2, and then gasped for air.

Felix looked around to see much the same scene playing out around him: those UN peacekeepers not having been killed by the horseback fusillade, or the direct fire from the pack howitzers, were being killed by blades. The Congregation men used their utilitarian machetes, and a few had axes, while Gerhardt finished off another shrieking soldier with his spatha. The barbarism was complete, and more importantly had a purpose. *They need to know we can be more brutal than they.*

"Elder Saul, collect your men, we need to be away from here before the UN can mount another patrol or dispatch air support."

FOB Pat Quinlan

Colonel Ready paced in his command post. The recorder had miraculously survived the Badger's destruction, but the memory for the device had been badly degraded by the high heat of the burning vehicle. Still, one of his techs tinkered with the recorder, trying to pull usable data from it.

He needed data. UN Command had been shocked at the ferocity of the attack on Powers's patrol. That shock prompted General Huff to order Colonel Nikolai Strelnikov to take over counterinsurgency operations at FOB Pat Quinlan, and the man was due to arrive soon with his team.

"*Got it!*" exclaimed the intel tech, and pointing to her screen continued, "Colonel, I was able to get a face scan off one of the rebels!"

Colonel Ready strode over to the console. He glanced at the screen and said, "Good work, Samantha!"

A low thrumming announced the arrival of four vertols off in the distance. Two of them were big transport jobs, but the other two were vicious looking gunships, with the distinctive look of being manufactured in the Russian Federation. The beefy insectoid appearance sent chills down Ready's spine as they came in low. The transports moved to the landing area of the base and set down. Troops poured out of them, moving with purpose.

Shortly, Colonel Strelnikov strode into the operations center with a confidence that Ready couldn't help but admire. Walking over to greet the colonel, Ready held out his hand, but the colonel gave only a perfunctory shake.

"Colonel Strelnikov, I have arranged quarters for you and your men, I would offer you a meal, but we haven't had fresh food in some weeks..."

Strelnikov wasn't a small man, but he also wasn't bulky. Hard years of near constant exercise had refined him and if he was impressed by Grainne's greater gravity, he didn't show it. He fixed Colonel Ready with a steady appraising gaze before he replied.

"While I appreciate that, Colonel, I am here to work. My Spetsnaz have come a long way and I would like to get to the bottom of your insurgent problem so that I can move onto the next hot spot." Strelnikov's voice was gravelly and while it was clear he was Russian, his accent was nearly perfect Oxford English, in contrast to Ready's Irish brogue.

Ready was troubled by this escalation. *Lethal force has been authorized and now Command has sent these men, these butchers.*

"Very well, Colonel, if you step this way. One of my techs has found something I think will help..."

Three Days Later

"That should about do it," said Brother Jacob as he tugged down on the last corner of the camo netting. Felix nodded his approval and the two men moved back to admire their handiwork. Before there had been a Bogtrotter with a pair of 20mm autocannons in the open, but now it sat snugly under camouflage netting that would hide its magnetic signature as well as its distinctive shape from prying eyes. A few meters to its left stood an identical setup, and the group of men were finishing a third such setup for equipment cases.

The men broke to eat, sitting under the shade of local trees. The food from the community was plentiful and fresh, though lacking in spices. It wasn't a religious matter. They were just that far out in the bush and had no way to resupply on such things now.

They were several kilometers away from the main community and off a maintained, if little-used road. Part of the team was also working to cover up any fresh tracks made by the pair of trucks, just in case the new UN commander got cleverer with his air patrols. All told Felix had about half of the forty fighters left, while Gerhardt had the other half disguising the other two trucks at another rally point. *I hate being separated by several kilometers from the other team, if the UN hit us now, they could defeat us in detail. I can't let them see I am concerned though, lest I kill their confidence in me now.*

Brother Caleb walked up to where Felix and Jacob were standing with an odd expression on his face.

"Is that a fire I smell?"

Colonel Ready was appalled at the level of violence employed by Strelnikov and his men. As he watched from the back seat of a command Ferret, a Spetsnaz trooper lobbed an incendiary grenade into another one of the surrounding homesteads. The building, nothing more than a simple one-story wood-frame house, burst into flames with the small detonation. To Ready's horror three people staggered out of the house, engulfed in flames. One of them based on stature had to be a small child, but he couldn't determine age or sex of any of the individuals as all were human torches. Ready violently threw up over himself and his gear. Outside the Ferret, Strelnikov directed his men to push on. The UN had come to call on the Congregation's community, and they had brought fire and death.

It had taken all of Felix's considerable force of personality to keep the men of the Congregation from racing back toward their homes. He had them uncover the trucks, though only start up one of them since they didn't have enough men to run both, and the other hardware he wanted to take back.

"Gerhardt, are you still at your site? Have you moved back to the community?" Felix commed to Gerhardt. But all he got was static on the comm net.

"My God, what have they done? What is happening?" cried someone from behind Felix, but he didn't have time for that.

"We don't know and won't know until we are back there. But what we need to do is be on our game, and not rush headlong into a trap set for us by the UN. Does everyone here get me on that?" Felix's voice was harsh and rose to a near shout by the end.

There were murmured assents, but only halfhearted ones. The Congregation troops were horrified that their families were left uncovered, and every fiber of their being cried out to rush back to their aid. Felix could understand their fears, but he knew that if they rushed in headlong, they wouldn't do any good.

"Here is what we are going to do, Jacob, you and your crew will run the truck. Caleb, you and your team are on the Gadflys..."

As Felix went over the details of his plan, they could hear the distinctive sound of automatic weapons fire coming from the direction of the community.

Elder Saul, upon seeing the first UN armored vehicles approaching up the road had gathered most of the remaining families at the big house with the attached community center and chapel. Not everyone had been able to make it though and he watched as several of the smaller outlying houses kept up a fusillade on the approaching UN troops. It pained him to see one of the houses go up in flames, and then another. He said a quick prayer for the souls of the Gerard and Loch families, then continued his commands to the women, older children and some elderly that were able to bear arms. He knew it wasn't much, but he had to buy as much time as possible for the men to get back to help.

"Sarah, you and the girls here take the LMG over to the east corner of the community center, and if it wears a uniform that doesn't look like one of ours you shoot it, do you understand, girl?"

"Yes, Elder," replied the twelve-year-old, toting a machine gun that was almost as large as she was.

"Good girl, now go," and with that the last of the commands had been given. Elder Saul put his fine hunting rifle to his shoulder and scanned the oncoming UN troops looking for a choice target. "Aha, those must be officers there."

Colonel Ready was standing next to his second in command, Major Chloe Harper, when he felt a splash of blood strike him in the face. He turned to Harper to see her shocked face, mouth wide open in a silent scream, as blood fountained from the right side of her neck. Something began to break inside Ready at this. He had known Harper since they were cadets back in Ireland.

Chloe doesn't deserve this, none of my people do . . .

A large-caliber round had punched through the gorget of Harper's armor and severed the right carotid artery and jugular vein. Blood poured down her armor, while spurts of it hit the front of Ready's plate. He grabbed the woman and gently lowered her to the ground.

"Shhh now there, Chloe. Just you lie down and take a rest now," Ready said in a surprisingly gentle voice, though it was lost on Harper who could no longer hear it. Once he had her on the ground Ready stood back up and for the first time in his military career, he fired a lethal round in anger. His submachine gun wasn't going to have any effect at this range, but he didn't care.

One of Strelnikov's Spetsnaz a few meters away shouldered an RPG and let fly with a rocket. This struck an outbuilding that had been a source of heavy machine-gun fire that had pinned one of Strelnikov's platoons. The thermobaric warhead entered the building with an effect like a small sun having suddenly appeared inside, and the machine-gun fire cut off with dreadful certainty. That almost all the fighters so far encountered had been women and older children still managed to bother Ready, but Harper's death had shocked him out of his reticence to engage them.

Felix and his men were just about in position. *Where are the UN aircraft? If they show up when we are crossing into the open, they are going to massacre us. I can't lose another team,* Felix thought angrily. Several of the community's buildings were on fire, and with each passing moment there was less and less return fire coming from them.

"Caleb, I want you to start dropping shells around those vehicles, I know you don't have much practice with the howitzer in indirect fire, but it doesn't need to be that accurate. I just want them to keep their heads down. Jacob, your job is to kill those trucks with your autocannons. Move your vehicle as you need to. Simon, stay sharp with those Gadflys, if and when the vertols show up you are our best defense got it?"

Simon and the other men nodded their understanding.

"Good, Ezekiel, you and your four men follow me. We are going to see if we can draw the UN forces off the main building and back toward us. Jacob, and Caleb, as they approach our position you all will take them under direct fire. All right men, let's do it."

Strelnikov and a squad of his Spetsnaz made it into the community center with Colonel Ready in tow. They had to detour around one side of it as a light machine gun kept up a steady stream of fire on where the Irish troops were cowering behind their vehicles. Strelnikov burst through a door right ahead of Ready. Strelnikov identified the group of young girls operating the machine gun and opened fire on them as they turned and faced him, startled and afraid. He stitched one girl with bullets, then another. One of the Spetsnaz also tossed a frag grenade at the group. Shockingly one of the girls was still alive, though grievously injured. Ready ignored her pained cries as he stepped back out to direct the rest of his men to come up. In another time and place he would have been disgusted with his actions, but no longer. Colonel Ready had given himself over to the savagery of battle. It was then that he heard the sharp boom of an artillery piece being fired. And then again, and again.

A line of explosions erupted behind the Irish troops and their thin-skinned Badgers. Ready gave out a pained cry as he watched the peacekeepers panic and begin to run in all directions. *I should have only used the Spetsnaz for this*, thought Ready. Strelnikov for his part was grinning, though why he should be was lost on Ready. *He has been doing this a lot longer than me, perhaps he enjoys it now?* That grin was short lived, however, when one of his thicker-skinned BTR 250s exploded in a hail of autocannon shells. Then another was taken under fire and Ready began to suspect that Strelnikov had bitten off more than he could chew.

"Maksim, call up the vertols, I think we have their main force pinned here," called Strelnikov to his comms operator.

"Aye Colonel!"

Felix grimaced as a round glanced off his armor and another singed his left arm. It took him a moment to catch his breath and he dropped to the ground and tried to make himself as small as possible. Brother Raphael wasn't as lucky as UN rifle rounds found their mark and left him bleeding out on the ground. Once Felix recovered enough to aim, he searched for the source of fire, and seeing it he engaged the Spetsnaz. The Russian had gotten a little too careless with his use of cover and Felix put a round through the man's right eye. Still the Spetsnaz knew where the remnants of Felix squad were and were pouring fire in.

Static burst painfully in Felix's helmet headset for a moment and then Gerhardt's voice crackled through. *"Want some help?"* he asked.

Felix laughed in relief and replied, "About time you showed up!"

"You guys decided to start the ball without us, how rude," Gerhardt radioed back.

A rocket leapt from the distant tree line on the other side of the community, centered on a knot of Spetsnaz that were trying to work their way around Felix's squad to take them in the flank. The weapon burst among the group peppering them with a hail of fragments and throwing the unlucky Russians to the ground in a welter of gore. Emerging from the tree line came Gerhardt's pair of Bogtrotters. The trucks both had dual 20mm autocannons ensconced in their beds while ersatz armor had been welded on to them. Their camouflage paint jobs did a pretty good job of blending them in with the background vegetation, and it was only the trucks' movement and the firing of their guns that gave away where they were.

With the cover of Gerhardt's forces, Felix's squad once again moved toward where he suspected the UN commander to be. They dashed from one outbuilding to another when they made a gruesome discovery. Brother Jedediah was only recognizable because half his face was still there, but none of the other individuals could be identified as they were far too badly burned. The three remaining Congregants with Felix let out anguished gasps as they recognized the dead. Worse, they could see other bodies that had to belong to members of the Congregation lying around other outbuildings. Felix recognized the look in these men and knew blood was in their eyes.

"No quarter, men. No one surrenders," he said quietly to them, though his face had twisted into a mask of rage.

How? How did they manage to have this much equipment on hand? Ready furiously thought. *They are butchering not only my troops, but also Strelnikov's Spetsnaz.* Another of the BTRs exploded when it tried to maneuver on the first technical that engaged them, and with its destruction the last of the armored vehicles was out of action. Ready at last realized they were going to lose. One of the Spetsnaz stood up with an SW-26 antiarmor rocket to engage the enemy truck when he was bowled over by a concentrated burst of fire from the low barn to his left. *We haven't even managed to kill all the people here yet!*

Another Spetsnaz ran over to the fallen rocket gunner and managed to snag the weapon away from the dead man. This soldier ran a few meters to another position and lifted the tubular weapon to his shoulder, sighted, and then let fly with the rocket. It streaked out and intercepted the first technical that had taken them under fire. The warhead impacted the lightly armored truck cab causing a pulse of superheated plasma to blast through the armor of the cab and into the vehicle where it ruptured the hydrogen fuel cells. The truck exploded, killing the driver instantly and dismembering the two men servicing the guns on the back.

The rocket gunner's elation was short lived though as another burst of autocannon fire shredded him. Ready and Strelnikov were down to less than twenty-five troops and they were making their last stand by the community center. Strelnikov ordered two of his men to proceed into the building and ensure that it was set afire.

I suppose I should be shocked by Strelnikov's order, but frankly

I just don't give a damn anymore. Let them burn, reflected Colonel Ready, almost sadly. His innocence and idealism had died this day in a welter of flame and gore. If teenage girls were willing to kill and die to avoid civilization, there was no reason to bother bringing it to them.

Felix shot down another Russian soldier, who had been trying to work his way back to what was left of the UN force clustered on the patio outside the community center. It was a dugout position with a stone retaining wall that formed a rather large patio with a large fire pit in the center. The Congregation often gathered there for outdoor picnics but now it served as an ersatz trench line for the remaining Spetsnaz. The other UN troops, who seemed to be from a different force based on their uniforms and altogether lack of discipline, had mainly panicked and run. A few were holding out around their thin-skinned ground vehicles, but their fire was largely useless. *We are going to win this, we are going to finish these bastards off...*

Felix heard two new sounds. Distinctive popping sounds came from the interior of the main house, not gunfire, but something else he could almost place when the other sound intruded. That sound was the thrumming of vertols.

Elder Saul lay in a pool of his own blood. He was growing very cold, and he knew it wasn't going to be much longer before he died. He had done his best for his people in peace and war, and was ready for God to receive him. His eldest wife, out of ammo herself, sat in the pool of blood beside him, holding his hand and crying. What he could feel hurt horribly. He tried to say something to her, to comfort her in his final moments but he was just too tired. As his vision began to gray out, he felt an intense heat coming from below him, so intense that it managed to burn through his shock. He used his final strength to gasp out, "Run, Mary, run."

"YES!" cried out Strelnikov.

One of the two vertols took out one of the technicals with a ripple-fired volley of rockets, while the other was hunting the position of the howitzer that was still firing on the Irish troops. Its rotary cannons whined to life and a streak of shells landed in the wood line to the west of them, silencing the howitzer. The last technical turned its guns on one of the UN aircraft, but the great insectoid machine sidestepped the tracers and responded with another volley of rockets. The pilot misjudged the bouncing technical and missed.

A streak of fire erupted from near that truck and raced up to meet the Werewolf, shredding its portside engine. The pilot tried to adjust for the sudden loss of power and overcorrected. The vertol flipped and inverted and came to a near standstill as the pilot attempted to right it. The battered technical took it under fire again and this time the tracers flared through the body of the aircraft and as Ready looked on in horror the MI 78 Werewolf nosed into the ground and exploded. The other vertol didn't fare much better as a second Gadfly missile struck it square in the cockpit, and it too folded up and nosed over into the tree line and exploded when it hit the ground.

Ready didn't have much time to reflect on the destruction of the Werewolves. Grenades bounced into the patio area and detonated. The remaining Spetsnaz were thrown to the ground, if not dead than concussed. For his part he was just starting to realize what had happened when a big man with a short sword was standing over him. The man said something but Ready could no longer hear through ruptured eardrums. Then the sword came down. Colonel Patrick Ready felt fire lance through his throat for the briefest of moments and then felt nothing else ever again.

■   ■   ■

Huff #17
Damn Russkies [October 210]

The Russians are fucking pissed and demanding answers. They want to know how we lost the better part of a Spetsnaz battalion and some of their most expensive vertols. The answer is simple enough: When things went really bad around FOB Quinlan, I sent in Nikolai Strelnikov. Colonel Ready and his Sinn Fein backers on Earth weren't happy about this, as they took giving lead over to the Russians as a slap in the face. I prefer to do things Ready's way, but after weeks of convoy losses and embarrassing attacks, all from the middle of nowhere, we had to do something. And Strelnikov? He's something. You don't call in Russians unless you want to make a point. I knew the strong possibility existed that he would just wipe out a whole village and call it a day, but considering the residents' behavior, I wouldn't lose much sleep over that.

The rebels' use of bladed weapons and their take-no-prisoners attitude are what put me over the edge. That's why they deserved Strelnikov. FOB Quinlan lies in the worst heart of fundie country. I'm amazed by the sheer diversity of weird cults and crackpot individualists in the countryside. The wilderness seems to enhance their viciousness. Quinlan was in direct conflict with a group called "CONL," who were augmented by Grainne SOF. They were far better equipped than we expected—howitzers and Gadflys. Losing the Spetsnaz, even losing Nikolai, the sick bastard, I can abide. Losing the Werewolves though, I'm going to pay for that. The Russians will want something on the back end, and they always get their due. I don't care what the Irish think.

Force Majeure
Part 6

Aboard FMS *Force*, the sourcing-in was limited by fuel and raw material. The delivery-out was limited by the number of deep-space-capable boats with sufficiently low profile, and not already compromised to the UN.

The crew was back on normal shifts, their frustration and tension somewhat relieved, though they'd been stuck in space for almost a year at this point, with no land or even habitat leave. That caused other issues.

Production, though, could increase again, if it weren't for the bottlenecks.

With transportation updates in hand, and the latest brief available, Yates started the latest command meeting.

"The first news, sadly, is that *Jack Churchill* was lost in combat. He took at least one UN operations ship, the *Gareta*, with him. The UN were hurt badly, but they have a lot more ships to spare than we do. I would like to pause for a moment so we can honor them privately."

For long seconds, no one spoke or moved. Yates wished their souls well, and reflected that they all faced the same fate.

He resumed with, "Thank you. First tactical matter. Tirza, can we fabricate an in-system boat?"

She made an expression and wrinkled her brow.

"Possibly. We can't do it aboard, even in the dock. The sections can be built there, but it will have to be assembled outside. Building a reactor is feasible, but I'm not sure we have enough magpoles. Then, it will be using our fuel pebbles."

"Damn. Well, can we adapt one of the rescue cutters?"

"Easier. What is your plan?"

He explained, "There's a smuggling ship we can meet halfway. They carry UN cargo, but can sometimes arrange to drop ours. We couldn't verify whose side they were actually on until the intel net cleared them."

"So the important question is, whose side are they on?"

"The UN is paying off their loan and has contracted them for cargo. Whenever there's a variance, they drop the excess somewhere it will be found. They also carry approved other cargo, and fit some of our production in amongst it. They've been effective. We have to fuel them, though, so they don't show short in UN space."

She commented, "Small amounts, but I suppose it's all cumulative."

"It is."

"How do you know the intel web is legitimate? Or won't be compromised? Or that these double agents aren't on the UN side?"

"That's a risk we're taking. I don't worry about that so much for us."

"We're a long way from the jump points and UN craft."

"Exactly. We can get further out, go quiet, and wait for *Sleepy*. Worst case, we can produce enough power to get in-system and surrender a hulk. But before I do that there will be no other alternatives."

"Well, Captain, I can't advise you further or offer anything else. Morale is determined, but tired. Fabrication Group will continue as we have been."

"Then let's convert a boat. If the smuggler never comes here, they won't know where we are. Not refined enough for a fix. We'll still have an escape margin."

"That's reasonable. I'll get the engineers on it at once."

He noted her formerly lithe muscle tone was suffering. So was his. Shipboard fabricated diet and lack of time or motivation to exercise was hurting them. There was enough slack in the schedule to add regular exercise back in.

"Dr. Okebe, can we schedule and implement some formal exercise?"

"In fact I intended to bring up that very item." The man grinned. "We can have a full-contact league, and both distance and endurance races. There are a few other options, too."

"Issue the order per me, then, as you feel it should be."

"Yes, sir. Also at my end, there've been four accidents this week. One badly lacerated hand in machinery, two crew crushed between cargo loaders, but they will recover. One welding splatter."

"Right. Commander Karanov, remind everyone of safety. They're not producing if they're hurt."

"Already have, sir. I will again."

"Good."

Injuries on normal rotations meant crew were burning out. Hopefully the sports and other rec time would help.

Of course, if more boats came online, they'd be back at emergency production levels until they ran out of sourced materials.

Captain Yates was tired, and if he was tired, the entire crew had to be exhausted to near failure. He'd had two brief meetings off ship at the space base in over a year. The medical clinic reported depression, strain, tension among the crew. Recreation was doing everything they could, from organized martial arts to dance to performance. The sex staff had reached the point of needing breaks themselves. The ship had been out here so long that porn access had dropped off in favor of video of mountainscapes and oceans. The crew needed space. Anyone with any talent at anything was requested to put in an extra div a week teaching or entertaining.

His first administrative detail the next shift was a report of a fistfight. The two spacers stood in his office, still faintly discolored from medical treatment.

"Gentlemen," he began tiredly. "You put me in an awkward position. Do I need the details on how this altercation started?"

They both turned fractionally to make eye contact, then back forward, and Corporal Machinist Andrews admitted, "It was rather stupid, actually, sir."

Yates asked, "Do you agree, Nasser?"

"Yes, sir. Entirely stupid."

"The problem I face is that I can't assign you extra duty. Everyone is maxed out. Base rations are not an option. Everyone is on field conditions. I can't pull you off duty for restriction. That would be taking a break. I can't even reduce your pay as we aren't getting any except as a bookkeeping matter at present. It would be dangerous to put the rec deck off limits. You'll just get more frustrated and angry. There's nothing I can do to punish you."

Andrews shifted slightly. "Sir, it will not happen again. I understand the urgency of the mission."

"I do too, sir," Nasser agreed. "It was just an overreaction. If we hadn't gotten dinged badly enough for the infirmary, no one would have known."

Hopefully this ended it. Yates ordered, "Stick to grappling in the gym, or make a date with padding and mark it down as unarmed combat practice. I need you fit for duty, performing that duty, and not eating my command time."

"Yes, sir!" they both shouted in unison.

"Dismissed."

At least they had some limited access to news. Inner-system broadcast was just detectible and could be processed. It was UN entertainment and news. Per intel, it was not well received below and the UN couldn't puzzle out why nobody wanted to watch their trite, statist pablum, or believe their professionally produced propaganda about how wonderful things were with government management of everything. It was hard to believe the people in those were locals and not imported actors. On the other hand, for money or food, one might say anything without believing it. Then, some of them were inserting coded messages in their delivery.

There were apparently issues over banned games. Interactive melee and shooting games were prohibited. Certain acquisition games were restricted and required lengthy disclaimers about how they did not represent a fair society.

In short, the UN was attempting to totally destroy the cultures of the Freehold in favor of the completely bland agonotopia it was turning Earth into, where each generation another culture was consigned to the dustbin.

It still seemed hopeless, but they had to persevere against it.

On the plus side, two stealth and one adapted gunboat rotated through cargo duties, bringing in what raw material they could, taking out whatever finished goods there were. *Force* turned the gunboat into a semistealth vessel with proper modifications. Every week one came in, loaded, departed. This last time, in addition to scrap metal and tanks of volatiles, 4J17 had brought a pallet of commercial candy and dried fruit. How they'd acquired it was a mystery, but it was very welcome, and the commissary rationed it out per person per week.

The ship was able to easily produce vodka, flavored into whatever else one might want, and Yates authorized a triple shot each down day. Recreation was important. Alcoholism must be avoided.

After command shift, he dressed for the gravity gym and went for exercise. Health and Welfare had coordinated with Commo, and come up with an aid. The gym was breezy by design, with warm and cool wafts punctuated with the occasional gust.

He stepped on a treadmill, donned a visor and headset combo, and started jogging, building up to a steady pace.

The rollers under him shifted, simulating country terrain. In front, he saw trees and grass, distant hazy mountains, bright clouds in a deep blue sky, and shadows. Around him the breeze added to the effect, and he almost felt as if he was outside.

It wasn't real, but it was a hell of a lot better than stark walls and artificial light. There were even wind and animal noises distantly in his headset. It took some of the edge off. Five kilometers of "cross-country" later, he reluctantly slowed and stopped, pulled the gear and blinked. Yes, he was still aboard ship, and there was a difference. Simulated it may be, but it helped.

The ship lighting was on three cycles. Factory decks were illuminated soft yellow, with daylight spotlights for necessary tasks only. Rec space used daylight frequencies with slow, random variance to mimic actual Iolight with clouds. Sleeping berths were dim red only, and every berth was sealable for privacy and complete darkness. If they got much lower on materials, they were going to have to dismantle half the bunks and go to hot cots, two spacers rotating through the same bed, and use the scavenged material for production. Already, as much of the ship as could be shut down was, to save power and oxygen.

It wasn't enough. Especially as everyone was working five divs/day officially, more often six. They had time to sit down for one meal, then shower and sleep. They needed R&R.

There was nowhere to go, though. They couldn't even approach The Rock. The UN had located one of the other clandestine facilities and destroyed it. The other two refueled and rearmed, performed repairs as they could to the few in-system boats left. *Force* had to remain where she was. Her sensor profile was not small, especially when the reactor was burning to power all the build crew. Her only defensive measure was distance against pursuit.

All crew had a maintenance day every eight days, to manage cleaning and caring for their personal gear, a small amount of extra rest, and whatever recreation they could fit in. *Sleipnir* was due to stop by with additional volatiles and fuel acquired through purchase, theft and guile by smugglers and SW craft in Govannon, NovRos and Caledonia. They should also bring fresh food, which would make a huge difference. The little left in stasis and refrigeration meant mere bites for each crew every few days. Everything else was reconstituted or packaged.

The duty schedule also included converting one of the empty holds into a hydroponics tank that should eventually lead to more fresh produce, and possibly even a meat vat. That would swap some of the ration issues for additional power drain—nothing came free.

However, current material stock on hand was impressive, and they actually were getting low on raw materials again. He didn't want to set any false expectations, but they all needed something.

The next shift, he took commo control to his station, and announced, "All hands, routine message from the captain," since it wasn't a combat or emergency warning. "Effective tonight at zero divs, First Shift will have a down day of no duty. Tomorrow at zero divs, Second Shift will also have a down day. There will be an additional down day each week until we acquire more raw material." He paused for a moment to let them realize what he'd just offered and let loose some of their tension.

He continued, "This is due to a combination of factors regarding schedule, but largely due to the amazing dedication the crew has put into accomplishing this mission beyond all wartime expectations, under extreme duress. I do expect that operations will continue enthusiastically before and after. When hostilities conclude, the entire ship and all crew are deserving of decoration for your devotion to duty and our nation. You each have my personal thanks, and the relayed thanks of the Forces command. Your efforts remain critical to the war effort and survival of our residents and way of life. Captain out."

There wasn't much more he could do, and they all knew it, but that precious day alone should be felt by everyone.

He hoped that after the hostilities concluded they were all still alive, and had the freedom to receive medals, rather than being shamed, mocked or abused by the UN.

Preparing to depart FMS *Force*, Commander Roy Brody ran through the launch checklist in detail. He was a skilled pilot or he wouldn't be command rated. Still, it had been some years since he conned a small craft between nav points, and he'd never done it between points that didn't have some sort of beacon. Then he had to get back to this exact mark.

The boat didn't have a name. He always felt a craft should. He turned to his assistant, Warrant Leader Sean Smock.

"What do we name the boat, Sean?"

Smock leaned back in his couch. "I hadn't really thought about it, sir. *Jawfish*?"

"Not bad. I was thinking of *Porpoise*."

The man shrugged. "Either is fine."

"Let's go with *Jawfish*. It's more aggressive."

"Sure, but we're hauling cargo."

"True, but it's violent cargo."

"Works for me."

He wanted to get along with his other crewman. They were going to be alone for three weeks.

With the rescue gear pulled, the cutter had space for a modest amount of cargo. The rear was full of bundles ready for the surface. Behind them were two pods with more supplies, as much as they could manage with the engines on this craft, even enhanced for the mission. It was never intended to be a freighter.

Well, that summed up the war.

"Everything checks. Please confirm, Warrant."

"Looks good to me, sir. Everything on my list is green."

"Then let's boost."

Spider's Web
Part 11

Damocles relayed to Moyra there was now a way to supply the freelancers. Naumann's side would deal with getting the equipment requests, as long as Moyra's handlers could arrange pickup. There was also an instruction that the units pick a name and emblems for official identification purposes. Once the "purchase orders" were filled, Naumann's team would coordinate to get the supplies to the appropriate destination.

:: So the freelancers aren't freelancing anymore? :: Moyra asked.

:: Being upgraded to bona fide militia and military reserves, in a way the UN can't deny, :: Damocles replied. :: So are you. ::

:: I what? ::

:: May I be the first to congratulate you on your commission-at-a-distance, Captain? ::

:: One, they nixed me joining years ago due to injury. Two, I haven't signed anything. Three, stop bullshitting me. ::

:: Not bullshitting you, Hesp. I remember how upset you were back then. I wouldn't do that to you. I admit I recommended you be given a rank above mine, for clarity down the road. Dal will get his notification matching my rank later. ::

:: I don't know what to say. ::

:: For now, we just need to make sure that everyone gets the rank/insignia needed. It helps with rules of engagement. You can marry me later. ::

Moyra snorted. :: Also didn't agree to that. ::

:: Later, of course. We still have a war going on. But your grandmother will agree with me. ::

Moyra just rolled her eyes, and redirected the conversation. She'd contemplate what a rank meant to her later.

Huff #18
This Is Real War [January 211]

My weekly small group strategy session: me, J3, J2, POLAD, CAG, JAG, deputy commanders.

The '3 let it all hang out. "They have standardized weapons and gear, including body armor, professional fucking uniforms. Intel. Obvious supply lines. Operational-level command and control. How are they doing this?"

J2 counted on her fingers: "One: Some of their pre-war chain of command survived, and, we assess, that includes senior officers with Mtali time. I'm sure it's Naumann. Two: From the high ground, we've recovered plenty of wrecks and done a lot of materials analysis. There's evidence of very recent low-G and extreme-condition fab work. Excellent, professional quality work. That means it's Factory Ship *Force*, we're certain. That's the largest remaining fab ship not in custody or destroyed. There may be some outside smuggling, but that's not where this stuff is coming from. S2 concurs. Three: I think we, collectively, underestimated their resiliency."

Wait a minute. I saw the order to take custody of that ship months ago. "Why is *Force* not in our inventory?"

Some nervous hand-wringing and throat clearing until J2 spoke up. "Sir, they...uh...well, they were able to boost their engines and evade our ships."

"They got away?"

"Yes, sir."

Un-fucking-believable. I stared at her and let the silence and my incredulity say more than I ever could without nominating myself for a re-education camp. Once again, the Spacy knew something, and neglected to tell me. Probably another "jurisdictional matter."

The JAG ended the silence. "The Red Cross/Red Crescent is unhappy."

Cue the '3. "Of course they're fucking unhappy. The savages don't respect their status!"

The CAG had a gleam in his eye. "We're not dealing with an insurgency anymore, they're crossing into conventional operations, field maneuvers and positional warfare. It's not consistent, not widespread yet, but they've organized. They're reconstituting a legitimate, armed combatant force. This should open doors for us, as far as LOAC goes. It should free us to be aggressive, pre-emptive, and use the right level of force. A uniformed force, led by Grainne military personnel, will have to follow LOAC too, if they want any legitimacy."

The CAG put the JAG on the spot, to give me an opening. "Unfortunately, right now, there's nothing we can do. They're terrorists in a sea of poor, helpless civilians. Legal says so."

Before the JAG could answer, I signified where I was going next: "If they're in uniform, and they're attacking uniformed personnel..." I left the space open for a moment. "Yes, they have terrorists among them, but now they are fielding lawful combatants, who are committing war crimes. They use *flamethrowers*, for fuck's sake!" Effective as they are, I despise the flamethrowers. We haven't encountered barbarism of that magnitude in centuries.

"If they want to play that game, we can oblige them, with loosened handcuffs. We can be proactive, we don't have to sit here and react, react, react." I snapped my fingers for emphasis.

I didn't let anyone speak. "You have your orders." Before they could leave, I added, "And, for the record, as I've noted before, I am undersupplied, second-guessed, and ordered to fight with one foot in a bucket. I'm taking steps to use force commensurate with the threat as it is, not how we'd like it to be. Even still, there are lines I will not cross, and you know what those are." I dictated my intent verbatim, and made it clear that we would not respond to war crimes with more war crimes, but we would be harsh. Still, for the sake of Grainne, better me than someone far worse, because that's who's waiting in the wings.

Spider's Web
Part 12

While Moyra, Damocles, and DalesOP frantically dealt with tightening up security which had admittedly gotten lax, Braknck became a problem. :: Man, those UN bounties just keep getting higher. Why aren't we getting in on some of that action? ::

:: We're earning plenty, :: Moyra replied. :: I know for a fact you got your share of this last payment just yesterday. ::

:: I'm broke. ::

:: How the hell, man? :: Jenkins asked.

:: Eh. My dealer got arrested by a UN patrol last week. I had to go to the other guy, who charges more. ::

:: ...So you want to risk selling information to the UN, who will arrest you for recreational drugs of any kind, so you can buy more recreational drugs? :: Jenkins' disbelief came through the text crystal clear.

:: Yeah? Why not? I'm sure you guys can find me plenty of good information they'd pay for. ::

:: Not likely. Why don't you tell them where the Sparkle comes from? :: Moyra replied.

:: That's why my normal dealer got picked up, heh. He wouldn't cut me a deal, so I got him back. Not sure they paid enough to make up the difference in cost from the other guy, though. I didn't realize he was that much more expensive. ::

Jenkins messaged Moyra privately. :: Did he just...admit to ratting out his dealer for a payoff, and then complain about how much the other dealer charges? ::

:: I think so. I think the Sparkle's finally fucked him up but good. ::

:: ...In that case, we should be giving him information that's safe to get shared. Before he rats us out, not that he knows anything else. But he does know about getting information about certain individuals in the UN to some businessman with money. ::

:: I've been dropping some, for just that reason. I guess we can "gossip" in the channel? ::

:: Don't like it, but it seems safest. ::

:: We're going to have to deal with him sooner or later. I just don't know how. ::

What It's Worth

Christopher L. Smith and A.C. Haskins

Sergeant Aram Sohigian crossed his arms, studying the Grainne soldier sitting across from him. The massive amount of bruises and small cuts on the man's face made it difficult to determine what he'd looked like before the damage.

"So." The word slurred through the man's split and swollen lower lip. "We're waiting for someone, then?"

"Major Neidermeyer should be here shortly," Sohigian said, "then we'll start the discussion."

"Ah. Don't see why we need to wait."

"The major has command of this unit, and any mission it takes is under his direct control."

"Still, seems to me like a waste of time," the rebel said. "You're going to be doing the hard work anyway, right?"

"We'll continue this conversation when the major gets here."

"Fine by me." He shrugged. "I'm just sayin', if it were me, I'd rankle at some stick-up-his-ass major telling me what to do."

"And if I had a 'stick up my ass,' rebel," Major Neidermeyer said from the entrance of the tent, pulling down the hood on his arctic coat and removing his gloves as he stepped inside, "I wouldn't be on Grainne."

Sohigian rose, snapping to attention.

"At ease, Sergeant," Neidermeyer said, walking around the table. He took the seat Aram had just vacated. "Let's not waste any more time, Corporal Davis, is it? I'm told you have information to trade for passage off Grainne?"

"Yep, and call me Lewis," Davis said, nodding. "One way ticket to anywhere but here, and I'll spill my guts."

"Depends on the quality of the information."

The rebel, smiling as much as his wrecked lips would allow, stayed silent.

"That's your cue to start talking," Sohigian said, glowering.

"See, here's the thing, man," the rebel said. "How do I know I'm dealing with you in good faith?"

"You don't really have a choice." Neidermeyer leaned forward slightly, steepling his fingers in front of his face. "But I will say this: I will guarantee safe passage to the nearest UN-held base for the duration of the war, simply for your cooperation. Anything further will be determined by the intel you give us."

Davis seemed to consider his options, then shrugged.

"Not much to go with, baby, but I guess it'll do for now."

"Excellent," Neidermeyer said. "Now, what is so valuable that you'd be willing to come to us?"

"Oh, I don't know...maybe a nice ripe target that no one's talking about? 'Cept me, of course."

"And?" Neidermeyer made a "come on" gesture with his hand.

"And, it's a place that a small element could take, easily."

Neidermeyer sat quietly, unmoving.

"I mean c'mon, baby, this is a great opportunity! Get in, hit 'em where it hurts, then lounge around drinking wine and eating cheese until backup arrives."

"Sounds too good to be true," Sohigian said. "What makes it such an easy target?"

"It's in the middle of nowhere, dude," the soldier said, grinning. "Only one road in and out. Even the people that live here don't want nothing to do with it. I mean, hell, it's not even strategically important, just one more place they have and don't want to give up. Skeleton crew, hard for them to get support. Probably just up and leave if anyone used harsh language on them."

He sat back, crossing his arms as much as his shackles would allow, grin still in place.

"So, do we have a deal?"

Neidermeyer stood, straightening his uniform.

"I'll take your offer into consideration. Sergeant, secure the prisoner, then meet me here."

"Hey, man, I need more than that to go on," Davis said, grin fading. He leaned forward, putting his elbows on the table. With a loud *clink*, a yellow coin landed in front of him. He quickly pulled his arms back, sweeping the coin into his lap.

Too late to keep the major from noticing, however.

"What was that?" Neidermeyer leaned forward, careful to keep out of the prisoner's reach, Sohigian noted.

"Nothing, just a good luck charm. Nothing to worry about."

"I'll be the judge of that. Sergeant?"

The prisoner hunched in on himself as Aram moved around the table, trying to protect the coin. His efforts were futile, however, as his leg shackles were secured to the chair. Sohigian grabbed the back of the prisoner's uniform roughly, jerking him to his feet. The coin hit the sheet plastic floor of the popup office with a muffled thud.

With one last, desperate move, the prisoner tried to cover the coin with his foot, coming up at least ten centimeters short. Major Neidermeyer picked up the coin and returned to his side of the table.

"Thank you, Sergeant," he said. Sohigian shoved the prisoner back into his chair.

"Hey man, no need to be that rough," the prisoner whined. "Could'a just asked."

The major turned the coin over in his hands, the bright gold catching the weak light inside the tent.

"Where did you get this?"

"Just found it, man. Like I said, it's my good luck charm. Can I have it back?"

After a few moments, Major Neidermeyer looked at Sohigian.

"Change of orders, Sergeant. Secure the prisoner, then meet me in my office in one hour."

"Yes, sir," Aram said, saluting. Neidermeyer returned the salute put his gloves back on, and strode out of the tent into the biting cold.

Aram released the ankle chains from the chair, locking them around the prisoner's ankles.

"Back to the brig, Davis," he said hauling the rebel to his feet. "And try to resist better."

"This happened last time I 'resisted.'" Davis made a gesture towards his face. "What more do I need to do, get shot?"

"Couldn't hurt," Aram said, shrugging.

"I draw the line at bullets."

"Pussy."

✧ ✧ ✧

The Major's office doubled as his sleeping quarters, and had the luxury of privacy, at least as much as a popup could afford. It was still chill in the vicious winter, though. Screens, hung on the plastic walls, showed various U.N. objectives, force projections, and supply lines. Neidermeyer seemed to be up to date with his intel; most positions had recent dates listed next to them. In the corner sat a perfectly made cot, the corners on the thin blanket sharp enough to shave.

Neidermeyer sat at a table in the center of the cramped space, a tablet computer and glossy satellite photos in front of him.

"Know anything about this good luck charm, Sergeant?" The major spun the coin in his fingers, carefully rolling it down his knuckles.

"First I've seen it, sir." Sohigian said. "We searched him for weapons, but he must have had it hidden. May want to sanitize it."

"Take a look." Major Neidermeyer flipped it towards him. Sohigian snatched it out of the air and examined it. "What do you see?"

The coin was fairly nondescript, gold, roughly two centimeters across, and hefty. One side stamped with a face he didn't recognize, in profile. Mustache, short hair, prominent upper front teeth, appeared to be singing.

The other side had a building and several numbers.

"Looks like currency, non U.N. of course. Dated on the back—maybe when it was stamped? If it is, it's recent. Not sure what the other set of numbers means."

"Did you know, Top, that the U.N. has only found a small number of coins, precious metals, and so forth, in any of the banks they've acquired? So why would the society here, that prides itself on independence and as little government as possible, have very little hard currency around?"

"They wouldn't."

"And when a war starts, where do you think they'd put it?"

"A bank, as far out of the line of fire as possible," Sohigian said, eyes widening. "In the middle of a wasteland, maybe. Like the forest where we captured our prisoner."

"I think your prisoner may know of the one place the rebels never want us to find."

"Major, are you suggesting that we knock off a bank?"

"Not 'a' bank, Sergeant. 'The' bank." He paused, face splitting into a humorless grin. "It would be a nice feather in my cap, as well as striking a blow to enemy morale."

"Yes, sir, an army lives on food and pay."

"Exactly." Neidermeyer said. He swiped the tablet a few times, opening various files. After a quick skim, he pointed to one of the photos. "In your after-action report, Top, you said that the prisoner was captured in this area, correct?"

Aram examined the image, compared it to the coordinates on the report, and nodded.

"Now, take a look at this one."

A few klicks north of the capture point, the major marked what looked like a small compound. As Davis had mentioned, only one road led to the cluster of buildings. It was snowed in with no recent traffic.

Neidermeyer pointed to several other images.

"Here you see several convoys moving into and out of the area in rapid succession, after the initial invasion. It appears that no one considered it important, as there was no further activity for months." He flipped through more images. "Only traffic in or out is one truck, at monthly intervals. I think it's a resupply transport, and maybe troop rotation."

"Looks like the last one was a week ago," Sohigian said, "Right before we found the deserter."

"Yes, it would appear that way. I'm thinking he made a break for it, knowing that it would be weeks before any attempt to find him could be feasible."

"So what's your plan, Major?"

"With a hard roll, we could be in that area in less than three days. With the inside information Davis gives us, we should have an edge on the forces guarding it." He paused, carefully stacking the paperwork in front of him. "Prepare the troops for a briefing in one hour, Top. Dismissed."

"Yes, sir. I'll get Capps on filing the initial mission plans with Command right away."

"I don't think that'll be necessary," Neidermeyer said, shaking his head, "I'm fully capable of handling that on my own. Besides, something like this is best handled quietly. The less people know, the more we have to gain, if you follow me."

"Just feels risky, sir," Sohigian said, "My people have only been here a short while, and yours seem green. What's to keep the brass from thinking we've gone AWOL?"

"I hand-picked these troops, Sergeant, with the intent of

molding them into my own personal, efficient, unit," Neidermeyer said, smiling, "Each one has qualities I find advantageous to advancing in the Peacekeeping Force. The least of which is following orders, and not asking too many questions."

It was clear from his tone that the "advancement" would be his, not those under his command.

"As to the brass," Neidermeyer continued, "They trust me to do what is necessary, without approving every operation."

In other words, Sohigian thought, *You've got something on someone, should you screw the pooch.*

"Yes, sir," he said aloud. He saluted and left the tent.

"All right, Peacekeepers," Major Neidermeyer said, striding toward the whiteboard purposefully, "let's get this briefing started."

Sohigian took a quick glance around. Eight people inside the tent made it uncomfortably cramped, but helped with temperature. The small heat pump still roared at max. The four newbies—Griffin, Capps, Henderson, and White—sat at rapt attention, focusing on the major. Urquhart and Tolle called on their years of experience and hid their boredom well.

"Our primary objective," Neidermeyer said, standing in front of them, "is to infiltrate the enemy's facility, secure any assets, and hold it until backup forces arrive.

"Basic intel shows that the objective is lightly defended, and should have no reason to expect an attack. You see here"—he pointed to the map behind him—"the only road is on the opposite side of our projected vector of approach. This should help to keep chances of enemy contact to a minimum."

He paused, pointing at a different location.

"I've arranged for a lift to here. From there, we should make the objective in two days local, on foot."

Sergeant Robin Capps raised her hand. Niedermeyer nodded at her.

"Will there be a secondary objective, sir?"

"Yes. We'll be escorting an asset. It is imperative this man be kept alive, and secure during the operation."

"Asset, sir?" This came from Specialist Xan White. "VIP or local contact?"

"Top, I'll let you answer that," Neidermeyer said.

"Two weeks ago, before we joined you," Sohigian said, "we

captured a Grainne deserter. He has since offered to provide intel and assistance for sanctuary."

"We're trusting a turncoat?" White's eyes went wide.

"The information he provided has checked out, so far," Neidermeyer said. "Taking him with us ensures his continued honesty and commitment. Also, he claims that he can get us in quietly."

"If you say so, sir," White said.

"How current is the intel, sir?" This was Griffin, their medic. "And how can we be sure this isn't a trap?"

"Current as of an hour ago, checked against past satellite sweeps." Neidermeyer turned to the maps on the walls, where the satellite images hung. "As you can see, these photos show that the OpFor has been in the same state of readiness over the last several months."

Sohigian caught Tolle and Urquhart's looks. OpFor was for war games, not actual combat operations. Tolle shook his head slightly. Urquhart's raised eyebrow seemed to say "I told you so."

The briefing continued, with Neidermeyer going over, briefly, each squad member's assignment. Sohigian's job over the next forty-eight hours was to make sure everyone knew their roles forward, backward, upside down and sideways. He tuned the major out, thinking ahead to his more detailed version.

"Any questions?" He focused on Neidermeyer again, catching the subtle shift in tone. Any queries would be directed to him, not the major. The others seemed to catch it too, as no one raised their hand or spoke up. Neidermeyer nodded. "Excellent. Top, you can take it from here."

Sohigian stood up.

"All right you lot, now I need you to pay real attention, not just act like it," he said, handing out the briefing packets. "We've got less than forty-eight hours to get this organized."

"Ain't it a couple days hike to the target, Top?" Henderson raised his hand as he spoke. "I mean, can't we study along the way? OW!"

"I'd prefer you didn't talk about the mission, *out loud*, while we're actually *on* the mission," Neidermeyer said.

Aram raised an eyebrow.

Rumor had it that the Major had used "unorthodox" motivational tools during various training exercises. Most famously, a large, neon purple, silicone sex toy. Apparently the one he twirled now. Just heavy enough to get a recruit's attention and to be embarrassing, without causing actual injury.

Various names had been attributed to it through the grapevine, but "Punishment Pecker" was the one that he'd heard most often. The rumor, it appeared, was true. Stifling a chuckle, he returned his attention to the major.

"Oh, uh," Henderson said, stammering and turning multiple shades of red, "I mean, I didn't mean…"

"It's all right, Henderson," White said, condescendingly. "We all know you're the brawn around here."

"Now, I'm sure there'll be more ignorant questions after we get into the details, but please hold them until we go over everything once." Sohigian took a map down from the wall, spreading it on the table. "Crowd around and bring your tablets."

After they had all approached, he pulled a small toy duck out of his pocket and placed it on the area marked "compound." The duck's sailor's hat and coat had faded over the years, from navy blue to something more pockmarked and patchy, but it was his good luck charm. The newbs looked confused, but his people nodded knowingly.

"The rubber duck," Capps commented. "Not to be confused with the rubber d—"

"Mr. Duck here represents our asset," Sohigian interrupted firmly. It was tradition to make Seaman Duck the positive objective—in this case, successfully escorting the Grainne deserter. It was bad luck to designate the enemy targets, or anything that was to be terminated, with the figure. Seaman Duck always came home safe.

"Now if you'll open the mission file, we'll get into the details…"

Sohigian's head was on a swivel, looking out for enemies or creatures like the one that had startled Capps the day before, but mostly he just focused on putting one foot in front of the other. That had been the only hiccup, so far, in the operation. He took a quick look at the younger woman, noting that she quickly dropped her gaze when he caught her eye.

It wouldn't have been so bad, except Capps had dumped an entire mag into the trees after hearing an animal scream. *That* wouldn't have been so bad, except they had spotted a rebel patrol only hours before, less than a klick away. They had been fortunate in that the patrol either hadn't been able to pinpoint their location, or had been far enough away by then to not hear it. The ass-chewing that followed had been thorough, colorful, and epic. Satisfied Capps wasn't going to do anything stupid—for now—he turned his thoughts back to the current situation.

Major Neidermeyer had ordered the squad to move high on a ridge above the tree line. Citing better mobility given the deep snow drifts in the valleys this time of year, and therefore decreased time to objective, he'd brushed off all concerns. Aram tried not to glare at the major's back. Tracks on a snowy ridgeline were easy to follow.

Neidermeyer himself seemed cheerful, his gait as relaxed as though he were strolling through a park behind his house. Aram shifted his pack, again, trying to get the largest lump to sit somewhere else for a while. The major didn't seem to have that problem, likely due to having the smallest load. He'd put Davis to use, loading the prisoner with everything he didn't want to carry. Air froze in his nostrils. It was like the Tibetan Plateau, with higher gravity.

"See, Top," Neidermeyer said over his shoulder, "I told you it would be easier going this way. Making good time, too."

"I stand by my recommendations, sir."

"You're being paranoid, Sergeant. There's nothing to worry about."

"Don't tempt Murphy, sir."

"Bah. Old wives tales and superstition, Top. No place for them in a modern military force."

A faint whine of engines in the distance rose over the biting wind. The squad stopped moving, each member scanning the air for its source.

"Fast movers incoming, three o'clock!" Urquhart yelled, just as Sohigian spotted a pair of dots in the distance. Small, but rapidly gaining size as they approached, they flew just over the trees.

Aram swore. The squad was a sitting duck, with nothing masking their thermal signatures in frigid weather. This was the worst possible position to be in.

"Get down!" Sohigian screamed, throwing himself to the ground. He curled up in the slush, trying to make himself as small as possible as the engines grew louder.

The craft buzzed almost directly overhead, without firing a shot. Sohigian risked pulling his face out of the snow, and glancing up, saw UN markings. He breathed a sigh of relief—friendlies.

Thank God for small favors, he thought, the whine of engines receding. He started to push himself to his feet and give the all clear, then stopped.

They were coming back for a second pass.

He felt the ground heave around him before he heard the first boom of impacting rounds. Dirt rained down on his back as he buried his face into the sharp, crystalized snow, praying none of the shells landed on his position. The concussion blasts buffeted him, but seconds later the pounding stopped and the muck stopped flying. For an instant, all Sohigian heard was a high-pitched ringing in his ears, replaced by the sound of engines fading into the distance. Apparently one strafing run had been enough for them to call it mission complete. For a moment, it was silent.

Then the screams started.

"MEDIC!"

"Who's hit?!" Sohigian shouted as he forced himself to his feet, the weight of his pack forgotten in the moment.

"Tolle!" Davis shouted back. "His leg's gone!"

Griffin ran toward Davis's position. The prisoner was on his knees in the red-stained snow next to the big gunner, frantically trying to get a tourniquet over the man's mangled right thigh, while Tolle screamed in pain. Griffin pushed him aside and got to work while Sohigian looked around.

"Anyone else?!" he yelled.

"Henderson! Lot of blood!" Capps answered.

Sohigian sprinted to where he saw Capps leaning over the bloody specialist. Pushing the panicking sergeant aside, he knelt to do a quick assessment of Henderson's wounds. Most of it appeared superficial, but there was a hole in the side of his chest. The man had terrible luck—the shrapnel had managed to hit the gap between his armor's plates. He stripped off the carrier, cut away the clothing around the wound, and pulled a chest seal from Henderson's aid kit, positioning it over the puncture. Then he carefully turned the unconscious Peacekeeper onto his other side.

"No exit wound," he said, handing Capps gauze and field dressings, "Patch up the rest and keep him warm."

Capps started to stand up, only to gasp and stagger. He stopped, noticing blood oozing from her calf.

"Cancel that. Let me see that leg."

She took a knee, favoring the wounded limb. A jagged tear

through her pants leg revealed a long gash; bloody, but not deep. Fortunately, he couldn't see any debris lodged in the wound. It would make walking painful and slow, but it wasn't life threatening.

"See to Henderson, then get that wrapped up," he said. She nodded, pale faced, as the major walked up.

"How is he, Top?" Neidermeyer's nonchalant tone had an edge. The officer was clearly freaking out and doing his best to hide it.

"Not good, sir," Sohigian said, looking the major in the eye. "He's got a sucking chest wound. I got it sealed, for now. He needs immediate evac or he's going to die."

"Have Griffin treat it when he's done with Tolle," Neidermeyer replied, waving a hand and turning away.

Sohigian froze. "What?"

"You heard me, Sergeant," he said, looking back at him. His face appeared calm, but his eyes showed otherwise. "Have Griffin take a look. I'm sure he can handle it."

The sergeant climbed to his feet and stared the major in the eye.

"Sir. Have you ever seen that before? A chest seal is a temporary solution. If we try to move him, he'll die. He needs a trauma center, and he needs it damn soon."

"Griffin will deal with it," Neidermeyer repeated. "We're a modern UN Peacekeeper force, Sergeant. He's got the best equipment in the galaxy. Henderson will be fine."

"No, sir," Sohigian answered, his voice quiet. "He will not. I'm telling you, there's nothing Griffin can do out here, except temporary measures. Henderson and Tolle need a trauma team. Now. Call the fucking evac for them, or I will."

"You'll do no such thing, Sergeant!" Neidermeyer snapped. "If there's nothing we can do for them, they get left behind. The mission continues."

"WHAT?!" Sohigian fought hard to get back in control, dropping his voice to keep the others from hearing, "You'll let these troops—my troops—die, rather than call in an evac?"

"That's exactly what I'll do, Sergeant!" Neidermeyer barked back, voice rising hysterically. "This is *my* mission. We will not compromise it for two men. They're Peacekeepers. This is war. It's called acceptable losses, Sergeant, and if you can't deal with it I suggest you find another profession!"

"You son of a bitch," Sohigian said, as realization dawned on him. "Those were UN birds. They hit us because they thought we were rebels. You never fucking cleared our route with Command."

"You're goddamned right I never cleared our route! What part of 'my mission' is so hard for you to comprehend?" His voice dropped. "You know how it works, Sergeant, everyone going for a slice of the pie. We keep this on the down-low, fake the paperwork and everyone walks away better for it."

Tolle's moan of agony cut through the still air.

"Stabilize them," Neidermeyer said, nodding at the wounded. "We'll come back for them later. They'll be happy when they're rich."

"It's going to take more than just a vague notion of 'rich,' Major," Sohigian said, after a moment of gritting his teeth. "I need hard numbers here."

"What, my word isn't enough?"

"Frankly, sir, no. We need to make this look like you're sacrificing something for the troops."

"Ah, I see," Neidermeyer said, chuckling softly. "A little theater for the grunts. Make it look like you care about their welfare. Very well, what's your offer?"

"I get ten percent, they get five percent each. Figure we report thirty percent to the brass, to keep anyone from looking too hard," he said, rubbing his chin. "That leaves you with twenty-five percent, splits the rest of it seven ways."

"Agreed. Now make it look good." Neidermeyer raised his voice. "I said five percent per person, Sergeant, and not a credit more!"

"Motherfucker." Sohigian took a step forward. Neidermeyer's hand fell to his sidearm.

"Take another fucking step, Sergeant, and I'll drop you where you stand," the officer hissed. Aram froze. "I ought to arrest you right here and now. You do *not* get to speak to me this way. You could be court-martialed and jailed for this."

Aram remained still, shifting his gaze between the major's hand and face. Neidermeyer's nostrils flared as his eyes remained fixed and unblinking.

"Fortunately for you," he continued, "I'm willing to overlook this little outburst as a moment of understandable passion. But we've still got a mission to complete. Get your Peacekeepers together, Sergeant. Seeing as you assure me there's no point waiting on the wounded, we move out in five."

✧   ✦   ✧

Sohigian took hind tit, partially because it was his turn, and partially so he wouldn't have to be anywhere near the major. This close to the objective, he didn't want to risk strangling the man by accident. Urquhart took point, with Major "I'm too important to put myself in danger" coming next. The rest of the squad had drifted back toward the rear.

Griffin, with White in front of him, was closest. Sohigian could hear their whispered conversation.

"I thought for sure Top was going to get cold cocked." Griffin looked around furtively.

"Yeah," White replied, "that was a wang-whacking offense if I ever saw one."

Griffin chuckled nervously, then caught himself. "It doesn't make sense, though. Why wouldn't the major at least tell someone in command we were out here? With Capps staying behind, it cost us three people."

"You heard him, Gabe, it's a secret mission."

"Yeah, but at least letting them know we were patrolling, so we wouldn't have been on the dangerous end of target practice."

"It's a war, there's always going to be a 'dangerous end,' especially in enemy territory."

"This whole planet can be considered enemy territory, Xan. The entire population is belligerent..."

"I'm not." That was Davis.

"...and the wildlife can kill you without breaking a sweat. And as far as sweat, this 'temperate' winter requires our arctic gear. Hell, even the gravity is against us. Worrying about everything else, I get, but our own side?"

White said nothing. They walked in silence for a moment.

"Kinda makes you wonder, though, doesn't it?"

"About what?"

"How bad the UN is seen. These people moved to one of the most inhospitable planets we know of, just to get away from us. And are defending it to the death."

"I've got eyes on two sentries at the main gate," Urquhart's voice came over the comm. *"They've got a twin heavy mount. No sign of other activity."*

"Roger," Sohigian answered. "Maintain position, let me know if anything changes."

"All right, *sir*," he said, turning to Neidermeyer. They hadn't spoken since the incident on the ridge. "Two sentries on the gate. How do you want to proceed?"

The major looked at him for a long moment, his eyes slightly narrowed, as if he were trying to decide if the sergeant's apparent attitude problem was worth the time to comment on. Evidently he decided not.

"We've got the advantage," he said, using a stick to sketch a crude map in the dirt. "You, me, Urquhart, Xan, and Griffin, versus two sentries and presumably a skeleton crew inside the compound. The prisoner here"—he nodded at Davis—"says no more than eight. So they've got a slight edge in numbers, but we've got surprise, and we won't be facing them all at once. Urquhart can take out the sentries, then Xan and Griffin can assault through the gate and take the compound before the rest of them figure out what's happening."

"Respectfully, sir," Sohigian replied, "That's risky as hell. First, it assumes the prisoner isn't lying. Second, three newbies, including a medic, who've never fired a shot in anger? Against six rebels with the advantage of a hardened defense? That's a lot of reliance on surprise and aggression, from a team that's never employed either outside of training."

The major looked impatient. "Are you telling me how to do my job, Sergeant?"

"No, sir." Sohigian shook his head. "But if I might make a suggestion, I wonder if these guards know what they're guarding?"

"What do you mean?" Neidermeyer looked somewhat puzzled.

"I mean that the insurgents are greedy. You know that, I know that, everyone knows that. Self-interested the lot of them, right? So I'm wondering how they might respond to an offer of a share, in exchange for opening the door?"

"Even if I were to consider paying them off, if they were so willing to turn on their own for money, why haven't they just stolen it already?"

Aram shrugged. "Possibly because they didn't have UN Peacekeepers offering them transport off Grainne after the deed was done. Can't hurt to ask, can it?"

"I suppose," the officer said, looking thoughtful, "that living defectors with potential intel look a lot better than corpses when we call Command."

"Exactly my thinking. So if you and I were to go and ask them..."

"No, not me." Neidermeyer shook his head. "We need someone to stay in command in case it goes badly, after all. Your idea, you get to ask. Take the prisoner with you. Urquhart will cover you."

Sohigian was mildly annoyed. Typical officer. Covering his own ass, yet again, and sending the enlisted man to do his dirty work. The credit for which, if successful, he'd undoubtedly claim for himself. It wasn't enough he'd probably gotten two good men killed already.

A few minutes later, Sohigian and Davis stepped out of the trees and started walking down the road. Top's rifle was slung at the low ready, his hand on the grip, but his posture relaxed. No need to set off itchy trigger fingers.

"You sure about this?" Davis asked.

"What's wrong, kid?" Aram looked over at him. He seemed nervous. "We planned for something like this, and it's too late to go back now."

"I know," Davis said, "It's just, what if they don't want to play ball? Hell, what if they shoot us on sight?"

"It's a possibility," Sohigian said, shrugging. "Not much we can do about it, honestly. Just stay in character, and hope they got the memo that they're supposed to be avaricious little traitors. If not, I guess we get remembered as the dumbest assholes ever to wear a uniform, and Urquhart avenges us."

Davis chuckled softly. Then he quieted down. "You think Tolle's gonna make it?"

"I honestly don't know." Sohigian shook his head. "I hope so. But he knew what he was signing up for, like the rest of us. Enough talk. Let's do what we came here to do."

When they came around the curve a minute later, they heard some curious yelling, followed by a shout.

"Halt! Who goes there?!"

"That's your cue to start talking," Sohigian muttered. Davis looked over, his hands held up in front of him.

"Here goes nothing," he said under his breath. Out loud, he answered the challenge, "It's Davis! Who's on the gate?"

"Davis? We thought you deserted! What the hell, man? Who's with you?"

Sohigian let out the breath he didn't realize he'd been holding.

The pair kept trudging toward the gate, slowly and carefully, even more than the snow dictated.

"Aww, baby, 'deserted' is such an ugly word. I went for a walk, is all," Davis said, smiling broadly. "This here's Sergeant Sohigian, UN Peacekeepers. And he's got an interesting proposition. You're gonna want to hear this... That *is* Greene yelling at me, isn't it?"

"Yeah, it's me," the sentry yelled back. "And I told your ass to halt, you fucking deserter!"

The pair stopped, about thirty meters shy of the gate, as the twin machine guns trained on them. The silence stretched for what felt like minutes.

"Your friend here said I have a proposition for you. Care to hear it?" Sohigian finally said.

There was another long moment. Finally, Greene yelled back.

"Friend of ours? He was an asshole, even before he left us to pick up his guard shifts." Greene's shift in tone notwithstanding, the mounted weapon didn't budge. "I'll hear you out. But if that rifle so much as twitches in our direction, the only thing your mother will have left of you are her memories, clear?"

"Crystal," Sohigian said, grinning and raising his hands. "And you're right about Davis here being an asshole."

The prisoner shot him a glare as they walked forward.

"...and that's it," Sohigian said, "No one gets hurt, everyone rides out the rest of the war in a nice, comfy cell, and when it's all over, you collect your share. Win-win, right?"

He could see the greed in the two men's eyes. He had them.

"The other option is the major falls back, we call in air support, and sift through the rubble for gold dust." He gave them a sharklike grin. "Which he'll do if we don't signal him in about sixty seconds."

"All right," Greene replied, wiping frost from his brow. "We'll get you in, and from there you've got a clear shot to the vault. Shouldn't even see anyone else; this time of day everyone's napping in the barracks."

"How many is 'everyone'?" Neidermeyer asked. He'd brought the rest of the team to join them after Sohigian gave the "all clear."

"Eight. Three shifts, four guards each—two on the gate, two in the vault itself. The LT's been pulling shifts like the rest of us since this fucker here"—he nodded toward Davis—"snuck out and left us shorthanded."

That matched up with what Davis had told them. The major nodded.

"All right, Sergeant. I'll take Urquhart to the vault. If the two inside don't want to play ball, Urquhart can get started wiring it. Top, you and the others take these two to the barracks and secure the rest of the insurgents."

"Woah," Greene said, holding up his hands. "Look, we're willing to let you in, but that's it. If this shit goes sideways, I'm gonna swear on my mother's grave I've never seen you in my life. For all I know, you snuck in through some secret back entrance with Davis's help. No way I'm implicating myself before you've even got the goods to pay me."

Despite Neidermeyer's glare, the other guard nodded in agreement.

"We're giving you a lot of money, and a free ride off this rock, and you won't even..." Sohigian held up his hand before the Major could finish.

"Sir, it doesn't matter. They're probably all asleep anyway, and even if they aren't we've got the element of surprise. They won't be expecting Peacekeepers inside the wire. Davis can show us the way, and we should be able to capture eight unsuspecting insurgents no problem."

The major shifted to face the sergeant, grinding his jaw. Even he wasn't stupid enough to let his emotions blow the whole mission when they were this close to success.

"Don't you dare interrupt me again, Sergeant," he hissed, biting off each word. "We will discuss your behavior when this mission is over." But after another second of thought, he nodded curtly. "Whatever. Fine. We'll see if the guards inside want to open the door. Meet us at the vault when the insurgents are secure."

"Wakey, wakey!" Davis shouted as he slammed open the door to the small bunkhouse. Top, Griffin, and White rushed through after him into the dim room, weapons at the ready.

The guards at the gate hadn't been lying—seven bunks were full, the men and women in them jerking awake at the loud noise, struggling to figure out what the hell was happening. An eighth man was already awake, sitting on his bunk working on a comm. His wakefulness, however, didn't make him any less surprised than the rest.

"Hands where I can see them!" Sohigian shouted. "Anyone goes for a gun, any sudden moves at all, and you die! Understood?"

A few seconds later all eight insurgents had their hands up. He nodded to White, who lowered her rifle and pulled out a pair of zip ties. Griffin covered her as she moved towards the nearest insurgent.

Aram lowered his muzzle slightly and looked over his sights, scanning around the room.

"Now," he said, "which one of you is the LT?"

"I am," said the man who'd been awake. "Why?"

"We need to talk. Alone. Outside. Griffin and White, you guys good here?"

"We'll be all right," Griffin said. White was already securing a third insurgent's wrists together. "So long as no one does anything stupid."

"You," Sohigian said, gesturing at the officer with his muzzle. "On your feet. Davis, you come with us, I want you where I can see you."

He led the way outside. Once they were around the corner, the LT spun around, putting his hands down.

"A bit over the top, don't you think?"

Aram lowered his weapon, grinning. "Sorry for the dramatics. Griffin and White don't know what's going on. They think it's just a raid. In the meantime, is everything ready to go?"

"Depends," the officer answered quietly. "Is he here?"

Davis nodded. "At the vault with Urquhart. We're supposed to meet them after we've secured your guys."

"Good, I'll tell Captain Reed you've delivered on your end, so he doesn't have the entire company smoke us all. Then I suppose you should head back inside, get over to the vault, and put this to rest." He chuckled softly. "Gotta admit, I didn't think you guys would come back, much less make it this far."

"A deal's a deal, sir," Sohigian said, grimly. "I gave my word, and I intend to keep it."

Urquhart connected the last wire, then turned and gave a thumbs up. She moved back to join the rest of the group behind the doorway. Neidermeyer stood on one side of the door with Davis, Sohigian and Xan on the other. Griffin was back at the bunkhouse guarding the zip-tied insurgents. Urquhart took position behind the prisoner.

"The way I see it, you've only got two choices here," Neidermeyer said, grinning. "Either you open the door and surrender, or we blow it and take what's in there."

"*This vault was designed to withstand professional attacks with hyperexplosives,*" the voice from the intercom said. "*Short of a tactical nuke, you're not getting in here.*"

"Option two it is." Neidermeyer nodded to Urquhart, then ducked down and covered his ears. Urquhart pressed the first button on the detonator.

The cutting charges that she had placed at the hinges and bolts blew with several *BANG!*s, making Aram's ears ring. Smoke and dust filtered out of the open doorway, to fill the small hall. Urquhart pressed the second button.

The next round of explosions was much louder, followed by a ground shaking thud. Even with his protection in place, Top's ears rang faintly for several seconds. He coughed in the sudden plume of smoke rolling past him. He and the others eased the muzzles of their rifles around the corner, careful to keep their bodies hidden. When no shots came toward them, he risked a quick peek.

The heavy door, still intact, lay on its face, leaving the vault behind it completely exposed. Urquhart knew her job well. The various explosives had, in order, severed the hinges and bolts, then blown the door forward. The occupants of the vault sat in disoriented silence, stunned by the concussion.

Neidermeyer stood, checked to make sure he was covered by the other members of the unit, and walked around the corner.

"You were saying?" Aram couldn't see his expression, but the tone of his voice implied a shit-eating grin. He and the rest of the unit fell in behind him, weapons at the ready.

"Now that we've gotten that out of the way, we'd like to finish our mission. Kindly fall out in a safe, orderly, proficient military manner, and no one gets hurt." He paused. "Well, any more than you already are."

The rebel soldiers carefully disarmed and made their way into the room. Neidermeyer handed his rifle to Sohigian and entered the vault. Urquhart's demo work had left the interior bars and door scorched, but still intact.

"Well, isn't this a fine sight," Neidermeyer said, turning slowly.

"Never seen this much money in one place, to be honest. Must be millions of creds' worth in here."

He walked to the back of the vault to stand in front of a large, heavy table filled with stacks of gold bars. He grunted slightly as he hefted one.

"White, call in our position, get some troops here to secure the facility, and let the brass know our mission was successful." He turned. "Top, you and the others secure the prisoners, while I take a few moments to relish the satisfaction of a job well done."

"I'll need the keys to the vault's cage," Sohigian said to the Grainne guard, holding out his hand. The other man handed them over, and stepped to the side.

Sohigian walked to the sliding iron door, closed it, and engaged the lock.

"Very funny, Top," Neidermeyer said, grinning.

"I'm not joking."

Neidermeyer whirled to face him, going for his sidearm. Sohigian raised his rifle before the other man's hand could touch the grip.

"You will hand that sidearm over now, or I will drop you where you stand."

"Top," Xan said quietly, "what are you doing?"

"Mutiny," Neidermeyer said, slowly drawing his pistol. "Peace-keepers, take this man into custody."

Neidermeyer's eyes grew wide as Urquhart trained her weapon on him, followed by Davis with one of the vault guards' rifles. White looked confused, her eyes going back and forth between Sohigian and Neidermeyer, her weapon aimed at neither.

The major paused, then apparently decided discretion was the better part of valor. He cleared his sidearm, and stuck it through the bars, butt first. One of the rebels stepped forward, retrieved the pistol, and immediately moved back behind Sohigian.

"Not a mutiny," Sohigian said, not taking his eyes off the major. "Defection. You have a choice to make, Xan, right now."

Niedermeyer growled, "I swear to God, Sergeant, I'll have your head for this!"

He turned to look at Xan.

"When I say your future depends on your decision, I mean it. Do you want to be a part of that anymore? Knowing that every day could be your last, simply because some 'elite' needed to cover their ass?"

Xan stood quietly for a moment, then let her rifle fall onto its sling. With slow, steady movements, she pulled at the insignia on her shoulder.

The unit patch fell to the floor.

Sohigian turned at the sound of the door opening. Freehold Forces Captain Mike Reed entered the room solemnly. He motioned for Aram to sit at the table.

"We found an unusual item, Sergeant, maybe you could explain?"

"I assume you mean the major's Walloping Wang?" Aram grinned. "The major liked to make an impression on his subordinates, sir. I've only occasionally witnessed it, but he'd use it to 'encourage' the troops."

"Ah. We'll designate it as 'Domestic Instrument, Lavender, Disciplinary, Occupational.'" Reed allowed himself a small chuckle, before growing serious. "The intel you delivered, it's actionable?"

"Yes sir," Sohigian said, nodding. "At least as of forty-eight hours ago."

"Excellent."

"Our forces won't know they've been compromised for at least another seventy-two to ninety-six hours, at the very least," he continued. "And that's a very conservative estimate. Neidermeyer had a certain amount of leeway in his mission parameters."

"That gives us a short window to act on it. Short, but usable."

"Sir, I hope this isn't out of line, but I have to say it." Sohigian paused, trying to find the correct words. With a sigh, he pressed on. "I need to know that this intel will be used as a scalpel, not a chainsaw."

"In what way, Sergeant?"

"I, and my team, ran this operation to defeat the UN's ideals, not to harm the people in it. We don't want any more casualties than absolutely necessary."

"Things happen in war, Sergeant."

"I understand that, sir, and that loss of life will happen." He met Reed's stare unflinchingly. "But the people doing the dying aren't the ones you're really fighting against. It's the ones safe behind the lines that are the real problem."

"You have my word, Sergeant, that your information will be used with as much discretion as possible. I can't put it in writing, but I can offer you this." Reed extended his hand. Sohigian took it with a nod. "Your courage, and that of your team, will save lives, on both sides."

He chuckled, shaking his head slightly. "Hell of a gamble, Sergeant. Using our man to set the trap was . . . risky."

"We needed to be able to sell it. Davis played his part perfectly."

"Indeed," the captain said. "Upon confirmation of the intelligence, and with the delivery of Major Neidermeyer, your payment will be considered rendered."

"Thank you. Sir, did the others make it?"

"Our patrol was able to find your transponder quickly. Corporal Tolle will survive but Specialist Henderson was dead when they arrived."

"What about Capps?"

"She's in our custody. Wounded, but stable." Reed snorted. "She had what the unit leader on site called 'a fully automatic enhanced panic attack.'"

Sohigian raised an eyebrow.

"She load dumped in the general direction of our people."

"I have a hunch she won't be asking to stay on Grainne."

"No," Captain Reed said, "I don't believe she will. On that note, you do realize that you and your unit won't be allowed free movement?"

"Yes, sir, it has come up." Sohigian grinned. "Good thing this place has grown on me."

"And the rest of your team? I understand White and Griffin both decided to defect along with the rest of you."

"We're all in agreement, sir. We've got more liberty in one of your prisons than we do 'free' in the UN."

"Is that so?"

"Yeah, it is," Sohigian said. "Thing is, here, you get what you earn. It's not given to you, you don't demand it just for breathing. I know that if you promise me three hots and a cot for the duration, I've earned it. We all have, just by risking our asses. But that's it. Everything else is on us, from here out."

"To a point, that's true."

"That's the thing. We couldn't count on that in the UN. Didn't matter how much blood, sweat, or tears we shed, nothing was guaranteed, even if you knew people. I like honesty, sir, and here, I know what it's worth."

Spider's Web
Part 13

Moyra Kelly's contact on Skywheel Two pinged her during the middle of a shift with concerning questions.

Skylight reported that the UN overlords aboard station were antsy and kept hammering them about "unauthorized landings."

:: What's weird, too, is all I can say is that, yeah, those landings aren't being authorized by US, :: she added to Moyra.

:: Keep your eyes peeled, I guess. I hope they don't decide to reverse their decision to leave you mostly alone. ::

:: Do YOU know what the landings are? I'm pretty sure there's some that neither the UN nor the Skywheels are seeing. ::

:: No. Sorry. :: Moyra felt terrible lying about it, but Skylight didn't need the extra risk. Truly, neither did anyone else.

:: Hrmph. OK. ::

Meanwhile, the contact for the latest "unauthorized landing" confirmed receipt of supplies and uniforms. If those UN fuckers were going to try to justify *bioweapons* against a civilian population because they weren't *organized*... Fuck them. Her jacket now said she was a captain, Freehold Forces Intelligence Branch. Most of the rest were a militia element named Spectre, because they were ghosts in the machine.

:: Number Six? :: Selene from Team 10 messaged Moyra. She normally stayed out of contact off shift. :: I have... concerns. ::

:: Yes? :: Moyra replied.

:: I think someone followed me home tonight. ::

:: Think or know? :: The comment *"That's not good."* didn't need to be said.

:: ... know. I think. ::

:: From the ops center? ::

:: Yes. ::

:: Can you execute your escape plan from your current location? ::

:: Not easily. Just... let the rest know? ::

:: I will. What other information can you give me? ::

Selene detailed what she had noticed about the person, and that building security confirmed they had denied an unknown person with non-Grainne accent entrance to the complex. Moyra detailed TripleShot to obtaining the security footage from the complex in question and reviewing it.

Moyra directed AI resources towards determining the severity of the possible compromise, but even if none were to be found, Team 10 had been coming up on a Shell Game move anyway.

Other channels alerted local neighborhood watch to be on the lookout for "suspicious persons." Most of the civilian peacekeepers hadn't really picked a side. They simply concentrated on protecting the residents under their watch, insofar as possible. One helpful member assisted in evacuating Selene and family out of the immediate area, under the guise of a medical emergency.

The remaining handlers from Team 10 were given different places to operate from, splitting the team into three, and retiring the designator. The new locations were less hardened than the existing safe house, but it had to be assumed that location was compromised. The safe house, purported to be a multiunit residence building on sale for several months, was vacated as thoroughly as possible.

A "renovation expert" team "acquired" the safe house within a week, and "renovated" the small apartments. Doing so removed most of the critical equipment that couldn't be easily recreated, while providing the option of more "low income" housing.

"Low income" housing which was previously unnecessary, of course, but the UN bureaucrats seemed puzzled why a functional society would start failing the moment they started imposing ever more draconian rules about "lawful enterprise." The "new" corporate owner of the building operated as a front for one of Naumann's finance people, who ran similar operations throughout Jefferson and the suburbs. The irony that military and paramilitary operations were being semifunded by collecting subsidized rent from those forced onto the UN's "welfare" was not lost on any of the command team.

It also provided a pathway for slowly moving key personnel back toward the population centers from the scattering caused by the initial invasion.

Teams were being evaluated for equipment versus availability versus standardization. Moyra put Selene on the task of collating that information from all of the in-field teams and forwarding that on to Naumann's personnel. From there, equipment swaps or regearing was determined, and orders cut to meet in passing to accomplish this, gather more or different supplies, and Selene updated the database.

The Danegeld
Part 3

"Captain? There's news from home." Sammy's voice lacked its usual brightness, the slow tone she'd had for months after her mother died. Ana heard it, and went right back to that time, every memory of Graciela screaming out from where she'd buried them.

She caught her breath with her upper body still inside the space hidden behind false conduits, clammy hands unable to grasp the neat stacks of nanos. Her heartbeat filled the enclosed space, and it took a few moments before she could acknowledge Sam's message.

Leaving the nanos in the cubby, she pushed out to the hall and nearly stumbled into Cal.

"Sam wants us," he said, reaching past her to slide the panel back into place. "You okay?"

"It's bad news." She allowed them both a moment of quiet, steadying herself against him. He rubbed her arms, moving up to her shoulders, and she sighed into his collarbone. "At least it's not incoming missiles. She would have been more specific."

"We don't have to keep doing this," he said softly, resting his head on hers. "If they catch us we lose it all, Ana. The ship, Graciela's island, the kids..."

"And if we don't do this, Cal. What does that make us?" Warmth from his hands mellowed her voice, and she held herself relaxed against him, taking the moment of peace.

"Smart." The edge in his voice brought the tension back to her limbs, and she pulled away to look up at him. Cal, gambler to his bones, considered the angles of their risks and rewards, which she appreciated even if it didn't change her mind. He stared back at her, intent, and continued, "Rid of debt. *Free.*"

"Free? Under the UN?" She turned her head enough to press a kiss into his palm, then stepped back, putting distance between them to clear her head. "We run their errands forever, or we slip our leash now and then and call it freedom. Free is what we were before. Now, we're just..."

"If you quote Hank's idiot Kipling at me—"

They both cracked small smiles at that, and Ana shook her head and started toward the deck.

"We're on borrowed time. The UN might catch us, and that will be awful. But it's worse if they win, and we're lapdogs for the rest of our life. Ship or no, they'll run ground and space, and there's nowhere to go."

"We do want to make money still though, don't we? Priority two."

"It's a priority, Cal, but not the only one. We'll figure out the ship, and the island."

He matched his pace with hers, silence somewhere between brooding and thoughtful as they walked. The downside of knowing him so long, and so well, that she read meaning into his damn silences. She'd almost distracted herself from why they were going to Sam when they reached the deck and the younger woman's unusually serious demeanor met them.

"The UN's claiming a win," she said, not bothering with a greeting. "Your friends, the ones near Jefferson? Winters, Drayman, Riggs, Seradu..." Her reluctance to say it made it clear.

"They're dead." No racing heartbeat now, she'd prepared herself for this the second she'd heard that flat tone from buoyant Sam.

"Killed in action, and all the leopards too. The official report doesn't go into detail, but word is it was messy."

"Nothing on Pieterse?" Cal asked, and Ana stilled next to him. Despite the small jump of shock at the word "messy," there was no surprise in Cal's tone. Noticing her attention, he went on hastily, "Or Seb?"

"Message from Seb says the hit came the day after he headed out to Harbor Hills. He's the one who said it was messy. Another UN point made." Sam's voice thickened, and Ana finished crossing the deck to put a hand on the girl's shoulder. Sam leaned against her for a second, then straightened. "You still want to take the overstock on the next Jefferson drop to Hazel's Bluff? I can tweak *Graci*'s approach so it's a little easier to get to the Hills."

"Keep the current course for now. If we change anything this soon after news of a UN win, someone might notice. Also, our people are expecting drops." She squeezed Sammy again and jerked her head at her husband. "Cal—my cabin."

He paused to kiss the top of Sammy's head, and then followed Ana, his silence clouding the air between them.

As soon as the door slid closed behind them in her cabin, she turned on him, clenching her hands to keep them from shaking.

"Good thing Seb got clear." She'd held her own with any

number of NovRos thugs, with assholes from every station and
dirt hill, so often and so well a Russie gangster had once deemed
her the woman with the cast-iron mouth to go with her cast-iron
balls. Now, facing her husband, she managed to keep her voice
steady with a massive effort.

"Nan—"

"Don't." Ana backed as far away from him as she could in the
small space, wishing she had small decorative items so that she
had something to hurl at him. "No sweet talk. *What did you do?!*"

"I didn't." He held both hands up, voice pitched low, eyes
warm on hers. "Ana, I wouldn't, not on purpose. I was playing
poker with Tennison, and I . . . I might have mentioned things got
a little hot for us outside Jefferson recently. Told them a good
story about wildcats in the woods. Maybe I said more than I
should have." The words spilled out a hair too fast, so smooth,
the Cal who eased ruffled feathers, who got reluctant clients on
board. The charmer.

"The fuck you did, Goderitch." She shook her head, needing to
grab something, shake something, and he took a step toward her.

"Ana." He stopped moving, took a breath, blew it out. "It was
a mention, not a direct location, not a *hit*. There was money on
the table, and we needed it. We're not close to breaking even, all
these side trips, all these costs to refuel. No one's helping us out
of the goodness of their hearts, and the UN's got all the money.
I thought the handlers would get chased out, maybe find a new
base. Roughed up a little, not . . ."

"The UN isn't a joke, you fucking reject. We talked ourselves
into thinking they were idiots, but we know better. We heard
about Mtali, we've seen how they run over the colonies, and here—
here, Cal, we know how dirty they'll play. You thought leopard
handlers would get taken in and 'roughed up'?" Her breath lost
its rhythm, and her stomach twisted, hunching her forward. It
was their fault. Not philosophically, running goods for the UN,
but directly. Actually. Because of them, a group of handlers and
their leopards were dead. Because of them, the UN had a win.

"I didn't sell them, Ana. I said too much, I'm sorry. It was
an accident, I couldn't have known . . ."

If she didn't vomit, she'd hit him, and it took a long moment
before she got enough control over herself to do neither. Losing
Graciela had unmoored them both, and here they were, caught

between the UN and home, bound to make everything worse for themselves or others, whatever they did.

"If you open your damn fool mouth one more time—"

"Never, Ana, never." Two steps closed the distance between them, and he dared to pull her close. "I'm sorry, I'm so sorry."

Cal had spent the last few runs keeping Sammy company on the *Graci*. Ana missed his easy hand with the UN soldiers, but Tico managed enough banter while unloading to keep the tension nominal. They'd put out word Cal had picked up one of the flus and was taking a while to regain his strength, which tended to give the UN soldiers a semblance of guilt.

She told herself keeping Cal spaceside gave Sammy a needed second set of hands for the velocity matching with deliveries from the factory ship. The girl was a brilliant navigator, but asking her to run the numbers, load the materials, and adapt the ship to get everything hidden bordered on unreasonable. Leaving Cal behind had nothing to do with keeping him dark on the locations they dropped to, the materials they portioned out across Grainne. She made a third set of books, inflating their profits in case Cal checked, to keep him content, buried the real information deep and coded.

"You think we can get more food rations?" Hank leaned back in his webbing, staring into nothing as the shuttle thrust itself back into orbit. All three of them had been quiet this run, still caught in the vision of hollow-cheeked sick kids and the desperate farmers taking outdated ammunition with blatant gratitude. How had they gotten here?

"We can ask for anything." Ana didn't recognize her own voice, breaking against the words. "We're running out of people to give it to."

Tico grunted, and no one had the energy for further conversation until they docked.

Ana left Hank and Tico to square away all the equipment, and started toward Sam to pick up the news and any updates on their latest appointment with the supply ship. After she'd staggered to a halt against the T-junction that offered a path to either the bridge or quarters, she realized she wouldn't be able to process anything. She'd go splash her face, maybe get Cal to rub some of the exhaustion out of her shoulders, then go to Sam. A break in routine would help.

When the door slid open, showing Cal hard at work, she felt

a smile tug at the corners of her mouth. He hunched over his slate reflexively, then saw her and smiled, closing whatever he'd been working on and standing to meet her.

But his eyes were still on the slate, not on her, making sure whatever had been opened was closed. A cold weight settled in her gut, and she tried to ignore it. But his movements were jerky, and his hand lingered on the table, covering the slate.

"How was Fa—the run?" he asked, nervous when she didn't say anything. "You're awfully quiet."

"Tired," she managed through numb lips. Her brain caught up to her senses—he'd been mumbling over his slate, as he always did when he was intent on something. Locations. Locations that he wasn't supposed to have, but of course he had been smart enough to figure out. Had she said they'd gone to Fall Creek? He was paying too much attention.

"You've been all up and down for weeks now, I'm not surprised. Would it hurt you to stay on ship with Sam for a stretch, let me pick up the slack?"

Why did he need to know where they were? Curiosity wasn't Cal's vice. She knew the answer. He couldn't sell off one resistance cell at a time, that would be foolish. He'd be found out by the crew as the UN snatched each one up, or their ship would be seen as the common denominator—no one would meet them anymore. He knew she wouldn't allow that.

She was the woman with cast-iron balls.

She stepped closer to him, wanted to smooth his hair back. Feel his slow smile against her palm. Would he have protected her and Sammy? Hank or Tico?

It didn't matter.

Cast-iron balls.

"Goddess, I can tell you're exhausted." His fingers twitched over his slate and he pushed it away, further from her. A useless gesture in such a small space. "Or did you just miss me?"

Only one entity needed to know the locations of the little patches of fight they dropped to, of the mysterious root of their refueling. Only one group would pay for the information. Pay so well, more than enough to buy back an island. Bigger payout for the quality of his information, how many groups he turned over.

"Cal." Her hand rested casually against her hip. It didn't shake. "I love you."

"I know, I know." He focused his attention on her, ignoring his slate. Rolled his eyes, a hint of a smile curling one side of his mouth. "But you don't li—"

The shot, perfectly centered through his forehead, finished the refrain for them both.

Shouldn't use ballistic shots on board, she chided herself, *could cause damage to the ship. Could punch an airtight. Disrupt a critical line.*

His body slumped to the deck. She didn't watch it fall.

She had work to do.

Damn, the military ships were stealthed stupid. If they hadn't gotten a ping, they'd never have seen it, and it was already within a thousand kilometers by then. Now it was alongside and still damned near invisible, black on black and flocked to soften the edges.

"*Seal's tight. We're good to start transfer.*" Sammy sent the message over comms while waving Ana out of the pilot's cabin.

Ana rolled her shoulders to ease the ache that had hounded her since she'd killed her husband. Killing a traitor shouldn't stay with you, but she couldn't seem to shake it. It just made her work harder.

"Any idea what we're getting?" Tico asked as she reached the loading bay. "Please tell me it's the big guns."

"We get what we get," Hank answered, leaning against Tico's favorite loader.

Ignoring them both, Ana hit the airlock release and stepped into the opening between the two ships.

"Welcome to the *Graci*."

"Did'ya bring us something nice?" Tico grinned, and Ana rolled her eyes, cutting in before either he could go on, or the two men in the other ship could react.

"I'm Captain Romdee. Tico here is cargomaster. Hank'll handle the...admin work." She gestured at her old friend, who ran his hand over his bald scalp and grunted. "We can get our pilot down if we need more hands for loading."

"Running lean," one of the men observed. "I'm Commander Brody, and this is Warrant Leader Smock. We've got a full load for you."

"And we're glad to have it. The leaner we run, the more room we have for cargo—and there are plenty of contacts we've got who will be a helluva lot happier." Ana gestured for Tico to get moving. "You have any instructions for where we're taking it?"

"Wherever Ground Control says," Smock replied, shifting out of Tico's way. "Mostly ammo and a lot of rockets, some commo, mixed other gear. We brought a fuel tank to gas you so you don't look short when you return."

"Let's get it, then." Ana set her shoulders, ignoring the ache, and readied to transfer cargo.

There was still a war to fight.

■   ■   ■

Huff #19
Intel (25 Feb 211)

The intel report was precisely worded, to the point of ridiculous exactitude. Translation: all but unreadable. Say again, everything after "The..."

Here's a real gem: "...rebel field elements in the southern north central region..." I had to read that description three times to make sense of it. Looking at a map, the locals call that area Darkwood Hills. There was no practical reason not to use a common local name, except to totally crush their culture, and knowing that, as they almost certainly did, they'd fight without restraint. They understood that the next phase of the game demanded cultural reformatting—cultural annihilation, frankly. They had to be broken. Not just defeated, but utterly broken.

Back to the report: "They employ three main modes of tactical transport. The primary element is typically mounted on turbine-powered field-improvised technical vehicles, hardened with polycermet plates around the engine, passenger compartment, and gunnery compartment; see Figures K through X." A detailed description of a truck followed. They could have just linked the factory specs, although that probably violated intellectual-property laws, even with "military necessity" exemptions.

"A second element is mounted on domesticated draft quadrupeds." Can you just say "horses"? The writers were purposefully obtuse, so they couldn't be accused of making gross assumptions if it turned out those were ponies, or gengineered breeds, or battle unicorns. Or, just in case there was some local animal unknown after 200 years that looked like a horse, but wasn't. There couldn't be, we'd have seen a monster like that by now. The "rippers" are bad enough.

The intel report then went into excruciating detail on the topic of rebel tactical use of wildlife: "Rebel use of stealthy, low-signature animals complicates force protection and security"... really, I'd have never guessed. "DNA detection devices are somewhat effective, in the range of 25.93% to 37.54%." Who needs that exact of an approximation?

However, it made the point that the native animals tend toward impressive, massive front ends like nightmarish hyena-bulldog combinations. Even the herbivores are hard to track due to the lack of sensor-observable mass and thermal exhaust indicators; they are also smart, tough, violent, and terrifying, especially to our urban recruits.

Oh, and then there are the leopards. Leopards have adapted well to the local environment, and the rebels seem to have a thing for them. Not long ago, we took out a rebel cell armed with hunting rifles, very skilled in woodcraft, and a number of them were leopard handlers. These maniacs have Military Working Leopards. The rebels make excellent use of those animals in combat, and as psychological warfare tools. The takedown of that cell was exceptionally messy, and we didn't get all of them.

[NOTE: *Digital entry with embedded pics and audio, partially recovered*]

[*Analyst 1*] "...some evidence suggests an increasing level of organization along the lines of light infantry and raiding forces, we have MEDIUM confidence in this assessment. Recovered opposition casualties this week included seven in professionally made uniform blouses with what appear to be unit identification on shoulder tabs (see Illustrations 1 through 7):

    —Northside Capital Militia (2)
    —Hinterlands Defense Force (1)
    —Dragontooth Mountain Irregulars (1)
    —Darkwood Provisional Guard (2)
    —Ripple Creek Security (1)"

[*Huff*] "Okay, *that* is interesting. Patch number seven is concerning, as it suggests one of the UN's primary personal protective services, a full-fledged cleared defense contractor, is assisting the opposition. This will cause a major scandal if it gets out."

[*Analyst 1*] "It's unknown if this is a local element that has chosen alliance with them, a chance choice of naming convention, a deliberate disinfo attempt, or, worst case, indicates a corporation-wide shift in allegiance. The last should be strongly considered as a potential threat unless and until evidence confirms otherwise."

[*Huff*] "Highlight that last piece and send to counterintel today. Let's ask the PSOs too. That community is tiny, and they all know each other, military and contractor alike."

Spider's Web
Part 14

:: Wow, Braknck, those bounties really are getting high, aren't they? :: Moyra mentioned in comm.

:: Told you. Surely there's some info we can dig up that they'd find useful, :: came the smug reply.

:: Maybe, :: DalesOP replied. :: I think Bowler Hat said he was running low on funds, and can't pay us for any information for a while. No one else is using our resources right now, either. ::

:: Can't believe there isn't a single company needing to get information on a competitor, :: Jenkins complained.

:: With the normal communication channels being down, how can anyone know what's going on? :: DalesOP asked.

:: Since YOU already have a reporting contact, Braknck, it'd be up to you to share the information we do find, without mentioning how you got it. And sharing that reward with us, :: Moyra suggested/reminded him.

:: I know, I know, :: Braknck said. :: Just get me info, I'll handle the rest. ::

:: We can do that, :: DalesOP confirmed.

:: Yeah, I'll see what I can pull up, :: Jenkins agreed. :: I've gotten bored of the normal stuff, anyhow. ::

Two days later, Jenkins shared "just some stuff he'd found while poking around."

DalesOP, in conjunction with the PsyOps and military intel teams, had carefully selected a set of verifiable information to "leak," which would reinforce Braknck's authenticity. From there, more information would be delivered—information true but not valuable, and disinformation designed to assist in determining the path of the delivered information.

Additional info packets existed, to be dribbled out via Braknck and two other scattered informants. The information varied just slightly, both to track the progress of the disinformation campaign and to allow the sources to act as "verifications" for each other.

It did not protect the identity of Hespera, but it made Hespera and her team a potentially useful resource. Since he might spill that he had "friends" assisting him in pulling the data, knowing it might go to UN sources, that further protected Hespera from being linked to Peterson or Kelly.

For once, Moyra felt exhausted trying to keep track of which moniker went with which operation.

Tension filled the atmosphere in the handlers' primary room in the newest safe house, while a rendezvous completed. Moyra Kelly had shifted all of her other tasks to subordinates to be able to focus on this critical shipment and retrieval. Multiple screens showed helmet video feeds, GPS coordinates overlaid by a map, all of the information she could cram into it. The UN had managed to obscure some of their units' nav coordinates from even their own satellites, so the known/suspected unit tags were incomplete. She hoped...

"*We're under attack!*" blared the audio feed. Sarah, the handler, sat in a different room while Moyra managed the voice channels for coordination, to minimize the risk of audio bleed over.

"Override the drones," Moyra ordered. "Protect our unit."

"*Scanning for nearby units. Units located. Drone override commencing,*" Ted, the operator, confirmed. "*Drone override and neural control appears to be functioning.*" Moyra watched the shared video feed wake up and spin around for target selection. Secondary feeds showed up as two other drones were slaved to the primary.

"*The drones are shooting blue-caps!*" the same distorted voice reported, mixed with the sounds of gunfire. Sarah confirmed at least some of the drones were co-opted.

The drones took out several UN soldiers before they recognized what had occurred. They took cover under and behind their vehicles, clumsy in cold-weather gear for the harsh winter. *Must not have been here the last go-round,* Moyra thought. The more experienced units still only trusted the drones as far as they could be thrown for target practice.

The firefight didn't last long. With the drones available as support, the Freehold unit managed to kill most of the UN unit and capture two. "*Cool,*" the speaker commented. "*We've got vehicles now. I was getting tired of walking.*"

"Give them the instructions for disabling the UN overrides on those vehicles. Make sure the primary and secondary transponders are left with the dead. We'll have a tech meet the team to verify nothing else exists later," Moyra ordered. Sarah relayed the information, including reading off the technical process.

Moyra switched over to text. :: Dam, let Boss-man know that LZ35 is assumed compromised. ::

:: Dammit, that team had some critical tech coming in. That's why it was a brand new landing site. Is anything salvageable? ::

:: All of it. We borrowed the drones for target practice. ::

:: Really? Good. Boss will be pleased to hear *that*, :: Damocles replied. :: Was this one sheer luck on their part? ::

Moyra hesitated for a moment. :: I don't know. New site, but really critical gear. Most of the landing teams have had at least one attack shortly after receiving goods. This team's had three, this makes four now. But all the others were at reused sites. ::

:: ...Do we have an unmanaged leak? :: Damocles asked. Only a few of the leakers had gone undetected long enough to actually inflict damage on resistance efforts. The rest were like Braknck, and being managed for disinformation campaigns.

:: If we do, they know more than we have been giving them credit for. Their counterintelligence people aren't complete morons, unlike some of their brass. Could also be insufficient trajectory obfuscation on the part of the landing craft's crew? I don't know. ::

:: Twitch. I'll see what Boss-man wants to do. Might need to do a bunch of verification reviews, and we don't have *time*. ::

:: Agreed. Not enough time and people. AI only goes so far for augmentation of hands. ::

Cry Havoc

Jamie Ibson

Part 1

February 32nd, 211
Sixty-One Kilometers East of Taniville

"What's the word?" Handler Corporal Dante Neumeier asked, following Sergeant Bill Michaelson into the clearing. Michaelson's cats had preceded them, and Kismet, Neumeier's leopard partner, trailed. Michaelson didn't answer the question; he merely frowned behind his beard and sat wearily on the log. Dante took a seat next to him, and Bill passed him a real wood-pulp paper note.

It was the first time they'd all been together in a week, each busy to their own tasks. Michaelson had spent four days patrolling west to Ridgeville to meet their intel contact, Anasazi, and another four days back. Neumeier and his lady friend, Corporal Helena Christiansen, had escorted an antiair missile team, brought down another Avatar interceptor, and the cats had had a merry time hunting down the crew.

Sergeant "Doc" Dixie and Corporal Tom Prince had gone north, to Falling Rock. Ranchers who had resisted the UN's intrusion into their day-to-day found themselves denied operating permits. Without permits, they were denied veterinarians, and without veterinarians, any herd deemed "infectious" would be slaughtered. After two such slaughters the Freeholders figured out the UN's game and began to seek, of all things, black-market veterinarian expertise. Anasazi would handle requests and some time between nine and one divs, Dr. Crystal Dixie would knock on the rancher's door for a late-night house call.

Blazer Specialist Risa Leifman and her field trainer, Operative Sergeant Stan Kirby, spent the week east in the foothills below the Boudicca Mountains, hunting and foraging. Risa was the junior-most member of the team and she and Stan were a study in contrasts; Stan's skin was such a dark black it was nearly blue, and the Operative was freakishly tall by Grainnean standards. Risa was petite and her skin had been porcelain-white until she'd covered much of it with ink. She liked to joke her tattoos improved her resistance to Io's harsh UV.

The meat they'd brought back would be smoked and preserved as homemade MREs and as treats for the cats. The leopards hunted for themselves as well, but having smoky meat snacks in the dump pouches helped gain their cats' interest and cooperation that much more easily. Leopards were smart, and knew exactly what they were doing; they'd trained their handlers well.

Iolight pierced the canopy from the west, indicating it was dinnertime and the seven handlers gathered around their dirt-brick stove for their "briefing." Bill bit into an elk-and-pepper kebab without answering Dante's question, and handed him the note.

> ~~Ghost~~
>
> ~~Fritz, Grenzland~~
>
> ~~Jack & Drayman~~
>
> ~~Magnus, Sheerah & Riggs (!)~~
>
> ~~Anubis & Serdadu~~
>
> ~~Winters~~

More casualties. Something had gone *very* wrong last week near Jefferson.

Warrant Leader Winters became the senior-most handler on the planet after Lieutenant Dave Hathaway was killed the spring before. Now Winters was gone, along with most of his team and they were losing this war of attrition. Handlers were the rarest of rare—after passing Blazer or Operative school, handler school took another full Grainnean year.

"Congratulations, Bill," Tom Prince said. "Looks like you're NCOIC, Freehold Combat Leopard Contingent."

The gallows humor went unremarked. It wasn't funny, because it was true. Bill Michaelson had more rank and time than any handler still alive. He was even starting to get silver streaks in his hair and beard and he needed to get *that* shit under control.

"Stop me if this is crazy," Risa Leifman ventured as she studied the note. "What if...what if we brought some of the ferals out of retirement? They've been thriving out in the preserve."

"You really think they'll remember us years later?" Helena Christiansen asked. "Or that they'll play nice?"

"I think it's worth trying," Risa answered simply. "I think it's better than letting the aardvarks pick us off, one or two at a time."

"I for one am sick of just *hearing* all these stories about what badasses Thor and Odin were, Bill," Kirby rumbled, a mocking grin on his lips. "I wanna see them in action for once."

"I second that motion," Dixie smiled. "I miss the little bastards."

"That's a long fucking walk," Neumeier objected. "Almost to Maygida, with two mountain ranges in between."

"We've been walking for a year, what's one more month?" Michaelson snapped. "Twelve hundred klicks divided by forty days' hiking means we only have to cover thirty klicks a day. Fit in breaks, and we can be there just after Equinox. I seem to remember one day in particular when Helena *jogged* that."

"To be fair," Helena retorted, "Capstick was dying, and it *sucked*. You're suggesting we do the same thing, every day, for forty days? In these?" She pointed to her handmade leather moccasins.

Bill paused, realizing his temper had gotten away from him. They'd been living austere, low-tech lives in the field as they'd been trained to do, hiding outside the edges of civilization. They'd had some guidance along the way, but "Commander's Intent" only went so far.

Maybe it's time to ask for help.

Bill exhaled and massaged his forehead. "No. You're right, the hike would be a major time commitment and we can do better. I'm not thinking outside the box. Anasazi mentioned they've got some transport available and proper equipment from somewhere. We'll see about getting trucks and whatever else we need. I want a wish list from everyone."

"Boots?" Risa asked, hopefully.

"Boots!" Helena Christiansen agreed. Before the war, she'd been a competitive ultramarathon runner. Hand-stitched leather was *not* cutting it. "And hair ties. I keep tying my own hair in knots," she grimaced. Her hair was done up in wind braids all over, hanging like scrim from a ghillie suit.

"It's a wish list," Bill said. "Whatever. Boots, toothbrushes, uniforms..."

"I, uh, kinda like this look, Bill," Kirby said. "It even comes in my size."

The handlers' ragged utilities were long abandoned and replaced with leather and hide they had harvested, stretched, smoked and stitched together from ripper, slasher and elk. Between the furs, leather, ghillie netting and judiciously applied camouflage dirt, they appeared to be completely feral. Their load-bearing harnesses and rucks were at odds with the rest of their clothing, but even those were more patch than original material.

"It's badass," Tom said. "Were I some aardvark with fur-clad barbarians and hungry, hungry war cats hunting me? I'd punch out the nearest NCO and get my ass over to the brig where it's nice and safe. I'm going to be grumpy as fuck when this is all over and I have to go back to wearing issue again."

Bill looked around the circle to see everyone nodding.

"All right, we keep the furs and hides, and anyone who wants new boots can give me sizes. But let's say we go collect a bunch of ferals. We can't just dump ten cats in the UN's lap here—the cats would go after civvies too. They're smart, but the ferals didn't make the cut. I doubt they'd be clever enough to discern Freeholders from aardvarks if we just cried havoc and let them slip. So...where?"

"There's Mirror Lake," Dixie offered. "One fat, isolated base with nothing but modular quarters and juicy targets? Central District's Quick Reaction team flies out of the airfac there and they rely on the relative isolation for security. The QRF consists of a company of infantry, a squad of Special Unit assault armor, and some vertols to get them where they need to be."

"Heh," Kirby chuckled. "There's a weak point on the rear of those suits. On Mtali, I deployed with a UN Special Unit and a squad of black ops to retake some seized artillery. There's a... lump, a dome, between the jump jets' fan ducts that houses the capacitors for the suit. It's a bit bigger than a rugby ball, you can't miss it. The armor's proof against small arms like the M5. But we don't have M5s, do we?" He grinned. It was generally understood that while the M5's 4mm rounds would at least take the bark off a tree, the M8's much heavier 8.6mm round would take it off *both* sides. The handlers had them to hunt for meat, use as DMRs, and in emergency, put down an enraged or mortally wounded cat.

"I like it. If we hit them from multiple angles to crack the power source," Michaelson said. "We're going to hunt the...third deadliest species on the planet: near-invulnerable power-armored suits with jump jets, crates of link for their machine guns and more visual overlays than you can use at one time. And we're going to kill them dead, because *we* are deadliest species numbers one and two."

February 41st, 211
The Janine Maartens Nature Preserve for Resurrected and Protected Species

Strange things are afoot.

Several sunsets ago, six or seven new humans broached our territory, bearing meat. They wired it to trees, where we could get it but not take it somewhere safe to eat without having to fight over it. I know better. *We* know better.

When the humans start stringing up food, it's because they're *hunting*. With Guns. Years ago, I knew some humans who stalked and chased and pounced like cats. I miss those days. It seemed so easy to get some of Dante's tasty meat bites and disappear up a tree until the Ioset. We hunted but we never ran low on food. I'd eat my fill, then I'd disappear. I'm *very* good at disappearing.

Then one day we flew through the air in a *vertol* and came here. Then he went back on the *vertol* and left Akuma and me behind. I thought he'd made a mistake, at first, that he'd come back. That it was more of the training, more of the games we would play, more hunting tricks.

He didn't come back.

Akuma was angry. I was sad. Akuma killed for *days*. Rippers, slashers, swamp crocs, bouncers, deer, elk, anything, *everything*. He didn't even stop to eat, he just hunted and killed and hunted and killed until he collapsed. I just wanted Dante back, his smoky snack bites and the games we'd play, stalking slashers, and that time we hunted a ripper? Good times. But winter has come and gone, I don't remember how many times. Five? Six? I miss those days. Hunting and not being hungry all the time is *hard work*. I wish I'd worked harder with Dante, maybe he wouldn't have let me go.

These humans don't smell right. Their scent is musky, and buried beneath a blend of *other* smells. They smell of smoke, oil, dirt, leather and fur. The meat they've wired up is sickly sweet, already rotting, but wired meat means humans hunting, which means we need to hunt them *first*.

I'm invisible on the jungle floor. It's warm and wet and everything is bright lights and dark shadow. The three of us, we make a good team. Akuma is bigger than me and he demands a bigger chunk of everything we kill but he's our best fighter. Little will flank and snarl and chase. She eats the leftovers but she's much smaller and doesn't eat as much anyway. I'm the one who will make the kill, unless they try to fight Akuma directly. The two of them channel the prey in my direction until I can ambush them when it's too late. I can smell Akuma now. He's close.

I dig my claws deep into the bark of the broadleaf. They're everywhere here and have nice fat leaves that hide me, and strong limbs for running upon. The rainfall masks the leaves as they rustle, and I move from branch to branch until I'm above the human. He sees Akuma, Akuma sees him, but they're just staring at each other. The human's head has streaks of dirt and mud and clay across his scalp and it helps him hide. He has a Gun but it's not in his hands where he can hurt anything. He reaches into a pocket, and I tense to jump in case it's a Gun. It's not. He throws food down onto the ground in front of Akuma. Akuma chuffs, but doesn't take the bait. Akuma doesn't trust anyone, not since Dante left us behind.

The wind shifts. I'm close enough to smell the sweet fishy smell of the food the human threw down, and separate out the smoke and oil and dirt and leather and fur from the humans' own musk and *I know that scent!*

DANTE!

HE'S BACK!

I jump down out of my perch and tackle him to the ground and I HAVE MISSED YOU and I nuzzle his face! He gets an arm free and strokes my forehead and folds back my ear, looking into it for a moment. "Ingwe!" Dante shouts, and there's relief in his voice. He probably thought I would kill him at first...but

YES! There is his treat bag and he's got candied trout! One of my FAVORITES! And...a small Gun in his hand. I hadn't seen it, and that would have been bad. But it's HIM and he has TREATS!

Dante rolls to his knees and now I know why he smells of smoke and oil and dirt and leather and fur. Humans don't have spots and they don't blend very well so they hide their skin under clothes that has spots and helps them blend. But now his clothes *are* spots, smoked and oiled furs from elk and gazelle and danger-cat and other prey. But right now that exquisite scent of candied trout is making me drool and he digs out a handful and he offers it to me in his hand. I lick them up in an instant and it is a FLAVOR RUSH and I head-butt him in the chest and he almost falls over. He's laughing. I rub my scent on him and bask in his.

Akuma's black fur slinks out from under the tall forker bush where he was waiting. He ignores the treats on the ground, and there's a low growl in his throat as he paces back and forth in front of Dante. He bares his teeth and the growl turns into a snarl. Dante doesn't back down, but he breathes deep and he sighs.

"I don't blame you, Akuma," he says. "I didn't want to cut you loose either, I won't do it again. Promise."

Dante holds out a hand, and Akuma reluctantly takes a bite out of the peace offering, but he's still angry. He opens wide and gnaws on Dante's hand, not hard, but hard enough. Dante doesn't pull away. Akuma walks away, turning his back on our Friend.

"Akuma, please?" Dante says, and Akuma turns and dashes across the clearing in three quick bounds and pounces on Dante, knocking him over onto his back, pinning him to the ground, snarling in his face. Dante doesn't say anything, but I see he's got one hand back in the pocket where he held the small Gun. Akuma swats Dante in the face, leaving thin red lines where claws broke skin. Then Akuma gets off him, and goes back to the trout still sitting in the grass.

"I suppose I deserved that," he says, sitting up. "Are we square?"

Akuma looks at him, and Dante tosses another treat, and Akuma catches it midair. The angry growling in his throat has changed to a contented sawing, and Dante turns back to me.

"And how've you been, my tree potato?" Dante asks. I don't know what a potato is, but I don't care because I will work SO HARD to make sure you keep me with you!

Little is perched on another korabi broadleaf. Her eyes are wide and her nostrils flare. She's unsure about this. She's been here in the wild longer than Akuma and me. I saw loudly and Dante gives me scritches and he follows my eyes up into the trees, and he spots her.

"Come on down, little war cat, there's plenty for all of you," Dante whispers. She hisses at him. "Oh don't be like that," he replies, and he gives Akuma and me another treat. He pulls himself up into the tree she's perched in, and she hisses again.

Dante carefully places a few treats on her branch near the trunk, then he climbs higher. She slinks along the limb, her eyes focused on him as she tastes the scent of the trout bits. She slurps one up into her mouth and chews. She tries another.

She likes them.

She jumps up to the same branch Dante is on and follows it out to him. He pulls out another handful of treats and she gently nips the fish bites out of his hand and swallows greedily.

"Friends?" Dante asks, and offers her the back of his hand. She sniffs it, tastes his skin, and then rubs her cheek on his knee before climbing back down out of the tree.

Friends.

1.2 Divs Later

Dixie was finishing Helena's new stitches when Neumeier got back into camp, and Dante dutifully joined his lady friend on the log next to her to get his face patched up. Her wind braids were a mess and she had a thin red line running from her temple to her jaw.

"You're all right?" he asked.

"Yes, we had a bit of a misunderstanding at first, but we got it straightened out. How're you?"

Dante nodded. "Good, except for this," he said, pointing to his cheek. "I hear chicks dig scars. I'm gonna be *irresistible* when this is over!" Christiansen rolled her eyes, but Dante had indeed collected a fair number of garish wounds all over his face and scalp over the last year. "I've got three new cats. Akuma, Ingwe, and a tiny clouded one, can't weigh more than thirty kilos. 53E16?"

Bill ran the service number through his comm. He had the old registry of cats, their lineage, and suitability scores, figuring if they lost the info, they'd never get the program running again. That she was one of the clouded leopards narrowed the candidates significantly—*Neofelis nebulosa* were smaller than *Panthera pardus*, and a completely separate genetic strain. The FMF was introducing them as light-reconnaissance cats and they'd proven up to the task—the smaller scout cats had once gone whole decades on Old Earth believed extinct in the wild, because they were so good at evading people.

"You've got to be shitting me," he said. "We need to get Minstrel down here."

"Who is it?" Dixie wanted to know. She knew Brad Ministrelli had been a brittle man since the KE strikes, doing everything he could undercover, distributing supplies, but he'd been gutted when his cats were killed in the KE strikes on Heilbrun.

"Xanadu," Michaelson said. "Most of her scores were excellent, but she washed out because she was too aggressive to be a scout."

"Oh goddess, Bill, he has to know! He's been dead inside for months!" Dixie exclaimed. "This'll mean the world to him."

February 49th, 2011
The Janine Maartens Nature Preserve for Resurrected and Protected Species

Minstrel stood by the side of a dirt track, second-guessing whether he was even at the right grid or not. His fears proved unfounded when fur-clad figure silently emerged from the bush. Bill's shaggy hair and unkempt beard were a shock. He barely recognized his old friend.

"Thanks for coming," Bill said. "Sorry to be so cryptic."

"It's fine, cryptic's kinda my thing these days. It's not that I don't love coming down here, but I'm plenty busy running around with my beard on fire up north. The madman's got a major push planned and shit's going to get real busy. What's this about?"

"Follow me," Michaelson said. The battered NCO ghosted along a hidden forest path. Minstrel followed close behind, feeling very out of his element. He'd been thoroughly urbanized over the last year in his jeans and plaid. Even seeing his old NCO in barbarian garb made him pause. He knew they'd been living rough, but he'd had no idea *how* rough.

A few segs' hike later, Brad entered the handlers' camp.

He looked around the clearing and saw leopards and panthers everywhere. They draped themselves over branches and snoozed in the shade. They wrestled and roared and purred as the mood took them. Three gnawed on a dead gazelle, and leather hides were being smoked over a fire pit.

The remnants of his old squad were there too. Everyone had shed weight they couldn't afford to lose and their uniforms were... not. Dixie was scritching a small clouded leopard's neck ruff. The blotchy gray-and-ochre fur stood out from the other cats, which were either a melanistic black or tawny with spots. Minstrel's augmented hearing let him hear her whisper "Who's that?" in the leopard's ear. The slim feline turned and locked eyes with Ministrelli before racing across the clearing and leaping into his arms. Ministrelli caught her and she licked his face with enthusiasm. Shocked, puzzled, he cradled the cat before kneeling, setting her down. He read her ear tattoo and froze. His eyes started leaking.

"Xanadu?" he gasped, hugging her close. Bill put one hand on Brad's shoulder and passed him a treat-filled dump pouch. Brad couldn't see, his eyes were blinded with tears, but he found the opening to the pouch and slid a handful out, offering them to the kitten who'd had *too much* fight in her, but was the only one who'd survived.

"How..." was all he managed to get out.

"Brad... we're getting clobbered out here," she said. Tears streaked her face as well. "We needed reinforcements, and we found some. If the cat's willing to listen, we're willing to take them along."

Bill nodded and picked up where she'd trailed off. "We've got twenty-eight cats here, ready to go rend some UN fat at Mirror Lake. Some are washouts, some are natural-born, we have cats again, and we need handlers. What do you say to swapping out your flannel for furs?"

Ministrelli swallowed hard.

"I... I can't."

Dixie opened her mouth to protest.

"Really. I can't," Minstrel stopped her. "You guys... this is too much. Naumann knows you guys have been tearing shit up, Anasazi updates us regularly. But... we've got a solid network going on in Capital District and I'm right in the middle of it.

I can't just cut out. I'd be...well, I'd be abandoning the Free-holders who've come to rely on me. I can't say more than that."

Minstrel's eyes hardened. "When I don't have to hide any-more? When I can put on a uniform again? Damn right I'm in. But what I've been doing is *important*. I can't. I'm sorry."

The handlers looked to Michaelson, and he nodded, processing.

"Respect, Brad. I get it. *Mors In Tenebris*," he said. The han-dlers' motto: *Death in the shadows.*

"*Disce Pati Quiete*," Brad replied with the Blazers' own motto, as he stroked Xanadu's fur. *Learn to suffer in silence.* "It's good to see you again, little lady, but I can't run with you right now," he told her. "They're going to take care of you, okay? Make sure you get lots of treats and don't let the bigger boys give you any shit."

Xanadu head-butted Minstrel in the chest, rubbed her cheek against his shoulder and squinted up at him, a faint purr in her throat.

"Dammit, kitty, you stop that, this is hard enough as it is," Brad said, his voice cracking even as a smile broke through the tears, "You just keep safe and I'll be back for you."

He stood and nodded to his old team before turning to head back to the air truck, back to a very different war than the one his teammates were fighting. Xanadu rose and made to follow, but Brad lifted a hand and grunted. She paused.

"Down," he ordered, and she knelt down into the weeds. "Wait," he whispered, and then disappeared back along the path he'd come from.

Spider's Web
Part 15

Moyra Kelly gave Jenkins the go-ahead to start needling Braknck while she waited on a complex query against the AI filters to complete.

:: Hey, Brak, when's that payment coming through? :: Jenkins asked.

:: Dude is holding out on me. Says he's not getting enough information, :: Braknck replied.

:: Not even a partial payment? :: Moyra asked, looking at Braknck's account at one of the banks, showing several large deposits, despite the low level of funds. *Did he NEVER change his password?*

:: Well, sort of. A small one. ::

:: Hrmph. I can't keep providing information for free, man, :: Jenkins replied. He messaged the command team. :: Does he really think we're that stupid? ::

:: He doesn't know that we gave him older code, :: Moyra replied. :: Nor does he apparently recall I actually have access to his main account myself. ::

:: Oh? :: came the question from the rest.

:: He's getting paid, all right. ::

:: And we know from a recruiter in the field that someone likely to be a UN operative attempted to use the information to gain access to the comm network, :: DalesOP said.

:: So they have some idea of how we're communicating, but haven't cracked it yet, :: Damocles added.

:: Right on both counts. The suspected operative was sidelined into one of the null spaces with a pure AI handler, and the original app interface, the most basic of encryption, :: Moyra replied.

:: AI harvesting information, then? ::

:: Trying. Also using that installation to pull more network info out and off. K-man's got the data. :: Moyra could never really think of Kozlov by any other name nor had he chosen one, but even to Damocles and DalesOP, she did not want to actually type it.

❖   ❖   ❖

:: To answer an outstanding question, :: Damocles messaged Moyra, :: we received a note from that smuggling ship with the most compromised deliveries. ::

:: Oh? :: Moyra asked.

:: The leak has been ... resolved. ::

:: How resolved? ::

:: My impression is "fatally." But we have shifted that ship to space force deliveries only anyway, :: Damocles replied. :: If one of the crew was compromised, others may be as well. The spacecraft can change locations more easily. ::

:: That means it is relatively safe to bring the new comm units in for dispersal. Data I'm gathering shows that the null-space operatives, emphasis on that S there, are figuring out that we're using a more advanced variation and are trying to track which all apps are in use. They have a few incompletely destroyed samples that they're pulling code from. ::

:: Fuck. Now is NOT the time to lose the network and deal with a shift. I'll let Boss-man know. Does Dal know, for the PsyOps angle? ::

:: Now that I've got two confirmations of that situation? He's next on the list, :: Moyra replied. :: We'll need to shift the existing comm network to noncombatant use only pretty quickly, I think. I have Jenkins, Salamander and TripleShot rolling the existing devices over to the next versions now. ::

Huff #20
Bonita [Early March 211]

Bonita—she's incredible. Probably the best thing about this whole fucking planet. Best sex I've ever had and just talking to her is almost as good. She's what the future could be. More like her, and we could probably reintegrate these people. Or, the hell with it, we can breed them out of existence. POLAD and I are floating an incentivized resettlement plan up through SecMil to take to SecGen—a call for brave, opportunistic, loyal citizens to help rebuild and alter the population mix on Grainne. I'd prefer the brave, but more refugees like those they sent here before hostilities broke out might have to do. This place is not densely populated, and given the culture, there's relatively few people who even *want* to move here, and none of those are sane.

That's the core of the problem. This is a war of nerves, of mindset. A war of culture. Now, a war of sex, one that involves lots of babies, might change the calculus. It might be better than this ugly mess that's soiled both us and them. I ought to ask Bonita what she thinks.

The core of *my* problem though, is that I'm violating my own General Order One by doing this. There's no way around that, but it has implications for long-term operations here. Long term is appropriate, because we're not going anywhere, anytime soon. I have to enforce discipline for a policy I'm blatantly ignoring. No going back now though, I think I'm falling in love with her. If my command sergeant major found out, he'd gut me himself.

Nevertheless, dating is a problem for us. Our standard morale efforts cause more problems than they solve. For example, if you turn someone down, they might claim prejudice, or that you're showing favoritism to someone else, and that causes months of work to investigate and resolve. Every claim gets a full investigation, regardless of evidence. That's not the real problem. The troops in the field—the ones not getting laid —are the problem. There is a lot of "unauthorized contact" with locals. The support folks in the main combat bases, those linked to the major cities? They don't face any shortage. Support and the "TOC-Roaches" have fuck all to do, except, well, fuck. And file complaints. And this is even after weaponized VD with contact toxins. I'd like to be outraged about that, but hell, we started the biowar.

It *always* comes back to sex when dealing with humans. Without fail. Who's getting it, who's not, and who's crying about it? This truth is thousands of years old; wars have been lost and won over it. Sex is just as zero-sum as politics. Ask the French girls who shacked up with their German occupiers during the big twentieth-century war how things went for them when liberation came.

Our regs explicitly prohibit local sex workers because of trafficking concerns, even though it's blatantly obvious that most of them are paid respectably, and are well-to-do compared to many people here. The contractors and media types have no compunction against partaking, and I've started sending them home by the dozens weekly. Not just for those reasons, but because they keep getting killed in rather creative and disturbing ways—like weaponized STDs, which we're also finding in our uniformed personnel. Nice, soft, squishy targets, and both a logistical problem and a liability for morale.

Claims of rape and abuse have popped on all sides. Civilians on Earth would be shocked at how much time and effort these cases consume. Hours per week of *MY* time. That's not even taking into account the complaints settled at lower echelons. I prefer to fight the actual insurgency. Instead, too much time gets lost fighting the blue-ball insurgency.

Spider's Web
Part 16

Damocles opened the door to the room let on Moyra Kelly's behalf, and gestured for the guard with them to run a security check. They chatted quietly while she cleared the first room, and then stepped just barely inside. A few moments later, the guard gave them an all clear.

"Thanks," Moyra said.

The guard nodded. "Should I go grab that pizza now?"

"Yeah, if you don't mind," Damocles replied.

"Sure thing."

The guard disappeared, and Damocles locked the door behind her. Moyra swung her personal pack down, and dug out her portable equipment. "You know the place is already equipped with a white-noise generator," Damocles commented.

Moyra didn't respond until the unit was running. "You know me and my trust of equipment."

"Quite." Damocles gestured at the sofa. "You look tired."

"And you look stressed."

He snorted. "Been a hell of a year, Hesp. Hell of a year."

She thought about watching the video streams of her handler team clutching each other as their safe house exploded around them, and the drone feeds of turning equipment on their erstwhile operators. "Yeah. Hell of a year. End game soon, eh?"

"That's why you, me, Dal, a bunch of others have been called in dribs and drabs to the area. I know you've deliberately stayed unaware of physical locations insofar as possible."

"Yeah. Can't accidentally slip a comment somewhere if you don't know. Only as much as I need to at any given time."

"How's your grandmother?"

"That damn virus left her pretty weak, even still. Partially paralyzed her diaphragm, and triggered a relatively minor stroke. 'Light respiratory infection,' my ass. She's being looked after by a couple of the handlers in that town. Says she's not dying until she knows the UN is gone."

"I would have thought she'd be saying she's holding out for you to have kids."

Moyra abruptly got up, and stood near the artificial window, looking out on a landscape that didn't exist. "The docs aren't sure why she didn't die already, Jeff. I know I downplayed it in chat and all, but she almost died. I watched babies die of that shit, too, while I sat there by her hospital bed. She insisted she needed less care than they did, and made them put her in the hallway when the worst influx came through. I was helping with the babies, when I wasn't helping with her, or running this whole...thing. Whatever this is."

"I would have come to help if you'd said," he replied after a moment. "I consider her my family, too. She's your family, that makes her mine."

"You were busy, Mick was busy, I was busy. It's a war. People die. I just..."

He came over and hesitantly offered a hug, which she accepted.

The tears weren't long behind, and for a while, her oldest friend just held her while she cried.

"Sorry," Moyra muttered as she struggled for her composure.

Damocles shook his head. "I've been buffered from a lot of the worst of it, being attached to Boss-man's ankle. You and Mick, you two have been through a lot. I know he's still not quite right after that long op."

"No, he's not." She half smiled, in bitter amusement. "Lot of therapists will be employed for life after this is said and done."

"Ain't that the truth." Damocles shook his head. "Want actual pizza, not a ruse to cover sending off a guard?"

"I think...I think that would be lovely, actually."

"Top-of-the-line frozen. Stocked the freezer myself."

"Sounds heavenly."

:: Brak's been awful quiet, :: Jenkins noted to the command staff. :: It's not like him to go quite *this* long without saying *something* stupid. ::

:: We'd better check to see if he got himself arrested or worse. :: Moyra sighed.

:: I already had a query running on his real and most common assumed names, :: Jenkins admitted. :: Nothing's popped. ::

:: Is there anyone we trust who can be trusted to check up on the idiot in person? :: Damocles asked.

:: He lives around here, :: DalesOP replied. :: I know his favorite bar; I can check there. See if anyone knows. ::

:: Worth a try. ::

Force Majeure
Part 7

With four boats in rotation and the cutter, and varied materials delivered for use, production steadied out. There were variations in requirements, though uniforms remained standard to equip resistance forces, and ammo demand was always as much as they could produce. Some of that was Freehold standard, some UN standard. The rebels had plenty of both types of weapons. Body armor, boots, rucks, hygiene. Based on Mtali levels of production from the ship's history, there were several decent-sized infantry battalions operating just on what *Force* produced. If the ground forces were managing local clandestine production and theft of enemy resources, they might be twice that. Respectable. Add in random elements and sheer noncompliance and the UN operational environment was not favorable.

Some support weapons had gone down: mortars, antiarmor rockets, thermobarics, plenty of squad and platoon machine guns. Yates assumed any marksmen were using civilian hunting rifles. No armored vehicles produced, though possibly some were built down below.

There were reports of vehicle and horse-mounted elements harassing the UN. There were reliable reports of a significant intel network. The Earthies were paying in blood and billions for every meter of ground they secured.

The incoming material appeared to be donations from Halo miners, scavenged debris from habitats—probably Greendoor and Breakout. There was even a decent amount of fresh food mixed in. After all, once consumed, the food byproducts, so to speak, remained useful organics for production. Fuel conservation remained an issue.

All this came through in a compilation for the command meeting. Yates took his seat and was ready to discuss all that. He figured knowing there was a sizeable resistance was good news that would cheer people.

Right then, Karanov's phone and his both alerted. He glanced at his.

"It appears we're needed at the dock."

They rose and made their way aft, pulling through emgee,

walking through the factory, pulling again along the companionway tethers.

The crew knew their orders and duty.

"Excuse me, sir." "Good to see you, sir, ma'am." "Gangway for the officers."

4J17 was back again, with supernumeraries. The dock area was crowded, but they found a cubby to pull into to talk.

"Captain, I'm Warrant Leader Coffman." The man was slight but fit, looked tired but very alert underneath.

"Good to meet you, Warrant."

"Thanks for meeting with me. This is Contractor Umair."

Umair was bulkier, muscled, about thirty Freehold years.

"And you, sir."

They made a point of greeting Karanov, too.

"Sir, we're special munitions experts. We're here to help you fabricate some dedicated mission devices. They're well within the capabilities of your crew and equipment. We're mostly to oversee and document."

Interesting.

Yates replied, "Very good. I'll need proper approval before we can let you anywhere, I'm afraid."

"Absolutely. I have confirmable documentation from Colonel Sansing and Colonel Naumann."

If so, they were clear. That was both Ground and Space Commands.

Karanov asked, "Do we get any hint as to your mission profile with these?"

"Only that they're for an offensive operation on a specific schedule."

"How is that schedule?"

Umair replied, "Long enough it shouldn't be a concern, but if we get short, it may pre-empt other production."

Yates said, "Let's verify your bona fides and find quarters. They will be sparse, I'm afraid."

"We assumed so. Your crew comes first, we're supplemental. A dark locker will be fine."

"Cabins are larger than that, but thank you for understanding. Here's our introduction." He handed over a tab.

"Let's proceed to Commo."

✧   ✧   ✧

He hadn't expected to need Commo AnLab any time soon. The staff were ready when he arrived, though. He locked in through a double hatch to the module that was completely vacuum-gapped from the rest of the ship. The walls were a very durable Faraday cage, and reinforced against most common explosives, though this was a tiny chip and shouldn't have any such risk. The oxygen system was internal. The comm they offered him attached to nothing else. If this contained hostile code, it could do nothing to the rest of the ship.

The tab had a confirmation code that matched his personal code. The second code matched the one handwritten on a sheet, kept in the vault here. Next was a valid number sequence for a STRATORDER. The text named the two men, and ordered him to provide all support possible within parameter 3. So, they couldn't risk the ship's survival, but they could pre-empt other operations.

There were video files.

He brought that up. First was Colonel Sansing. She spoke. "Captain Yates, thank you for your consideration in this project. OPSEC prohibits details, but it is critical to the war effort. As the orders note, this operation is not above the safety of your ship, but please render all support to the utmost of your resources. Also please relay to your crew that your actions so far have resulted in the award of the Citizens' Unit Citation and the Forces' Operational Excellence Award with Combat 'C,' which I never thought we'd ever have a reason to issue. You and your ship have been critical and essential to everything fought and held so far. Put directly: The war would have been over last year without you. I've recorded a separate message with that last information that you may share with the crew. Thank you again."

He actually had damp eyes. To hear that kind of feedback, with no administrative dress up was just stunning.

Commander Naumann he knew slightly. The man was pure Special Warfare, regarded as a complete genius and a complete sociopath, but he accomplished his Mtali involvement with astonishingly few casualties, a massive combat bootprint, and an enemy thoroughly demoralized, until the Freehold Forces withdrew. They'd never met in person, but this ship had provided munitions support to him.

Naumann looked like a gym rat, and utterly exhausted. That was what a thousand-meter stare looked like.

"Captain Yates, with all that's been said, I'm only going to add that there absolutely is a concrete battle plan, and I can't afford to waste any resources. Everything you're sending is critical on the surface and in some of the habitats. I'm not guaranteeing victory, but I am guaranteeing everything is worth the effort. Please proceed as you have been. I can't ask for more."

That was honest and direct. It was also concretely verified.

He'd work with the techs on whatever unique materials they needed.

There was another file, that summarized operational accomplishments. It didn't show Freehold losses of course, but it did show known UN casualties and damage.

He'd have to study it later, but yes, if this was correct, the invaders were being hammered mercilessly, dragged through the mud, and kicked in the teeth. If they won, they were going to regret it.

He realized he'd thought "if" the UN won.

Well, damn. It was still a war.

He looked around and saw the AnLab crew were waiting on him.

"We're good," he said. "There will be an announcement shortly."

Outside, he directed the billeting chief, "Make these experts as comfortable as we can." He turned and noted, "We're at your disposal, gentlemen."

"All hands, routine message from C-Deck. We have a communique from Space Command that all crew are ordered to watch at their earliest operational availability. We will play it now for crew on hand."

Sansing's video and voice started with, "Crew of FMS *Force*. I am Acting Space Commander Colonel Sansing. Attention to orders:..."

She read off a summary of the awards and he watched the entire command crew cling to the wording.

"...Put directly: The war would have been over last year without you. Thank you all. For Space Command, Sansing ou—"

The last consonant was drowned out by the sound of a thousand spacers screaming cheers.

There was knowing one mattered, and then there was knowing

how much one mattered. Beyond that was others knowing it and recognizing you.

Yates was pretty sure their already record productivity just improved fifteen percent.

Tirza contacted him just as he went off shift.

"Captain, did you hear anything recently about our guests?"

"Not since they arrived, why?"

"They're already at work."

"Good?"

"I believe so. Their schematics are for high-intensity, focused-burst EMP warheads, a couple of very clean tritium-boosted devices, several extremely compact, super-compressed thermobarics that I didn't even know existed conceptually, and stripped-down, all-out, nothing-but-brute-power drives to deliver them all."

"Interesting. That's certainly offensive weaponry. Anything bothering you?"

"Not bothering me, no, but I'm wondering why build them all here? Unless we're the only source of materials, which is possible. Or unless they're all for use out here. I'm also wondering how we'll get a chance to use those. There's enough to damage, wreck, and piss off most of the larger UN facilities. Collateral damage is obviously going to be present. I'm not sure it's the right approach when they will just send another round of occupation when we have nothing to even slow them down, and they're angry."

"Possibly it won't be cost effective for them?"

"I assume there's some strategic calculation we're not in on, yes. But this is like firing a full complement of missiles at something, and flipping the finger."

"It worked for *Hate*."

"And it took us a week to put her back together. I don't know. We're going to run out of exotics and REE on this, but that's why we have them. It's going to get hot soon, though."

"Win or lose, that's better than fading into the night."

"It is. Do you want more info if I get any?"

"Yes. Ping me if it's urgent. Otherwise, during routine briefings. Find out what you can, but don't dig into anything we shouldn't have a need to know."

She half smirked. *"Sure. And a chocolate bar while I'm at it?"*

"Rum preferred. I realize it's tough. I trust your judgment."

"*Thanks. Karanov out.*"

"Out."

Commander Brody and Warrant Leader Smock closed in on the point that should be within sensor range of *Force*, or at least her reactor output.

Nothing.

Smock said, "She is pretty heavily shielded."

Brody replied, "Yeah, but there's nothing above background level."

They'd made a good delivery. The smuggling craft was a commercial freighter with cube to spare for a load this size. They were competent and professional, and damn, it was good to talk to someone else. Someone not crew.

But now he really wanted to talk to the Commo section of his own ship.

Nothing.

Smock was busy with his screen, and said, "I've narrowed as much as I can. Permission to tightbeam?"

"Go ahead."

Smock nodded and transmitted, "Home, this is Courier. Confirming delivery."

They should be within a few light-seconds. They waited.

Brody checked coordinates again. They could get slightly closer, and inevitably drift happened, but this far out it should be minimal. Had they overshot? He clutched the inertials, took them through an orange-slice maneuver, and looked for anything emitting anything.

Wait, was that something?

Smock saw it too, and transmitted again.

No response.

They had oxygen for a while, but fuel for another few days. That should be plenty. If not, it wouldn't get them in-system.

Had *Force* been destroyed? There was no debris—the density in the volume would change if it had been, and there should be background from a missile or her reactors.

"Let's head for that...cool spot." It wasn't a hot spot, but it was above background.

"Agreed."

He nudged the course. They were several light-seconds from whatever it was, and it was possibly just within their margin of error.

Something swept them then came back with, *"—is home. Delivery confirmed."*

Sighing hard and slumping, then reaching back to his controls, he took a better bearing and conned toward it.

Smock had signal. "Courier inbound. Good to see you."

The next day they pulled up alongside the dead black mass of *Force*.

Both men grinned at each other, shook hands, and prepared to debark.

Once aboard, Commander Karanov was waiting, drifting between two struts, out of the way of the loaders.

"First Officer, good to see you again," she offered.

"Thanks. We got nervous at the end there. I can confirm the ship is very well hidden. At least from our sensor array."

"That's good, though I understand their warships have better resolution."

"They do, but I'm reassured by what we do have. I hope we can swap off or refine course from our data. That was rather grueling.

She asked, "How was delivery?"

"Perfect. They were very glad to see us. If it's at all possible, we really need a bigger boat."

"We'll see what the engineers can do."

Cry Havoc
Part 2

March 35th, 211
1.25 Divs / 3.5 Hours After Local Midnight

Private Wu dozed off in the northern guard shack. His watch-partner Private Tamashiro was dead when he woke up. The floor was thick with already-congealing blood and claw marks and bites had left Tamashiro's uniform in ragged tatters. Blood, bile and partially digested food tainted the air.

Wu bolted forward in his seat, but he crashed to the floor when zip ties around his wrists and ankles went taut. He shattered a tooth on impact and tasted blood. He recoiled and retched when he realized it wasn't necessarily *his* blood he was tasting—he'd landed facedown in the pool of Tamashiro's gore. He thrashed and strained and eventually, managed to get his chair over sideways, which left him on his side, immobilized, less than a meter from the guy he'd been partnered with for most of the tour. He raged, screamed for help, shouted and sobbed.

The squad on foot patrol never checked in on him, but he didn't find out why until later. His relief never came for him, because the ones on duty were supposed to wake their relief. Wu shivered there, trapped, until Iorise.

3 Divs / 1 Hour After Iorise

Captain Castle took another drink. The whiskey had burned when he cracked the bottle; it didn't now, and the fact that it didn't worried him. He watched the external video feed for the southern gate and shivered when one of those fucking FMF jungle cats vaulted the fence next to the shack and circled the building. Some fur-clad, barbaric wild man followed the cat over the fence and into the shack. He was in and out in no more than a minute. It was no coincidence his men kept having lethal "animal attacks"—it was enemy action.

Why hadn't the motion sensors tripped?

He pulled up the command app for the supplementary

laser-fencing system and confirmed yes, it had been active. The trip log was pages long and they'd happened all over the base. They'd had so many, the OCC dialed the trip threshold down and called it a glitch in the system. When the glitches continued, they bypassed the OCC completely and sent the advisories directly to the foot patrol. In retrospect, it was clear they'd been probing response times and testing the fence's sensitivity.

He pulled up a second video and watched as the foot patrol rounded one of the sandbagged positions out by the airfac. There was no audio, and it was probably better that way. Seven of the troops ducked and dove for cover simultaneously, but Corporal Wang dropped in place, limp. All seven huddled in a fighting position meant for three. Puffs of rockrete and sand indicated enemy fire was hitting the cover, keeping them pinned. Nine point four seconds passed, and then...

More cats.

One moment, his squad was ducking sniper fire, the next, four times sixty kilos of tawny spotted death leapt into the sandbagged pit. It was no contest, and fifteen seconds later, two of the cats carried Sergeant Jonathan Nguyen and PFC Duc away with them. Nguyen hadn't even gotten in a contact report before he died.

Castle stabbed the play icon again, this time for the northern guard shack. The time stamps for all three videos were identical—the foot patrol came under fire at the same time the first cat and his barbarian partner vaulted the south fence, at the same time another cat and another barbarian pulled off the same trick that had left Wu a gibbering mess.

They were being hunted by hunters who were coordinated, and watching.

March 36th, 211
Midnight

Lopez was eyes-bugged-out terrified. He could feel his pulse pounding at his throat and every snap and pop as they swept through the woods had him convinced he'd be next. *He'd* seen the master sergeant dig Chan's locator beacon out of his boot tread. *He'd* known what that meant. It wasn't fair. They weren't fighting *soldiers* with *guns*, they were fighting *animals* that would *eat* him. He wasn't any sort of Special Unit hard-ass, he was a *clerk* who'd fucked up and been sent to a security unit "to shape up." The captain had spun them some bullshit about "Operation Wolfpack," but in truth, he felt more like a lamb being led to the slaughter.

Sweat kept dripping into his eyes inside his helmet, stinging them. He unbuckled his chin strap and slid the full-face helmet off for a moment, wiping his forehead and his visor with a shirtsleeve.

The visor came away streaked.

"The fuck...?" he said aloud, unsnapping a flashlight from his harness and turning the light on.

"Hey, HEY, HEY!" he shouted. "I GOT SOMETHING OVER HERE!"

The Special Unit troops flanking him left and right both snapped inward, scanning him and the area through their night optics.

"*What've you got?*" the suit labeled ARNOLDS asked over his external loudspeaker.

"I got, uh, a lotta blood," he stammered. "It's on my sleeves and, uh, yeah it's on my pant legs too."

The power-armored troops stomped through the alien ferns, around ancient trees that stretched upward for tens of meters. Mauser kept watch as Arnolds and Jensen turned on an external lamp and lit Lopez up.

"Hey, c'mon guys," he pleaded, "Why you gotta do that?"

The bright white light burned away the darkness and rendered Lopez temporarily blind. His utilities glistened where the dark stain of blood shined under the light. Arnolds pointed his blinding lamp at the trail Lopez had left in bent and broken grass. The four of them backed up until they located a dark, damp patch of deeply stained grass and dirt.

"*The fuck have we got here?*" Jensen said, and he swept the lamp around in a slow three-sixty.

Nothing.

Lopez glanced up and then...

"Oh... Oh fuck," he said, and collapsed to his knees, face down in the brush. He retched and puked, splashing his helmet with vomit. He stretched out an arm, pointing *up.*

Ten meters above them, the bodies of Sergeant Jonathan Nguyen and Private Duc hung from a tree branch. Or rather, they'd been *hanged* from a tree branch.

With their own intestines.

Mauser staggered forward as a heavy round struck his armor near the waist, and he got an amber icon warning him that one of his jump jet's ducts was damaged. The round hadn't penetrated deeply enough to hurt *him*, but that they'd penetrated the ducts was scary enough. Mauser didn't care for that *at all*. He spun in place and noted Lopez was now wisely prone in the dirt and tanglewoods.

"Contact! Stay down!" he shouted over his external speaker, and hosed the forest down with his forearm-mounted machine gun. The rest of Three Platoon dove for cover as Mauser, Arnolds and Jensen fired into the woods. He couldn't see anything on thermal overlay, so he just picked a direction and loosed a long burst.

"Clear," he said, then looked down at Lopez again. *Shit,* he thought. The round that had damaged his jump jet got there by way of Lopez's head first, leaving the young soldier's head a cratered, bloody mess. "Man down."

"Contact!" Sergeant Hardip Bajwa shouted as he ripped off a burst from his rifle.

"*Sitrep!*" Lieutenant Randhawa ordered.

"*Caught a flash of something in the brush, sir!*" Bajwa replied.

Randhawa was already orienting his platoon back east. Mirror Lake was only a kilometer distant, so if they acted quickly they could pin the enemies against the lakefront with no escape. Master Sergeant Pandis and Senior Corporal Norris from the Special Unit broke off to anchor the flanks of Two Platoon, to catch their enemies before they could slip away.

Well, they're not exactly tame leopards, Dante thought. *This is why they say "no plan survives contact with the enemy."* He slithered out from under his hide, and raced down a dry creek bed that ran perpendicular to the UN's firing line; no one ever outran a train by running down the tracks. Kismet was staying tight to him, darting around the featherferns and under fallen logs. Ingwe was up in the trees, staying high, and he had lost track of Akuma already. He would let the UN blunder on past until they gave up the chase. Then Helena would reach out and touch someone, and the chase would be on again.

1 Div / 2 Hours, 50 Minutes After Local Midnight

What the hell?

Lieutenant Randhawa knelt for cover behind a thick tree and immersed himself in his HUD. Down the left side of his display, he saw the status indicators for his troops. Patel had just gone gray, indicating he was KIA, but Patel's GPS was moving deeper into the woods.

"Sergeant Bajwa, what's the status on Patel?"

"I've, uh, lost PFC Patel, sir, he was anchoring the left flank. There seems to be something wrong with my readout sir. I'm showing him both KIA and mobile, fifty meters to my front, sir."

"I've got the same thing here. Tighten your troops up into two trios, I'm going to request the heavy armor move forward and figure out what the hell is going on."

"Oh, shit," Dante whispered to himself. He was invisible in the mud, brush and leaves, but anyone with a lick of sense could have followed the trail Akuma was making with his most recent kill. He'd always been an aggressive, uncontrollable, mean-spirited sonofabitch, which was why Akuma had been cut from the program. Kilo for kilo, leopards were one of the deadliest man-eaters evolution had ever produced, with massively powerful jaws that allowed them to carry away prey too heavy for lesser predators, and Akuma was the largest cat in living memory. "Wait wait wait!" Dante whispered at the top of his lungs. "Akuma, drop it! Drop it!"

The big panther snarled without loosening his grip.

"Wait," Dante admonished, and drew his seax. He pulled the dead man's arm over a fallen branch, and chopped hard. The soldier's forearm bones succumbed to the blade, and he threw the now-dripping hand away into the brush back the way Akuma had come.

"Okay," he told the big black cat, and received another growl before Akuma disappeared back into the darkness with his trophy.

"Mystic, Initiating now," Stan Kirby growled. He lay in a low "trench" he'd reinforced with boulders and sand, because he was about to poke the ripper. All other things being equal, a two-meter-tall man needed a deeper trench, and he was deep enough

into the forest he was hitting rock a bare meter down. His trio had bumped, sniped and drawn one of the platoons deeper and deeper into the woods, away from their comrades. This part of the forest had thick overhead coverage and relatively little ground cover, allowing for much longer engagement ranges. Three hundred meters south, the heavy assault armor was conspicuously tall and glowed bright under thermal vision, despite their active camouflage system. The UN wasn't used to fighting enemies of a comparable tech level, and still thought of the Freeholders as backward, barely civilized colonists, despite a year of combat proving otherwise. The handlers had soaked their leathers, further dampening their own thermal signature, wore ghillie netting, and used terrain and cover to stay out of sight. Stan took a deep breath, let it half out, then fired off five quick shots at the power armor, riding the impact of the powerful 8.6mm M8 rifle against his shoulder. He didn't need to kill the armor—he just needed them to look his way. The suits immediately turned to respond, hosing his position with bursts of machine-gun fire. Rounds sparked off the heavy rock fortifications he'd laid out as he slipped back into the ravine behind him.

"Royal, green," Dixie heard Tom Prince update.

"Doc, green-two-one," she replied, and squeezed the trigger on her rifle just as Tom did the same. While Stan weathered the assault suits' answering fusillade, his teammates had an unobstructed view of the *rear* of two of the suits, each glowing hot in their goggle overlays. Each handler sent eight thousand joules of brute force downrange, smashing into the conspicuous domes between the jump-jet turbines, cracking the armor of the capacitors and penetrating the volatile metals inside. Twin chemical fires immolated Arnolds and Jensen while Dixie slipped away to another fighting position. They'd chosen this part of the forest for its numerous creek beds and shallow ravines, allowing them to move around invisibly.

Chaos and panic filled the forest with terrified screams behind her and she paused, her enhanced hearing telling her the story. At first, she thought it was these ill-disciplined troops panicking, but there were snarls and hisses of cats in the mix. Bagheera and Khan were at her heels, but the two young ferals were gone. She heard one sustained burst of machine-gun fire, then another. As the gunshots echoed and faded, moans of injured UN troops wafted through the trees. Then someone cursed.

"Mierda. *Fox Six, this is Fox Three Five, uh, sitrep, over.*"

Dixie listened for a moment as some young idiot updated aloud that the two natural-born leopards had taken out the platoon commander and five more troops before they'd been killed. More importantly, additional suits were inbound. She slipped away south, ready for their inevitable retreat.

Lieutenant Randhawa was pissed. Pandis and Norris had abandoned them to back up Three Platoon, leaving his ass hanging in the breeze. Without the suits and the incessant whine of their musculature, the night was suddenly very quiet. He heard a distant exchange of gunfire and explosions, but they were far away and then the shots echoed to nothing. There were no birds, no bugs, no wind, nothing.

Reddy's status indicator blinked from green to gray.

How...?

He'd just checked on the young corporal, twenty meters away, not three minutes ago. He'd heard nothing. He gestured to the weapons section commander to get his attention, pointed and motioned for them to get moving. They crept through the shadows and the tall grasses, but couldn't see Reddy anywhere. Randhawa switched from starlight to thermal, and blanched when he realized there was hot blood splatter all over the grasses to their front. A meter from his feet was *another* severed forearm.

There was a strangled cry from the far end of the platoon's position, which abruptly stopped when Goswami's indicator blinked out as well. Staccato gunfire followed the scream, and then a female voice shouted.

"I got it! I—"

Randhawa heard the muted cough and hiss of a suppressed pistol round sizzle through the air. It put a stop to Sergeant Chaudhry's brief moment of victory, destroying what little morale his platoon had gained by killing one of the leopards. Chaudhry's section blindly fired into the dark, and as Randhawa joined them on the line, he scanned the forest in starlight and thermal.

Nothing.

The insurgents were *invisible*.

Three members of Two Squad turned tail, and ran. Sergeant

First Class Sharif made to chase after them, but Randhawa ordered him to stay put. They hadn't made it fifty meters before Deol's indicator turned gray. Singh's turned yellow, and Malhotra's went gray as well. In the distance, Randhawa heard Singh's wailing cry of agony. He screamed, and was abruptly cut off.

"No one runs!" Randhawa ordered. "Do you hear what happens to cowards who run? *No one runs.*"

2 Divs / 5 Hours, 40 Minutes After Local Midnight

Three dead leopards, a dozen missing or mutilated troops, multiple Special Units killed in action, and how the Grainneans had managed *that*, he still didn't know. The platoons were kilometers apart, so far from each other they may as well have been by themselves. Castle felt a head rush like he'd stood up too fast—*that had been their plan all along, those bastards.*

"All callsigns this is Fox Six Actual. Fall back," Castle ordered. "Special Units, return to your assigned platoons and escort their withdrawal. Regroup here," he said as he dropped a pin on the AOR map. "Bring it in."

"*Roger that, sir,*" Master Sergeant Pandis answered. "*Be advised, we're bingo on fuel though, sir, we've got enough to make it back to base and not much more.*"

"I don't care right now if you make it back to base, Petra, because at this rate *none of us are*," the captain snarled. They were supposed to be the QRF for the region. Rockville had been quiet, more or less, for the entire duration of their tour. And now . . . *this*. This colossal donkey-humping clusterfuck would end Castle's career, guaranteed.

If they could just escape this death trap, he could call in an Avatar fire mission and drop incendiaries on the whole accursed forest, which, in retrospect, he should have done in the first place. Of course, for that level of destruction, he would have to call in local xenoarborists and the envirogeeks to do a proper environmental impact statement, ensure the ensuring firestorm wouldn't endanger anything protected, that it wouldn't put undue risk on the civilian population in case the winds shifted . . .

The admin *still* would have been worth it.

A trio of Guardians roared overhead, and Castle sighed with relief. He hadn't expected backup, but he wasn't about to question it, either. He cued up the emergency channel on his comm and hit the transmit button.

"Guardian flight, this is Fox Six Actual, I need overwatch and ground support, and I need it three hours ago. Sending grid coordinates now, how do you copy?"

"Roger, Fox Six, we'll be landing at the airfac, you wanna send up a flare?" the replying voice answered.

"Will do, Guardian, thanks!" Castle said, digging a pen flare projector out of his harness. He puzzled out the mechanism, loaded it, and fired a shooting star high into the sky above his position.

"Don't mention it," the crewman replied. *"We copy your flare, we'll come find you."*

Cowards, Stan Kirby thought to himself. "Mystic, I've got suits covering the platoon's retreat, heading southeast," he said over his comm. "Looks like they're taking their ball and going home. I'm green for a shot if I can get a second."

"Royal's up," Tom Prince sent back. *"I'm green on the one to the east."*

"Viking, take it," Bill whispered. *"If we push now, they shatter."*

"Mystic green-two-one," Kirby replied, and squeezed the trigger on his M8.

In his suit, Mauser stunk of sweat and fear. He'd originally signed up as a line infantry thug, which was a pretty solid resume builder to join a law enforcement group back home. He loved shooting machine guns and blowing shit up, but the walking and digging thing was bullcrap. Special Units had assault armor, *they* didn't have to dig, and that was guaranteed to land him a spot with the choicest departments back home. He'd fought hard to join a Special Unit. He wanted to be in the heaviest armor where he'd be safest, if they were going to send him to the goddamn Freehold to fight. It had been a good plan, right up until tonight. Another salvo of armor-piercing rounds shattered Ross and Sylvestre's power sources, penetrating the capacitors and turning the suits incandescent.

Caution abandoned, Mauser fled.

Stan Kirby was rather pleased. The suit he'd hit triggered his external loudhailer as he died. The SUQR's screams were macabre, echoing through the trees at a hundred and forty decibels. The fiery pyre broke the aardvark's will to fight, and terrified troops tucked tail and ran. He had to slide his goggles up; the thermal bloom rendered them temporarily useless. The fleeing soldiers dumped the litters carrying their wounded and threw away their rifles. They tripped over logs, rocks, and fell facedown into the creek beds and ravines that cut through the forest carrying icy snow melt from the Dragontooth Mountains.

"Fight!" Stan bellowed to his cats as he broke cover.

Rasputin and Merlin led a feral along the arboreal highway, leaping from stout branch to stout branch. Theirs was a stern chase, racing southbound from Kirby's hide, but the cats were far faster in the trees than humans were on the ground. Merlin leapt down on one soldier, grabbing him by the base of his skull, whipsawing past him. The impact broke the soldier's neck and flung the limp body off into the brush. Rasputin crushed a soldier to the forest floor, raking him with his claws and tearing him to shreds.

Stan loped south, a hulking wraith between the trees. He was five kilometers deep into the woods, and had no doubt they'd catch the fleeing soldiers. In all the time they'd spent spying on the base, not once did anyone see the UN troops out for a run.

More screams ahead. The cats were tightening the noose. Rasputin, Merlin and the feral drove them forward. Tom's cats, Scout, Apache, and two more ferals flanked them on one side, Dixie, Bagheera and Khan flanked the other. The slowest of them died, one by one.

To the east, Risa Leifman and Helena Christiansen opened fire on the densely packed members of Two Platoon. Two volleys later, Randhawa's platoon broke and fled as well. Machinegun fire stitched their hide, sending them scrambling for cover. Leifman slithered into one of the well-camouflaged fighting pits they'd prepared throughout the area, while Christiansen rolled into a ravine and turned her rifle to spot the just-arriving suits. *Oh well, why not?*

She centered the scope reticle on the feed cover for the machine gun and squeezed. The heavy rifle round tore into the mechanism and the weapon was instantly ruined. She watched the SUQR study the weapon dumbly, before he turned and ran. Next to her,

Risa emptied a full magazine into the second armored suit, riding the recoil as she pounded it with rapid fire. She reloaded as her target fled, but the suit was still visible in thermal when she chambered her next round. She found the weak point, squeezed, missed, reacquired, squeezed, and saw the round spark off the armor, but with no further effect.

"Kismet," Dante calls, "time to hunt."

We have been patient. We have remained quiet, hidden, as the host of prey passed by. I hear Guns boom, and the panicked screams of frightened prey. I heard the rush of leaves and brush as the enemy flees.

Patience is the tool of the hunter.

This enemy is many, they have Guns. They are the single greatest threat I have seen since the Great Hunt began. Akuma, Ingwe, Xanadu and I are all far up the trees, so high the prey below never suspect us. We work our way down through the branches of the pillar trees until we are low enough to jump. Xanadu and Ingwe go wide, to better corral the prey. Akuma and I wait.

Xanadu snarls, and a few gunshots reply, but she is tiny, well hidden, protected. For one so small, she is an excellent hunter and the frightened prey flees directly toward us. They are clumsy, fleeing through the brush, crashing through thicket and bush and branches. They never once look up. It is too easy.

Now.

Ingwe leaps on the slowest from behind. Akuma and I pounce from above. One carries a machine Gun; he is the greatest threat, but he collapses as I land on his chest and shoulders. My hind paws slash downwards, tearing through his armor and harness. His throat is exposed beneath his helmet and I tear it out and bounce clear as he bleeds out in the dirt. There are more, another one runs past me and I race after him, up and over branches, under logs, through the ferns and grass. The enemy cannot run for long and mere moments have passed before this one stops to lean against a tree to breathe. He gasps like a winded deer, until I crunch his neck bones between my teeth.

I lick my lips, taste the air, and my ears twitch. Sounds of chaos reign all around me, but we hunt as a pride and I need to rejoin mine. I claw my way back up into the trees to get a better vantage. The prey wear helmets, and almost never look up.

Snapping branches and rustling grass indicates movement to my left. I can taste Akuma's, Ingwe's and Xanadu's scents nearby, and we move toward the enemy, silent as shadow and invisible as the wind. Below us, Dante follows. Even he knows we are the better hunters, he is there to cover for us; we are there to hunt.

More enemy follow a dry creek bed as deep as a man is tall. I take the last one in line, slashing his hamstring and tearing out his guts. I jump onto a fallen tree, race up the log, then off into open air to come down on the next prey from above. He still has his Gun, so I bite down on his Gun hand and he screams. *Sloppy.* Screams are better than gunshots though, and I drag him down and rake his chest with my claws. Akuma races past me, a whisper of black in the shadows, and kills the next. He catches another tall prey by the head and flings the body into his partner, knocking him down. I kill another before he can regain his feet, and then we're running again. Xanadu and Ingwe are still up in the trees and the whine of the armored suits is closing in fast. I turn and flee down the creek bed, staying below the line where the suit can see me until I round several bends. Then I'm up into the bushes and away.

2.25 Divs / 6 Hours, 20 Minutes After Local Midnight

Captain Castle and most of One Platoon waited at the tree line. Sergeant First Class Sharif limped into view, and collapsed against a tree, breathing hard. Behind him, Master Sergeant Pandis and Senior Corporal Norris crashed through the brush in their armor.

"You took your sweet time, Pandis," Castle growled.

"We're all that's coming, *sir,*" Pandis said, failing to keep the contempt out of her voice. "I am *out of juice.* I need to exit my armor *now* or I'll be deadlined and trapped."

"I'm about out too," Norris said. "Another minute, maybe two, and my weapons are wrecked."

"God DAMN it," Castle shouted, "FINE!" He turned to his comm and stared at it for a moment. "Guardian flight, Guardian flight, this is Fox Six, where is that cover I ordered?"

"We're shaking out now, Fox Six, we'll meet you at the tree line."

The two Special Unit troopers disengaged their armor next to Lundgren's, already abandoned. E&E packs on the legs of their suits held carbines, knives and helmets. They took up position watching the forest for threats and friendlies. Castle checked his map and saw it was littered with immobile beacons scattered through the woods in two long lines, converging on his location. A handful of soldiers from Joachim's platoon were on the move, and they were less than a hundred meters away.

"Royal, in final position," Prince sent. *"I'm green, eyes on the SUQR with the beard."*

"Viking is green as well, tall blonde bastard," Michaelson whispered back. "Sitrep all."

"Inferno," Dante said, *"Red, I've got the airfac but that's all. Have eyes on three new Guardians unassing troops. Step it up."*

"Myrmidon and Titan, just in position now," Helena said. *"Red."*

"Doc's here," Dixie said. *"Red, no shot, they're not where we thought they'd be. I confirm a hundred or more troops. Some are heading into the base, not this way. Gunfire."*

"Mystic, half a seg until green," Stan Kirby whispered.

"We'll go with three then." Bill replied. "Mystic calls it."

Bill Michaelson had just made the most difficult stalk of his life. The two teams of handlers had drawn the platoons off in opposite directions, allowing him to sneak past the "front line" with all five of his cats—Dutch, Capstick, Freya, Odin, and Thor. The UN didn't think of forest fighting and close terrain as being a 3D battlefield like urban operations, but leopards did. He'd crossed the last fifty meters high above the forest floor, moving quietly from branch to branch. The pillar trees had thick, stout limbs that interwove like ancient steel trusses, and Bill had picked up a pair of climbing *tekagi-shuko* during an exchange with the Hirohito special forces several lifetimes ago. That part of the stalk took nearly forty segs, but the gambit worked.

Below Michaelson, Stan Kirby, Rasputin and Merlin slipped through the grass. They were close enough to hear one of the UN officers having a temper tantrum, jacking up one of his troops for having lost his rifle while fleeing for his life.

"Green—" Kirby whispered. For the first time in months, he triggered his CNS implant and rode the euphoric wave. *"Five-four-three-two-one..."*

One SUQR's head came apart on cue in a spray that splashed hot in Kirby's thermal overlay.

High above him, he heard the boom of Bill's unsuppressed Peregrine and the second SUQR dropped like a pithed frog. Kirby rushed from the undergrowth, *kataghan* in one hand, pistol in the other. He put a trio of shots into the last SUQR's chest—he recognized her, she'd been on the Mtali mission with Ken—but then the tide of battle carried him away. He hacked down another soldier and leapt to carve a bloody hole through the heart of One Platoon. Rasputin and Merlin crashed the line with him, and the surviving UN troops turned, running for their lives. Above him, Bill's cats, annoyed that they'd been denied the joy of the hunt until now, leapt down to finally get their slaughter on.

Bill swung down like a gymnast and tumbled to the ground, rolling to his feet with his langseax in hand. He started hacking down fleeing aardvarks and fired until his pistol was empty. He holstered it with the slide to the rear and hamstrung a fleeing soldier who collapsed, screaming in the dirt. With no targets in immediate reach, he slid a fresh magazine into the butt of the holstered pistol, drawing it and thumbing the slide release. Odin sprang from a bush to his right and tackled a soldier he hadn't seen. Freya tackled another fleeing aardvark, breaking his neck, and he passed Thor who was muzzle deep in an enemy's chest cavity. Bill met Stan in the middle and they fought their way through the woods for a hundred meters, killing every UN soldier they saw until they separated again. The loudmouth asshole officer had been the first to run and Bill wanted his head on a pike. He caught a flash of movement ahead and a pair of high-intensity flashlights shattered the darkness. He dove behind a tanglewood bush and crawled for cover, listening and catching his breath. Capstick and Dutch were by his side, covering his flanks. The flashlights were mounted on rifles, and the rifles weren't pointed at him. A strange voice ordered a surviving UN soldier's hands up, and Bill heard the ratcheting of binders being snapped on.

"Viking? It's Hammer! Hope you've been taking good care of Dutch for me!" a booming voice shouted. At Bill's side, Dutch crept forwards a couple short steps, then dashed away and Bill heard his old squad commander laughing.

"This is Viking," Bill said over his comm. "The Guardians are delivering friendlies, again, they're *friendlies*. Bring it in."

Bill was still buzzing from the CNS boost when he emerged

from the brush with his hands raised. "Viking's here, Hammer," he declared. He moved into the open and saw Joe Carpender kneeling as Dutch headbutted him and nuzzled his chest.

"Hey, boyo, how've you been? You still running around with this old man?" Joe asked his former partner, smiling widely.

"Says the crusty old *retired* recruit instructor," Bill said. "You'll have to excuse me, but my troops and I just took out a company of aardvarks, I'm still high on CNS, and where did you come across a company of infantry? *Ques-ce que fuck?*"

"Give a crusty old retired recruit *instructor* some credit," Joe retorted. "I spent four years teaching handlers how to cat, and two more teaching maggots how to soldier. Retirement didn't suit me."

Carpender nodded to Kirby and Rasputin as they approached, and sent the rest of the Freehold militia troops to press the attack at the base itself. The resistance was minimal, but there were a *lot* of noncombatants to account for. Prince, Christiansen, Leifman and Dixie trickled in with their partners, Neumeier joining them last.

"I have orders, *Warrant Leader* Michaelson, to ensure your good deeds here don't go unpunished. We're taking you home to Jefferson area at Naumann's personal request, he has a valley full of aardvarks to flood and Winters's team was Plan A. Now it's *your* problem. My Coastal Independents will handle mopping up from here, you've got a flight to catch."

■   ■   ■

Huff #21
Rules of Engagement [Late March 211]

"We don't waterboard." I tried to drive this home.

"Well, not officially."

"No, we don't. At all." This was when I hated the J2 folks most of all. What if they really are, but hiding it from me? I wouldn't put it past that bitch to try and manipulate me into giving tacit approval of such things without realizing what I'd done.

"But when you need answers in a hurry..."

"We tried it once." This stuffed shirt was quibbling about how I ran *my* command. You really don't get how much this stuff doesn't work in the real world, do you? Especially when you've forced us to play half-assed, but they're full throttle.

"And?"

I'd like to wipe that smug look off his face. Baldy held a look of barely controlled contempt. "Do you really want to know? The next day they released two prisoners."

"Well...that's good, isn't it?"

He's getting a little nervous. Good, he should be. "The prisoners told us they'd been 'boarded, cloth over mouth and nose, eyes exposed. Then—then! They were used as the unit urinal for a full day. They were 'urine boarded.' They're still tranq'd, in therapy, and we're afraid to send them home in case they ruin morale among the rest, or go public."

He looked properly horrified. "So, what do we do, then?"

"We don't become grotesque ourselves, no matter how tempting. We don't interrogate. We'll go through the motions of trying to get information, but none of them know anything outside their own group. They mainly use a cell structure, classic guerilla warfare, but the reason that's been around for so long, is how effectively that protects OPSEC. So, what they tell us is mostly irrelevant, and by the time we get to a named location, they've all unassed."

"No names?"

"Never." Not one. We've tried.

"Have you tried other encouragement?"

"Same thing. We had a couple of interrogators rough a detainee up. The next day, the rebels gave us the location of a doctor's office where another four captives were held, for exchange."

"Roughed up worse?"

That's one way to put it. "They were restrained, hyped up on stims. Then, the bastards worked two of them over with hammers from toe to knee, millimeter by millimeter. Up to the patella, they were literally pounded to flat goo. Those two are in regen. The other two had to watch. They were force fed 'go pills,' and will be staying with Emotional Health for a long time. We're also trying to keep that story quiet, but the rumor mill is persistent."

"So, nothing?"

"This is . . . very old-fashioned, do you understand? Have you ever heard of a twentieth-century Irishman named Michael Collins? Maybe Carlos Marighella in Brazil? Or, my personal favorite, the Stern Gang, the *Lehi*, in Palestine? This is right up there in that level of spite and contempt, and evil."

"I'm not following you, General."

I struggled to hold my bearing, because if I lost patience here, it could be the end of me. "Look, whatever we do, they're ten times worse. They've got a standing assassination order on flag officers and generals! You saw what happened to me! They've got hits out on several bureaucrats. They murder cooks in the field. They've had their animals eat our casualties. Military-trained leopards! They've made it more terrifying to be support than a combatant. Nothing that I, nor the officers, nor the senior NCOs say to the troops can counteract that. No one here has *ever* encountered anything like that. It's brilliant in execution. Thus far, there is no line they won't cross, and if there is, I don't want to find it."

I thought about one of the latest patrol PARs briefed to me at the RC Commanders Conference. A forward observation base practically empties itself out with a full-blown reconnaissance-in-force. The commander decided he'd had enough of the harassment, the sniping, the probing attacks, drones, hacking, and PSYOP material, so he decided to smoke out the insurgents, to try and funnel them into open battle. While he and his combat command are away, the base is completely overrun. The enemy decides the REMFs all look better with only one arm apiece, courtesy of bladed weapons. They took the arms, preventing reattachment. Entire unit in regen treatment. This now-former commander's recon expedition accomplished fuck all.

The toady broke my reverie. "But casualties are reported to be quite low now. Lower than early on."

Yes, and I'll tell you why. "That's not because of pacification. That's us keeping our heads low and avoiding contact. I don't want to escalate this to a point where I can't follow through, because then we cease being human. I'm not ready to throw our dignity in the toilet."

"General, listen carefully. They must accept UN control. There is no debate on this point. It has to happen in the next year, before the election gets underway. They must be pacified."

"They're more effective all the time. I'm hamstrung on budget and means."

"Means are open now, as long as they are discreet."

"Discretion? That's not possible anymore. Their intel apparatus is at least as effective as ours, enhanced by tens of thousands of sympathetic HUMINT reporters. That, and they sniff out and kill our collaborators in spectacular fashion."

"Then what do you propose?"

I only wish I had the right answer. "Don't escalate. Resupply me, arm me with heavier forces. I won't play dirty pool though. We're too outclassed in that department and we're still recovering from the last time you sold me a 'nonlethal' bill of goods."

"There was no way to know how virulent those infectio—"

"Do *not* lie to me!" I reached the limits of my professionalism. Dial it back, Jacob, now! "I've seen the preliminary research and the early field tests. The whole *system* has seen those reports. You and your Dr. Phillipi knew exactly what those agents would do to vulnerable populations before implementation."

"It was only supposed to make them feel like hell for a while, keep their heads down long enough for us to regroup. Maybe convince them to let us provide some humanitarian aid. We had to pacify them."

"Well, what it did was set us up for our own potential Nuremberg. A bioweapon offensive on combatants, even terrorists, could be forgiven. That's war. But this?" My hands trembled with barely controlled rage. I threw some pictures on my desk, hard copies I'd kept from the data flood, of small bodies stacked in barns, waiting for burial. "These are children. Innocents. We can never take that back. If we're going to kill people, let's at least do it honorably, on a battlefield."

He breathed deeply, staring at the pictures, avoiding eye contact with me. He knew I was right. "Very well, General. I'll support your request."

Bonita was waiting for me. I didn't dare tell her anything, just in case. But I needed company in the worst way.

Force Majeure
Part 8

It was yet another staff briefing aboard FMS *Force*. Warrant Coffman and Mister Umair were present.

Yates told them, "Please go ahead."

Coffman said, "Thank you, Captain, and you also, Fabrication Commander. With no motive at all, I'd like to thank you and your crew for the most dedicated and righteous production I've ever heard of. Utterly brilliant and awe inspiring. Our mission is ready for its next step, which honestly we weren't positive of. We'd expected at least fifty percent, would have been ecstatic at seventy, we're at ninety-five percent only due to a material shortage, and Commander Karanov says even that may be resolved in time."

"We thank you. Hopefully this matters.

"With all that said, our next step involves delivering the munitions. We were told it is possible, and to ask if you can make a kinetic pass in system? This would involve three steps."

That was a big jump. From fabrication to delivery platform.

"I see. Explain away. We'll take notes."

"First, drop your boats with supplies to be delivered to our forces. Second, proceed in-system with the best concealment your experts and we can devise. Additional protection would involve decoys, which will also be used as distractions close to Grainne orbit. En route, our payloads would be separated to find their own destinations. Third would involve gravel saturation of several orbitals—just dumping some of your silicates, iron or tungsten. Fourth would be dropping anything left supply wise to burn in reentry over the continent. We can estimate an impact zone, but it's more useful there than here."

It took time to process all that. Yates had silence while he did so.

Finally, he replied, "That's an extensive operation."

"It is."

"I don't see how we can stealth this ship that much."

"Likely not. Your crew know more about that than we do."

"Where does that leave us after the event, other than empty, low on fuel, zipping out of the gravity well with maneuvering margin only?"

"That's what it leaves, sir."

"With no plans for recovery?"

"Sir, this is a single massive counterattack. I don't have all the details, but I know the intent is that the UN is going to be hit massively. Everything they have in-system, and some outside, all have elements aligned. Even if we're only half successful, they'll be bleeding bad. Even a quarter is enough to change the entire dynamic of the war from occupation back to conflict. The intent is they can't fight beyond that."

Very good, he thought, *if* it works, but... "That doesn't solve my fuel problem."

"No, sir. The intention and hope is that there will be elements able to assist in recovery of the crew at least. Obviously, a valuable asset like this should be saved as well. But mission first, crew second, craft third."

It didn't take much thinking out loud to lay it all out. "Morally I don't have a choice. If this will further the war, and you say it will, backed up by Space and Ground Commands, then yes, we'll do what we can. Also morally, I am very reluctant to waste my crew on a possibility, but without information I can't get even if you have it, that's a matter of trust. Technically, I have no idea if this is possible. I suppose my astrogators, hull and sensor specialists, engineer and dock techs need to discuss it."

Coffman seemed to relax fractionally.

"Thank you very much, sir."

"I suppose we must schedule that conference. What is your time frame?"

"It doesn't have to be today, but sooner is better. There may be modifications necessary."

"Modifications?"

"Sir, with respect, I'd prefer not to run through it all multiple times. You'll be present and we need your support. It won't be behind you."

"Fair enough. I'll schedule it."

Yates really wanted the details of the mission, and he scheduled the conference for the next morning. He considered that the refusal to discuss it otherwise might have been a prompt. If so, it wasn't an issue. This was a war. Time was a resource.

The conference room was spartan at this point. Everything

that could be stripped for material or crew use had been. The table was a sheet of polymer with dogs for comms to mount. The chairs were standard extrusions from their own production, possibly made this morning and to be recycled immediately. There was good cocoa, and a tray of pastries and sausages from the mess. It reminded him of the stripped down nothing at Space Base.

It was almost amusing the way they all converged within a few seconds. Yates waved them in, then followed.

The discussion included Yates, Brody, Karanov and her operations officer Kaciri, both senior astrogators, Engineer Anderson, and Tactical Officer Rievley. He hoped that was enough, and he'd call for more if he had to.

"Gentlemen, the floor is yours."

Coffman stood carefully in the low G. At his height, standing up fast might possibly cause hydraulic issues with his circulation.

"I can't thank you all enough, once again, for getting us this far. You've built the weapons we needed. The reason all the work was done here was to simplify delivery. In other words, we hope you can make a high-speed in-system pass and deploy them en route."

"I wondered if we were coming to that," Yates replied. He waited a few seconds, glanced at key people, and said, "We'll need more details."

He assumed the request was technical, not permissive. If the ship could do it and he refused, they probably could get a call in to have him relieved. However, if it wasn't at least as safe as some of their more desperate recent maneuvers, he'd have to consider the validity of the proposal.

Umair fingered his comm and said, "I have released the summary profile. We thrust against orbit, then directly in-system, to achieve a cometary trajectory straight down. This keeps the thrust as shielded as possible. Run silent, deploy munitions in set places as we go. Those will activate on delay, which draws attention to them, but not immediately to us. It's a close-in hyperbolic past Grainne, dropping all available finished materials to the surface, dropping kinetics against certain orbital material and other targets. Then back out the other way."

It sounded straightforward. The math was going to be lengthy, but wasn't that complicated. It was straight orbital mechanics plus delta V.

He took the lead.

"I would like any objections first. I don't see an astrogation problem. Farana?"

"Lots of problems, but all calculable, sir. We can do it."

"Structural issues, Commander Anderson?"

"I can't think of any. It's less strain than a lot of our maneuvers have been."

"Sensors?"

Rievley offered, "I see several elements relevant to us. I understand the boost profile to minimize energy signature. However, once we're dropping loads, those trajectories can be calculated, and shortly, that leads to us. Exactly how they found *Malahayati*, but we'll be giving them more signatures to work with, and we're not a warship for either thrust or weapons. Then, I assume we can't stray much from the groove. I don't see how they won't locate us. I can't say if they'll have time to do anything—they'd have to match vectors. Though they can easily toss mass in front of us."

Coffman started to speak, but Yates raised his hand. "One moment. Fabrication?"

Karanov said, "Well, we managed to dampen *Hate*'s signature. We stealthed the gunboat. We can probably do something to ourselves."

"Very well. Warrant Coffman?"

He grinned and shook his head. "Nothing, sir, Commander Karanov has addressed my point."

"Very well. Do you have any kind of estimate of our odds of survival?"

The man shook his head. "None at all, sir. I can't offer anything. I'm sorry. The awkward point there, too, is that we won't be aboard."

"Oh? That is a bit awkward. Where will you be?"

"On a small craft, conducting a raid. Our odds of success are pretty good. Of surviving and being recovered ... are lower."

There was silence.

Yates inhaled and said, "I see. You did say this is a major push on a lot of fronts."

"I can say that. I don't know much more. It's supposed to be significant, and most units aren't being informed until go time."

He wondered about that. "That doesn't seem wise."

"Commander Naumann says the units who need to move or know are advised. The ones in place are in place for a reason, and will know what to do when the shooting starts."

"Fair enough, with the little we know." He turned. "Exec, am I missing anything?"

Brody said, "No, sir, we have a profile we can meet, reasonable odds of harming the enemy, and the means to do so. Beyond that we don't know, but it's a war. That's what we're here for."

He turned back. "Gentlemen, it appears we can support the mission. If I may ask, though, which unit are you from?"

The two of them stared at each other for a moment.

Umair looked back. "Sir, we're instructors from the Special Warfare, Special Projects School. We teach unconventional fabrication of everything from false identification and lock cracking to—"

He cut in with, "To field-improvised fission warheads and high-velocity space drives."

"Yes, sir."

"I'm very impressed. If you'll give us the information you have, we'll start planning and fabrication. Staff, of course, everything here is need to know. Specifically, I don't want the crew worrying over odds we can't calculate. Let's get to it."

Astrogation had an updated solution for boosting, and earlier was better, with increased odds of avoiding detection. As soon as that was confirmed, he had them thrust.

"Warn the crew and boost on schedule."

"Aye, sir."

The first maneuver was very short and low G. There really wasn't much to it at all. Their orbital velocity was tiny, and this was more an astrogation correction than a real maneuver. In close to Iota Persei, they'd have dropped like a rock. Out here, grav-only acceleration would take weeks to be relevant.

The ship precessed on maneuvering thrust on all three axes, pointed near enough directly in-system at this distance, and drive power increased. It was definitely present, but not significant yet.

It was time for that announcement.

"All hands, routine message from the captain, though this is a bit more than routine." He waited a few moments for everyone to be attentive.

"You are all aware we are under low boost. Our intent is to reach a particular velocity with minimal signature. Our trajectory will take us in-system, then back out, where we should be recovered by *Sleipnir.*" He hoped.

"In between, we will be releasing the entire remainder of our production cargo, attempting to deliver it where needed. This is why much of our own structure has been utilized for material. We are advised that the war may end shortly thereafter due to a concentration of power.

"While this crew has had its share of morale and discipline problems since this began, those have not diminished our accomplishments. Every member of this crew, even those of you I've had to address on these matters, has performed their duties beyond the highest expectations. The ship has already been decorated. I hope when this does conclude that you can all be properly individually recognized for your performance.

"With thanks and congratulations to you all, Captain Yates out."

They were on standard watch, off the frantic production schedule, until the end of this operation. He had no idea what to do with actual free time in his command schedule.

He decided he'd start with a hot shower.

On max tempo, the work was done in a week. Engines for one payload had to be stripped from a lifeboat, then there was a heated discussion over a second. Yates relented when Fabrication said they could build a short-range engine that would be good enough for near space around Grainne, just enough to put it on the ground. He ordered an extra for good measure.

He did not want to reach a point where bailout was necessary and there weren't enough seats. He would stay with the ship if he had to. He wasn't going to order his officers to do so if it was at all avoidable.

The trip in-system would take fourteen days, but their velocity built early. Their exposure should be minimized.

Force Majeure
Part 9

Before May 211

FMS *Force*, encased in vacgel fluff that so far kept her undetected and near invisible, was within visual range of Grainne
and Gealach. Ahead were multiple UNPF targets. Inside the one
exposed dock lock were multiple warheads, vessels and masses.
It was her turn to engage as a combatant, starting now.

Coffman and Umair, suited up, were ready to board one of
the boats. Yates caught up to them before departure.

"I'm glad we could help, and hope it works to best effect," he
said, offering his hand. "I hope we can meet when this is all over."

Coffman paused and blinked, then said, "Thank you, sir. And
you. Please relay it to your officers and crew."

Umair shook hands, and they both turned for the hatch to
the dock.

As they left, Yates realized what that hesitation of Coffman's
had meant.

They weren't expecting to meet up afterward.

Yates fingered his display and adjusted his mic.

"All hands, routine message from the captain. We are commencing the actual operation now. Regardless of the outcome, it
has been a privilege and a pleasure to serve aboard *Force* with
this crew. In the names of all our spirits and deities, may we
be blessed."

The next div would decide it all. If their track was still discreet,
they'd drop cargo, avoid any detection, and be through, free of
any pursuit. Less ideal was avoiding any weapon intercept but
being captured. Below that was destruction while accomplishing
the drop. At the bottom...

There was nothing anyone could do at this point. Any notice
of trouble wouldn't arrive more than moments before the event.

Success, or vapor. Though neither guaranteed a victory. Nor
could he estimate without knowing what was where, who was
what, and how it would be used.

Astrogators Farana and Mathews were both on the deck, Mathews in the couch normally used by Commo, since there was no reason to communicate before this concluded. This allowed backup and cross-checking. Helm was crewed, but it was almost certain that if any course changes were made it would be directly from Astrogation. Sensor Engineer Bates was seated, but under the circumstances was likely unable to receive anything useful or offer input they could act on. However, the possibility existed, so it was covered. Tactical Officer Lieutenant Rievley was adjoining Sensors in case they needed analysis.

Yates had no real task other than to approve or disapprove a necessary variation that would take a matter of seconds. He had no reason to second-guess his astrogators. They were more recent on practice and had the data ongoing. He was unlikely to counter any maneuver they came up with.

There was no physical sensation of anything. They boosted at low G, at a very high speed, along their chosen trajectory, in complete placidity.

Farana said, "Sir, as you can see on clock, we're about to commence."

"I have no supplemental orders. Proceed."

"Aye, sir."

Clatters and thumps indicated launches and releases from docking clamps. Faint shoves against the ship marked mass changes as the payloads departed. In seconds, every item of their entire cargo on hand was in its own trajectory, and their fabricated warheads aimed at a good chunk of the Freehold's own hijacked infrastructure.

The fabrication vessel was now a warship.

The most under-armored, complicated, over-equipped warship ever improvised, he thought.

Farana crowed, "In the groove! All drops complete at our end."

How many would survive to the surface and their targets he couldn't know. But their mission was accomplished.

He offered a thought for the two technicians, and hoped either his interpretation was wrong, or the tactical calculations at the other end were wrong in their favor.

Now *Force* had to survive.

"Reactors to minimum, sensors passive only, decouple all other external antennae as a precaution."

Engineer Anderson confirmed. "We're dark," he said.

"Crew to standard underway shifts. They've earned a break."

The payloads needed enough velocity to arrive on schedule, using minimal maneuver thrust for low signature. That meant *Force* was moving fast in the same cone, and had limited maneuver options. Doing nothing on a ballistic course was their safest bet.

Four days later they and their devices entered the immediate area around Grainne. Everything was within a few million kilometers.

Now they had to keep an eye out.

"Sensors, report." Every div was a dedicated check, with tactical staff alert for any craft changing trajectory or appearing to respond.

Bates was a specialist in low-order signatures and residue. She was following tiny variances in output, reflection, emission.

She noted, "Lots of activity, sir. Active scans, multiple craft."

Rievley said, "Sorting. Few capable of pursuit or launch solution. Local volume is clear. Medium range is unrefined. They seem aware of the existence of the attack. I can't determine to what degree."

He then added, "Refining. UNS *Lagos*, hull 419. Breaking orbit and attempting to pursue."

"Advise me on envelope and options. Can we run?"

"That will quickly get into fuel limitations, sir, hold on, please." He fingered his controls and ran figures, which he dumped to Yates and Farana.

"She can intercept. It's going to take her a couple of weeks, but she'll match us easily at that boost."

"Understood."

"Sir, our only survival options are surrender or run. If we run, we can't boost enough Gs, dump enough mass. Even if we try, we're dependent on recovery, and it's going to take weeks and a lot of power for anyone to get us. We can eventually make it to Jump Point Three, but if we don't own it then, we're a target on approach. With her chasing. If we surrender...that's your call on how we might be treated."

Neither option was pleasant.

He noted, "Before the attack, we might have managed fair treatment. Conducting a military attack and attempting to surrender before the smoke clears...is usually not received well."

"However," he continued. "I gave this some thought. When they contact us, we'll stall until they sound serious, like last time. Then, we'll pretend the crew has taken over, and is gradually bringing us back around. We'll start feeding them a list of emergency supplies we need for survival, make them split their resources, and hope for a good outcome for our forces. If not, we'll abandon ship in the boats we have as close to Grainne as we can risk, land, and go to ground. That buys us time, harasses the enemy, and gives us a potential bolt-hole."

"Very good, sir. I'll bring Mati up and we'll coordinate with your orders."

The stern chase by UNS *Lagos* started exactly as predicted.

"*Hostile craft, you are identified as a probable combatant and ordered to stand down at once. Your vessel is engaged in illegal combat operations against the UN government in UN space. All officers will consider themselves under arrest, charged with piracy and terrorism.*"

Yates snickered. "Well, that was pretty direct. It's also a rather stupid order, since we know how they're going to treat us. On the other hand, they did comply with the legal niceties, so there's that."

The strident messages continued through the second watch. They were direct, angry orders. Meanwhile, *Lagos* was boosting at high G, probably her maximum available power.

By the time Yates resumed watch, her orders changed down to where they expected.

Even the camouflage and concealment was only effective for a while. There were no other craft with the dimensions of a factory ship, she was known to exist, and the UN narrowed down the options.

"*Any crewmembers of the ship formerly identified as FMS Force, you are authorized and ordered, on UN authority, to use any means available to seize control of the ship from the officers. A substantial reward is offered to any and all crew who assist in the apprehension of the officers, who are charged with piracy and terrorism. In addition, no charges will be filed in the event those suspects are harmed due to their own resistance.*"

Well, that was an interesting turn. Yates did feel a bit of tension, and wondered if he should unlock weapons for the officers.

He didn't think they could all be detained, or that anyone would, but the offer was designed to tempt someone. Even a failed attempt would be ugly.

"Sir, we're approaching a really good point to commence a return to Grainne orbit. It will still take a couple of weeks, but it saves fuel and puts us in a good trajectory."

"Then let's proceed. Tech Mati, you know what to do."

"On it, sir."

Farana fiddled controls, wrapped a scrap of cloth over her mic and thumbed up.

She spoke on his cue. "Hello, *Lagos*. This is *Force*. I will repeat this message periodically until we make contact, I hope. This is Spacer Rochelle Boise. A group of us have managed to seize the C-deck. We are locked inside and have it secure. We wish to surrender. We lack food, but do have water and toilet facilities for now. The crew has split into at least two factions. The officers are in the passageways with others and we think they are attempting to get equipment to force entry. The other group seems to support us, but wants to know how much the reward is. Also, none of us are C-deck crew and we need instructions on operating the ship. We think we've figured out how to reduce thrust. We will try to do that now. Please respond. We understand it is several light-seconds."

She closed her mic and tried not to laugh.

"Well done," he commended. "That was very believable. Now let's make the thrust a bit erratic. Down, up slightly, down a bit more. Then whatever you can get away with that suits our own needs."

"Yes, sir."

He felt the thrust oscillate and steady. It was definitely reduced. The reply came in shortly.

"*Crew of UNS* Force, *this is* Lagos. *Well done. You are commended. If you can receive a data packet, we can furnish approximate handling instructions you should be able to adapt to use. We can advise in detail by radio.*"

Farana noted, "That was pretty fast and astute. I don't think we can string this out more than a couple of days, three at the outside."

"Blast. Well, we can stall until orbit. Advise the crew we will load boats in two days, and we'll need to engage in denial procedures starting this time tomorrow."

"Yes, sir."

It tore at him. The ship had done everything they asked and more, beyond every design spec, beyond any hypothetical dreamed of. It was something to record in the history books.

Tomorrow they'd destroy her from the inside out so the enemy had nothing to salvage.

"Stall them on their requests as long as you can, and bring us into the planned orbit. I suppose I should rest now. I won't be able to tomorrow or the next day. Medical officer, please bring me whatever tranquilizer you recommend. Commander Brody, I stand ready to be relieved."

Yates had barely gotten into a medically induced sleep when his alert woke him.

He grabbed his phone before he was fully awake, sat up, and heard, *"Captain report to C-deck. Urgent."*

He rolled out, struggled against thrust and maneuver, and got oriented.

"On my way."

He staggered in at a lope, dropped into the couch that Brody had just vacated, just as Tech Brown announced, "Captain on deck."

He pulled his mic and asked, "What do we have?"

The medic on duty handed him a neutralizer for the trank, and a bottle of water. He popped the pill and chugged.

"Sir, this is a replay from three segs ago."

He heard *Lagos*'s communication specialist.

"FMS Force, we are no longer able to support your transfer."

Farana asked, "*Lagos*, what do you mean?"

He'd addressed them as FMS *Force*, not "Ship formerly identified as." That was interesting. The communique suggested their own resources were tapped.

"FMS Force, you should be aware of the recent counterattack by your forces. The UN mission is unable to provide support or recovery to any non-UN personnel at this point in time. When... if it becomes possible, we will do so. You may still surrender per your request, but we do not have the capability for prisoners at this time. Per Geneva and Mars, you would be released on your own parole. We are unable to assist in stabilizing your crew struggle. We are sorry."

Translation: They'd just had the crap kicked out of them.

Naumann or whoever was managing the Freehold side of this was a strategic fucking genius.

Brown said, "Sir...I have a status update from our side. We have control of the commo net back. I'm dumping it to your visual, and...holy fuck."

He was about to ask as the display filled in.

Transport UNS *Kalama*, destroyed. Cruiser UNS *Montevideo*, destroyed. Command ship UNS *London*, destroyed. All jump points back under Freehold control, except JP1, destroyed earlier. Gealach habitats, under control. UN Force Command in Delph'...utterly crushed. More than half the unmanned orbital elements were destroyed.

"Ho-ly fuck," he echoed. Whatever they'd just been part of had wiped out tens of thousands of UN troops, most of their ships and most of their occupation.

In fact, it might be time for them to offer the UN terms for their surrender.

"Let's rub some salt in that wound," he said. "Inform them that as we have not yet met for surrender, we are retracting the acceptance. We will engage in no hostile acts, but don't agree to any stand-down. If they wish, they may surrender to us, with fair treatment and adequate facilities until we can reach basing. Thank them for their decency in this exchange."

Brown replied, "Yes, sir. Do you want to send it personally?"

"I specifically do not. If their captain requests, I will reply. But their status is 'supplicants.' They can speak to a junior officer. If you'll take that in context and not as derogatory."

"I understand perfectly sir," the man grinned. "No offense taken."

■   ■   ■

Spider's Web
Part 17

DalesOP arrived a week after Moyra. He brought old news that their wayward asshole Braknck disappeared after walking out of a bar with a UN bureaucrat of some kind. No one could confess to feeling too much grief if his disappearance remained permanent.

Apart from one brief initial meeting, where DalesOP clung to both Damocles and Moyra for several divs, the trio was logistically unable to gather as three again. The risk to the operation at this late stage dictated their continued separation.

Damocles and Moyra took turns keeping DalesOP company at odd times, when not on duty. She witnessed some fairly horrible things, but her actions haunted her far less than Dal's did.

TripleShot and Jenkins were pulled in next, arriving together. Moyra was forcibly reminded of how *young* Trip really was. He was good, but *young*. She greeted them with DalesOP with her, and TripleShot all but glued himself to DalesOP's side. With Trip and Jenkins around, Moyra and Damocles could take a slight stand-down from suicide watch.

Not that they'd admitted to themselves or anyone else that's what they were doing. One day, Moyra hoped to see the Mick of her childhood again, but the boy was buried under a man who hated himself right now. He just hated the UN *more*.

Moyra also brought Selene into the outskirts of Jefferson, along with a handful of the other handlers. Families were left behind in the relative safeties of the outlying areas. Kozlov lived nearby, and had just kept his head down for the duration. Salamander lived on the other side of the continent, so he did as much as he could from a programming aspect. Once the attack started in earnest, he would try to assist with communication pipelines, but there was a limit to how effective he could be.

Officers, soldiers, fighters who'd proven their worth, professionals of various stripes, all dribbled into a few primary areas, with the largest concentration in Jefferson. The new comm units and other issue gear stayed hidden in the city, unless an individual was on an active attack pattern.

Meanwhile, Moyra noticed the few UN soldiers to be seen

patrolling the streets of Jefferson looked scared. Some were the trigger happy kind of scared. They were weeded out quickly. Others simply did as little as possible to meet their orders before scurrying back to the relative safety of the UN base.

A base they believed secure from more than the occasional nuisance, harrying missile attack, although the perimeter was known to be dangerous.

The team quietly worked on determining how much data the UN had unscrambled or hid from their long-term intrusion. Questioning where and how the new drones were deployed without any kind of notification on the known network, or the manifests which Skylight continued to provide as fast as possible, led to the question of how much equipment Freehold forces did not yet know about.

Between visual observation and scouring every bit of data possible, Moyra worried that the report of "only a bit more than the drones" was inadequate. The remaining items couldn't be quickly compromised, but their remote controllers could be blocked. It was currently unclear whether or not the local operators could force a fail-open on the weaponry.

All the pieces that Moyra could move or direct were now on the board for the final play.

Now, it was a waiting game. She knew that Naumann's other leaders were finalizing their preparations. All she could do was wait.

When the order came, it was nearly anticlimactic. A bit after midnight local, Naumann first ordered Moyra to wake and/or summon her critical team members. As soon as she confirmed presence, or at least attempts at consciousness, of those individuals, Naumann gave the initial order.

Moyra gave her own to DalesOP, Damocles, Kozlov, Skylight, and others.

The Tech Command room filled with the rapid *tak-tak* of keys, followed by muttered commentary and curses. Moyra soon had a rolling verbal report from each team and their current status.

The base's jamming field fell first, followed by the inactivated drones waking up under Kozlov's team's command. Video feed showed phalanx formations as multiple drones were slaved to chained primaries for ease of control. One phalanx blasted its way through a storage room wall, where the drones had been left dormant. UN troops scattered away from it. A glimpse of the initial Freehold artillery battery hitting targets flashed across one feed.

Commands to shut down all connected smart guns and force UN remote-controlled weaponry over to Freehold control were issued. The lockout couldn't affect every UN unit, in part because some had disabled the networked aspect on their own after the drone rebellions. However, a large percentage of UN soldiers discovered their autoaiming and locked guns were malfunctioning, if not outright failing. As they tried to report this information back, the UN satellites were taken down. A few were taken down programmatically, and others were physically destroyed. A distributed denial-of-service attack initially saturated the hardwire lines, while lines were physically cut or edge devices such as firewalls were corrupted beyond use.

A few of the Freehold satellites were destroyed. Communications shifted to the Sister Station networks, over-the-air broadcasting, and relays via Skywheels One and Two. Surviving hardwire links enabled the remainder of communication flow.

Drone operators and teams using the remote targeting systems got network priority in an attempt to decrease their lag time. Most were experienced gamers, however, and quickly settled into the groove of anticipating the next needed move versus an enemy with lower lag times.

The primary handlers worked with Naumann's communications team to handle field reports and coordinate physical, human-based attacks. Skylight reported Freehold Forces ships arrived "out of nowhere," and were engaging UN ships and orbitals, and protecting the skywheels.

Snippets of reports into the communications team overlaid Moyra's focus on the reports from Tech Command.

"Reservoir dam explosives detonated. Structure confirmed damaged; breach imminent."

"Huff's dead. Agent reports but can't evac."

"The leopards are OURS. DO NOT FIRE on the leopards or the humans with them."

"Dam is breached. Levees should hold and direct toward base. Clear your people out of the valley!"

Divs passed, how many Moyra would never be sure. As members of her teams started fading from exhaustion and better-rested made it in, she ordered them to shift around. Several catnapped along the walls.

At some point, Naumann directed her to hand over oversight to the more rested Damocles. Moyra made it as far as the back wall before sliding down to pass out.

When she woke, Tech Command was eerily quiet, only a few key taps here and there. DalesOP and Damocles sat waiting across from her. "Status?" she asked.

"Mostly over, Boss-man thinks," Damocles replied.

"Isolated pockets of fighting still," DalesOP agreed. "Mostly centered around the remnants of the bases. Clearing some of the more saturated areas will take several days. A few UN ships are trying to outrun ours for the jump point. They're not faring well."

"And we have a couple of ships guarding the JP anyhow," Damocles added.

Moyra nodded. "Better check in, see what Boss-man needs from me next."

Her friends got to their feet and helped her up. "How's the hip, after sleeping on the floor?"

"Stiff." She winced while trying to move. "I was locked in one position for a while, earlier."

"Want your arm crutches?" Damocles asked.

She shrugged. "Do I ever?"

DalesOP snorted, and offered her an arm to lean on. "No."

The trio was permitted entry into the main command room immediately. "Ah, Captain Kelly, Corporals." Naumann did not comment on her limping or their support. "My aide will provide you with the information you require for the next phase of the operation."

"Yes, sir," Moyra replied.

Huff #22
I'm tired (April 31st, 211)

I read a lot of old books between meetings. I found an obscure one on my tablet that I must have kept from some old staff course, and it made such an impression that I made the staff print a whole copy. I prefer hard copy because the act of physically marking paper makes the content stick. The author was a British diplomat named Thomas Meadows, known as a "sinologist," before terms like that became unfashionable. He died young, and spent his career in China during the "Opium wars" of British imperialism. The book is *The Chinese and Their Rebellions*, and this quote bothers me:

> Revolution is a change of the form of government and of the principles on which it rests; it does not necessarily imply a change of rulers. Rebellion is a rising against the rulers which, far from necessarily aiming at a change of government principles and forms, often originates in a desire of preserving them intact. *Revolutionary movements are against principles, rebellions are against men...*

I circled and underlined that last line again and again. I descend from Afrikaners. A long time ago, my family lived through both revolutions and rebellions, and now, here I am. I'm staring, right now, at the two display cases on the wall behind me. One is full of exceedingly rare and priceless National Scout relics, and the other, British South Africa Police relics. The BSAP flask I keep with me. Few people today are well read enough to know the story behind these items, but looking at it all makes me want to believe in reincarnation.

The rebels absolutely hate *us*, and their tactics reflect that. They target people who aren't directly hurting them, but enable our forces to operate. They love going after the reconstruction bureaucrats, the UN administrators who enforce our cultural power. The rebels are cruel in their methods; everything from poison, to food, to sex. *They hate us. And we've learned to hate them, too.* For me, I finally started to hate them when they fed one of our casualties *to his own comrades—from a damn FOOD TRUCK we allowed on base for months!* I tried explaining this to a SecGen lackey here on "fact finding":

"Everyone knows. We can't put this genie back in the bottle." Instead, the counselor berated me for making a "coded racist statement" with the "genie" remark. Then, the insurgents uploaded a vid of one of their cells dumping out caskets of our casualties, and putting slaughtered pigs in them. It's happened more than once. This place is destroying our souls.

Now, there's one contingent here, I suspect, that doesn't hate the insurgents and perhaps even *loves* them: the North Americans. They hate the violence being done to them, but I suspect many of them secretly wish they could *be* "Freeholders." I need to transfer them out of theater. I don't need that undercurrent on top of everything else. There are reports of small-scale *defections* from the NorthAm troops. Never, in a million years, is that something I would have thought possible, but with the Americans, maybe I shouldn't really be surprised. They were birthed in perfidy, so we should expect nothing less. It's settled: they go home. Tomorrow, the J4 will get that underway.

Leadership—command—is about both *love* and *hate* in the right measures, and at the right times. This is an old lesson from a massive document of leadership maxims I've kept and added to over my whole career. Ironic, given my earlier comments, that it comes from a piece by an early twenty-first-century American armor officer named Captain Michael Few, who served during one of the Southwest Asian wars that sparked the creation of the modern UN. It's not original to him, as he was citing a superior: "Sometimes you got to give the love, and sometimes you got to give them the hate."

To Captain Few and your anonymous colonel, what would you think of this whole thing? Not enough love, or not enough hate?

[NOTHING FOLLOWS]

Reviewer's comments: This was General Huff's final entry. Three days later, he was assassinated in his quarters aboard Jump Point Three by his paramour, a specially tasked FMF asset: "Bonita."

While initially seen as a victory for the Freehold Military Forces, the situation deteriorated much more quickly and chaotically than expected. UN command and control was briefly frozen as Huff's deputies were either reluctant or unable to assert authority, and formation commanders on both sides exercised their own initiative to inflict as much damage on the enemy as possible. Casualties on both sides, military and civilian, were heavy.

■   ■   ■

Spider's Web
Part 18

Moyra Kelly sat in Tech Command, reviewing the information her AI filters were pulling a third time, making a frustrated sound as she did so.

Major Sarkosky spoke up to her side. "That doesn't sound promising, Captain."

Moyra looked up, startled. She gestured at her interface. "The colonel wishes an update, and I...don't like what I am seeing. But it's not conclusive."

Sarkosky nodded her head. "That's why I'm here, of course. We trust your intuition. What do you *think* you're seeing in the data?"

"The movement patterns of the in-system ships have abruptly shifted. Decrypting further reports, as well as reviewing the encapsulated news transfers...nothing is explicit. But my gut? My gut says the UN is mobilizing to invade in even more force. Not immediately, but certainly sooner rather than later. Probably much sooner. We know they were already irritated by how long the subjugation was taking, so it's not unreasonable to assume they already had that ball rolling. Most telling is the complete lack of information about the resistance battles. The encapsulated news transfers previously mentioned something at least in passing about the 'humanitarian mission on Grainne,' but there's been nothing since they got word."

Sarkosky looked surprised. "That is interesting. I will provide your verbal report to the colonel. If you can pin down specifics for a written report, please do."

"Yes, ma'am."

Naumann leveraged the communications network that Moyra's team built over the duration of the invasion to notify citizens of the expected secondary, larger UN invasion. A vote was called to authorize stopping the next wave at the source.

DalesOP, Damocles, and Moyra clustered in her small room to watch the official tally count. The "nays" numbered few indeed.

"May the Goddess forgive us," DalesOP sighed, when the tally was finalized.

"Babies suffocated to death from that virus. Others rotted to death," Moyra replied. "No amount of political war justifies that. We're still dealing with it, even with the antivirals."

"And now we'll do even worse."

Moyra shrugged. "Depends on your definition of worse, I guess. They insisted on starting this war. We have to finish it."

DalesOP nodded slowly. "I can't do any more. I've done all I can."

Damocles agreed. "You have. Others still have their tasks to do."

Moyra dispatched a single unencrypted message to the address Naumann provided, supposedly containing an old family recipe from a "cousin."

A second address received an encrypted message, from a different source, using the recipe as the decryption key. The decrypted data packet provided the orders to agents on Earth. A countdown provided synchronization, initiated by the response from the primary agent.

With those sent, Naumann considered Moyra's part of the task complete, and she was given the option to leave. But, much as she felt compelled to stay with her handlers, she bore witness to the results. She sat in Tech Command as the countdown neared the finish. What they were watching was almost thirteen divs old, she reminded herself, physically carried through jump points and then beamed with a speed-of-light delay.

A few ratty, tattered Freehold Forces ships, with barely more than engines and weapon systems remaining, materialized in Earth system, near Earth proper. Phase-drive drones also appeared, nearly in atmosphere. Recon drones and an observation point at a station known as Starhome provided video feed.

There was nothing preventing this kind of attack, as Earth had demonstrated. It was now being taught that some lines were not crossed with good reason.

The AI-driven ships provided cover for the drones, attacking orbital craft and defenses, attracting attention and inflicting damage on the UN's space projection. Drones dropped straight down for their target cities.

The first UN ship broke apart from the onslaught. One lucky UN orbital platform managed to hit one of the decrepit ships, to be promptly opened up to vacuum themselves. Other orbital stations also suffered catastrophic damage, and satellites were vaporized. A handful of drones were destroyed before they could descend.

The rest made it through the defenses, multiple per targeted city. Nightside views showed explosions followed by entire cities winking out into blackness, then glowing from fire. The blossoming explosions were pretty, if one didn't know what they meant.

Earth had tried to break them. It had to be broken to prevent another round that would obliterate what was left of the Freehold.

Dayside views showed the devastation. Kinetic bombs and nuclear warheads slammed into first-tier cities. Under the kinetics, buildings disintegrated, or crumpled from the blasts. A multilevel elevated freeway pancaked all the way to the ground as warheads targeted the vehicular arteries that kept a megacity alive. Elsewhere, a skyscraper's glass exterior shattered outward, millions of glittering shrapnel falling below, and then it slumped over, crushing the smaller buildings in its path. A stadium imploded in the middle of what appeared to be a game, with the entire exterior structure falling in. Moyra winced as she saw the people raining down to the ground, before the walls collapsed completely.

Once the drones delivered their payloads, they were programmed to reactivate their phase drives... right into the city below them. Bolts of unseen energy vaporized ground almost down to the mantle. Vacuums that were left as the drives literally vacated atmosphere in their passage were then slammed with thunderous pressure rebound and steam explosions from the crust.

Shortly, the cities were full of rapidly cooling molten rock and dirt. Dust clouds roiled above the rubble. What Earth had inflicted on Grainne was returned a hundred times over.

News relays across Earth broke into scheduled programming to report destruction of food supplies, grain and vat stores both, as more explosions took out facilities. The most densely populated areas would only know afterward, as they starved and rioted among the shambles, their life-supporting infrastructure demolished.

Those that survived, at any rate.

Within another day, Earth conceded and begged for peace talks.

■   ■   ■

EPILOGUE:
Post Action Review

It was a hot summer evening with clear air, made muggy by the sheer number of people present. They were of no particular group and of all demographics. The liquor and recpharm was present in enough quantity he could smell it. Whisky, beer, that was a red wine, pot, dusted sparkle. Everything.

Captain Francis Yates was in uniform, at least as far as a logoed shirt for FMS *Force* ("Ex Pulvere Ad Gladii") over standard field pants. The fresh air was intoxicating, after two years without it.

Around him were any number of uniforms with Freehold Residents' Provisional Forces tags. As they milled about he saw Northside Capital Militia, South Islands Alliance, Hinterlands Defense Force, Central Independence Group, Dragontooth Mountain Irregulars, Free Resident Element, Darkwood Provisional Guard, Coastal Independents, one group apparently named GFY, numerous others. Among them were any number of people without blouses, many armed, others not. He could pick out some of the actual military cadre who'd trained and organized a bunch of cranky loners into a functional, if colorful, force.

There were another handful in uniform, surviving reservists. At the retaining wall, four lean and leathery leopard handlers, with their leopards. The cats seemed unsure of the crowd, but were under control. Those uniforms were other Spacers, who simultaneously appeared to love the fresh air and be uncomfortable in it. One group wore a commercial ship uniform of coveralls with tags, and next to them were three people in Skywheel oversuits.

The elation, though. It surrounded all of them. They'd done it. Outnumbered a hundred or more to one, operating on wit, guile, viciousness and sheer refusal to quit, they'd recovered their independence.

He could hear them, too.

"Wait, what was your callsign?"

"Ninja Three," said a woman in a cluster of four, uniforms marked SHINOBI.

"Yeah! You got us that map of their perimeter cabling."

"I remember, yes!"

"So, where's Ninja One and Two? Or shouldn't I ask?"

"There never were Number One or Two. We had Three, Seven, Eight and Twelve." She indicated the others.

"Ahah. That's fantastic."

"Yep, their intel spent months going through files trying to figure out our TOE."

Clever. Over there was another group.

—"Wait, you did what?"

"They set up a decoy to prove the threat level, to their own bureaucrats. We turned it into a real ambush."

"Right. That unit eventually reached us. We had time to get all the noncombatants out first. You saved them. Thank you."—

—"You were inside their perimeter the entire time, sneaking out data. How did you handle that without melting down?"

"That's why I'm drinking and lit now, dude." Her words sounded slurred. She looked barely adult.—

—"It's a better party if everyone is involved," a voice muttered. Arika Santiago turned her head and saw another woman standing there, a drink in one hand. She made a waving motion at the large group around them. "Most of these are Militia uniforms. You're Skywheel. Come, tell us what happened up there."

Reluctantly, Arika allowed herself to be dragged into the group. One of the men looked her over once and nodded.

"So what'd you do?" he asked without preamble. "Espionage? Worked on some seedier stuff?"

"I was in Payload Control...I brought down Skywheel Three," she responded in a quiet tone.

For a brief instance the entire group went silent.

"By the Goddess," a muted whisper came from somewhere in the group. "That was you? That was fucking *epic!*"

Not just me, she silently corrected as she thought back to the only man who had ever made her feel truly alive. *Oh Ranil, you have no idea how much I miss you.*

"Not just me," she said aloud. "I would like to toast a friend."

Around her, a hundred glasses were raised.—

—"What happened up at Mountainside Village? The retirement home?"

"Apparently it's a retirement home for Special Warfare and spooks."

"And that's where the UN put their biowarfare people?"

"And that's why all the casualties."—

—"He didn't make it? Gods, I'm sorry. He was so damned brave."

"We lost so many. But it was obvious they were going to round us up and slaughter us even if we just gave up."—

—"We *melted* Earth. I can't imagine there wasn't some less horrific way to end it."

"They kept coming. Remember, this was the second attack. Then they lost several ships, but they just kept coming. The only ending was a boot on a neck."

"Yeah. And they hurt us, but damn, have you seen the vids of Earth? They've lost billions."

An almost angry voice retorted, "I have. I guess they shouldn't have started a war if they couldn't take a joke."—

—Captain Prassert Dean wandered through, with Matt Campos hanging nearby, unsure how to interact, and worried about his Earth accent.

He paused and looked at a woman in a body brace, in uniform. He'd have expected her to be in his element.

"Funny to finally see faces, isn't it?" the slight redhead said. She leaned against a much older lady's wheelchair. Captain's insignia. Her jacket said she was Intelligence, as did the jackets of the two men beside her. They were lieutenants.

"After months of hearing distorted voices and moving camera views only, yeah, it's almost disconcerting," replied another woman, militia element SPECTRE.

"What element are you guys?" he asked.

The redhead flicked a glance at one of the obvious guards, who tilted his head. She looked back at him, and gestured at the jacket. "Intelligence."

"I guessed, but never knew we had a functional chain."

"Then we did our job." She smiled. "But everyone spoke with at least one of us, often several times a day."

He blinked. "Beth?"

"Was not pure AI," she replied.

"I never even guessed."

"Then we did our job."

"*Who* are you?" he repeated.

She smiled and looked away, returning to observe the crowd. "Tired. But they're alive." Murmurs of agreement, tinged in sadness and anger, came from the rest of the team.

He took the hint.—

—That was Colonel Naumann.

"Sir, do you have a moment?" Captain Dean asked as the commander and his guard detail passed by.

The colonel turned. "Yes. Dean. Logistics, right? You brought stuff into the Bluff."

"Yes, sir. This is one of our wartime recruits. He's all in for career. This is acting Transportation Specialist Matt Campos."

Naumann extended his hands and Campos shook them vigorously. "It's just amazing to meet you, sir."

"And you, Specialist. Well done. I saw your bio a couple of days ago. I think I can get the Citizens to waive your obligation. Welcome to the Freehold, now that we have it again."

"Thank you, sir."

The kid was tearing up.—

—The Wandering Minstrel negotiated the crowd with ease, clasping forearms here, exchanging hugs there, with his ladyfriend and fellow spy, Siobhan "Anasazi" Ceallaigh, at his side. When he caught Lieutenant Michaelson's eye and noted the small clouded leopard at Dixie's heels, he crossed the intervening space and braced himself at attention.

"The war is over, and I don't have to skulk around anymore, sir. If you'll have me back, I would be honored."

"Of course, Brad." Michaelson engulfed his friend in a tight hug. "We have a sore need for skilled handlers, and we have a program to rebuild. Assuming you're up for raising kittens again?"

Siobhan's eyes lit up at the mention of kittens, and Brad laughed. "Absolutely."—

—"You're from *Force*! You guys were the whack! What did you do aboard?"

"Fabricated about six billion rounds of carbine ammo."

"No, shit. I shot about six thousand rounds. So I guess I owe you. Beer?"

"Sure, anything. As long as I never look at a fucking 'Matrix Caster, Small Arms Ammunition, set for 7mm by Fifty Rounds, Unitized Charger Bloc' for the rest of my life."—

—"What's next for you two?" asked a worn looking Brother Simon. He had been the man to bring down the last Werewolf and was the new leader of the Congregation.

Senior Sergeant Felix Tolstoy replied, "With this over, it's time to pick up the pieces of the Blazer regiments and train the next generation."

"I hope you two don't take this the wrong way, but I hope to never see you two again," Simon said in a rather neutral tone. The expression of hurt that briefly flickered across Felix and Gerhardt's faces was allayed when Simon went on, "Not in your official capacity. If you heathens ever want to visit, you are most welcome!"—

■　　　■　　　■

ABOUT THE AUTHORS

Jessica Schlenker holds an M.S. in Information Security & Assurance, a bevy of industry certifications, and a B.S. in Biology. She works as a professional nerd in the field of IT Security. Sadly, she is too much of a white hat to actually combine these specialties into creating her own cyborg army. But she's thought about it.

Chris "MOGS" DiNote has served twenty years so far in the United States Air Force and Air National Guard (Pennsylvania and Ohio). He has deployed for Operations Enduring Freedom and Iraqi Freedom. Chris is a graduate of the US Air Force Academy and the USAF Weapons School. He holds an M.A. in Military History from Norwich University, and a Master's in Strategic Studies from the Air War College. A (very) amateur musician, Chris has also played saxophone and bass in several bands. He was born in Philadelphia, PA, raised in South Jersey, and resides wherever the Air Force tells him to with his wife and coauthor Jaime, and their daughter Remy.

Jaime DiNote is a veteran of the Florida Army National Guard and US Army Reserve. She mobilized for Operation Noble Eagle in Washington, DC. Jaime is a graduate of Seattle University ROTC and holds a B.A. in Criminal Justice. Due to the demanding PCS schedule, she is a stay-at-home mom and military spouse, and is working on her first novel. She also enjoys cooking, shooting, and singing. She currently resides wherever the Air Force sends her with her husband and coauthor Chris and their daughter Remy.

J.F. Holmes is a retired Army Senior Noncommissioned Officer, having served for twenty-two years in both the Regular Army and Army National Guard. During that time, he served as everything from an artillery section leader to a member of a Division-level planning staff, with tours in Cuba and Iraq, as well as responding to the terrorist attacks in NYC on 9/11.

From 2010 to 2014 he wrote the immensely popular military cartoon strip, *Power Point Ranger*, poking fun at military life in the tradition of *Beetle Bailey* and *Willy and Joe*.

On a dare from his beautiful girlfriend, after complaining about a popular TV show, he started to write a militarily realistic zombie apocalypse story, which is now in its tenth volume. In 2017 two of his books were finalists for the prestigious Dragon Awards.

Rob Reed inherited his love of reading from his parents. He'll read the cereal box if nothing else is available. He loves SF, fantasy, mysteries, thrillers, and military history. His diverse employment history includes working as an emergency room clerk, a reporter, and a firearms instructor. As a "professional projectile launcher enthusiast," he writes about guns and shooting for a variety of publications. He lives with his wife Marie and their cats in the Metro Detroit area.

Jason Cordova, a 2014 John W. Campbell Award finalist, has been previously featured in *Forged in Blood*, the national bestselling Freehold anthology. He currently has over thirty works published over a variety of genres, including the military science fiction series, the Kin Wars Saga, and his YA series The Warp. A US Navy veteran, he is a high school basketball coach in his spare time and currently lives in Virginia.

Kacey Ezell is a USAFA graduate and active duty USAF instructor pilot with 2,000+ hours in the UH-1N Huey and Mi-171 helicopters. When not teaching young pilots to beat the air into submission, she writes sci-fi/fantasy/horror fiction. She's contributed to multiple Baen anthologies, including the story "Family Over Blood" which was featured in the Freehold-universe anthology *Forged in Blood*, and winner of the Year's Best Military and Adventure Science Fiction, Volume 4. In addition to writing for Baen, she has published several novels and short stories with independent publisher Chris Kennedy Publishing. She is married with two daughters.

Robert E. Hampson, Ph.D., turns science fiction into science, with over thirty-five years' experience in animal and human neuroscience, culminating in the first neural prosthetic that boosts memory by enhancing the brain's own neural codes for memory. He has advised more than a dozen SF/F writers, game developers and TV writers, and writes fiction ranging from military SF to zombie apocalypse. Some of his work previously appeared under the pseudonym Tedd Roberts.

Larry Correia is the award-winning, *New York Times*–bestselling author of the Monster Hunter International series, the Saga of the Forgotten Warrior epic fantasy series, the Grimnoir Chronicles trilogy, the Dead Six thrillers (with Mike Kupari), the Monster Hunter Memoirs series (with John Ringo), and several novels in the Warmachine universe. A former accountant, machine-gun dealer, and firearms instructor, Larry lives in the mountains of northern Utah with his wife and children.

Marisa Wolf was born in New England, and raised on Boston sports teams, *Star Wars*, *Star Trek*, and the longest books in the library (usually fantasy). Over the years she majored in English in part to get credits for reading (this... only partly worked), taught middle school, was head-butted by an alligator, built a career in education, earned a black belt in Tae Kwon Do, and finally decided to finish all those half-started stories in her head. She currently lives in Texas with three absurd rescue dogs, one deeply understanding husband, and more books than seems sensible.

Jamie Ibson was born in London, Ontario, Canada and joined the CF Army Reserves as an infantryman while still in high school. A six-month tour of Bosnia in 2001 impressed upon him just how awesome things are in North America compared to most of the rest of the world, which was an important lesson for a naive twenty-year-old kid. In 2007 he joined Canadian law enforcement and has been posted to the left coast ever since. He is married to a very supportive wife and has two shockingly supportive cats.

[Jamie also served as the Deputy Vice-Assistant Editor in Charge of Continuity and Stuff, keeping the entire timeline for the Freehold universe correct. The Editor is indebted.]

Michael D. Massa has lived an adventurous life, including stints as a Navy SEAL officer, an investment banker and a technologist. He lived outside the US for several years, plus the usual deployments. Mike is married with three sons, who check daily to see if today is the day they can pull down the old lion. Not yet...

Brad R. Torgersen's award-winning, award-nominated science fiction has appeared in numerous magazines and anthologies. A veteran and Chief Warrant Officer in the United States Army Reserve, Brad has also served in half a dozen different countries. His latest novel, *A Star-Wheeled Sky*, is a military space opera with hard SF leanings, released by Baen Books. Married for twenty-five years to his very first audio narrator, Brad lives with his family in the Intermountain West. He can be found most often at his Facebook page, and occasionally writes nonfiction for both his personal blog and the Mad Genius Club group blog.

Justin Watson grew up an Army brat, living in Germany, Alabama, Texas, Korea, Colorado and Alaska, and fed on a steady diet of X-Men, *Star Trek*, Robert Heinlein, DragonLance, and *Babylon 5*. While attending West Point, he met his future wife, Michele, on an airplane, and soon began writing in earnest with her encouragement. In 2005 he graduated from West Point and served as a field artillery officer, completing combat tours in Iraq and Afghanistan, and earning the Bronze Star, Purple Heart and the Combat Action Badge.

Medically retired from the Army in 2015, Justin settled in Houston with Michele, their four children and an excessively friendly Old English Sheepdog.

A native Texan by birth (if not geography), **Christopher L. Smith** moved "home" as soon as he could. Attending Texas A+M, he learned quickly that there was more to college than beer and football games. He relocated to San Antonio, attending SAC and UTSA, graduating in late 2000 with a B.A. in Literature. While there, he also met a wonderful lady who somehow found him to be funny, charming, and worth marrying. (She has since changed her mind on the funny and charming.) Chris began writing fiction in 2012. His short stories can be found in multiple anthologies, including the bestselling and award-winning *Forged In Blood* (Baen). His two cats allow him, his wife, their three kids, and three dogs to reside outside of San Antonio.

A.C. Haskins is a former Armored Cavalry Officer and combat veteran, who now earns his living in a much more sedentary (read: boring) fashion, working as a management consultant, economist, and occasional defensive firearm instructor. He has a lifelong love of speculative fiction, having written his first science fiction novel as a class project in eleventh grade. His interests include (but are not limited to) ancient and medieval history, applied violence studies, tabletop gaming, and theoretical economics. He lives in Michigan with his fiancée and their two cats.

Philip Wohlrab is a veteran of both the US Army and the US Coast Guard. He continues to serve as a medic and medic instructor for the Virginia Army National Guard. He did two tours in Iraq, where he earned the title "Doc" the hard way. He has a Master's of Public Health and is a registered EMT. When he isn't working as a medic, he spends his time writing and attending various science fiction conventions.

ABOUT THE EDITOR

Michael Z. Williamson is variously an immigrant from the UK and Canada; a retired veteran of the US Army and US Air Force with service in the Middle East; a consultant on disaster preparedness and military matters to private clients, manufacturers, TV and movie productions, and occasionally DoD elements; bladesmith; award-winning and bestselling editor and author. His hobby of collecting weapons has led him into an arms race in which he outguns Barbados and Iceland, so far.